PATRICK HENRY JONES

CONFLICTING WORLDS

NEW DIMENSIONS OF THE AMERICAN CIVIL WAR

T. Michael Parrish, SERIES EDITOR

PATRICK HENRY JONES

IRISH AMERICAN, CIVIL WAR GENERAL, AND GILDED AGE POLITICIAN

MARK H. DUNKELMAN

LOUISIANA STATE UNIVERSITY PRESS
BATON ROUGE

Published by Louisiana State University Press

Manufactured in the United States of America
FIRST PRINTING

Designer: Mandy McDonald Scallan
Typeface: Whitman
Printer and binder: Maple Press, Inc.

Library of Congress Cataloging-in-Publication Data are available at the Library of Congress.
ISBN 978-0-8071-5966-8 (cloth: alk. paper) — ISBN 978-0-8071-5967-5 (pdf) — ISBN 978-0-8071-5968-2 (epub) — ISBN 978-0-8071-5969-0 (mobi)

The paper in this book meets the guidelines for permanence and durability of the Committee on Production Guidelines for Book Longevity of the Council on Library Resources. ∞

For Annette,
with me from the start

CONTENTS

ILLUSTRATIONS

(following page 108)

PATRICK HENRY JONES

INTRODUCTION

Faded Memory

Biographers rarely chronicle a significant class of nineteenth-century Americans: the several hundred men who led brigades and higher commands in the Civil War and governed at the municipal, state, and federal levels in the postwar years. Like no other group, Civil War veterans influenced the politics of the Gilded Age. Today a handful of the former generals who wielded postwar political power remain firmly lodged in historical memory, but for every well-known Ulysses S. Grant, there are hundreds of men whose lives have gone unexamined and whose influence has been overlooked. Despite their noteworthy public service, most of them have long been forgotten.[1]

A small subset of that coterie consists of generals of foreign birth. Over the past seven decades ethnicity has steadily emerged as an analytical factor in Civil War history. Most recently, scholars have questioned the military effectiveness of ethnic soldiers, whether their allegiance was devoted to their ethnic group or their cause, and if their service advanced or retarded the assimilation process. What is clear is that ethnicity was a matter of great importance in nineteenth-century America. The questions relating to the military service of certain foreign-born Civil War generals can also be asked of their postwar political careers.[2]

Patrick Henry Jones was one such ethnic general and postwar politician. A native of Ireland, from all appearances he readily assimilated as an American and achieved remarkable success in his adopted country. But even successful Irish immigrants remained somewhat estranged from American culture, unable wholly to adapt to life in their new land and harboring homesickness for Ireland. Irish clannishness and suspicion of American ways combined with American stereotyping and mistrust worked to retard Irish social integration. Jones's family personified the estrangement. Repelled by nativist prejudice in New York State, they became pioneer members of an Irish Catholic colony in the West. Jones remained behind and prospered.[3]

When the Civil War erupted, Jones had the Irishman's legendary good luck to be attached to a largely Irish regiment. He rose in rank and within sixteen months was colonel of a new regiment that followed him to the end of the war. He served in significant campaigns; survived wounding, injury, capture, and illness; and emerged from the ordeal with an exemplary military record and a commission as brigadier general. Of the twelve Union generals born in Ireland, only Thomas A. Smyth—an outstanding brigade and division commander who was mortally wounded during the war's final days—produced a better overall military record than Jones.[4]

In the postwar years Jones was one of the most prominent Irish-born politicians in New York City, enormously popular during a time when his ethnic group was consolidating political power. His career sheds light on the political ins and outs of the age and the machinations of the spoils system. Initially a Democrat, he rose to prominence as a Republican—an anomaly for an Irishman. New York State congressman, governor, and senator Reuben E. Fenton and the influential editor of the *New York Tribune,* Horace Greeley, mentored Jones in his rise to political prominence. At their urging President Grant appointed Jones—by then a veteran of elective and appointive offices—to the prestigious and patronage-rich office of postmaster of New York City. Jones was thus presented with a dilemma when in 1872 Greeley challenged Grant for the presidency. Two years later the Irish vote helped elect Jones to office as a two-party candidate. In the following decade he became disenchanted with the Republicans and, like many Irish Americans, drifted to third parties.

In his heyday Jones was a nationally known figure, acquainted with many of the best-known Americans of his era, frequently mentioned in the press, and pictured in the popular illustrated newspapers. On his death in 1900 a paper in his former hometown remarked, "His memory shall not fade among men." But in the century-plus since then, his name has lapsed into obscurity. In the many books that have chronicled the deeds of Irish Americans, he has gone unmentioned. Nor is he remembered in Ireland, where the Civil War service of Irish American soldiers remains largely unrecognized and little understood.[5]

Having attained prominence, Jones was not immune to its perils. Gilded Age corruption enmeshed him in the embezzlement of a post office subordinate, which hurt him financially, and a scandal involving a protégé, which besmirched his reputation. Then he was dragged into a peculiar involvement in the most sensational crime of the era, which indelibly tainted his name. Nagged by the scandals, plagued by the crime, troubled by alcoholism, he fell into a downward spiral that cast him from the limelight into darkness. Jones was an honorable man undone by circumstances. In the end his life was a tragedy of ambition gained and dashed, of steady rise and precipitate fall, of hard-earned plenty reduced to poverty.

This biography portrays Jones the public man, offering only hints of his personal life. His career as a soldier and public servant is amply documented by contemporary press coverage and other sources. His personal papers were allegedly lost after he died; his widow claimed mice ate them. But enough Jones letters survive in the papers of his correspondents to add personal perspectives to the copious press reports. In addition, reporters interviewed him during certain pivotal chapters of his life, recording his opinions on key events.[6]

Nineteenth-century America teemed with promise and pitfalls, and Patrick Henry Jones partook of both. America offered prosperity to the ambitious, able, and hardworking; Jones possessed those attributes and reaped the benefits. Americans presented obstacles to immigrants; Jones overcame them. American fought American at great cost in the Civil War; Jones served the Union cause valiantly, suffered severely, and emerged from the conflict with high rank and reputation. American postwar politics offered opportunities to war heroes; Jones seized them. American politicians became enmeshed in Gilded Age corruption and scandal; Jones was so tainted. Americans were shocked by a horrific crime; Jones's involvement in the case cast a pall on his reputation. Patrick Henry Jones strove for success in America. He grasped it and held it for some heady years, but eventually it slipped from his hands. Jones's rise and fall reflected a society in which anything was possible—including some very good things and some very bad.

CHAPTER 1

From County Westmeath to Cattaraugus County

That Patrick Henry Jones made a name for himself in the United States was a significant accomplishment for a nineteenth-century native of Ireland. The great waves of Irish and German immigrants who arrived in America during the midcentury decades met with an often-hostile reception. Ethnicity mattered in nineteenth-century America; the melting pot was a twentieth-century conceit. In 1840, when young Jones arrived with his parents in the United States, native-born residents found much to dislike and distrust in the religion, language, and customs of foreign newcomers. As xenophobic sentiment coalesced into a political movement, Know-Nothing agitation disrupted the Jones family. Jones's parents and siblings fled New York State to the promise of a Roman Catholic colony in the West. Jones remained behind, assimilated, and thrived. In his first two decades in America he successfully joined a society that was difficult for many immigrants to penetrate.

Jones's boyhood decade on the Emerald Isle defined the rest of his life in the United States. Despite his deceptive Welsh surname, in his heyday the American public knew him as an Irishman. His ethnicity was both a burden and a boon. During his early years in western New York he studied and worked hard, overcame prejudice, found his way to an influential and lucrative vocation, climbed the social ladder, and made his first forays into politics. He thrived in his new country, an antebellum ethnic American success story. In years to come, his ethnicity would color and propel both his military and political careers. Eventually, however, it would constrain him from further advances.

Being Irish was important in framing Jones's story in America, but ironically, little is known about his life in Ireland. His antecedents there are clouded in obscurity, as are details of his formative years and the circumstances of his family's emigration. His youth must have entailed considerable hardship. Ireland was a poor country on the verge of a devastating catastrophe when the Jones family—poor themselves—departed. Once Jones established himself in America, he apparently never returned to the beautiful but melancholy isle of his birth.

When the distant Jones forebears left Wales for Ireland is unknown. Like many others, by the late 1700s they had intermarried and assimilated into Irish society. They had converted to the distinctive Irish brand of Catholicism infused with folk religious practices, in which believers made pilgrimages to sacred places and performed rituals at thousands of holy wells. For generations the Joneses lived some fifty miles west of Dublin in County Westmeath, a fertile, scenic region of lakes and bogs in Ireland's central plain.[1]

At the time of Patrick Henry Jones's birth, most County Westmeath residents lived on farms. Aristocratic landlords owned huge estates and rented plots of various sizes to tenants of varying means. The landscape, dotted with the ruins of ancient castles and monasteries, was sparsely inhabited. A visitor recorded walking for miles through lordly demesnes without seeing another person. Cattle, pigs, and horses were abundant, however. Westmeath's judicial seat and commercial center, Mullingar, regularly hosted cattle and horse fairs, and Westmeath livestock and butter were shipped via Dublin to the British markets. Manufacturing was limited to the home production of woolens and linens.

A guidebook of the era called Westmeath's peasantry healthy and robust, but a visitor described worn, thin men and poorly clad women and children. All went barefoot. Women shared work in the fields and performed other outdoor tasks such as hauling peat in carts. All but the elderly spoke English. Landlords provided tenants with nothing but soil, generally less than five acres. Tenants had to construct their own houses, barns, and sheds. Their homes were poor cabins built of limestone rubble or mud, with dirt floors and straw-thatched roofs. Furnishings typically included damp straw beds, a few stools, a rough wooden table, a dresser with a few plates and vessels, and an iron pot. Oatmeal and potatoes were staples.[2]

For generations the Jones family belonged to the Roman Catholic parish church at Clonmellon, a County Westmeath market and post town of about nine hundred inhabitants. Patrick Jones married Catherine Flynn there in 1797. Between 1798 and 1808 they baptized five children in the Clonmellon church. The eldest, James Jones, married Ellen Lynch at an unknown date and place. By 1830 the couple resided in Mullingar, where approximately forty-three hundred residents crowded a mile-long main thoroughfare and several side streets. Some inhabited well-built stone houses; the less fortunate huddled in one-room cabins, typically filling the squalid spaces with six to ten humans and a pig. A coaching and market center, Mullingar was reputed to be the filthiest town in Ireland, known far and wide as "Mullen-Dirt." It became an ecclesiastical seat in 1830, when a newly chosen bishop located his diocese there and set about building a cathedral.[3]

James Jones was not registered as a voter, indicating he was an impoverished tenant. He and Ellen were part of a population that Clonmellon's priest described as "those unhappy beings," the unemployed and evicted that crowded County Westmeath's villages and towns. Consequently, they were living in humble circumstances when their first child was born. American biographical sketches consistently have given Patrick Henry Jones's birthday as November 20, 1830 (as did Jones himself), but Clonmellon parish records list it as November 18. He was christened after his grandfathers, Patrick Jones and Henry Lynch. James and Ellen Jones had two more sons during their years in Westmeath, Edward C., born in 1832, and Richard, born in 1835. Then the growing family caught the emigration fever.[4]

Ireland's people were fleeing decades before blight devastated the potato crops from 1845 to 1847, setting off the Great Famine and propelling the largest wave of emigration. Between 1815 and 1845 more than a million people left Ireland, primarily for economic reasons. Despite the loss, the population almost doubled during that period to more than eight million, while a decline in agricultural prices simultaneously depressed the economy, making Ireland one of the most densely inhabited and poorest countries in Europe. The population was ravaged by five famines before the great one struck. As the 1830s waned, the economic plight of County Westmeath's small farmers and laborers was worsening, and emigrants were streaming to New York City and Buenos Aires.[5]

Enticements to emigrate spread throughout the land. Encouraging handbills were plastered from Dublin to County Westmeath and beyond. Irish newspapers carried notices of forthcoming sailings. American papers such as the *Boston Pilot*, a Catholic journal aimed at the Irish in both the old and new countries, promoted Irish emigration and provided advice to prospective emigrants. Agents in major towns such as Mullingar were commissioned to collect and forward emigrants to Liverpool, the main seaport of the Atlantic passenger trade, to sail for North America or Argentina. By the time the Joneses decided to leave Ireland, Irish emigration was marked by some distinctive practices. Most Europeans emigrated in family groups; only about half of Irish emigrants did. A common Irish practice was chain migration, in which family members took turns emigrating as funds became available, the money often sent by relatives who had already relocated. The Jones family appears to have adapted this practice to their own needs.[6]

For Irish emigrants bound to the United States, including the Joneses, New York was the port of choice. According to Ellen Jones's obituary, she and husband James emigrated in 1837. Family lore relates that a son was born and died during the voyage. James and Ellen apparently took young Edward and Richard with them but left Patrick in Ireland. As the favored first son of Irish tradition, he was to receive an education in his homeland. Biographical sketches agree that at the age of seven Patrick was sent away to school for three years; one states he studied at a monastery in County Wicklow, another that he attended a grammar school in Dublin. During that period his parents had a fourth child, Catherine, in New York State in 1839. Then it seems they returned to Ireland, leaving Edward and Richard with family or friends but taking infant Catherine, to retrieve their eldest son.[7]

James and Ellen Jones, with nine-year-old Patrick and baby Catherine, made their way to Liverpool, where emigrants often boarded in shabby flophouses while waiting for a ship. There the family took passage aboard the *St. Mark*, one of the largest of eight packets operated by James D. Roche running between Liverpool and New York. Advertisements in the *Boston Pilot* described Roche's New York–built ships as first-class vessels, constructed from the best materials for speed and comfort, and commanded by men of character and experience. Almost two hundred men, women, and children boarded the *St. Mark* along with the Jones family. Most of them were Irish, but there were more than thirty from Wales, a half-dozen English, and a solitary Pole. Virtually all of the men were listed as laborers; many of the women were described as spinsters.[8]

Jones's biographical sketches give no accounts of the voyage, which typically took five to six weeks. Many ships in the trade were originally built to carry timber or grain, but if Roche's advertisements were accurate, his vessels were superior. On any ship, however, life in the crowded steerage deck was unpleasant and dangerous. It was rarely more than six feet high, damp and foul, with no openings for fresh air or light other than the hatches, which were kept closed at night and during bad weather. Flimsy berths were constructed of rough lumber. Steerage passengers had to provide their own provisions and cook their meals as best they could. The long voyage across the often stormy Atlantic could be frightening. Passengers were plagued by disease, chiefly typhus, cholera, and smallpox. About one out of every twelve of them died. For the Joneses the ordeal ended on June 5, 1840, when the *St. Mark* arrived at New York and young Patrick got his first sights of the city he would eventually call home.[9]

During the nineteenth-century canal building boom, thousands of Irish immigrants worked in the industry digging ditches, blasting rock, and building locks. The canal companies advertised for workers in Ireland; it is possible that James Jones was drawn across the ocean in response to such a notice. He worked on the early stages of the Genesee Valley Canal, which was authorized by the New York State legislature in 1836. When completed in 1856, the waterway linked the Erie Canal near Rochester with the Allegheny River at Olean, in Cattaraugus County. Labor on the canals was physically grueling, dangerous, and poorly paid (most workers earned eight to ten dollars per month). Room and board was provided in raucous, violent, disease-ridden camps of wooden bunkhouses. According to Catherine Jones, the family was living in Monroe County, along the northern stretch of the canal, when she was born in 1839.[10]

The 1840 census listed the Joneses as residents of the Cattaraugus County township of Hinsdale, through which the canal ran on its way to Olean. That September a man named Judd, who had contracted with the state to complete certain sections of the canal, hired James Jones and his brother Edward as subcontractors to do excavation and embankment work. Ten percent of their pay was to be withheld as a reserved fee, to be paid on completion of the job. According to Catherine Jones, when her father finished his work, Judd kept the reserved fee "and ran away to Canada," leaving James Jones with nothing but the horses and carts he had used on the job. Court records corroborate part of her story. Judd paid the Jones brothers their wages but withheld the reserved fee, which amounted to $85.30. Irish canal workers were not afraid to speak out when they believed they were being exploited—protests and strikes were common—and the Joneses displayed this militancy by suing Judd to recover the fee. When the Cattaraugus County Court of Common Pleas ruled in the brothers' favor, Judd appealed to the state supreme court, which affirmed the ruling, and then to the state's highest court, the court of appeals, which also found for the Joneses. The case became somewhat of a landmark in contract law. Coincidentally, the New York State Court of Appeals came to be an institution of importance in Patrick Henry Jones's life.[11]

James and Ellen Jones's family grew during the 1840s with the births of Thomas B. (1841), Mary (1844), and Ellen (1845). At some point during the decade, the family moved to a farm in the Cattaraugus County town of Little Valley, where they were recorded in the 1850 census. Almost a century later an old-timer asserted that the Joneses lived on rugged Fish Hill, which rose steeply near the corner of three townships: Little Valley, Mansfield, and Ellicottville, the county seat. Numerous Irish families carved farms into the wooded hills surrounding the village of Ellicottville, lured to the area by a land speculator who held Roman Catholic services in his office until a proper church was built in 1851. Today's Irish Hill Road and Dublin Road commemorate their settlements.[12]

In her recollections Catherine Jones stated that her father, after being cheated by Judd, traded some of his horses and carts for a thickly forested, forty-acre property. James Jones felled and burned the timber and sold the resulting potash. After a few years he rented four hundred acres and operated a dairy farm and sugar bush. Patrick and his siblings worked with their parents, performing chores according to their abilities, helping to make brooms, candles, soap, and maple sugar. Catherine Jones recalled an amusing incident from those years. It was common at the time for dogs to tread large wheels to power churns, but the Joneses' lazy dog could not be made to do the work. So, James Jones trained four sheep to run the churn. One day little Mary and Ellen Jones were out watching the sheep crank the contraption. The sisters were clothed alike in polka-dot dresses made by their mother and belts obtained from Indians (the Seneca tribe lived on nearby reservations). A traveling circus happened by on the road that passed the Jones farm. "Well, we haven't all the circus," one of the troupe called. "See there!" The procession stopped and admired the colorfully costumed girls and their trained sheep—and the girls no doubt stared wide-eyed at the curious circus folk and their caged animals.[13]

Patrick worked on the farm until his parents sent him to the Union School in Ellicottville, where he continued the formal education he had begun in Ireland. He was reportedly a diligent student. He worked to earn his tuition and in the process became familiar with village life. Ellicottville embraced the young Irishman, praising him for his "more than ordinary promise and ability," for raising himself from poverty by dint of "indomitable perseverance and application." With the benefit of an education, Jones was ready to seek employment away from the family farm.[14]

He chose journalism, a profession inextricably entwined with politics, with which he would be actively involved for much of his life. Jones's interest in politics developed as he matured into young adulthood during the 1840s. That period marked the emergence in America of a distinct two-party system. As the decade progressed, both parties entered a period of upheaval over the most disruptive issue facing the nation: the debate over the expansion of slavery into western territories. The Whigs stressed restrictions on slavery and voiced support for a strong national government and the Union. The Democrats defended slavery and states' rights and opposed federal funding of internal improvements. They championed white supremacy but were otherwise ethnically and religiously tolerant, welcoming the Irish into their fold. Consequently, the Joneses were Democrats.[15]

In 1850 Jones turned twenty and began his journalistic career. His first job was with the *Cattaraugus Republican*, a weekly Democratic newspaper published in Ellicottville. (The paper's name referred to republicanism; the development of the Republican Party was several years in the future.) Its publisher and editor, Robert H. Shankland, was a prominent Democratic functionary widely regarded as an able, kind, and honorable man. After his initiation with Shankland, Jones traveled through the western states as correspondent for a leading New York State newspaper, presumably another Democratic publication. Unfortunately, the name of the paper is unknown; thus, it is impossible to know the extent of what must have been an impactful western journey.[16]

On returning to western New York, Jones settled in the region's largest city, Buffalo, and became local editor of a Democratic daily, the *Buffalo Republic*. In June 1853 native Irishman Bernard Doran Killian hired Jones to edit his new weekly Catholic paper, the *Buffalo Sentinel*. Robert Shankland described Killian's paper as neatly gotten up and edited with ability by Jones, who well deserved success. But Jones's editorship under Killian was short-lived and proved to be his journalistic coda. A biographical sketch speculates that he lost interest in journalism. He quit the newspaper business and the city of Buffalo and returned to Ellicottville.[17]

In 1853 he began to study law in the Ellicottville office of Addison G. Rice. Nine years Jones's senior, Rice became an influential figure in the Irishman's development as a lawyer and (later) a soldier and politician. By the time he took Jones as a student, Rice was a leading attorney in Ellicottville. He was a Whig who became a Republican when that party was organized in Cattaraugus County in 1855 and was a delegate the following year to its first national convention. The Republicans—a coalition of former Whigs, Free-Soil advocates, and antislavery Democrats—upheld many of the tenets of the Whigs, among them free labor and internal improvements. As the political landscape shifted, the Democratic Party increasingly split along sectional lines over the slavery issue. In remaining loyal to the Democrats, Jones stood by his fellow Irish Americans, who disliked the Republicans and regarded them as anti-immigrant, antislavery, pro-temperance, and representatives of the propertied classes. Despite their political differences, Rice and Jones established an amicable relationship. After three years of working together, the mentor made his student a partner, and in August 1856 the firm of Rice and Jones began advertising in Ellicottville newspapers. On November 18 of that year, Jones was admitted to the bar at the general term held in Buffalo. At age twenty-six the former farmer, student, and journalist had found the profession he would follow for the rest of his life. In the meantime he had parted with his family.[18]

By the time the Joneses arrived in America, the native-born Protestant majority perceived the Irish to be exclusively and devoutly Roman Catholic. Not all Irish immigrants were Catholic, of course, and those that were had left a large part of their religion behind at Ireland's holy wells when they came to the States—only about half of them were active parishioners. The Irish were also stereotyped as friendly, generous, and good-hearted, but those admirable attributes were overshadowed by their perceived shortcomings as violent, clannish, and dependent. Influential ethnological and phrenological theories painted them as an inferior race, brutish and simian, and as such they were portrayed in the popular culture onstage and in fiction. Such prejudice would dog the Irish to the end of the nineteenth century and beyond.[19]

Most Irish immigrants came from rural areas, but lacking cash and encouraged by parish priests, they tended to settle in cities. New York City was the Dublin of America, with almost one out of four residents of Irish descent. Often illiterate and unskilled, holding the lowest-paying jobs and hindered by discrimination, the newcomers struggled to climb the ladder of economic success. Xenophobic American antipathy to the massive growth of Irish and German immigrant communities evolved over the years into a political movement of considerable power. Nativist clout reached a zenith in the Know-Nothing craze of the 1850s—a phenomenon that had a major impact on the Jones family.[20]

Nativist fraternal organizations sprang up throughout the North in the early years of the decade. They condemned Irish and German immigrants as criminals and paupers, blamed them for economic decline, and doubted their patriotism. Nativists also believed that America was meant to be a Protestant country; they opposed Catholics and feared Catholic political power. They distrusted traditional parties at a time of schisms caused by the sectional crisis. Around 1850 a secret organization calling itself the Order of the Star Spangled Banner was founded in New York City. By 1853 it was the largest nativist group in the country and had adopted the informal moniker "Know-Nothings." The name was made public that fall by the famous editor Horace Greeley in the pages of his nationally distributed *New York Tribune*. Greeley opposed the movement, but despite the persuasive influence and wide reach of his editorials, the Know-Nothings spread from urban to rural areas throughout New York State.[21]

The Know-Nothings were notably successful in Western New York, particularly in Cattaraugus and neighboring Chautauqua Counties, where they often captured their largest electoral majorities. Jones's former employer Robert Shankland deserted the Democrats for the Know-Nothings and trumpeted them in his newspaper. In 1854 the party's nationwide membership soared from fifty thousand to more than one million. Many of them were dissatisfied Whigs and Democrats attracted by the Know-Nothings' adoption of the temperance and antislavery causes. The party's explosive growth generated widespread newspaper coverage and inspired a host of Know-Nothing branded products, from candy and cigars to tea and toothpicks. In the 1855 state election the party showed strength, but it had lost control of Western New York, where its supporters had largely swung to the Republicans. By then, however, nativism had goaded the Jones family out of the area.[22]

By 1853 James Jones wanted to escape the widespread prejudice his family faced in New York State. A subscriber to the *Boston Pilot*, he was intrigued by articles promoting Irish Catholic settlements in the West. Writers particularly touted Iowa, the fertile expanse of prairie between the Mississippi and Missouri Rivers, a state since 1846. The Roman Catholic bishop of the Diocese of Dubuque was encouraging settlements. A *Pilot* correspondent reported that hundreds of Irish emigrants were entering Iowa and there was "plenty of room for more." Another correspondent described a settlement at Garryowen, Iowa, about twenty miles from Dubuque, that was said to have inhabitants from every county in Ireland. Inspired by such news, and perhaps influenced by son Patrick's assessment of western prospects from his journalistic tour, James Jones sold his Cattaraugus County property, packed up his wife and children, and headed west.[23]

Embarking on their great adventure, the Jones family left Patrick behind. The dynamics of the split are unknown. Did Jones consider joining his parents and six siblings? Did his trip through the western states as a correspondent influence their decision to emigrate or his decision not to join them? While the circumstances remain hidden, the end result is clear—Jones and his family parted, never to reunite.

Consecrated in 1837 as the first bishop of the new Diocese of Dubuque, native Frenchman Mathias Loras set to work to encourage European immigrants to establish farms on Iowa's vast plains. By the early 1850s Loras was widely promoting the effort in the *Boston Pilot* and other Catholic publications. The bishop warned potential emigrants of the hardships of frontier life. Prospective settlers should have ample means to sustain themselves through at least a year or two of serious privations, he observed, and should not expect to have a priest and church in every settlement. Other Catholic clergymen proposed immigrant colonization plans, but Bishop Loras proved to be the leading figure in the movement. He and his fellow promoters met with opposition from clergy in the eastern states, who doubted spiritual efficacy in the colonies. In the end western Catholic settlements would result more often from the individual initiative of families than from any church-sponsored program.[24]

On April 20, 1853, a team of horses hauled a wagon carrying the Jones family and their belongings to Buffalo, where they spent the night at an Irish-owned boardinghouse. Perhaps they had a farewell get-together with Patrick, who was living in the city at the time. The next morning, accompanied by other Irish families on the same mission, the Joneses boarded a steamer and sailed to Toledo, Ohio. From there they took a train to Illinois and stopped for a night at Chicago, where they stayed with Irish friends. The group then spent several months in Illinois on rented farms. But James Jones was dissatisfied with the situation, and in 1854, lured by the reports from Iowa, he traded his horses for oxen, and the family and their companions moved on. When the pioneers reached the banks of the Mississippi River opposite Dubuque, they took quarters for the night at an Irish-owned hotel.[25]

James Jones and his son Edward (known as Ned) called on Bishop Loras in Dubuque and told him they had left their home in New York State to settle in a new country near a Catholic church. Providentially, the Reverend Jeremiah F. Trecy joined the conversation. A native Irishman, Father Trecy ministered to the Catholic colony at Garryowen. With the bishop's support, Trecy planned to found other colonies. Loras, Trecy, and the Joneses talked of forming a colony, but the bishop declared he could not then spare Trecy; the colony would have to wait. In the meantime, Trecy suggested, the Joneses and the rest of their party could rent farms at Garryowen. They did so, giving their landlords portions of their crops for rent.[26]

In the spring of 1855 Father Trecy, Ned Jones, and six other men set off to found their colony, heading west across Iowa in a mule-drawn covered wagon painted with the slogan GOING WHERE NO ONE LIVES. They arrived at Sioux City, an untidy cluster of log houses and hotels, in June. There they crossed the Missouri River into Dakota County, Nebraska Territory. They followed the riverbank northward for a few miles to a grove of cottonwoods surrounding a spring. They had found their spot. Scouting the area, Ned Jones made claims for his family.[27]

Leaving some men to hold the claim, Trecy and Ned Jones returned to Garryowen. In February 1856 Bishop Loras sent Trecy to the Irish Immigrant Aid Convention in Buffalo, which advocated a unified approach to Catholic settlements in the West. When Trecy returned to Iowa, a formal colonization society was organized, with Loras as president. Trecy named it in honor of St. Patrick. He was confident that Irishmen were no longer disposed to submit to a state of drudgery in the East; western migration would give thousands of his poor native countrymen a home. A *Boston Pilot* correspondent thought the settlement would succeed "if Catholics go together and aid each other as Yankees do."[28]

On April 21, 1856, Father Trecy and his colonists began the three hundred–mile trip west across Iowa. On the morning of their departure from Garryowen, Bishop Loras blessed them at Mass and requested that they hoist a cross and the American flag at their destination. Twenty-five families—some sixty people, mostly Irish immigrants—and their belongings filled eighteen ox-drawn wagons. Off they rolled, the women and children riding and the men walking and driving the oxen. After an arduous trek of forty days, they reached Sioux City. The party crossed the Missouri on a flatboat and camped for the night by the riverbank. The next day, June 2, 1856, St. Patrick's Colony arrived at its new home. They named the place St. John's, after John the Baptist. Father Trecy performed Mass, and, fulfilling their promise to Bishop Loras, the colonists raised a fifty-foot cross and the flag on a high bluff. That month a 240-acre town site was surveyed and platted in a rectangular grid, with streets named after saints. Some of the colonists settled in the town site, but most of them took claims in the surrounding countryside.[29]

The pioneers immediately began to build dugout homes in the hillsides, with log walls and sod roofs. They broke ground and planted acres of corn, a crop that was lost to grasshoppers. Then came a bitter winter and more hardship and want. Deep snows imprisoned families in their dugouts. Men strung lines to guide them through blizzards to their crude barns. Families lived on parched corn and milk. After the dreary winter came spring rains and floods and mud. Summer brought another menace—Indians, who stole crops and livestock and filled the colonists with fear of killings and burnings.[30]

At a meeting of the colony on New Year's Day 1857, a committee of five, including Ned Jones, drafted a letter to be sent to Catholic newspapers in the East. The missive made no mention of hardships. Instead, it extolled St. John's location on the Missouri River, its salubrious climate, fertile soil, pure water, and abundant timber. There was ample space for five hundred families; prospective pioneers were urged to lose no time in making their move. The colonists sought fellow Irish Catholics whose savings could support their families for three months while they established themselves. A committee would welcome them as long as the newcomer had a letter from his priest attesting to his moral character and temperance. The St. Patrick's Colony was "a model of temperance, and not subject to broils and contentions." In the November 1856 election the colony had chosen its own officers, and Ned Jones had been elected to Nebraska's territorial legislature. Forty-nine colonists signed the letter, including Ned Jones, his father, and his brother Richard. Most of the colonists were farmers. All were Irish except for a handful of Germans.[31]

When published, the letter set off a flurry of correspondence to the *Boston Pilot*. Two visitors to Nebraska made a string of negative assertions about the "disgraceful deception" of the settlement and its "wretched inhabitants." Other correspondents branded this letter a fraud; Father Trecy called it "an unmitigated fabrication." Another visitor who spent six weeks at St. John's described fine land, abundant crops, fifty houses, and commercial structures and a church under construction. For his part the *Pilot*'s editor denied any responsibility for claims made about western settlements by the paper's correspondents.[32]

Father Trecy experienced an embarrassing incident in March 1857 during an eastern lecture tour meant to garner support and pioneers for St. Patrick's Colony. At the close of his speech in New York City, a member of the audience rose to voice disapproval. He was Archbishop John Hughes of New York, the most influential Irishman and Roman Catholic in the United States. Hughes asserted vehemently that Trecy's effort would impede and perhaps prevent Catholic immigrant assimilation into American society and subject pioneers to discomforts, afflictions, and mental and religious evils. When the archbishop finished his diatribe, the audience filed out of the auditorium in stunned silence. Trecy made no more appeals for his colony in the Archdiocese of New York.[33]

In the summer of 1857 grasshoppers again devoured most of St. John's corn crop, and Indians stole what was left. A year later St. John's peaked as a village of almost two hundred inhabitants, with stores, a sawmill, and a log schoolhouse. But the hardships continued and discouraged pioneers moved away. Others abandoned their claims when the federal government demanded payment for the land. Many residents moved about a mile and a half to the southwest, to the newly established town of Jackson. By 1859 only the Joneses and two of the other original families remained in the area. The colony's symbolic death occurred in July 1860, when a storm knocked down the church under construction. During the Civil War years the Missouri River threatened to wash away the site. By the war's end all of St. John's buildings were gone—some of them had been moved to Jackson—and the town was abandoned.[34]

Historians have pointed to Father Trecy's frequent absences as the single greatest cause of the failure of St. John's. His missionary work covered most of Nebraska Territory, and he left St. Patrick's Colony without a priest for long periods of time. In a letter to the *Boston Pilot* one disgruntled colonist revealed that seventeen people had died in the settlement without receiving the last sacraments. Here was an example of the religious evil that Archbishop Hughes had warned of in his attack on Father Trecy. A eulogist proclaimed Trecy "an active, energetic and zealous priest of the early days," always spoken of by the pioneers of Garryowen and the Missouri River Valley "with words of sincere praise." But according to one account, the St. John's residents became so bitter against Trecy that he fled the colony.[35]

The Jones family stuck it out on their claim near present-day Willis, Nebraska. They struggled to get by, borrowing money at usurious interest rates. The girls were sent to Sioux City to attend school. Mary Jones took a teaching job in nearby Ponca. Ned and Richard Jones worked for a while at Omadi, a now vanished settlement opposite Sioux City. In 1857 Ned Jones took his seat as Dakota County's first representative in the territorial legislature. He sent newspapers and government documents to Ellicottville to keep the folks in Cattaraugus County informed of doings in Nebraska.[36]

St. John's did not vanish entirely. It left a hilltop cemetery, where many of the St. Patrick's Colony pioneers were laid to rest. Among them was James Jones, who died in 1864, his wife, Ellen Lynch Jones, who died in 1888, and their four youngest children: Thomas B. Jones (a Civil War veteran of the Second Nebraska Cavalry), Catherine Jones Twohig, Mary Jones McHenry, and Ellen Jones Boler.[37]

While his family escaped bigotry in the East to encounter hardships in the West, Patrick Henry Jones prospered as a lawyer and ingrained himself in Ellicottville society. He and his partner, Addison Rice, joined ten other village men to call for the founding of a lyceum or debating club. A cofounder was the Reverend Thomas Morris, a native Englishman who came to Ellicottville in 1834 as minister of St. John's Episcopal Church. When he retired in 1848, the congregation presented Morris with a farm outside the village. By the late 1850s he had emerged from retirement to ride the circuit in the northern district of New York State, ministering to scattered Episcopalian congregations. Consequently, Reverend Morris was often away when Jones was courting his daughter Sarah.[38]

On the morning of December 20, 1859, twenty-nine-year-old Patrick Henry Jones wed twenty-two-year-old Sarah Morris in Ellicottville. This marriage of a Catholic to a Protestant must have stirred controversy. At the time religiously mixed marriages were considered unthinkable, sure to result in disaster. If there was opposition to the match, however, Thomas Morris apparently did not share in it. He officiated at the ceremony, which was held in his home. Sarah later recalled her wedding as very quiet, attended only by a sister and three family friends. "Good luck to our old *young* friend Patrick," congratulated Jones's former boss Robert Shankland. "We began to mistrust he would be an incorrigible old bachelor, but this last move on the matrimonial board has certainly dispelled our fears. Long may he live to practice *honesty* instead of LAW, in our midst, and prove a worthy husband of a worthy 'charming young wife.'" The newlyweds settled into rented quarters in Ellicottville. In the absence of their correspondence or other evidence, it is impossible to assess Patrick and Sarah's marriage beyond one certainty—it proved to be a till-death-do-you-part bond.[39]

Jones's political path in the late antebellum and Civil War periods is traced in the pages of Ellicottville's three weekly newspapers. The oldest was the *Cattaraugus Republican*, the Democratic organ published from 1835 by Robert Shankland, where Jones had started in journalism. When Shankland deserted the Democrats for the Know-Nothings in 1854, he sold the *Republican* to a pair of partners who continued to run it as a Democratic sheet. Delos E. Sill founded Ellicottville's second oldest newspaper in 1840 as a Whig Party organ. When the Whigs dissolved, Sill became a Republican and named his paper the *Cattaraugus Freeman*. Robert Shankland bought the *American Union* in 1855. Two years later Shankland abandoned the Know-Nothings and returned to his old party, whereupon the *Union* supported the Democrats.[40]

With the pivotal presidential election of 1860 looming, Shankland's *American Union* recorded the formation of a Democratic club in Ellicottville. Jones was one of thirteen vice presidential appointees and sat on a committee on resolutions. Three months later Shankland charged his rivals at the *Cattaraugus Republican* with having Jones write an editorial. In the competition between the two Democratic papers, Jones apparently had aligned himself against his erstwhile employer Shankland, the former Know-Nothing.[41]

The law firm of Rice and Jones underwent change around the turn of the decade. In 1859 the partners had two students under their tutelage, Dan B. Allen and Alanson Crosby, both Cattaraugus County natives. That year Crosby was admitted to the bar, and in 1860 he joined his mentors' practice. The firm of Rice, Jones and Crosby would be short-lived, but Jones, Crosby, and Allen would be reunited within two years in the military.[42]

At this point in his career, Jones had reached a modest prosperity. The 1860 census valued his personal estate at three hundred dollars. On November 17 of that year he bought his first piece of property at a public auction in Ellicottville. Townsman and fellow attorney Allen D. Scott had been appointed receiver of the parcel in a land fraud case. It consisted of fourteen acres abutting the Allegany Indian Reservation, home to the Seneca tribe, in the Cattaraugus County town of Cold Spring. Jones was high bidder, at twenty-five dollars. A week later he and Sarah sold the parcel and pocketed a tidy fifty-dollar profit.[43]

The Joneses' first year of marriage played out against a backdrop of national turmoil. Weeks before Patrick and Sarah's wedding, the antislavery zealot John Brown was hanged in Virginia following the failure of his raid on Harpers Ferry, meant to spark a slave uprising in the South. Split over the slavery question, the Democratic Party's national convention in Charleston, South Carolina, adjourned without agreeing on a candidate. Northern Democrats subsequently convened in Baltimore and nominated Stephen Douglas for president. Southern Democrats met in Baltimore days later and nominated John C. Breckinridge. Former members of the Whig and American Parties also met in Baltimore, formed the Constitutional Union Party, and nominated John Bell. The Republican Party met in Chicago and nominated Abraham Lincoln. The divisive questions of slavery and sectionalism dominated the subsequent presidential campaign. Within days of Lincoln's election southern leaders proclaimed secession inevitable. It became a reality on Patrick and Sarah's first wedding anniversary, December 20, 1860, when South Carolina seceded from the Union.[44]

As 1860 ended, the three partners in Rice, Jones and Crosby went their separate ways and opened individual practices during deeply unsettling times. Other southern states were on the brink of joining South Carolina in leaving the Union. The sectional crisis had led to secession, secession would lead to war—and war would lead to opportunity for Patrick Henry Jones.[45]

CHAPTER 2

The Irish Rifles

Within days after the firing on Fort Sumter, the *Cattaraugus Freeman* announced Jones would take up arms in defense of his adopted country. Republican editor Delos Sill called Democrat Jones an "esteemed and patriotic friend" who would leave behind a large and lucrative law practice to defend the flag on the battlefield. Sill offered a prayer for the new soldier: "God grant that his life may be spared, and that he may return to us and his family again at some future day, when the honor of our country shall have been vindicated, and peace shall again smile throughout the land." On a more mundane note Sill reported that Ellicottville attorney Allen Scott would handle Jones's unfinished business during his absence.[1]

Like communities throughout the North, Ellicottville was electric with excitement at the war's outbreak. In response to proclamations by President Abraham Lincoln and Governor Edwin D. Morgan, an enthusiastic crowd filled the county courthouse on the evening of April 23, 1861, to rally for the cause and to organize a volunteer company. A resolution pledging support for the Constitution and the Union passed to thunderous applause. Jones had a lifelong reticence when it came to addressing the public and did not speak, but a series of orators, including his associates Allen Scott and Alanson Crosby, stoked the crowd's enthusiasm. A letter from Jones's former partner Addison Rice pledging six hundred dollars to benefit the families of volunteers was read to loud applause. Scott offered one hundred dollars, and other men voiced pledges. The meeting closed with songs—the Marseilles and the Star Spangled Banner—and cheers for the volunteers, the Union, the flag, and Maj. Robert Anderson of Fort Sumter fame.[2]

Ellicottville's few commercial blocks were adorned with patriotic mottoes, flags, and bayonets. Recruiting was brisk. Men drilled to the sound of fife and drums and slept in makeshift barracks in the concert hall. But there was a problem, as Jones explained on May 10 in a letter to John Manley, a clerk in the Interior Department in Washington, D.C. "We are in the fog here," Jones wrote, about how the enlistees were to be mustered into the federal service. Could Manley—Cattaraugus County's only federal employee at the capital—obtain the necessary information from the War Department?

There was another issue. "Cattaraugus wants to furnish a regiment if they can go under their own officers," Jones reported, but under the state call the county was limited to only two companies. Was a regiment possible? "Our men are anxious to know," Jones informed Manley. "An early reply will oblige the citizens of this place."[3]

Jones's letter was one of the first of thousands Manley received during the war from Cattaraugus County soldiers and civilians seeking his aid with federal government matters. He soon was dubbed the "Soldier's Friend" for his work on the county's behalf as a tireless cutter of bureaucratic red tape. A Republican, Manley became a regular correspondent for the *Cattaraugus Freeman*, keeping the homefolk up-to-date on their men at the front. Over time he also became a staunch ally and advocate for Jones.[4]

Jones asked Manley to have duplicate information sent to Capt. Luke G. Harmon, an Ellicottville man who had matriculated at the U.S. Military Academy and served in the state militia. Manley consulted at the War Department, and Maj. Irvin McDowell—soon to be a general commanding a Union army—forwarded army forms and regulations to Cattaraugus County. There would be no regiment, Jones was told, just the two companies authorized under the call. They were quickly organized. Captain Harmon recruited the Chamberlain Guards in Allegany, and Capt. William T. Clarke raised the Cattaraugus Guards in Ellicottville.[5]

Jones enrolled in the Chamberlain Guards in Allegany on May 15, 1861, to serve two years. He joined that company rather than the one recruited in his hometown of Ellicottville because of his relationship with Luke Harmon. He and Harmon were allied in the recruiting effort, and on May 16 the *Freeman* reported that Jones had been commissioned a lieutenant in Harmon's company. He would serve under a West Point–trained officer whom Delos Sill described as "a brave-hearted, cool-headed, resolute young man." Captain Harmon offered Jones the best chance to learn army procedures. Jones took the advantage and proved to be an adept pupil.[6]

The Chamberlain Guards departed Allegany by train on the morning of May 22 in high spirits. Addison Rice accompanied the company as a file closer. They arrived in Elmira that afternoon and were greeted with cheers by the Cattaraugus Guards, who had preceded them by two days. Approximately ten thousand troops jammed Elmira, and more appeared with each arriving train. Most of them were in organized regiments, unlike the two Cattaraugus

County companies, which were "hanging around loose," quartered in a church and taking their meals at a hotel. "There is no discontent here," wrote one of the Cattaraugus Guards, "but every man is anxious to travel south, where he can climb the ladder of fame, and enroll his name where it may live through time."[7]

They took a step closer on the night of May 25, traveling by rail to New York City. The two companies marched to a barracks in City Hall Park for breakfast. Then they whiled away the day until late afternoon, when their mascot, a bulldog that delighted in parading to fife and drum, won onlookers' attention during a march to a barracks on Thirty-First Street. The men looked "rather hard" after two days without rest, an observer noted, but remained in "tip-top spirits." They enjoyed sightseeing and visits to Barnum's American Museum.[8]

On May 26 the city commemorated Col. Elmer E. Ellsworth. The dashing young friend of President Lincoln had been killed two days earlier after removing a Confederate flag from atop a hotel in Alexandria, Virginia, consecrating him as the Union's first heroic martyr. His remains lay in state in City Hall and attracted a mob of mourners. Jones and a visiting Ellicottville friend attempted a viewing. They made it halfway up the City Hall steps, tired of fighting the crowd, and left.[9]

Addison Rice left for home on May 30. By then the two Cattaraugus companies were quartered in houses at Ninety-Fifth Street and Bloomingdale Road. A military board at Albany had assigned them to the Thirty-Seventh New York Volunteer Infantry. Seven of the regiment's eight other companies consisted of the Seventy-Fifth Militia, composed of Irishmen from New York City. Consequently, the Seventy-Fifth was called the "Irish Rifles"; the Thirty-Seventh Regiment would carry on the name. Through happenstance Jones found himself a member of an organization composed largely of his native countrymen. With the Irish Rifles, Patrick Jones of County Westmeath would fight under a harp-spangled green banner. As a western New Yorker, he was an outsider among the Manhattan men, but as a native Irishman, he was one of their own.[10]

The Irish, as an immigrant ethnic group, were underrepresented proportionally in the army owing to their allegiance to the Democratic Party and their opposition to abolitionism. Nevertheless, almost 150,000 Irishmen fought for the Union during the course of the war. Before Fort Sumter the Irish in the North were ambivalent regarding secession and the Confederacy; after Sumter they solidly supported the Union. Some of them served in all or largely Irish regiments such as the Thirty-Seventh New York; most served in nonethnic units. They were motivated by patriotism, a thirst for adventure, economic considerations, and the desire for military experience that could be used in liberating Ireland from Great Britain. Thus, they had dual loyalties, to the United States and to Ireland. They would emerge from the war with a reputation as fighters. Jones had been part of an ethnic minority in western New York. Now, in the regimental milieu, he enjoyed a bond with the ethnic majority. Life with the Irish Rifles, however, presented difficulties for the Cattaraugus County men and consequently for Jones.[11]

They were unlucky when it came to their commander. A native of Ireland, John H. McCunn had risen from poverty to become a New York lawyer of dim repute. Elected a city judge in 1860, he proved to be a corrupt tool of the notorious Tammany Hall Democratic political boss William M. Tweed. McCunn had commanded the Seventy-Fifth Militia during the 1850s, which led to his commission as colonel of the Thirty-Seventh. The Cattaraugus men initially anticipated "conspicuous and pleasant duty" under Colonel McCunn. "If there is anything good going," one of them conjectured, "we will have our share." But the favorable first impression quickly faded, and the men came to regard their colonel as a "tap-room politician," "utterly worthless and incompetent," "a man profoundly ignorant of all military matters," who was "of questionable loyalty to the Union, but of boundless conceit and overbearing in his disposition." McCunn in turn expressed his contempt for the Cattaraugus contingent—which included abolitionist Republicans—by calling them the "Niggeraugus Boys."[12]

On June 3 McCunn's regiment marched to the foot of Manhattan and camped near Castle Garden. There the soldiers lounged in their tents, buffeted by sea breezes, enjoying first-rate meals of seafood and roast beef, and welcoming visits from friends. The enlisted men had yet to receive their uniforms (Jones and the other officers clothed themselves), so they drilled in their civilian togs. The Thirty-Seventh New York was mustered into the service of the United States on June 7. The Chamberlain Guards were designated Company H; the Cattaraugus Guards became Company I. Jones was mustered in as Company H's second lieutenant. (His commission would be dated July 4, 1861, with rank from May 17, 1861.) After taking the oath, the men gave three cheers and a tiger for the Stars and Stripes. "Our boys are all in good spirits," one of them wrote, "and only anxious for a chance to spread themselves and show what green Cattaraugus boys can do for the Union."[13]

Cattaraugus County district attorney William Pitt Angel, who visited the Thirty-Seventh's camp on June 9, recorded similar sentiments. Angel spent an hour touring the site and conversing with his old friend Jones, who assured him that the enlisted men were content with their rations and satisfied with their treatment by the officers. They were in good health and spirits, Angel reported in a letter to the *Cattaraugus Freeman*, patiently waiting to be armed and equipped and "anxious to be off to the wars," adding, "You need have no fears for the Cattaraugus boys. If any men are disgraced in this contest, it will not be them."[14]

While the men waited to go south, Captains Harmon and Clarke and Lieutenant Jones were granted leaves of absence with orders to report at its termination to headquarters in New York City. The three officers returned to Cattaraugus County. They were still absent when the enlisted men finally received their uniforms, arms and equipage, and pay. Passing the time, the soldiers went sightseeing and gawked at celebrities. They named their camp after Thurlow Weed, the editor of the *Albany Evening Journal* and statewide Republican Party powerbroker. Thus far, the members of the Cattaraugus contingent were pleased with their regimental comrades. "The Irish boys are the most free hearted on the ground," one of them wrote. "They will do anything you ask of them." William Angel visited the Cattaraugus companies a second time and again reported them "anxious to get away to the war." With their muskets now in hand, "the boys *feel* very much more like soldiers, since they can make a soldierly appearance." Jones would return to a transformed regiment.[15]

Reflecting its commander's ineffectiveness, the Thirty-Seventh New York's departure from the city was delayed to allow many absentees to report. Jones, however, remained absent. On June 22, 1861, an immense crowd witnessed friends give Colonel McCunn a sword and revolver and city merchants and schoolgirls present the regiment with flags. The next morning, a Sunday, Chaplain Peter Tissot, a native Frenchman and Jesuit priest, said Mass. That afternoon, as a band played traditional Irish airs, the regiment marched past a dense, cheering, largely Irish crowd to a steamer, crossed the Hudson River to New Jersey, and boarded a train to Washington, D.C., via Philadelphia (where they were received with great goodwill) and Baltimore (where they were not). Southern sympathizers in Baltimore, Pvt. Nelson Loomis of Company I found, "look daggers but keep their mouths shut."[16]

The Thirty-Seventh arrived in the capital on June 24 and marched through oppressive heat to the White House and a review by President Lincoln and Secretary of War Simon Cameron. Then they settled in for the night on Pennsylvania Avenue, "some in the street, some in houses, some sober, some drunk," according to Chaplain Tissot. The Cattaraugus men marveled at the large numbers of African Americans in Washington, D.C.; black people were virtually unknown back home. Some of the soldiers visited John Manley. The next day they moved to a hill overlooking the Potomac River east of the city and established Camp Mary, named after the first lady. When Mary Todd Lincoln and her husband dropped by an evening later to review the regiment, Colonel McCunn broke a bottle of champagne over a wagon wheel to officially christen the camp.[17]

Jones missed it all. The *Cattaraugus Freeman* of June 27 reported that he and a lieutenant of Company I were in Ellicottville on a brief visit to their families. "They both look as if camp life agreed with them," the squib noted, "and are as hale and hearty as they could reasonably desire." Soon Jones was back in New York City, where he discovered the regiment had proceeded to Washington. He bought a ticket to the capital and rejoined the Irish Rifles at Camp Mary on June 30. There he and the other line officers began an education in military science, drilling the men six hours daily and studying tactics in their spare time. Owing to the experience of Captain Harmon, Company H bested Company I on the drill field.[18]

Soldiers fainted during a sweltering Independence Day review of New York regiments by President Lincoln and Gen. Winfield Scott. That day Nelson Loomis noted that the Cattaraugus men, in an early sign of trouble, had "had a row" with some Irishmen of the regiment and had "cooled them off in a short time." Loomis now cursed the Irish. Later that month Governor Edwin Morgan reviewed and addressed the regiment. Companies H and I also welcomed a visit from Reuben E. Fenton, the congressman representing Cattaraugus and Chautauqua Counties, who presented the men with a thousand franked envelopes. Jones would come to know both men well. Morgan would become his political associate, Fenton his political patron.[19]

Morgan had made a fortune in New York City as an importer of sugar and coffee and a shareholder in railroads and clipper ships. He had served as a Whig alderman and state senator until the formation of the Republicans in 1854, when he was named state party chairman. Two years later he became national chairman, presiding over the Republicans' first two national conventions, in 1856 and 1860. Morgan was elected governor of New York in 1858 and reelected two years later. At the outbreak of the war President Lincoln appointed him a major general of volunteers, in command of the Department of New York.[20]

Born in Chautauqua County on the Fourth of July in 1819, Fenton personified the self-made man and the ambitious politician. As a teenager, he had been forced to abandon his legal studies when his father's business failed. After rescuing his father financially, he made a modest fortune in the lumber industry. Fenton was elected a colonel in the militia, but his true interest was politics. Initially a Democrat, he served terms as a town supervisor and state assemblyman before going to Congress in 1852, where he split with the party over the slavery issue. In 1854 he ran for reelection on a combined Whig-Democratic ticket but lost to a Know-Nothing candidate. The next year Fenton presided at the first Republican Party state convention, and the year after that he went back to Congress, where he remained.[21]

Ethnic tensions increased between the Cattaraugus companies and the Thirty-Seventh New York's Irishmen. As 1st Sgt. William Bird Jr. of Company I complained, "Our men are not very well satisfied" with the regiment and certain of its officers. Nelson Loomis noted that the western New Yorkers "had a fight about every day with the Irish cusses." Their ultimate nemesis was the insufferable Colonel McCunn. So, the Cattaraugus men mustered their political allies in Washington, D.C. John Manley relayed their dissatisfaction to Addison Rice and Representative Fenton, who extracted a promise from Secretary of War Cameron to detach Companies H and I from the Thirty-Seventh. Rumors of the detachment reached camp on July 14. "Bully good news," crowed Loomis in his diary. How Jones navigated the turbulent sea of ethnic strife is unknown. The situation must have been difficult for him.[22]

Before the detachment of the Cattaraugus companies could be effected, circumstances intervened. Brig. Gen. Irvin McDowell—just ten weeks earlier a major sending enlistment forms to Jones—now commanded the Union army in and around Washington, D.C. McDowell organized his force into five divisions. The Thirty-Seventh New York, however, remained unassigned and consequently was in a sort of military limbo when rumors began buzzing that a big battle was looming at Manassas Junction, Virginia, about twenty-five miles south of Washington. As McDowell hurried his army out of the capital in that direction, the Thirty-Seventh was left alone at Camp Mary. On July 17 the regiment received marching orders but remained in camp. Finally, on July 21, as its band played "Dixie," the Thirty-Seventh crossed the Potomac by ferry to Alexandria, Virginia. That night John Manley sent a report to the *Cattaraugus Freeman:* "Our boys left Alexandria at 5 p.m., cheering and being cheered."[23]

A half-century later, one of the Cattaraugus men recalled there was much muttering in the Thirty-Seventh during the march from Camp Mary to the ferryboat. The regiment had been promised new rifles but had never received them. At the wharf the Irish companies refused to board the boat over the issue. Some of the Cattaraugus men joined the mutiny, and anarchy threatened. During the ruckus Cpl. William H. Clark of Company H squabbled with Colonel McCunn. Years later Clark recalled, "Pat Jones, the great pacifist," stepped between the two and quieted them down. After much delay Jones and other officers managed to herd the regiment aboard. When the still-angry Clark and McCunn continued to spar, Jones again proved to be a good mediator. "Pat got it fixed up," Clark remembered.[24]

The men rode a train of cattle cars from Alexandria to Fairfax Station as distant cannons roared. They disembarked about eight in the evening and marched into the woods. During the day McDowell's army had fought the Confederates not far from Manassas Junction, near Bull Run. Now the Thirty-Seventh encountered fugitives from the battlefield who brought unnerving tales of a disastrous Union defeat. The army was falling back to Washington a confused mob. Expecting the Confederates to attack at any minute, the jittery Irish Rifles spoke in whispers. Colonel McCunn sent panicked messages to Generals McDowell and Scott: "Things are looking ugly here" and "What shall I do?" After midnight Scott ordered McCunn to return to Washington.[25]

A heavy rain was falling as the Irish Rifles trudged back along the railroad toward the capital. The Cattaraugus companies were assigned as the rear guard. "The regiment behaved very badly and retreated in great disorder and many of them threw away their arms and baggage," William Bird wrote, "but our company drove in all the stragglers and brought our men in all safe." The road was crowded with fugitives, including many wounded. "This tries a man's pluck," observed Nelson Loomis. The Thirty-Seventh arrived in Alexandria at daylight on July 22 to find ambulances disgorging their wounded passengers in a downpour. The Cattaraugus companies were assigned to garrison Fort Ellsworth (named after the late hero), a hilltop earthwork commanding the town and the river, where the drenched men huddled in the mud without food or shelter. The rest of the Irish Rifles, many of them drunk, moved to Alexandria's slave pen. Stragglers and deserters overran Alexandria. The Cattaraugus men rounded up hundreds of them and destroyed whiskey throughout the town.[26]

Companies H and I moved on July 24 from Fort Ellsworth to a vacant hotel. Reflecting on recent events, Pvt. Jerome Andrews of Company I admitted the extent of the Union disaster at Bull Run but voiced a determination to forge on to victory: "[We] will try this 69 times before we give up (if necessary)." "If it ever comes that the Cattaraugus boys meet the Rebels on the field of battle," Musician Harry L. Bailey of Company I mused, "never fear but that they will give a good account of themselves." He lauded the officers for their demeanor in the debacle, praising them "for their energy, and the care which they took of their men." Bull Run showed Jones and his fellow raw soldiers the ugly aftermath of battle, but the Irish Rifles had yet to fire a round.[27]

Within days, however, Jones came under fire for the first time. On July 27 the Thirty-Seventh New York moved to an abandoned estate a couple of miles from Alexandria. An order on July 30 directed forty men from each of the Cattaraugus companies to reconnoiter the position of the enemy at Bailey's Crossroads. The officers drew lots to see who would go; the duty fell to Captain Clarke and Lieutenant Jones. The detachment marched three miles to the crossroads and posted pickets for the night. The next morning about half of the men, including Jones, moved out along the road toward Falls Church, fronted by skirmishers. As they crested a hill, they met Confederate scouts and exchanged fire. A Confederate officer was killed, and the enemy fell back. The Cattaraugus men, fearing an advance by rebel reinforcements, likewise fell back upon their reserve. That night they were ordered back to camp.[28]

Four days later Colonel McCunn sent Jones on a special mission. Under a flag of truce Jones carried a letter from McCunn to Col. J.E.B. Stuart of the First Virginia Cavalry. The missive sought permission to search for the body of Col. James Cameron of the Seventy-Ninth New York, a friend of McCunn who was killed at Bull Run. Stuart replied the next day, stating that the matter had been brought to the attention of the Confederate army commander and that a decision was forthcoming. The Confederates later informed McCunn that Cameron's burial site was marked and promised to deliver the slain officer's personal possessions. Meeting Jeb Stuart may have been unremarkable at the time, but Jones had the unusual distinction of having had a peaceful encounter with a soldier who became one of the Confederacy's most legendary generals.[29]

Jones got a lesson in political influence when the Cattaraugus companies were detached from the Thirty-Seventh New York on August 5 and ordered to Washington, D.C. Addison Rice and Reuben Fenton had swayed Secretary Cameron to permit the transfer. The news set off a celebration in the two company streets, with the men applauding and tossing their hats in the air. They quickly packed up and left "Camp Hell or Irish," as Nelson Loomis called it. Jones's dilemma in the Cattaraugus versus Irish feud ended with the separation of the two factions. Companies H and I were sent to Fort Washington, fourteen miles downriver on the Potomac's Maryland shore. The detachment outraged Colonel McCunn. He branded Fenton and Rice as deceitful politicians seeking to break up his regiment in order to get one of their own.[30]

Fort Washington was a fifty-year-old masonry structure that offered sweeping views up and down the Potomac and across the river to Mount Vernon. There the Cattaraugus companies joined two companies of regulars under the command of Maj. J. A. Haskins, a fine officer who had lost an arm in the Mexican War. Haskins was in several regards McCunn's opposite: quiet, dignified, considerate, possessed of "a noble Christian character." The men immediately noticed an emphasis on discipline that was sorely lacking in the Irish Rifles. "We have to toe the mark here just the same as the regulars," wrote William Bird. The strict attention to regulations was a great change, for as Bird explained, "In the 37th everybody did just about as he pleased." Haskins quickly won their respect and esteem. The major gave Jones a military education that John McCunn was utterly incapable of providing.[31]

With the end of the "hasty and unfortunate alliance" with the Irish Rifles, the Cattaraugus men vented their gripes with the regiment in letters to newspapers at home. McCunn had reneged, they charged, on promises of promotions. Poor rations had caused men to desert. Their shoes were worn; some were barefoot. The lack of discipline was deplorable. Only an eyewitness could believe the "disorder, abuse and misconduct" that prevailed in the regimental camp. There was much dissatisfaction with uncaring officers. One had taken a potshot at a drunken soldier in the guardhouse; others had cursed their men and struck them with swords. Generally demoralized, plagued by desertions, infected with a mob mentality, McCunn's regiment was a disaster. Hence, they had appealed to Rice and Fenton.[32]

In a letter to the *Cattaraugus Freeman* John Manley weighed in on the subject. He castigated "the graceless, godless, unmitigated, forward and backward, blarneying, duplicity-dealing McCunn" as an utterly insufficient commander. Manley had informed Fenton of "the grievances and the insults to which our boys had been subjected, their desire to get detached from the cause of their troubles, and their willingness to assume any position the War Department might order, even to joining the regular army." Despite McCunn's opposition—he had lodged a protest at army headquarters—Fenton and Rice had managed to effect the detachment. "It was an awful blunder," an Ellicottville man confided to Manley, "which placed our boys in that regiment." The Cattaraugus men now were happy to be "in responsible and honorable positions" at Fort Washington, declared Robert Shankland in the *American Union*. "Free from the Regiment they were formerly with, their ambition is aroused and they are trying to learn their duties." Jones and his comrades were enjoying a boost in morale.[33]

The hapless McCunn continued to prove Manley's assessment correct. After a run-in with a provost marshal in Washington, he was charged with conduct unbecoming an officer and gentleman and conduct prejudicial to good order and military discipline, found guilty by court-martial, and sentenced to receive a reprimand by the Army of the Potomac's new commander, Maj. Gen. George B. McClellan. In confirming the court's sentence, McClellan stated that McCunn "has yet to learn at least two things before he becomes competent to command a regiment, and these are self-command and respect for proper authority." Thus chastised, McCunn was ordered to return to duty.[34]

But the colonel's misadventures continued. Spurred by a petition from the regiment's officers, McCunn submitted his resignation, which McClellan accepted. Governor Morgan intervened, however, and asked that McCunn be allowed to continue in temporary command of the Irish Rifles for an extraordinary reason. Five of the regiment's ten captains had been accused of making out false payrolls to pocket extra cash, and Morgan wanted McCunn to purge the miscreants. The captains were tried by court-martial and dismissed from the service. McCunn then leveled spurious charges against other regimental officers and spread more discontent in the Thirty-Seventh and elsewhere in the army, criticizing McClellan and blathering that the Irish would no longer support the Union cause. McClellan finally ordered McCunn's arrest and banishment to the North. Escorted by provost marshal guards, the disgraced former colonel left the capital aboard an evening train.[35]

McCunn was incorrigible. On his return to New York he blustered to the press about the unfair treatment he had endured. A decade after his Civil

War shenanigans, he was found guilty of judicial misconduct and malfeasance by the New York State Senate and voted off the bench. He told his family that the disgrace would kill him, but the pneumonia he brought home from Albany took him instead. He took to his bed and two days later died in his sleep. The *New York Times* closed its obituary bluntly: "In person Mr. McCunn was agreeable and popular with the rougher classes of society, being always anxious to keep them favorable to him. As a politician, he was mistrusted, even by those with whom he labored."[36]

Throughout Jones's military career circumstances occasionally took him away from his command. He had already returned home to Ellicottville once, on his jaunt in June. On September 9 Captain Harmon wrote to Adj. Gen. Lorenzo Thomas in Washington requesting that Jones be sent to Cattaraugus County to recruit sixty-four men for Companies H and I, which had been depleted by attrition. Three days later a special order assigned Jones to the task. On September 21 he left Fort Washington and headed north to seek volunteers. "I trust he will have no difficulty in obtaining the requisite number," commented 2nd Lt. Constant S. Trevitt of Company I in a letter to the *Cattaraugus Freeman*. "Right heartily, I assure you, will our old friends and neighbors be welcomed here."[37]

But the impulse to volunteer, so strong five months earlier, had diminished. Jones reached Ellicottville around October 1 and placed an eye-catching advertisement illustrated with an eagle and flag in the *Freeman* seeking recruits. They would be allowed to choose which of the two companies they preferred to serve in, he promised, and they would enjoy comfortable and healthy quarters at Fort Washington. Jones was "indefatigable in his labors," the *Freeman* noted, and met "with very good success." On October 7 he accompanied twenty-six recruits from Ellicottville to Elmira, whence they were forwarded to Fort Washington. Another round of recruiting yielded sixteen more volunteers, whom he delivered to Elmira on October 24. Jones returned to Ellicottville and continued recruiting until Lieutenant Trevitt arrived in early November and assumed the duty. Jones returned to Fort Washington on November 28. The next day Major Haskins appointed him the post's acting adjutant.[38]

Jones found the Cattaraugus companies had changed significantly during his absence. The western New Yorkers—veterans and new recruits alike—were adorned in new uniforms and armed with new Springfield muskets.

They presented themselves spit-and-polished for morning guard mountings and afternoon dress parades. A visitor from Cattaraugus County found them to be perfectly drilled and in "excellent good spirits . . . You can hardly imagine the improvement made in the men since they left Ellicottville." Major Haskins had transformed them into soldiers.[39]

While Haskins trained the Cattaraugus companies, a significant change occurred about four miles from Alexandria at the Thirty-Seventh New York's Camp Michigan. Governor Morgan appointed a regular army officer, West Point graduate and Mexican War veteran Capt. Samuel B. Hayman, to the colonelcy of the Thirty-Seventh. Hayman took command on September 28. "As soon as Hayman made his appearance amongst us," Chaplain Tissot noted, "the regiment began to look different." The new colonel discharged several incompetent officers and instilled the discipline that had been lacking under McCunn, steadily transforming the mob of wild Irishmen into a well-trained, reliable unit. "Our men have been gradually assuming a more 'regular' and military character," one wrote, "owing to the strict and thorough system to which we are now made to conform." Tissot described Hayman—a widower, Episcopalian, and avid chess player—as "a fair, honorable man." Like Jones, Hayman was a so-called War Democrat, a supporter of the Lincoln administration's effort to suppress the rebellion (unlike Democrats who opposed the war, later dubbed "Copperheads"). In contrast to the inept McCunn, Hayman would be an ideal military mentor to Jones.[40]

In shaping the Thirty-Seventh's officer corps to his liking, wrote one of the Irish Rifles, Hayman set three standards for promotion: "That the candidate belong to the regiment, that he must know his business, and finally that his moral character and educational acquirements are such as to fit him for the responsible and honorable position of an officer in the army." Hayman inaugurated an "excellent system of promotion for merit alone, in opposition to the *regular* and stupid system of promotion according to seniority." Jones met Hayman's criteria and thus earned his first promotion. One of the officers Hayman purged was the regimental adjutant. Jones was mustered in to replace him on November 8. With the promotion came a move from Fort Washington to regimental headquarters at Camp Michigan. As first lieutenant and adjutant, Jones was Hayman's chief administrative assistant, responsible for the copious regimental correspondence. With Hayman as his tutor and having a natural aptitude for the post, Jones thrived.[41]

On December 4, 1861, Jones became a parent, when Sarah gave birth to a boy and named him Thomas M. Jones, after her father. It is possible Jones was home on a leave at the time. After an absence of uncertain duration, he returned to regimental headquarters on December 19. A favorite of Colonel Hayman's, Adjutant Jones soon received a second promotion when he was mustered in as major on January 21, 1862. Clearly, Hayman had been pleased with Jones's performance during his two months as adjutant. Now Jones had risen to the third highest rank in the regiment. As major, he would learn how to maneuver the unit in drill and in battle, which would supplement the administrative skills he had mastered as adjutant.[42]

Politics was never far from the surface in Civil War armies. In the *Cattaraugus Freeman* Delos Sill attributed Jones's latest promotion to the instrumentality of Congressman Reuben Fenton. Sill also ran a glowing tribute to the new major. "There is hardly one [Cattaraugus County soldier] whose course we have watched with greater pride and pleasure than that of our esteemed friend," Sill wrote. Jones's townsfolk knew that "patient perseverance and unceasing toil" had enabled him to overcome the disadvantages of poverty, acquire an education, and rise to prominence as a lawyer. They were certain those traits would also bring him "an enviable reputation in the profession of arms. And we have not been disappointed." Jones was now regarded as one of his regiment's "most thorough and accomplished officers." Sill closed with a prediction: "If his life is spared, still higher honors await him."[43]

A week later the *Freeman* printed a letter from Jones under the headline "A Correction." Congressman Fenton had had nothing to do with his promotion, Jones asserted; politicians had no influence when it came to promotions in the army. Fenton was a friend who would do anything for Jones, and Jones owed Fenton gratitude for many favors (as did many soldiers from Fenton's district). "But," Jones insisted, "I am not indebted to him, or any other politician, for any rank that I ever held in the army." He admitted that bad political appointments and promotions had been made in the volunteer service. But he claimed disingenuously that political influence was "played out." "For my own part," he emphasized, "I desire it to be known fully that I have not sought and will not ask political influence to be exerted in my behalf to the detriment of others." This dismissal of political support to secure promotions was specious. Jones's military career would surely benefit from Fenton's influence and that of other politicians as well.[44]

In the wake of Jones's promotions, word reached the Cattaraugus companies that he had been appointed assistant adjutant general to Brig. Gen. James Henry Lane of Kansas. "I am very glad to hear it," William Bird wrote on hearing the news. Bird considered Jones "the best officer we had" and "a very good fellow" and predicted that "he will distinguish himself" in the new post. Lane had served his native Indiana in the Mexican War and as a conservative Democratic lieutenant governor and congressman. He then moved to Kansas Territory and transformed into a radical abolitionist. At the start of the war President Lincoln had authorized Lane—a newly elected senator from the fledgling state of Kansas—to raise a brigade. Lincoln had appointed Lane a brigadier general, but Lane did not formally accept the commission, which by law would have cost him his Senate seat.[45]

When Bird wrote, Lane was in Kansas expecting to be put in command of a southern expedition. When another general was chosen, Lane lobbied in Washington for the post. But he never got the command, and Jones never joined his staff. It is plausible that Jones knew Lane. During his western travels as a journalist in the early 1850s, Jones could have encountered Lane in Indiana. Or he could have met him in Washington during the war. Lane spent the latter part of 1861 in the capital and was there off and on in subsequent months. Jones, too, was in and out of Washington during that period, and it was then that the staff officer story circulated. While the rumor indicates a connection between the two, their relationship remains a mystery.[46]

The approach of spring brought a flurry of activity as the long-dormant Army of the Potomac stirred in preparation for a campaign. The two Cattaraugus companies remained at Fort Washington when Major Jones and the rest of the Thirty-Seventh New York left Camp Michigan on March 14, 1862, and marched to Alexandria. Four days later the regiment boarded a steamship, part of a great flotilla bound to Fort Monroe, at the tip of the peninsula formed by the York and James Rivers. From there General McClellan planned to maneuver his army up the peninsula and attack the Confederate capital at Richmond. The Thirty-Seventh was now part of the Third Brigade, Third Division, Third Corps, commanded by Brig. Gen. Hiram G. Berry, Brig. Gen. Philip Kearny, and Brig. Gen. Samuel P. Heintzelman, respectively. As the ships passed Fort Washington, they were cheered heartily by the Cattaraugus companies. The Thirty-Seventh reached Fort Monroe on March 19 and gradually crawled up the peninsula with the rest of the army, arriving at the defenses of Yorktown on April 5. Two weeks later the Cattaraugus companies left Fort Washington and rejoined the regiment, arriving by ship. Jones met them at the landing and escorted them to camp. Over the next few days the Thirty-Seventh built roads through the marshy terrain and guarded other work parties.[47]

On the morning of May 4 it was discovered that the enemy had deserted its works and retreated. Rumor had it that the Confederate troops had retired to Williamsburg, about twelve miles distant. That day the Irish Rifles passed through Yorktown and halted in the woods for the night. Reveille sounded at three in the morning on May 5. The march got under way five hours later in a heavy rain and deep mud, to the distant sounds of battle. The Confederates had paused in their retreat to check the Federal pursuit. At the front they were driving Union troops in disorder. Kearny's division rushed forward, Berry's brigade in the lead, and arrived just in time to save the day for the Union forces. The Irish Rifles formed a line of battle under heavy fire and advanced slowly, gradually driving the enemy back into its breastworks. Then, together with the Fifth Michigan of its brigade, the Thirty-Seventh made a bayonet charge that drove the rebels from their entrenchments into an open field beyond. Darkness brought an end to the battle. Soaked to the skin, the men spent a miserable, chilly night under arms in the mud, without fires or food, listening to the cries of the wounded between the lines.[48]

Jones survived his first battle unscathed. A member of the Irish Rifles reported that he "did his whole duty in every respect." The enemy troops retreated during the night, leaving behind their dead and wounded. The next morning members of the Thirty-Seventh walked among the fallen, sickened by the sight and the stench. The regiment's casualties at the Battle of Williamsburg amounted to ninety-five killed, wounded, and missing. Theirs was the first Irish blood shed in the Army of the Potomac. The Cattaraugus companies lost four killed and eleven wounded. Congressman Reuben Fenton sent a man to look after the wounded, and John Manley visited them when they reached hospitals in Washington and Baltimore. The soldiers were proud of the praise they received for their role in the fighting. General McClellan complimented Berry's brigade and ordered it to inscribe *Williamsburg* on its colors. General Kearny declared the brigade was the best in the service and lauded the Irish Rifles in a letter to Governor Morgan. Wrote Lieutenant Trevitt, "Cattaraugus need not feel ashamed of her representatives on the bloody field of Williamsburg." When the casualty lists reached Ellicottville, Robert Shankland noted in the *Cattaraugus Union* (formerly the *American Union*), "This community was thrown into deep sorrow."[49]

While the homefolk mourned, the Thirty-Seventh continued to advance toward Richmond. Believing the Confederates to be dispirited, the men did not expect to do any more fighting. The route of their march took them to Cumberland Landing on the Pamunkey River, where they stopped for several days, then to Bottom's Bridge on the Chickahominy River, where a long bridge spanned the river with impenetrable swamps on either side. On May 25 the Thirty-Seventh crossed the bridge and camped in the woods. Over the next few days the regiment moved within eight miles of the Confederate capital, near a crossroads called Seven Pines.[50]

Early in the afternoon of May 31 an explosion of musketry startled the men. It came from the west, in the direction of Richmond. Two advanced Union divisions were struck by a massive Confederate attack and sent reeling. As the fighting drew nearer, the Thirty-Seventh was ordered to occupy some rifle pits near its camp. While the men rested in the shelter, Chaplain Tissot rode along the line and gave them absolution. At four o'clock in the afternoon the regiment was suddenly ordered into the fight.[51]

Colonel Hayman was directed to join the Third and Fifth Michigan regiments in a wood to the front. Under a heavy artillery fire he finally located the two regiments, but the Thirty-Seventh's right flank was in danger of being turned, and Hayman ordered the regiment to turn in that direction to meet the threat. He was surprised, however, to see his left wing heading straight to the front, led in a charge by General Kearny. Hayman followed the movement with his right wing, and the combined force checked the enemy in its front. A severe firefight ensued. Kearny eventually ordered the Thirty-Seventh to incline to the right to thwart Confederate flankers. But the enemy did not follow, and the regiment's role in the battle ended.[52]

"We got pretty roughly handled," wrote William Bird of the Battle of Fair Oaks (as it came to be called in the North; southerners dubbed it "Seven Pines"). The Thirty-Seventh reported eighty-two casualties. Major Jones narrowly escaped being one of them, as he explained in a private letter that was shared with the *Cattaraugus Freeman*. He was hit in the shoulder by a spent rifle ball, "but it did not penetrate the flesh." A cannonball passed near him, rendering him senseless for some time and deaf for about twenty-four hours. "But I am now recovered," he wrote, "and feel no bad effects from it." Jones judged the Battles of Williamsburg and Fair Oaks to be "the heaviest infantry fights, I suppose, that ever took place on this continent . . . The carnage [at Fair Oaks] was terrible on both sides. On the field where we fought, we buried more of the enemy than of our own men."[53]

Jones noted a couple of the regimental officers had been hospitalized with "Miasmatic Fever"—malaria—and added, "I should be sick myself, under any other circumstances, but am well, thank God." He thought his temperament enabled him to stand Virginia's climate better than more robust men. Malarial symptoms include chills, shakes, nausea, headache, an enlarged spleen, and a fever that spikes every one to three days (hence, names for the ailment such as "intermittent fever" and "ague"). With a disorganized medical department and a shortage of quinine, malaria was widespread in the army during the campaign. Jones was healthy when he wrote to the *Freeman*, but he too fell victim to the disease. He suffered attacks for the rest of his life, bedridden with chills and fever for a week or two every spring and fall.[54]

Jones also divulged some news about his brothers. "My brother Edward has returned from the South," he wrote. "I had a letter from him a few days ago. Richard is still in the South—perhaps in the Confederate Army." According to Jones family lore, the two had gone to Vicksburg, Mississippi, in the antebellum years to conduct business. After his return to Nebraska, Ned Jones served for two years in the Union army. Richard Jones reportedly did serve in the Confederate army—so remembered Patrick's wartime comrades in the postwar years. Jones's sister Ellen related that Richard returned to Nebraska after the war in his Confederate uniform and their mother dyed it so he could continue to wear it in peacetime. In the postwar years federal authorities sought to keep Confederate veterans from wearing their gray uniforms, which lends plausibility to Ellen's story.[55]

Did brother meet brother on a Civil War battlefield? It is possible, but proof of Richard Jones's service has yet to be found. (Nor has Edward Jones's Union regiment been identified.) None of the several soldiers named Richard Jones who served in Mississippi regiments match Patrick's brother in age or nativity. Of course, Richard could have served from another state or enlisted under an alias. While the family legend puts him in prewar Vicksburg, no Richard Jones born in Ireland was recorded in Mississippi in the 1860 census, nor was any Richard Jones listed on county personal property tax rolls—which would have been virtually impossible for him to escape. Alone of Jones's six siblings, the fate of Richard Jones is unknown.[56]

Jones had performed well in his first major combats, passing the soldier's ultimate test. In his official report of the Battle of Fair Oaks, Colonel Hayman praised Jones "for advice as regarded the movement of the enemy" and "for his general good conduct." Over several months at the rank and in two significant battles, Jones's performance as major had been commendable. But with a lieutenant colonel of Hayman's choosing above him, another promotion in the Thirty-Seventh New York was unlikely.[57]

In mid-June the Irish Rifles moved to the extreme left of the army and pitched camp in an area of dismal swamps. June 25 opened the great Confederate offensive known as the Seven Days, which drove the Army of the Potomac from the vicinity of Richmond to the safety of Harrison's Landing on the James River. The Irish Rifles reported eighty-one casualties for the week, about evenly divided between wounded and captured, most of them incurred on June 30 at Glendale. Thus, the Peninsular Campaign ended in abject failure. Army commander McClellan bragged that his retreat was unparalleled in the history of warfare, but the Cattaraugus men described it as an inefficient muddle that dispirited the troops. One of them sarcastically called it "*our victorious retreat*," another more acidly described it as "the skedaddle."[58]

The army languished at Harrison's Landing for more than a month. Finally, the Thirty-Seventh New York spent a week marching back down the peninsula to Yorktown. On August 21 the men embarked on a steamboat to Alexandria, arriving the next day. McClellan's army was being sent to aid the army of Maj. Gen. John Pope in the campaign that culminated in the Second Battle of Bull Run. From Alexandria the regiment shipped by rail to Warrenton, marched to Centerville, and on August 30 and 31 was in reserve at the Bull Run battle, with a loss of four men. With Pope's defeat the regiment retired to Centerville. On September 1 Kearny's division met the enemy at Chantilly, and a fierce combat ensued that lasted until after dark as a thunderstorm raged. Although the Thirty-Seventh was again kept in reserve and suffered no casualties, it mourned the loss of Kearny, who was killed leading his men. The regiment spent the night on the sodden Chantilly battlefield before marching to Alexandria.[59]

The end result of the Second Bull Run campaign was another dispiriting defeat. "Now instead of [us] threatening Richmond," a Company I man wrote, "the Rebs are threatening Washington. The soldiers in our army don't care a cuss which way the war goes. They are discouraged and sick of fooling in the way they have been at it for the last few weeks." Fortunately for Jones and the Thirty-Seventh Regiment, the Third Corps was left in the vicinity of Alexandria when the rest of the Army of the Potomac marched into Maryland and battled the Confederates at Antietam on September 17 in the bloodiest single day of the war. During that month the regiment occupied some large forts in the Alexandria area and enjoyed a rest after a busy and brutal summer.[60]

Writing from Harrison's Landing in August, an anonymous member of the Irish Rifles declared, "We are, I am afraid, likely to lose our gallant major, whose distinguishing characteristics can be more accurately summed up in Latin than in English: *Suaviter in modo fortiter in re*"—gentle in manner, resolute in action. It happened on October 8, 1862. Per a special order from the War Department at Washington, Jones was honorably discharged from the Thirty-Seventh New York to accept an appointment as colonel of a newly formed regiment. In the first year and a half of the war he had persevered with his unit while other officers were discharged or resigned. He had performed well enough to earn two promotions. He had experienced an amazing transformation in his regiment, from the anarchic mob led by the buffoonish John McCunn to the crack outfit commanded by the steady Samuel Hayman. He had absorbed the influences of fine officers in Luke Harmon, J. A. Haskins, and Hayman. Now Jones's military education with the Irish Rifles had earned him command of his own regiment.[61]

CHAPTER 3

Colonel and Brigadier General

Political maneuvering was behind virtually all appointments of volunteer officers, whose commissions were issued by state governors. Jones was no exception, as the path to his colonelcy demonstrates. After President Lincoln issued a call for 300,000 three-year volunteers on July 1, 1862, Governor Edwin Morgan assigned most of New York State's senatorial districts to each raise a regiment. Among them was the Thirty-Second Senate District, composed of Cattaraugus and Chautauqua Counties. At a convention held in Mayville, the Chautauqua County seat, the district delegates resolved to raise the assigned regiment and designated nearby Jamestown as site of the rendezvous. They also requested that Governor Morgan appoint Maj. William O. Stevens of the Seventy-Second New York, a Chautauqua County man, as colonel of the new unit, Jones as lieutenant colonel, and another Chautauquan, Capt. Jeremiah C. Drake of the Forty-Ninth New York, as major. The *Cattaraugus Freeman* stated the proposals "cannot fail to gratify the citizens of both counties, and produce a most favorable effect towards inducing enlistment."[1]

From Washington, John Manley informed the *Freeman* that the selection of Stevens and Jones produced great satisfaction in the capital and was fully approved of by Secretary of War Edwin M. Stanton. Manley also reported that Congressman Reuben Fenton had recommended Jones's appointment in a telegram to the Mayville convention. Jones's erstwhile law mentor and partner, Addison Rice, a newly elected state assemblyman in Albany, wrote to New York State Adj. Gen. Thomas Hillhouse asking that Jones be detached to assist in organizing the regiment. Nothing came of the request, however; Jones remained at the front.[2]

Almost a month later the appointment of regimental officers had yet to be made. Stevens had declined to be colonel. Among the men suggested for the post, the *Jamestown Journal* stated, only Jones and Drake were worthy of consideration. "We have raised a splendid regiment and now let us have men worthy to command them," the editor declared. "And of all curses do keep out political favorites and party hacks."[3]

But the contest for the colonelcy was highly political, pitting county versus county. When Cattaraugus delegates nominated Jones for colonel, Chautauquans countered by supporting Drake. Cattaraugus magnanimously withdrew the name of its favorite son, and the organizational committee elected Drake. An order from Secretary of War Stanton voided such elections, however, so the matter remained unresolved. Then the *Cattaraugus Freeman* suggested a compromise candidate, Assemblyman Addison Rice, whose name would "meet with a hearty response in every part of Cattaraugus." But Rice pulled off a coup in Albany that changed the situation dramatically. He received approval to raise a second regiment in the district and was appointed its provisional colonel. Command of the district's first regiment, designated the 112th New York, went to Jeremiah Drake after all.[4]

Cattaraugus County's war committee recommended Jones for the permanent colonelcy of the second regiment, and from the start that apparently was the arrangement. When the editor of the *Jamestown Journal* fretted about Rice as colonel (his only military experience was in the prewar militia), Jones's former employer, Robert Shankland, offered reassurance in the *Cattaraugus Union:* Rice was only the interim colonel; Jones would take command after the regiment was organized.[5]

The newly minted 154th New York Volunteer Infantry, consisting of eight companies from Cattaraugus County and two from Chautauqua, was mustered in at Jamestown in late September. The regiment left western New York a few days later by train for the front. Acting Colonel Rice was "exceedingly popular" with the men, the *Freeman* observed, "and they will follow with alacrity wherever he may lead."[6]

The 154th New York arrived in Washington on October 2. Ten days later the regiment marched to the vicinity of Fairfax Court House, Virginia, where it joined the First Brigade, Second Division, Eleventh Corps, Army of the Potomac. Rice remained with the regiment, but his popularity had waned. He was "about played out," wrote Musician Charles W. Abell of Company E, who only hoped Jones would be as good as the 154th's lieutenant colonel, Henry C. Loomis. "If so," Abell noted, "we won't ask the government to change our officers, I assure you." Loomis, a Cattaraugus County resident and veteran of the Sixty-Fourth New York, was extremely popular with the men, who called him "Uncle Henry."[7]

At the end of October, Acting Colonel Rice wrote to Adjutant General Hillhouse, asking him to send Jones's commission without delay. When the document arrived, it was dated November 3, to rank from October 8, the date of Jones's discharge from the Irish Rifles and now the official date of his muster-in as colonel of the 154th. But Jones had yet to report for duty with his new regiment—he was absent, at an unidentified hospital, suffering what John Manley described as a serious illness. Most likely, it was an autumnal bout of malaria.[8]

Addison Rice left the regiment in the hands of Lieutenant Colonel Loomis and returned to his Ellicottville home. Early in November the 154th embarked on an inconsequential movement to Thoroughfare Gap, Virginia, where it remained for a couple of weeks before backtracking. It arrived at Fairfax on November 19 and was met by its new colonel. Jones had recovered enough from his ailment to return to duty.[9] Now he would pass along the lessons he had learned from Luke Harmon, J. A. Haskins, and Samuel Hayman to instill discipline and efficiency in his green regiment. In his first days of command he established a strict regimen of daily drills, inspections, and recitations in tactics by the company officers, among them his former law associates Capt. Dan Allen of Company B and 2nd Lt. Alanson Crosby of Company A. Jones expected the officers to pass a military board's examination by the end of the year.[10]

The men honored their new colonel by naming their village of tents "Camp Jones." Their first impressions of him varied. "I think he will be more to the comfort of the regiment than it has been heretofore," opined Pvt. George Eugene Graves of Company D, adding, "He is a fine fellow." Pvt. George W. Newcomb of Company K had a less favorable opinion: "I do not like him as well as I do our Lieutenant Colonel Loomis."[11]

Jones found his new command embroiled in ethnic antagonisms not unlike the Cattaraugus-Irish conflict in the Thirty-Seventh New York. The ranks of the Eleventh Corps included a large component of German immigrants. The 154th's largely American-bred members generally disliked the Germans, and vice versa. According to Cpl. Joel M. Bouton of Company C, Jones thought the German commanding officers showed preference to their countrymen. Consequently, he was trying to get the 154th detached from the "Dutch" corps. "Colonel Jones is a man not to be run over by the Sauerkrauts," Bouton declared. But nothing came of Jones's petition to have the regiment transferred. To their distaste the 154th New Yorkers continued to serve in Maj. Gen. Franz Sigel's Eleventh Corps, in Brig. Gen. Adolph von Steinwehr's division, and in Col. Adolphus Buschbeck's brigade, together with three largely or entirely German regiments, the Twenty-Ninth New York and the Twenty-Seventh and Seventy-Third Pennsylvania.[12]

Political partisanship intensified in September 1862 as New York State's gubernatorial election approached and both parties held their state conventions. In the interim President Lincoln changed the course of the war when he issued his preliminary Emancipation Proclamation. The United States forces were no longer fighting solely for the defeat of the rebellion and restoration of the Union—they were also fighting to purge slavery from the land. This profound change in policy was a contentious issue.

Republican governor Edwin Morgan had decided not to seek a third term, leaving the field wide open. (Morgan instead sought to be chosen U.S. senator by the state legislature in 1863, which he was.) The Democrats convened in Albany and nominated Horatio Seymour, a conservative lawyer who had served a term as governor in the 1850s. In accepting, Seymour denounced Republican policy as unwise and dangerous. The Democratic platform called for suppression of the rebellion and restoration of the Union, as it had been antebellum (in other words, with slavery intact).[13]

A rift split the Republicans. Thurlow Weed and Henry J. Raymond, state assemblyman and editor of the *New York Times*, led the conservative wing. Horace Greeley, the renowned editor of the *New York Tribune*, led the radicals. The chief difference between the two factions was the Greeley wing's support for emancipation. Amid hints that the conservative Republicans might ally with the Democrats, the fractured party convened in Syracuse.[14]

Greeley worked for the nomination of Brig. Gen. James S. Wadsworth, a zealous Free-Soil man, for governor. Wadsworth's backers urged a resolution favoring emancipation. Weed's faction proposed a more conservative platform and nominated Maj. Gen. John A. Dix, a former Democrat with a lengthy record of public service at the state and national levels. Wadsworth beat Dix on the first ballot, and his nomination was made unanimous. As finally adopted, the Republican platform urged a vigorous prosecution of the war, hailed the preliminary Emancipation Proclamation, expressed gratitude to the armed forces, and pledged to support them. Greeley's radical faction had won a complete victory over Weed's conservatives.[15]

Both parties stressed the importance of the gubernatorial election. In an acrimonious campaign war issues predominated. Republican Party orators and editors condemned Seymour and the Democrats as antiwar, disloyal, treasonous rebel sympathizers. The Democrats called for bipartisan support for the war effort, portrayed themselves as conservative constitutionalists, and attacked the Republicans as radical abolitionists who were also corrupt and incompetent.[16]

New York State law disenfranchised its soldiers at the front, but Jones's inability to vote did not deter him from participating in the campaign. Back home in Ellicottville, Democrat Robert Shankland took Jones and 1st Lt. Commodore Perry Vedder of Company G to task in the *Cattaraugus Union* for urging their friends to vote for Wadsworth. The two had always "pretended" to be Democrats, Shankland charged; Jones had been "quite shaky, politically, before he went into the army, and required the best kind of watching." Jones and Vedder probably supported Wadsworth to ensure further promotions, the editor added. "We have had already too much politics and too little military science in the army," Shankland grumbled. "Politicians have been the bane of the army—they have brought us defeat and disgrace—and we advise Col. Jones and Lieut. Vedder to turn their faces towards the south, and no longer look backwards toward home to regulate matters clearly not within the scope of their military calling."[17]

Jones did not respond publicly to this criticism, but Republican editor Delos Sill came to his and Vedder's defense in the *Cattaraugus Freeman*. The two officers knew that Seymour's election would be joyfully welcomed by the Confederates and would encourage and strengthen their armies and aid in prolonging the rebellion. "They frankly and freely stated their opinions upon the subject, and urgently appealed to their political friends to rally to the support of Wadsworth." According to Jones and Vedder, "The army would feel rebuked if Seymour were elected." Heretofore, Jones had been known as a Democrat. Now he publicly backed a Republican, the party of his patrons Addison Rice and Reuben Fenton. In supporting Wadsworth, Jones turned his back on his fellow Irish Americans, who were largely and adamantly opposed to emancipation. Jones's efforts were to no avail, however, for Seymour was elected governor in a Democratic sweep.[18]

At the front the war ground on. Days after the election George McClellan—a favorite of most Irish American soldiers, including Jones—was removed from command of the Army of the Potomac and replaced by Maj. Gen. Ambrose E. Burnside. In mid-December the 154th New York marched from Fairfax Court House to the vicinity of Falmouth, Virginia, fortunately arriving too late to participate in Burnside's disastrous defeat at Fredericksburg. An incident of the march demonstrated Jones's willingness to relax discipline to ensure the comfort of his men. At the end of a day's tramp the German regiments of the brigade plundered nearby barns of hay to sleep on. In the 154th Jones interrupted roll call to advise his men: "If you don't get such things as you want here to make yourselves comfortable, it is your own fault. Other regiments are doing it—but you must commit no depredations." The men gave a cheer for the colonel and set off on a run to secure their bedding.[19]

Such acts increased Jones's popularity in the regiment. Alanson Crosby stated the colonel was "universally liked by officers and men." Pvt. Barzilla Merrill of Company K, however, called Jones "a rough wooden kind of man, [with] no refinement," and Pvt. Alansing Wyant of Company B thought Lt. Col. Uncle Henry Loomis was better liked. In January 1863 Jones obtained a twenty-day leave from division headquarters and visited Washington and Albany on regimental business, much of it concerning promotions. (As colonel, he made recommendations to the governor to fill vacancies in the officer corps, thus shaping it to his desire. He thrice promoted his friend Alanson Crosby, for example.) During his absence the 154th took part in one of the most miserable movements of its service—the Mud March—when Burnside attempted to negate his Fredericksburg debacle and was defeated by torrential rains and oceans of mire. Jones returned to the 154th's Falmouth camp on January 26, a few days after his bedraggled regiment slogged back.[20]

Early in February the 154th New York marched to the vicinity of Stafford Court House and set up a new winter camp. Anyone in the regiment was welcome to receive a hearing at the colonel's headquarters. Jones continued to teach the officers tactics and settled squabbles among them. He consulted with enlisted men regarding various issues. He kidded one private, saying he had gotten so fat that his family would no longer recognize him. He corresponded regularly with Governor Seymour and the state adjutant general regarding promotions. His routine drilling of the men paid off. When Maj. Gen. Joseph Hooker, who had replaced the hapless Burnside in command of the army, reviewed the Eleventh Corps, a private wrote proudly, "The general told our colonel that we done as well in our movements as the old regiments did." Hooker took a shine to Jones. They shared a bond, having both served in the Third Corps during the Peninsular and Second Bull Run campaigns. The two men became friendly.[21]

On the day of the review Jones was granted a ten-day leave of absence, and two days later he left for home. A few days after his return he commanded the First Brigade for ten days in the absence of senior officers. He was back at regimental headquarters on March 16 to welcome John Manley, who came from Washington, D.C., to visit the members of the 154th and to deliver an immense amount of food sent from home and a personal gift of a barrel of whiskey. As thanks, the regiment named its camp after the Soldier's Friend. Manley was pleased to see—and to puff in the *Cattaraugus Freeman*—his "warm friends" Jones and Loomis, who for two years "had manfully battled for the salvation of this country, and we had been in a position to know their aspirations, their severe trials, their disappointments, and to rejoice at their success and advancement." Manley admired "their acknowledged merit, their tried patriotism, and their prestige won in the campaigns of 1861–62."[22]

On St. Patrick's Day, Jones, Manley, Surgeon Henry Van Aernam, and other officers rode some sixteen miles through the army's camps to the bivouac of Brig. Gen. Thomas Francis Meagher's Irish Brigade. The party arrived too late to attend morning Mass, but they made it in time to see the steeplechase races. As each new race started, Manley wrote, "the excitement ran wild among the spectators." Thousands of them followed the action, surging on horseback in great mud-splattered tides within the track's two-and-a-half-mile ellipse. During an intermission the revelers feasted on a sumptuous repast and downed more than thirty gallons of whiskey, rum, and champagne. In the afternoon the enlisted men competed in foot, sack, and wheelbarrow races; chased a greased pig; and tried to outdo one another in Irish dancing. General Meagher, dressed as an Irish gentleman, was master of ceremonies. Among the spectators were General Hooker and several of the corps, division, and brigade commanders. Jones reunited with comrades of the Irish Rifles, who "were among the jolliest of our lively, gay, sprightly and muddy soldiers on 'St.-Patrick's-day-in-the-morning!'" It was probably the most festive day Jones spent in the army.[23]

As spring commenced, a campaign neared. Jones was granted a leave of absence for ten days and left Camp John Manley on March 26 for an unknown destination. A private speculated that he was "off seeing about getting us back to Washington and other things," perhaps still attempting to have the 154th transferred out of the Eleventh Corps. Jones was back in camp by April 8, when he prepared the regiment for a review the next day by Maj. Gen.

Oliver Otis Howard, who had replaced Franz Sigel in command of the corps. The most memorable review occurred on April 10, when President Lincoln visited the Eleventh Corps. The men felt well prepared for the coming campaign. "Colonel Jones has been indefatigable in his exertions to place the regiment on a good 'fighting basis,'" wrote a sergeant, "and I presume the first band of rebels we meet will testify that his exertions have not been wholly without effect."[24]

The meeting was soon to come. On April 13 and 14 Buschbeck's brigade marched to Kelly's Ford on the Rappahannock River. During the first day's march Jones heard an angry Colonel Buschbeck threatening to punish a member of the 154th who had milked some cows without permission. Jones came to the man's rescue with "a merry twinkle in his bright eye," a veteran recalled in the postwar years, a look that told the miscreant, "It's all right to milk the cow, but don't get caught at it again."[25]

On the evening of April 28 the 154th New York crossed the Rappahannock in boats and drove enemy pickets from the opposite shore, spearheading the movement that culminated at Chancellorsville in one of the bloodiest battles of the war. The regiment's baptism of fire came around sunset on the evening of May 2, when the Eleventh Corps was routed during Confederate general Thomas J. "Stonewall" Jackson's famous surprise flank attack. Buschbeck's brigade, the farthest from the initial point of impact, made a stand of approximately twenty minutes in a rifle pit near Dowdall's Tavern before being driven into the tangled woods to the rear. The 154th anchored the left of Buschbeck's line and lost 241 casualties out of 590 engaged, a 40 percent loss rate and the fourth highest regimental casualty count in the Army of the Potomac. One of them was Jones. That night Sergeant Horace Smith of Company H noted in his diary, "Our colonel—brave man—was wounded and I fear taken prisoner."[26]

When the battle ended in defeat for the Army of the Potomac, the dispirited regiment returned to Camp John Manley. Many of the survivors speculated about their colonel's fate. As Henry Van Aernam put it, "Colonel Jones is known to be wounded and is probably a prisoner, as he has not been seen since the night of the fight." For days no word arrived regarding the men who had been left on the battlefield, and the uncertainty about Jones persisted.[27]

Meanwhile, the soldiers commented in letters home about Jones's conduct on the battlefield. Sgt. Samuel D. Woodford of Company I described how Jones had ordered the men into the rifle pit as soon as the attack erupted and how they had fired for about fifteen minutes, holding the Confederates in check until "the enemy were on three sides of us and were pouring destruction and death into our brave boys. The colonel gave the order to fall back twice before our boys left." Pvt. Oscar M. Taylor of Company E stated: "Our little colonel walked behind his regiment and cheered them. He said that we had got to leave the ground, but when we left we would leave with honor." Indeed, the 154th was the last Eleventh Corps regiment to leave the field, and Jones was the last officer to order the retreat.[28]

Finally, on May 14 Gene Graves wrote: "We have heard from Colonel Jones. He is a prisoner." Jones was paroled on May 15 at United States Ford and returned that day to Camp John Manley. He had been wounded in the upper right hip; Surgeon Van Aernam described it as a severe flesh wound but not dangerous. The entrance and exit wounds were four inches apart. Jones was silent, his head bowed, as Van Aernam stitched them. Sgt. William Charles of Company F made him a pair of crutches. Jones reported that during his days of captivity he had received rough fare. But the enemy "treated him very kindly," William Charles wrote, "and took first rate care of him." The men did not expect Jones to remain in camp. "I presume he will go home in a few days," guessed Cpl. Truman Harkness of Company H, who added proudly, "We have the best colonel that ever was in the field."[29]

Addison Rice arrived at Camp John Manley on May 16 and the next day accompanied Jones to Washington, where he was admitted to a hospital. Within days he was granted a thirty-day leave of absence on a surgeon's certificate of disability. Still accompanied by Rice, Jones traveled to Philadelphia to receive more medical treatment and probably to visit his family. His father-in-law had moved to Philadelphia in 1861 and was living there with a daughter. It seems likely that Sarah Jones and the toddler Thomas were there too.[30]

Back in camp members of the 154th lamented Jones's departure. "We miss him," wrote Pvt. James W. Washburn of Company C. "He was a fine little fellow. He was an Irish, but he was smart." "He has gone home for a few weeks," wrote an anonymous soldier to his hometown newspaper, "but we hope, to return soon. He is a noble officer and worthy of a much higher position than he now holds."[31]

Henry Van Aernam had similar thoughts about a promotion for Jones but sensed that ethnic politics would prevent it from occurring. "It seems the 'Dutch' powers that be are determined to make a general of Col. Bushbeck [*sic*]," he noted. "That is all right and proper if it can be done with justice to other parties, but if any officer in the 11th Corps has earned a commission as general for anything that was done in that rout [at Chancellorsville], Col. Jones is entitled to the position." Buschbeck was a fine officer and continued to serve as such for another year, but he never was made a general. Jones, meanwhile, had to wait until the senior Buschbeck was discharged before he could advance to brigade command.[32]

From Washington, John Manley praised Jones in a letter to the *Cattaraugus Freeman* as a "dauntless, Christian soldier . . . than whom no braver or magnanimous man lives." The 154th New York had won enduring fame at Chancellorsville, Manley declared, and made a proud record amid the most adverse circumstances, a panic on the battlefield. "I know of the pride of Col. Jones in his command, his faith in his men, and of their good discipline," he added. The men held their colonel in "as near to affection as men are capable." For their heroic devotion to the Union, both commander and soldiers "merit the plaudits of their kinsmen and friends on the far-off hills of Cattaraugus and Chautauqua!" A week later Manley cited "the obstinate bravery of Col. Jones and the 154th boys. All honor to the Heroes!" The *Freeman*'s Delos Sill chimed in with praise for Jones's "coolness and intrepidity," which entitled him to "all honor."[33]

After his wounding and capture at Chancellorsville, Jones entered a period of enforced inactivity. Regulations proscribed paroled prisoners from taking up arms or discharging any duty until they were exchanged. Consequently, Jones was prohibited from conducting official business. That did not stop him from making "unofficial suggestions" regarding regimental promotions to the new state adjutant general, John T. Sprague, during a visit to Albany in early June. His recommendations were enacted. Jones had promoted his former law student Dan Allen once, from captain to major. Now, on his suggestion, Allen was commissioned lieutenant colonel to replace Henry Loomis, who had resigned after Chancellorsville. Also moving up in the regimental hierarchy was Jones's erstwhile law student and partner Alanson Crosby, now first lieutenant and adjutant.[34]

Jones was still in Albany when he wrote to the *Cattaraugus Freeman* on June 12. "I am getting much better," he reported, "[and] can travel with great ease now. Perhaps I may yet see my friends in Ellicottville before I am returned to duty." But on June 18 he was admitted to a Washington hospital for further treatment. A surgeon declared him unfit for duty on July 2, and by July 10 he was in Ellicottville on a twenty-day leave of absence. Delos Sill noted in the *Cattaraugus Freeman* that Jones "has nearly recovered from the effects of his wound, and appears to be in excellent health and spirits." A rumor circulated that he planned to resign. "If so," wrote Commodore Vedder, "it is with unfeigned regret and sorrow that I part from him. He is one of the best soldiers, and the most honorable and magnanimous man I ever met." Jones denied the rumor. "He entertains no such purpose," Sill stated in the *Freeman*. "He is much attached to the gallant Regiment which he commands." "Good for the Colonel!" chimed Robert Shankland in the *Cattaraugus Union*. During his stay at home Jones learned that the 154th, under Dan Allen's command, had suffered grievously at Gettysburg, losing 205 casualties of 265 engaged. He would return to a much-reduced regiment when he was exchanged. Meanwhile, with his leave nearing a close, on July 20 he reentered a hospital in Washington, D.C.[35]

Jones left the capital on July 24 and two days later reported at Camp Parole, a facility on the outskirts of Annapolis, Maryland, that housed paroled prisoners until they were exchanged and returned to their units. Prohibited by oath from performing military duty, the seven thousand parolees had fallen prey to disciplinary problems, with drinking and gambling prevalent. Just days before Jones arrived, Col. Adrian R. Root of the Ninety-Fourth New York had been assigned to command the camp. Root banned the sale of liquor in Annapolis and cracked down on discipline, which eventually resulted in much better order. The parolees were divided into four battalions, based on their regiments' home states. Root assigned paroled officers to command the battalions. He put Jones in charge of one of them, which included the 154th New York's Chancellorsville parolees.[36]

Health issues plagued Jones during his time in Annapolis. Early in August he was hospitalized with a case of temporary blindness. He was again hospitalized during the first half of September. After returning to duty, he yearned to resume command of his regiment. According to John Manley, the long restraint from active service weighed heavily on his "active temperament." Aided by Congressman Fenton, Jones made repeated efforts to effect a special exchange for a captive Confederate colonel. Finally, on October 1 he was exchanged. But more frustration awaited him. He again appealed through Fenton to be sent to the 154th, which had been transferred with the Eleventh and Twelfth Corps under General Hooker to the western theater of the war and was then camped at Bridgeport, Alabama. But the authorities deemed it in the best interest of the service to detain Jones with Colonel Root at Camp Parole, "where his authority and his example should have a very beneficial influence on the discipline and good order of the Camp." Jones was assigned to escort groups of exchanged prisoners from Annapolis to the Army of the Potomac. On his return an officer wrote to the War Department that Jones's "anxiety to return to duty entitles him to most favorable consideration." Secretary of War Stanton concurred, and Jones was assigned to conduct the exchanged prisoners of the Eleventh and Twelfth Corps to Nashville, Tennessee, whence they would be delivered to their commands. After a lengthy hiatus Colonel Jones would soon be reunited with his regiment.[37]

He left Annapolis with his charges on November 1 and arrived in Nashville six days later. When news of the colonel's imminent return reached the 154th New York, Maj. Lewis D. Warner wrote, "We shall all rejoice to greet him once more." But the regiment moved from Alabama before Jones arrived. The 154th spearheaded a movement of the Eleventh Corps from Bridgeport to the vicinity of Chattanooga, Tennessee, opening the famous "Cracker Line" and lifting the siege of the city. The regiment then camped at the foot of Lookout Mountain.[38]

After shipping the exchanged soldiers to their regiments from Nashville, Jones rejoined the 154th on November 21. The next day the Eleventh Corps moved to the outskirts of Chattanooga. Then ensued the dramatic battle in which the Union forces, under the overall command of Maj. Gen. Ulysses S. Grant, routed the Confederate army from seemingly impregnable positions atop Lookout Mountain and Missionary Ridge. The Eleventh Corps played a minimal role in the fighting. At daybreak on November 24 the enemy drove in the 154th's pickets near Citico Creek. Six men were wounded.[39]

With memories still fresh of the numerous losses at Chancellorsville and Gettysburg, several of the men described the regiment as lucky at Chattanooga. One of them, Pvt. Stephen R. Green of Company E, attributed the good result to Jones. "It was very fortunate for us that he was with us," Green wrote. "He is a noble officer and knows his business and cares for his men." The soldiers were delighted to have him back in command. Observed Pvt. Emory Sweetland of Company B, "Colonel Jones is very popular in the regiment." William Charles noted that Jones had been personally lucky: "Our colonel had a ball put through his boot and another took a piece of mane from his horse's neck," but Jones was unhurt.[40]

There was no immediate rest for Jones and his men following the battle, for the Eleventh Corps was ordered to accompany Maj. Gen. William T. Sherman's troops to the relief of Union forces in Knoxville, Tennessee. The march proved to be one of the most difficult of the regiment's service. For much of the trek—which commenced on November 29 and ended on December 17, when the 154th returned to its old camp in Lookout Valley—the men were poorly provisioned and inadequately shod. During the movement Jones briefly commanded the brigade in the absence of Colonel Buschbeck.[41]

As the regiment settled into winter camp, Jones wrote his report on Chattanooga and corresponded with New York State adjutant general Sprague, Secretary of War Stanton, and other officials regarding various matters. He also presented himself as a candidate for promotion to brigadier general in a letter to the army's adjutant general in Washington. He submitted his military history, he asserted, on the suggestions of his superiors. Generals Howard and Hooker endorsed Jones's petition. "He has proved himself a brave and efficient officer," wrote Howard. Hooker cheerfully commended his long and distinguished service. Jones had fought often and fought well, Hooker declared; as a regimental commander, he was unexceptionable. Hooker closed with a flattering tribute: "If good Colonels of Regiments make good Brigadier Generals—which is the safest rule to follow—Col. Jones will make an excellent one."[42]

In January 1864 the 154th was sent to Kelley's Ferry on the Tennessee River to unload boatloads of rations. On returning to Lookout Valley, General Hooker ordered the regiment to take over an abandoned camp near headquarters. "Joseph and Colonel Jones are pretty good friends and I don't know but he wants us all for staff and bodyguard," Cpl. Martin D. Bushnell of Company H wrote proudly. "Joseph knows that we are about as good as they make." "Hooker's affection for the Regiment was always the source of greatest pleasure to us," Jones reflected years later, "indeed I may say of pride." The general's choice of the regiment as headquarters guard was "a mark of affection which we greatly appreciated and in which we cordially reciprocated—you bet."[43]

Jones was detailed as member of a court of inquiry requested by two German officers to investigate aspersions on their commands made in a report by Hooker. The forced relationship with the Germans of the Eleventh Corps continued to rankle the men of the 154th. Jones twice petitioned army chief of staff Henry W. Halleck to have the regiment transferred from the corps. The first time, Halleck referred the matter to Eleventh Corps commander Otis Howard, who refused to allow the change, declaring the 154th could not be spared. The second request was likewise denied. Commented a regimental officer, "So we have had to Dutch it through."[44]

Colonel Buschbeck was absent when Jones took command of the brigade by seniority on January 30. "We expect soon he will get a star," wrote Capt. Arthur Hotchkiss of Company K, referring to Jones's potential promotion to brigadier general. Hotchkiss added: "He is a noble officer and can lead this regiment where no other can, for all love him. He is firm but kind. He is ambitious to do for all, all that is in his power to do." Buschbeck outranked Jones as colonel, however, and had led the First Brigade competently since its inception. The German seemed more likely than the Irishman to receive a promotion to brigadier.[45]

By this time many Irish Americans were losing faith in the Union cause. They had concerns about the mistreatment of Irish soldiers in the Union army, they were dismayed by Irish soldiers' horrific battle losses, and they disliked emancipation. But Jones remained faithful. He hoped to return to Cattaraugus County to recruit for his regiment. But when he was granted a twenty-five-day leave of absence on February 26, he instead went to Philadelphia to visit his family. Arthur Hotchkiss noted that Jones was not well, perhaps troubled by malaria. The colonel returned to Lookout Valley on March 22 "looking somewhat better than when he left," according to Major Warner.[46]

The campaign to secure Jones a promotion entered an important new phase that month when Reuben Fenton and seventeen other men signed a petition to President Lincoln recommending his appointment as a brigadier general. The document stated, "He is a gentleman of education, a lawyer by profession; honorable and moral; a devoted soldier, a gallant officer, and a tried patriot; and a man of ability and integrity." Lincoln turned over the petition to Secretary of War Stanton, and there the matter languished for the time being.[47]

On the last two days of March and the first of April, the 154th marched to Trenton, Georgia, on a reconnaissance and returned to Lookout Valley. The men reached camp footsore after the roughly fifty-mile tramp. Jones noticed that the soldiers who danced jigs to fiddle music in camp stood the march better than their comrades and jocularly proposed to detail fiddlers to keep the men in shape. More fun was had when the 154th played a series of baseball games against other regiments. After losing one contest to a Massachusetts team, Jones bet two hundred dollars that his men would win a rematch. (Whether the game was played went unrecorded.) A spring campaign soon ended the fun and games.[48]

After General Grant was called to Washington to command all the Union armies, General Sherman assembled three armies for an offensive in the western theater. In April the Eleventh and Twelfth Corps were merged to form the Twentieth and became part of the Army of the Cumberland. The rest of the army—commanded by Maj. Gen. George H. Thomas—consisted of troops from western states, so the easterners of the Twentieth Corps were an anomaly. The 154th New York was assigned to the Second Brigade, Second Division, of the new corps. Many of the Eleventh Corps' German officers were purged in the consolidation, but Adolphus Buschbeck retained command of the reorganized brigade, which included the Twenty-Seventh, Seventy-Third, and 109th Pennsylvania; the 119th, 134th, and 154th New York; and the Thirty-Third New Jersey. Brig. Gen. John White Geary commanded the division. Jones's friend Joe Hooker commanded the corps. "Hooker told Colonel Jones that he did not think that we should have any fighting to do here," Emory Sweetland noted, "that all of the fighting would be on the Potomac." Events soon proved Hooker wrong.[49]

A draining and bloody campaign ensued. Sherman's army left its camps near Chattanooga and confronted the Confederate Army of Tennessee holding Rocky Face Ridge, a lengthy mountain that shielded the town of Dalton, Georgia, and the railroad that ran to Atlanta. Four days after the campaign opened, on May 8, 1864, Geary's division was ordered to assault a spot atop Rocky Face called Dug Gap. The soldiers of the 154th New York clambered up the steep mountain under fire from the enemy at the crest, who also sent huge boulders careening down the slope onto the attackers. Jones, who had been ill for several days, led the men to the shelter of the palisades that gave the ridge its name, where they halted briefly to catch their breath. Then he ordered them to attack the crest. The color-bearer reached the summit, planted the flag, and was instantly killed. Others in succession were killed, wounded, or captured while scrambling to rescue the fallen flag. Finally, a corporal secured the banner, and Jones ordered him to carry it to the rear. The regiment retreated down the rugged slope, having suffered 55 casualties out of roughly 240 engaged. The battle was a tactical defeat for the 154th, but it would endure in the veterans' memories as a proud moment in their history: a valiant charge climaxed by a daring rescue of the regiment's most precious emblem.[50]

Among the injured was Jones, whose right side was severely bruised in a fall from the rocks. Attendants pitched a tent for him at the field hospital at the foot of the mountain, but he refused to take it, saying the wounded men should have it. Unfit for duty, he left the next day for medical treatment in Chattanooga. John Manley noted that Jones's numerous friends in Washington were pained to hear of his injury and hoped it was not serious.[51]

Jones spent twenty days convalescing at the officers' hospital on Lookout Mountain before heading back to the front. On June 7 he reported for duty near Brown's Mill and assumed command of the Second Brigade. Colonel Buschbeck and the Twenty-Seventh Pennsylvania had been discharged from the service, their time being up, and Jones was now the brigade's senior colonel. Meanwhile, Samuel Woodford reported that Jones was going to join General Thomas's staff. "He says he will try to do something for the boys," Woodford noted, adding, "I think he intends trying to get us in as [Thomas's] bodyguard. If he could it would be a good position." The rumor proved to be untrue. Until the end of the war, with a few exceptions, Jones would continue to lead the Second Brigade.[52]

A week after Jones took command, the brigade moved to the vicinity of Pine Mountain. On June 15 it charged the enemy's entrenchments at Pine Knob. The next day it remained pinned down in disadvantageous terrain under a galling fire. Brigade losses over the two days totaled more than two hundred, among them Jones's former law student and partner Capt. Alanson Crosby, mortally wounded. In his official report of the action, based a month and a half later on his own "rough notes and memoranda," Jones detailed the maneuvers of his regiments, praised the stubborn gallantry of his officers and men, mourned the loss of Crosby and other officers, and thanked his staff officers for their assistance during the fighting—a formula he would follow in reporting subsequent battles.[53]

The Pine Knob fight brought Jones a new and influential champion in the press. David Power Conyngham was a native of Ireland who had taken part in the uprising of 1848, fled briefly to America, and gone back to Ireland and began a literary career. When the Civil War broke out, he returned to the United States and was sent to the front as a correspondent for the *New York*

Herald. Following Sherman's army, Conyngham naturally gravitated to his fellow Irishman Jones. An officer described the reporter as "a pure Celt . . . large, cheerful, winning, plump and ruddy, and as genial a companion as ever." In his *Herald* dispatches (also published as a postwar book) Conyngham puffed Jones for his bravery and his dashing, daring impetuosity at Pine Knob. He would continue to laud Jones as the campaign wore on.[54]

The Atlanta campaign was unlike any Jones had participated in—an almost constant grind of maneuvering and fighting. In the days after the Pine Knob battle, Jones's brigade confronted the Confederates along Mud Creek and at Greer's Farm, where David Conyngham reported it had "a dashing brush with the enemy." Jones's horse was shot, but the brigade commander escaped personal harm. During a brief halt on June 24 he composed a letter to the *Cattaraugus Freeman*, enclosing a list of the 154th New York's casualties "in order to relieve the minds of the friends of the regiment of apprehension" and noting: "After a fight, matters are reported worse than they really are. God knows it is bad enough as it is." He proudly reported, "Hooker and Thomas speak of the command in the highest terms—the poor fellows deserve it." "We are as well as could be expected," he added, "[and we] don't complain since we are drubbing them up, and driving them splendidly as we move on." His old regiment was "doing its full share and getting its full compliment of glory. No one is jealous, however, since they deserve it so fairly."[55]

More combat occurred late in June near Kennesaw Mountain before the brigade pushed on toward Atlanta, arriving near the Chattahoochee River on July 5. There the men rested until July 17, when they crossed the river and approached the city. On July 19 the brigade crossed Peach Tree Creek, moved to the crest of a ridge, and entrenched. At some point during the day Jones was relieved of command and placed under arrest by division commander Geary, who was known as a hot-tempered and physically abusive disciplinarian. What caused him to arrest Jones is uncertain. According to a member of the 109th Pennsylvania, Jones had drawn Geary's ire by misplacing the brigade's skirmishers "so that they fired on our own men." Lewis Warner stated that "alleged disrespect" had led to the arrest. In the postwar years an officer of the 154th New York recalled Jones telling Geary to "kiss my ass" in response to an order, and although he recollected it as having occurred elsewhere, he might have been misremembering this incident. It was the only recorded instance of Jones being disciplined during the war.[56]

In any case Jones was back in command of the Second Brigade the next afternoon, July 20, when he and Geary accompanied the Thirty-Third New Jersey through the woods south of Peach Tree Creek to a hill in advance of the other regiments. The men were working on an outpost when a massive Confederate attack swept them back and sent the rest of Jones's brigade reeling. General Hooker rallied the troops at the edge of a ravine, and the restored Union line repulsed the attack with great slaughter. The Second Brigade lost 164 casualties at Peach Tree Creek, Jones's largest battle as a brigade commander. Of the moment of crisis David Conyngham effused, "Jones's noble brigade, admirably led and fought by its brave commander, was nearly decimated, and could not hold out much longer." A desperate rout was averted by a rally for a signal victory. Jones wrote feelingly in his report of "the readiness and alacrity" with which his regiments had re-formed and turned upon the enemy, which was a credit to "their discipline and steady valor." Jones's horse was wounded, but Jones was unhurt. To the *Cattaraugus Freeman* he sent a list of the 154th's casualties and a quick note that stated, "The command fought bravely of course, and repulsed the attack made upon us handsomely."[57]

As Sherman tightened his noose around Atlanta, Jones wrote an official report of the Second Brigade's operations under his command. In a paean to the brigade's "uniform gallantry," he regretted that too many deeds of valor had gone unrecorded, too many heroes unheralded. He praised the survivors and eulogized the lost.[58]

The next day he entered the Second Division Hospital with a case of chronic diarrhea. According to Arthur Hotchkiss, Jones was thinking of seeking a new position and still "waiting for a star" of a brigadier general. In his absence Col. George W. Mindil of the Thirty-Third New Jersey took command of the brigade. Jones admired Mindil as a soldier; at the end of the war he wrote a warm letter to Secretary of War Stanton recommending that Mindil receive a brevet promotion to brigadier general. Some Second Brigade men, however, disliked Mindil because he was a Jew. Members of the 154th New York particularly regretted the change in command. Jones lingered in the hospital during the August dog days, taking care of routine business and presiding over a court-martial. In the meantime the campaign came to a successful end when the Confederate army evacuated Atlanta in early September. Jones returned to brigade command in a suburb of the fallen city on September 17.[59]

Another election loomed in the autumn of 1864. The previous year the New York legislature had granted the state's qualified military personnel the right to vote by proxy. Republicans supported the measure; Democrats opposed it as unconstitutional. Governor Seymour vetoed the bill, but a special election endorsed it as a constitutional amendment, and it became law. As the 1864 elections approached, the state's Republicans—calling themselves the Union Party—met in September at Syracuse. The nomination of Reuben Fenton for governor was widely expected. New York secretary of state Chauncey M. Depew described Fenton as a "a master of all current political questions and in close touch with public opinion," a "shrewd judge of character," who "rarely made mistakes in the selection of his lieutenants." Although Fenton was a radical, he had gained the support of the conservative Thurlow Weed, retired as an editor but still a powerful force in state politics. Fenton handily won the nomination, defeating former War Democrat John Dix and another candidate. Party resolutions supported continuing the war until the rebels submitted, emphasized Union military victories, and heralded the right of soldier proxy voting.[60]

The Democrats convened a week later in Albany and nominated incumbent Horatio Seymour for another term. The platform endorsed the party's candidate for president, former Army of the Potomac commander George McClellan, pledged to seek peace while supporting the preservation of the Union, and denounced the Lincoln administration. At both the state and national levels the election became a referendum on the war. The Democrats were generally conciliatory to the South and included a plank in their national platform condemning the war as a failure and calling for peace. McClellan saw fit to repudiate that resolution, which lost him support among the Copperheads. The national Republican platform endorsed unremitting war until the Confederates surrendered and backed a constitutional amendment to abolish slavery. Surveying the mood of a war-weary North, President Lincoln had resigned himself to defeat in the election until Sherman's army took Atlanta and Republican prospects brightened.[61]

During the campaign Fenton worked on behalf of Jones, and vice versa. Fenton wrote to Secretary of War Stanton regarding Jones's proposed promotion to brigadier general. Stanton in turn had the adjutant general query Jones's superior officers about his fitness. General Sherman passed the request to General Thomas, and Thomas sent it on to Gen. Henry W. Slocum, recently assigned to command the Twentieth Corps. (To the dismay of the corps' rank and file and no doubt to Jones's regret, Hooker had resigned when Sherman passed him over for a promotion.) New to the corps, Slocum felt unqualified to judge Jones's merits but noted his brigade was in good order. General Geary lauded Jones as a gallant officer, well educated, an excellent regimental colonel, and a competent brigade commander. Meanwhile, Jones chaired a meeting of the 154th Regiment to support Fenton for governor, passing resolutions to be published in the hometown press. Days later Fenton begged Lincoln that Jones receive a thirty-day leave to return home. Jones could be of great service in the political campaign, Fenton advised, as "an educated man, a good speaker, and formerly a Democrat." Taking a different tack, Jones applied for a leave to return to Ellicottville to settle an old law case. Both requests were rejected. "No officers can at present be spared from General Sherman's command," Stanton noted on the verso of Fenton's request. Another campaign was in the offing, and Jones was needed at the front.[62]

Irish Americans, their devotion to the Democrats deepened by their opposition to Republican policies, overwhelmingly backed George McClellan in the presidential contest. Who Jones supported is uncertain. Arthur Hotchkiss stressed that Jones was an admirer of McClellan. But soldier sentiment was against McClellan, who received only a handful of votes in the 154th New York. In any case the election put two Jones allies in power: Reuben Fenton as New York's new governor and Surgeon Henry Van Aernam of the 154th to take Fenton's seat in the House of Representatives. A rumor spread that Jones was to be made a brigadier general. Jones expected the promotion, Hotchkiss noted, and his chances were good—he had the best recommendations of Generals Hooker and Howard.[63]

In November the members of the 154th raised six hundred dollars to buy Jones a saddle and related horse equipment and sent their former lieutenant colonel, Henry Loomis—now the regimental sutler—north to make the purchase. Henry Van Aernam noted that Jones's health had much improved. Days later Jones led the Second Brigade out of Atlanta on Sherman's legendary March to the Sea. Proceeding via Georgia's state capital, Milledgeville, the brigade wrecked railroads and bridges and a vast amount of other property and encountered plenty of resentment from women but met with no military opposition until it reached Savannah. During the ensuing siege of the city, on December 12, 1864, as proposed by Secretary of War Stanton six days earlier, President Lincoln nominated Jones to be a brigadier general.[64]

Savannah had fallen when Jones visited the brigade's chief surgeon on Christmas Day 1864 and was diagnosed with chronic diarrhea of six months' standing. "A change of climate and mode of living is necessary to prevent permanent disability," the doctor stated, recommending a thirty-day leave. Jones followed up the next day with a formal application of his own. His leave was granted on New Year's Day 1865. On January 4 he procured transportation on a steamboat to Hilton Head. That day Governor Fenton wrote to Senator Edwin Morgan urging Jones's confirmation as a brigadier general; Morgan quickly voiced his support. Meanwhile, news swept through the 154th Regiment that Jones had received the long-sought promotion. "Bully for Pat!" exulted 1st Sgt. Francis M. Bowen of Company I. The *Cattaraugus Freeman* hailed the news: "He has earned this mark of distinction by long service and meritorious conduct, and we most heartily congratulate him upon his good fortune. General, we salute you!" Officially, however, Jones had yet to receive the promotion.[65]

On January 30 a doctor in the Cattaraugus County town of Randolph recommended a twenty-day extension of Jones's leave. He was still afflicted with chronic diarrhea. Two days later the Senate's Committee on Military Affairs and the Militia reported favorably on his promotion. Newspapers issued another round of congratulations. "We are proud of him as a man, a citizen and a soldier," boasted the *Freeman*. On February 14 the Senate confirmed Jones's nomination as a brigadier general. He was still too ill to return to his command, however; within days he applied for another ten-day extension of his leave, citing another physician's certificate. Chronic diarrhea would trouble him for the rest of his life, limiting his diet.[66]

Toward the end of February, Jones traveled to New York City, whence he expected to take a steamer south to rejoin his command. He had yet to receive his commission as brigadier and was anxious to have it and the concomitant raise in pay. So, he turned to a friend for a favor. A staff officer for Gen. John Dix, headquartered in New York, wrote to the adjutant general's office in Washington requesting that Jones's commission be sent to the city immediately, before Jones left for the front. Otherwise, with his brigade on the move, Jones might not receive the document for weeks. Such proved to be the case.[67]

While Jones languished in the North, his brigade, commanded by Colonel Mindil, took part in the epic Carolinas Campaign, spreading desolation and making inexorable progress under adverse conditions. By March, Jones's string of leaves had expired, so he traveled from New York to North Carolina to rendezvous with his command. On March 24 he found the 154th New York and 109th Pennsylvania in Kinston. Jones brought each member of the 154th a pair of socks and a lump of sugar. They were pleased to reunite with him. Wrote Sgt. Marcellus W. Darling of Company K, "We all think a [great] deal of him."[68]

Jones resumed command of the entire Second Brigade on March 30 at Goldsboro. Journalist David Conyngham welcomed his return. "Few officers have done more to merit a star than General Jones," he informed the readers of the *New York Herald*. One week later word arrived of the fall of Richmond. The delighted members of the 154th surrounded Jones and gave him three cheers. When news arrived of Confederate general Joseph E. Johnston's surrender to Sherman on April 16, Jones donated a keg of whiskey to his old regiment's celebration. Sherman's lenient peace terms, however, were subsequently rejected in Washington. On April 18 Jones was officially appointed brigadier general of U.S. Volunteers, to rank from December 6, 1864—the date Stanton had proposed him for the promotion. As he had feared, however, his commission had not arrived, and consequently, he was not mustered in at his new rank. In a letter to Fenton he complained about the delay.[69]

On the night of April 26 news arrived of Johnston's official surrender to Sherman. Jones sent his compliments to his joyful old regiment, with another barrel of whiskey. In subsequent days he led his brigade on a lengthy and punishing march in torrid heat and choking dust from Raleigh to the vicinity of Washington, D.C. On May 19, at Cloud's Mills near Alexandria, Virginia, Jones was finally mustered out of the 154th to receive his promotion to brigadier general. Five days later he led the Second Brigade in the Grand Review, the triumphant victory parade through the thronged streets of Washington. The celebration continued when Governor Fenton visited the brigade's camp near Bladensburg, Maryland, on May 30 and made a speech to the New York regiments. An enlisted man saw a lot of civilian visitors mingling with hundreds of drunken officers at Jones's headquarters.[70]

The jubilation at the war's end was tempered for Jones by troubles regarding his commission as brigadier general. From North Carolina he had written to Congressman Henry Van Aernam to see if Van Aernam could expedite its delivery. But it was not until May 20 that he accepted a certified copy of the document and signed his oath of office. His actual commission arrived two days later. On May 26 he wrote to the adjutant general, requesting that his pay as brigadier date, like his rank, from December 6, 1864. The adjutant general denied the request on the grounds that Jones was entitled to pay only from the date he had accepted his commission, May 20. That decision denied Jones more than five months' pay as a brigadier—at least $620—he had hoped he had coming.[71]

The 154th New York was mustered out near Bladensburg on June 11. That day Jones drew up a certificate to allow his five staff officers to retain their horses. It was one of the last bits of official army business that he conducted. On June 17, 1865, he resigned his commission as brigadier general and was honorably discharged from the service. He listed an address on F Street in Washington as his temporary residence.[72]

Independence Day found Jones in Albany, where he attended the presentation of New York State regimental flags to his friend Governor Fenton. More than ten thousand soldiers and citizens packed a specially erected building on the city parade ground for the solemn ceremony. Among the guests were Ulysses Grant and more than a dozen other Union generals. Grant insisted that every one of the more than two hundred flags be presented to Fenton individually.[73]

Two days later Jones arrived back home in Ellicottville. Veterans who had preceded him fired a cannon salute in his honor. This type of festive welcome was typically given by civilians to groups of soldiers returning to their hometowns from the front. In Jones's case his fellow veterans bestowed an individual honor, a hero's welcome. He was "a great favorite" among the men of his old command, Delos Sill noted in the *Cattaraugus Freeman*. "The returned soldiers all speak well of him," Robert Shankland reported in the *Cattaraugus Union*, "which is a sure sign that he did not send his men where he dare not go himself." The general looked well, the editors observed. Jones told them he intended to reside once again in the village.[74]

CHAPTER 4

Politics Beckon

Jones had outgrown Ellicottville. His reputation now extended far beyond Cattaraugus County's borders. As a respected veteran with powerful connections, a Democrat turned Republican and a Republican Irishman at that, new vistas opened for him in politics. His patron Governor Reuben Fenton was organizing one of the most potent statewide political machines ever seen. Fenton valued his advice. A political career for Jones was logical, feasible, and promising.[1]

New York State Republicans convened in Syracuse on September 20, 1865, to nominate a slate of candidates for November's off-year election. The influential Thurlow Weed controlled the proceedings and, aided by Senator Edwin Morgan and Congressman Henry Raymond, selected the ticket. To identify themselves as the party that had stood by the Union, the Republicans referred to their slate as the "Union State Ticket," implicitly branding all Democrats as Copperheads. At the afternoon session a delegate from Chautauqua County nominated Jones for clerk of the court of appeals. Other delegates offered praise, and when a suggestion was made to make his nomination by acclamation, it was spontaneously and enthusiastically approved. Weed had urged the convention not to nominate former Democrats, but he let Jones pass. The clerkship of the state's highest court suited Jones's legal, administrative, and leadership abilities. If he won the election, he would gain a steady foothold in state politics—and the clerkship could be a springboard to other offices in the judiciary or elsewhere.[2]

Jones's Democratic opponent, Edwin O. Perrin, was an Ohio native who had migrated via Tennessee to New York City. He had been an active Whig until 1856, when he bolted to the Know-Nothings. He then completed his political metamorphosis by becoming a Democrat. In 1857 he served as private secretary to the governor of Kansas Territory. A year later he returned to New York and was appointed an assistant clerk in the state assembly. At the outbreak of the Civil War, the secretary of war sent him on a secret mission to New Mexico, where he associated with Col. Christopher "Kit" Carson. A critic wrote of Perrin, "He seems to be one of those ubiquitous chaps who are *always* 'on hand' *where there is light work and good pay!*" Another observer noted that Perrin "has not a *large*, but an *active* brain, is not a profound man, but has an excellent and ready use of all his faculties."[3]

The short political campaign was marked by the usual partisan warfare in print. In the *Cattaraugus Freeman* Delos Sill scoffed that the Democrats expected their Irish followers to vote for the nativist Perrin; Jones stood in "beautiful contrast" with his opponent. The candidates' war records also contrasted. Perrin's New Mexico venture notwithstanding, he had not served the Union cause in uniform. Jones, Sill noted, was a war hero. Loved by the officers and men under his command, "he was as popular in the army as he is worthy, and that worth and popularity will win him thousands of votes" from veterans across the state, whether Republicans or Democrats. Cattaraugus County would, Sill predicted, "rally to his support with a zeal and energy that shall tell in the canvass of the estimation in which he is held at home."[4]

The *Irish-American,* a popular ethnic weekly published in New York City, generally supported the Democrats but voiced dismay with the party's ticket. An editorial suggested that its readers disregard party and vote for the candidates who best presented "the true worth of manhood and integrity." Thus, it supported Jones, who the paper described as "proud of his Irish birth and a credit to it," while excoriating Perrin as a man who had stubbornly sought to deprive immigrants of the right to vote. The *Albany Evening Journal* praised the *Irish-American* for refusing to swallow the "disgusting pill" of Perrin in favor of Jones, "the brave Irish patriot." The *Evening Journal* also accused a rival Democratic paper in Albany of concealing Jones's ethnicity by neglecting to print his first name, referring to him instead as "Henry Jones."[5]

A Republican campaign pamphlet compared Jones to his opponent. Jones "went into the army with a Musket and came out with a Star; and when war was ended and rebellion crushed, he laid down the Sword and returned to the quiet and peaceful pursuits of his Profession. Contrast the conduct of this patriotic young man, born in another country, but grateful for the prosperity and happiness he enjoyed under our Government—volunteering his services and periling his life for the Union—with that of his competitor, the candidate of the hybrid Democracy, a 'Know Nothing' in Peace and a 'Copperhead' in War."[6]

During the canvass Jones covered the state from Ellicottville to Albany to New York City. A month after his nomination he wrote to the state adjutant general: "Everything is looking favorable and I entertain no serious apprehensions. I trust the Republicans are not all too confident. It might relax their energies." He also reiterated a request to Fenton that his journalist friend David Conyngham be commissioned in a regiment in order to become a citizen. Conyngham apparently had an angle on a federal job if he became naturalized. Jones readily vouched for him as "an excellent and gallant gentleman." As usual, Fenton endorsed Jones's request, and Conyngham was commissioned a first lieutenant.[7]

The Republicans swept the state offices with strong majorities in the November 7 election. The numbers in the Jones-Perrin contest were not reported but probably approximated the voting in the other statewide races, about 302,000 for the Republicans to 272,000 for the Democrats. The *Irish-American* alleged that New York City Republicans had "basely deserted" Jones because he was Irish while city Democrats had voted for him to make up the difference. Perrin's name was omitted from the Democratic ballots in one county, which was said to have cost him from 8,000 to 10,000 votes, too few to affect the outcome. Only months after the war had ended and Lincoln had been martyred, the Union State ticket was unstoppable, and Jones won his first office.[8]

Jones's three-year term as clerk required him to spend much of his time in Albany, overseeing the operations of the New York State Court of Appeals and its staff. Four times a year, however, court sessions were held elsewhere in the state's eight judicial districts, and he traveled with the judges. Time between sessions offered more travel opportunities. Jones was able on occasion to visit his family in Cattaraugus County. More often he was drawn to Manhattan. During his clerkship he made the great leap from bucolic Ellicottville to the nation's bustling metropolis, the teeming stage upon which the rest of his career would unfold.

He arrived in Albany in late December and commenced his duties on New Year's Day 1866 at his office in State Hall. (The court met at the Old Capitol.) The court of appeals had been established in 1846 in reaction to widespread dissatisfaction with an antiquated judicial system. Two decades and five clerks came and went before Jones took office. During that time increasing numbers of cases led to excessive workloads. By the time Jones became clerk, the court had fallen years behind in its business and was an institution in crisis. Reforms initiated by a constitutional convention during his term led to a thorough reorganization of the court and its clerkship after he left office. The court was given the power to appoint and remove its clerk; the clerkship was no longer an elective office. Ironically, the first man appointed to the post was the man Jones had defeated, Edwin Perrin, who would serve for twenty years and die in office.[9]

Jones made more money as clerk of the court of appeals than he did in the army. As a colonel, he was paid $1,140 a year, from which he purchased his own provisions and clothing and paid a servant. The clerkship paid an annual salary of $2,000. By custom the clerk also pocketed the interest on monies in the hands of the court, which had been the principal profit of the office. Jones, however, interpreted the law strictly to prohibit such payments and instead donated the money—thousands of dollars—to charitable institutions. Such largesse would prove to be a lifelong habit, amounting as time went by to a problem. Politically, however, Jones's generosity would prove to be golden.[10]

A booklet of biographical sketches of the state officers described Jones as "a gentleman of slight proportions, but plainly possessing powers of great endurance. He has a mild, calculating eye, a pleasant face, and a courteous, modest mien." After summarizing and praising his military career, the sketch concluded: "We cannot refrain from adding that Mr. Jones' course, from boyhood to the present time, has been marked by integrity of purpose and bravery of spirit. Born in a land where the oppressions of hundreds of years has not been able to crush out the longings of the people for liberty, and coming to a country where every man is a sovereign, and where eagerness for distinction, wealth and power, is remarkable, he has, in reality, 'won his way' in a praiseworthy manner." In the eyes of the establishment Jones was an Irishman who had taken good advantage of America's promise.[11]

Albany city directories listed his residence as Ellicottville in 1866, New York City in 1867, and Randolph in 1868. Sarah and little Thomas apparently lived with relatives in Randolph. Sarah gave birth to twins James Morris and Anna on June 27, 1866, but the baby girl died on November 25 and was buried in Randolph's cemetery. Jones bought a house in Randolph in 1868; it turned out to be the only home he ever owned. The 1870 census valued his real estate at thirty-five hundred dollars and his personal estate at five thousand dollars. But by then he was firmly ensconced in New York City, where Sarah and the boys would eventually join him.[12]

In the summer of 1867 Jones opened a law office in New York. A year later his former partner Addison Rice moved to Manhattan, and the two formed a firm with a third associate, Edward J. Wilson. A native of the West Indies who was about twenty years Jones's senior, Wilson had come to New York at a young age and studied law with the celebrated Irish radical exile Thomas

Addison Emmet. Jones moved from the fashionable St. Denis Hotel to board at Wilson's West Eleventh Street home.[13]

Soon after Jones's 1867 arrival in Manhattan, he was elected counsel for a state agency, the Commissioners of Emigration and Quarantine. This job gave him a philanthropic mission as well as an extra salary. The agency's purpose was to protect newly arrived immigrants from the predatory practices of swindlers. "Runners" habitually bullied and cheated victims by steering them to shady boardinghouses, confiscating their luggage, or charging them a bogus fee for entering the country. Runners logically preyed on their own countrymen, Irish cheating Irish, Germans hoodwinking Germans, and so on. Crooked forwarding agents—who purported to aid immigrants heading west—overweighed baggage, overcharged for transportation, and in general treated victims brutally.[14]

Up to the 1840s Irish and German aid societies had looked after the welfare of immigrants as best they could. Over time, however, the great tide of new arrivals overwhelmed them. The societies consequently supported the state legislature's 1847 act establishing the Commissioners of Emigration. Board members included community leaders and the presidents of the ethnic aid societies, who served without salary. To finance the operation, the board inaugurated the collection of "head money," a per capita tax on each immigrant, to be paid by every ship's commander within twenty-four hours after arriving in New York. These fees constituted the board's entire income and provided Jones's salary as its lawyer.[15]

In 1855 the commissioners leased the old fort on the Battery, Castle Garden, and outfitted it as the Emigrant Landing Depot. There the immigrant met with a state-sanctioned, institutional introduction to America, rather than the historic chaos of the waterfront. No longer did runners plague new arrivals. Instead, immigrants were inspected at a quarantine station below the city and accompanied to Castle Garden, where their luggage was checked and they were transferred from ship to shore via barges and tugs. Following a medical examination, they were registered in the depot's huge central rotunda. There they could buy railroad tickets, obtain lodgings in licensed boardinghouses, exchange money, have their baggage delivered anywhere in the city, receive mail, meet with waiting friends, write letters with the aid of multilingual clerks, or find a job. City policemen were on duty day and night to keep order.[16]

Jones turned over much of his commission work to a young protégé, Michael Nolan. The two had met during the Atlanta campaign, when Nolan was a staff officer for General Geary. After the war Nolan served Jones in Albany as a clerk at the court of appeals. When Jones went to New York, Nolan followed and became managing clerk of the firm of Rice, Wilson and Jones. Most of Nolan's commission work consisted of cases concerning swindlers and abandoned children. He handed off much of the routine caseload to a Castle Garden policeman. Jones stuck to writing opinions; he only took on "a few extreme cases" at the express orders of the commissioners and did not pay close attention to everyday matters.[17]

Jones remained politically active while juggling business in Albany and New York. In February 1868 he was at the New York State Republican convention in Syracuse, which selected delegates to the party's upcoming national convention. The Republicans were split between three factions—the radicals, led by Fenton, moderates, and conservatives. About two-thirds of the chosen delegates were Fenton men. Among them was Jones, who represented the state's Thirty-First Congressional District, Chautauqua and Cattaraugus Counties. Fenton was named as first choice for vice president on the national ticket. At the national convention in Chicago in May, both the radical and conservative wings of the party enthusiastically backed Ulysses S. Grant for president, and the delegates nominated him on the first ballot. A split between the factions in the New York delegation helped to doom Fenton's chances for the vice presidential nod, which went instead to Speaker of the House Schuyler Colfax of Indiana.[18]

Grant ran on a moderate Republican platform that championed congressional reconstruction and black civil rights in the South. The Democrats held their national convention in New York City at Tammany Hall, Boss Tweed's bailiwick. They endorsed an early end to reconstruction and nominated former governor Horatio Seymour for president. The Republican press presented a stark choice between the candidates. Grant was the hero who had masterminded the Union victory and would preserve the gains won at high cost in the war; Seymour was the Copperhead who had opposed the war and played an equivocal role in the bloody New York City draft riots. The Republicans made an intensive bid for the Irish vote, establishing campaign clubs, founding an Irish American Republican newspaper (the only one of its kind in the country) in New York City, and branding the Democrats as the party of conservatism and tyranny. But the Democrats had little worry of Irish defections—Boss Tweed had the city's Irish firmly in his grip, and he had created tens of thousands of new Democratic voters by means of fraudulent naturalizations. In the end Seymour took close to half of the popular vote in the election, but Grant won by a landslide of electoral votes. He failed to carry New York State, however, anchored as it was by its populous and largely Democratic metropolis.[19]

Much of the Democrats' strength in New York City rested in its large Irish population. In Manhattan, if not elsewhere in the country, the Irish wielded political clout. By Grant's election Jones had made a name for himself as a prominent son of the Emerald Isle. He had also established a foothold in Manhattan, the country's Irish stronghold and media capital. He was ready to step into a leadership vacuum caused by the deaths of two nationally celebrated Irish Americans. Gen. Thomas Meagher of Irish Brigade fame was lost overboard from a Missouri River steamboat in Montana Territory in 1867. Bvt. Brig. Gen. Charles G. Halpine, who had made his name during the war as a writer, died during the 1868 presidential campaign. Halpine's death led to a major turning point in Jones's life.

Halpine was a well-known humorist. Born in County Meath a year before Jones, he had arrived in the United States in 1850 and began his American life shilling for showman P. T. Barnum. He began writing witty verse and prose for the New York newspapers and became a darling of the major editors. In the Civil War he was a staff officer to a succession of generals and to Governor Seymour. Halpine was moving in Washington's highest circles when he invented his most famous character, an Irish Union soldier named Miles O'Reilly. His creation was a hit in the *New York Herald*, the city's most popular newspaper. When a collection of O'Reilly tales became a best-selling book, demand for Halpine's writing skyrocketed. He resigned from the army in 1864 and became editor of a city weekly. He also continued a downward spiral into alcoholism.[20]

Always politically active, Halpine ran for the office of register of the County of New York in 1866. The register's office recorded deeds, mortgages, and titles—work that had grown exponentially with the city—and charged fees for the service. Said fees fattened the register's wallet by between forty thousand and ninety thousand dollars per year. The register was, in fact, America's highest-paid elected official, earning much more than the president (whose annual salary was twenty-five thousand dollars) or a congressman (who earned eight thousand dollars a year). Halpine was handily elected. He took office on New Year's Day 1867 and lived the good life for a year and a half. He vacated the office at a city hotel on August 2, 1868, when he killed himself with an overdose of chloroform. He left a wife and six children.[21]

Governor Fenton faced the task of appointing someone to complete Halpine's term as register, which ended on December 31. Influential men urged him to name a man willing to donate the fees of the office to Halpine's widow and children. If such an appointment were made, Maj. Gen. Philip H. Sheridan assured Fenton, "you will place thousands of admiring friends under lasting obligations." Generals Grant and Sherman echoed the plea in telegrams to the governor. Horace Greeley—who had become a good friend of Halpine's family—appeared in person to discuss the matter with his political crony Fenton.[22]

The press voiced support for the proposal. The *New York Times* declared that such an appointment would bring satisfaction to all parties "with the exception of the office-seekers"—and Fenton had a score of friends who would gladly agree to succor the bereaved family. The *Irish-American* praised Sheridan's suggestion as "a noble one, and we trust the Governor will accede to it." Senator Edwin Morgan suggested to Fenton that it would be politically expedient to appoint a prominent German citizen to replace Halpine. But Fenton, urged by Horace Greeley, had decided to replace an Irishman with an Irishman. The Irish claimed Greeley (whose mother was Scotch-Irish) as one of their own. For his part the editor was ambivalent about the Irish. On one hand, he disliked their clannishness and political bullying and believed they should be assimilated and indoctrinated with American values. On the other hand, he had always been their friend. He fought nativism and defended their rights as citizens, and he staunchly supported the cause of Irish nationalism, considering it part of a crusade for universal freedom in the Western world. He described America's Irish immigrants as "the best of Ireland's population." Now he and Fenton decided on a prominent Irishman and mutual friend for the post: Patrick Henry Jones.[23]

Thus, Jones came into the orbit of one of the most interesting and influential men of the era. Nineteen years Jones's senior, Greeley had worked for newspapers in Vermont, western New York, and Pennsylvania before moving to New York City in 1831. During his early years in the city, he set type and became friends with a temporary resident, Robert Shankland—the future Ellicottville editor and Jones's journalistic mentor. In 1841 Greeley launched the publication of the *New York Tribune*. By the 1850s he and his paper were American fixtures, with the largest nationwide audience of any newspaper in the country. For many years a Whig, Greeley joined the Republicans on the formation of the party. He made monthly trips to Albany or Washington, D.C., to wield his considerable political influence. An eccentric who dabbled in spiritualism and vegetarianism and was a teetotaler, Greeley was known for his fringe of white whiskers, thick spectacles, and rumpled white overcoat. He was one of the best-known men in the country, constantly hounded by politicians, reformers, advice seekers, and beggars. A workaholic, he spent long hours in the *Tribune* offices at Nassau and Spruce Streets—a neighborhood that Jones came to know intimately. He and Jones shared a common attribute: notoriously indecipherable handwriting. According to a recent biographer, Greeley "had few friends and no cronies"—but it appears that he and Jones grew to be closer than merely political allies.[24]

On receiving his commission as register from Fenton, together with a letter explaining the arrangement to turn over the fees to Halpine's family, Jones responded with a missive that was widely reprinted. He praised Halpine and assured Fenton, "I accept the trust you have devolved upon me—for such I consider it—and will see that the recommendations are fully carried out." Jones now had two powerful political allies in Fenton and Greeley.[25]

He took the oath as register on August 14, 1868, and immediately commenced his duties at the Hall of Records. His appointment and his agreement to donate the fees to the Halpines were widely covered in the city newspapers and beyond. It was reported that the family benefited from Jones's largesse by sums ranging from eighteen to twenty-five thousand dollars. The *New York Evening Post* noted that Jones's personal financial circumstances rendered his act of generosity "a serious matter."[26]

While his generosity to the Halpines was universally applauded, his handling of patronage aroused controversy. The Republican editor of the *New York Dispatch* expected him to follow tradition by removing Democratic employees and replacing them with Republicans, specifically veterans: "We shall expect that the political influence of the department, *throughout*, shall be wielded in behalf of those loyal defenders of our Union who marched, and still march, under the banner of Ulysses S. Grant." Eight days after he took office, Jones composed a letter to Robert B. Roosevelt, the Democratic owner and editor of the *New York Citizen*. Roosevelt claimed that Jones had decided to make no personnel changes during his truncated term. Not so, Jones declared. He might not make changes, but he would exercise his right to party patronage if it could be done "without detriment to the public service." Roosevelt had spoken kindly of Jones as a candidate for register in the upcoming election. Jones responded that he was grateful for the suggestion but stated, "I am not a candidate for this or any other office."[27]

According to reports, Jones quickly wielded the patronage power. The *Herald* wryly stated that he had "raised a very unexpected commotion in the City Hall Park by erecting a guillotine for the decapitation of clerks in the City Register's building." Jones removed six or seven clerks and the examiner, janitor, and watchman—Democrats all—and replaced them with Republicans. Observed the *Herald*, "Such are the checkered fortunes of politicians." Less temperate in its analysis was the *New York Mercury*, which deemed Jones's actions an "outrage on the memory of Miles O'Reilly." "Who is Jones?" asked the *Mercury*. He was a "military popinjay," a hypocrite who had created "fat places for some of the vile vampires" of the rotten Republican Party. The paper added a prediction. Because of Jones's outrageous act, "he will secure the reputation of the reckless wretches who rob the dead."[28]

DeWitt Van Buren's Democratic *New York Leader* likewise slammed the new register in "The Captain's Political Gossip" column. To show his disdain, the Captain (presumably Van Buren) nicknamed Jones after Seth Pecksniff, the sanctimonious, hypocritical, and treacherous conniver presented by Charles Dickens in *Martin Chuzzlewit* as "soft and oily," a man who "knew what a good man he was, and what a blessing he must be to anybody," a man of "philanthropy, forbearance, piety, toleration, all blended together in a flexible adaptability to anything and everything." The Captain knew his readers would be familiar with this well-known villain and understand perfectly his characterization of Jones.[29]

So, the Captain wrote, "Pecksniff Jones is making things stagger in the Register's office, and makes no bones of snatching the bread and butter from the mouths of the friends of poor 'Miles O'Reilly.' No doubt, if it was not for fear of public opinion, the widow and orphans of the 'poor Boy' likewise would stand but a slim chance with the pious Pecksniff." Jones was following the dictates of his masters—to "kick all the Democrats out, and appoint 'red-hot' Rads"—and "you may bet Patrick will follow up his instructions to the letter, and more so." Concluded the Captain, "Let us all be thankful we shan't be troubled with Jones long; but while he is among us, can't we have a 'smelling committee' appointed just to look after Jones and his 'carpet-baggers,' for fear that too many of the stamps that should go to poor Charley's heirs might not stick to their dirty fingers?" Criticizing Jones for playing the political patronage game was one thing. In this attack the Captain insinuated that Jones could and would steal money he had promised to the Halpines.[30]

When Jones took her husband's place, the widow Margaret G. Halpine promised not to interfere regarding appointments in the register's office. Nevertheless, she asked Jones to keep a "faithful friend of poor dear Charlie's" in his job at the Hall of Records and importuned Horace Greeley to intercede with him regarding another. According to the *Leader*'s Captain, the minds of Democratic politicians were "fearfully agitated" regarding the upcoming election for register. Many were anxious and willing to hand walking papers to Pecksniff Jones. The Captain continued to complain about Jones's personnel changes. "Patrick has been doing the beautiful in the Register's office; that is, in his own estimation, by removing all the intelligent Democrats from position there, and appointing an illiterate and ignorant set of 'carpet-baggers' in their stead, some of whom knew scarcely how to write their own names. Paddy should send these fellows to school."[31]

The intemperate language and ethnic slur illustrated the passions aroused by the so-called spoils system of civil service. For generations political parties, in assuming power, had removed opponents from government jobs to give the posts to the faithful. Appointees were assessed a tithe on their wages for the party's coffers. Such partisan patronage was entrenched at the federal, state, and local levels. Considering the numbers of people involved—the federal workforce grew from 50,000 at the end of the Civil War to 150,000 in the Gilded Age—the spoils system impacted many lives. Since the war voices had urged reform and the hiring of governmental employees based on merit. As president, Grant called for civil service reform, but Congress failed to enact a permanent civil service commission. True reform would not take place until the 1880s. Jones would spend his entire political life operating within the parameters of the patronage system, as both recipient and dispenser.[32]

More than seemed possible at the time, the circumstances of Jones's four-month interim term as register would come to be crucially important to him. Meanwhile, Tammany Democrat Michael Connolly, one of William Tweed's henchmen, soundly defeated his Republican opponent in the election that

Jones had shunned. Under Connolly's rule as register, Jones's appointees were routinely purged, Tammany men took their places, and the office became a major source of income for Boss Tweed's "ring." The vast corruption of Tweed and his associates would benefit Jones in that he was usually seen as an honest man in contrast to the Tammany Hall thieves, soiled exemplars of the need for civil service reform.[33]

On October 1, 1870, Jones tendered his resignation as counsel to the Commissioners of Emigration. The board accepted it on December 22. His three years' connection with the commission had been lucrative as well as altruistic, but it would come back to bother him. At the time, however, leaving the position appears to have been nothing more than a practical matter. Jones had much to occupy him. His terms as clerk of the court of appeals and register had paid dividends, serving as rungs up the political ladder. By the time he resigned as the emigration commission's lawyer, he was immersed in his latest endeavor, having been appointed to a notable position by President Grant.[34]

CHAPTER 5

Postmaster

President Ulysses S. Grant came to be saddled with a stereotype, in historian Joan Waugh's words, as "a political dimwit, watching helplessly as his administration became awash in corruption and chicanery." Right out of the gate the newly inaugurated Grant stumbled in making appointments. Republican Party leaders were displeased by the president's failure to consult them, his choice of military men for staff posts, and his cabinet selections. Grant was flummoxed when the appointment of his friend Alexander T. Stewart as secretary of the Treasury did not pan out. Congress cited an obscure old statute that prohibited anyone in trade from holding the post—Stewart was a department store magnate. Grant had to name another man. Stewart consequently became a footnote in Grant administration history, but he would come to play an important role in the life of Patrick Henry Jones.[1]

A. T. Stewart amassed one of the largest fortunes of the early Gilded Age. An Ulster Protestant, he came to New York City as a teenager, opened a small dry goods store, and over the years expanded to ever larger quarters, culminating in a six-story emporium covering an entire block on Broadway. The "Merchant Prince" was a creator of the modern department store and one of the great innovators in retailing history. From 1860 to 1871 A. T. Stewart & Company sales rose from eight million dollars to forty-eight million dollars per year. At the height of his career Stewart had more than five thousand employees serving an average of fifteen thousand shoppers daily, in a store so well-known it was unmarked by a sign. Generally forgotten today, Stewart's name was instantly recognizable to Americans of his era.[2]

If choosing seven cabinet members was difficult for Grant, distributing the patronage of the vast federal executive branch was an even bigger headache. Although an important task for him as party leader, Grant loathed the process. Hounded by aspirants and their backers, he lamented: "Office-seeking in this country, I regret to say, is getting to be one of the industries of the age. It gives me no peace." He shunned self-seekers, looking for loyal, useful, manageable colleagues, men who submerged self to mission without consideration of risk or reward. Jones was such a man, and the president found a job for him, but the curious way it came about indicated a certain ineptitude and indifference on Grant's part.[3]

Grant turned to party leaders for help in the gargantuan task of office filling. At his request Horace Greeley came to Washington, D.C., to discuss appointments in New York State. Greeley hoped to have Jones chosen as marshal of the southern district of New York. To further that end, he wrote to Grant's influential secretary of state, New Yorker Hamilton Fish, recommending Jones and soliciting Fish's support. Greeley also had Senator Reuben Fenton hand deliver a letter to Grant's good friend General Sherman seeking an endorsement of Jones for the post. Sherman complied and voiced the hope that Jones would be named. He was extremely reluctant to make any recommendations to Grant, Sherman added, "but whenever he selects for Marshals, Governors of Territories and other purely executive offices, men who served well and faithfully throughout our Civil War, I think he can't go wrong." When Greeley met with Grant, the president reportedly promised him that Jones would be made the marshal.[4]

Greeley's relationship with Grant was problematical. Greeley had supported Salmon P. Chase for the Republican presidential nomination in 1868, his *Tribune* had given Grant lukewarm support during the campaign, and leading Republicans were increasingly shunning his advice. Greeley admitted in private that he disliked the president personally, but he also smarted from Grant's handling of New York State political affairs. Greeley's ally Fenton was engaged in a spirited battle over the state's patronage with his fellow New York Republican senator but bitter rival, Roscoe Conkling. Conkling and Fenton had served together in Congress in the early 1860s and apparently disliked each other from the start.[5]

Although Grant disliked Fenton and admired Conkling, he split the New York patronage evenly between the two. Conkling, however, joined Fenton in endorsing Jones for marshal. Not everyone was pleased with the prospect. Some New York City politicians complained that Jones was from the country. As the inaugural month of March 1869 waned, Washington remained filled with office seekers. Trainloads of aspirants arrived in the capital daily, many of them veterans seeking a favor from their former commander. Erstwhile general Alfred Pleasanton was mentioned as a rival of Jones in the contest for marshal. Grant surprised the backers of both men by appointing James W. Wadsworth (son of the 1862 gubernatorial candidate). But the congressional judiciary committee rejected Wadsworth, whereupon Grant withdrew him from consideration and pondered the matter anew.[6]

Following the Wadsworth debacle, Grant quickly appointed another man as marshal: former general Francis Barlow. Fenton expressed his objection to the choice in a meeting with Grant and followed up with a letter of "earnest protest." Barlow was a friend of Fenton's foe, former governor and senator Edwin Morgan, who in Fenton's opinion had already been granted all the appointments he deserved. Jones was "all that can be desired in respect of integrity and capacity," Fenton argued; he saw no reason why Barlow should be preferred. Jones also had the support of the state party, Fenton reminded Grant. He closed with a suggestion: "In my judgment it would be wise to recognize the loyal Irish sentiment of my state as represented in the person of Genl. Jones; a true man & a brave & devoted soldier of the Republic."[7]

It was said that Horace Greeley was "terribly incensed" when he got word of Barlow's appointment and traveled with Jones to Washington for an audience with the president. Grant, who seemed curiously casual and unconcerned about many appointments, informed the two that his promise of the marshal post had "slipped his mind." Leave the matter to me, Grant told Greeley, and I will try to find something for Jones. Grant's forgetfulness—whether real or feigned—would redound to Jones's favor. To appease Greeley and Fenton, the president would present Jones with a more prominent position than marshal.[8]

By mid-April 1869 the large crowd of office seekers who had been hanging around Washington since the inauguration was fast disappearing. New Yorkers headed home to the city to court Grant's new appointee as collector of the port, Moses H. Grinnell, for posts in the customhouse—the epicenter of the spoils system, with more than a thousand workers. Like the register, the collector raked in huge fees. An early convert to the Republican Party, Grinnell had staunchly supported the Union war effort with his labor and wealth (his fortune—made in whale oil, shipping, and insurance—was estimated at more than $100,000). His supporters looked to him to reform the corrupt customhouse.[9]

With Grinnell in office as collector, the only important New York City post Grant had yet to fill was postmaster—not a lucrative office like register or collector but one of the top political patronage dispensers in the country. The incumbent was Lincoln appointee James Kelly. On April 20 Grant ended much speculation by nominating Kelly to continue as postmaster. Within days a delegation of New York Republicans descended on Washington to lobby for Kelly's defeat, accusing him of being a lukewarm Republican at best, only in the party to save his political neck. They presented a petition to Fenton and Conkling protesting Grant's choice. While Kelly's nomination languished in a Senate committee, his opponents took the upper hand. "It now seems probable that his confirmation will be smothered," reported the *Times* on April 23. It was. A day later Grant had chosen a new man, and word went out to a select few. Horace Greeley telegraphed the president: "I heartily thank you for the appointment of Gen. Jones. No better selection could be made." Making amends for his earlier oversight regarding the marshal's office, Grant had found a prominent job for Jones. One of thousands of Union veterans the president appointed to positions in federal agencies, Jones had been awarded the plum prize.[10]

The appointment reportedly surprised him. He later stated that the first intimation he had that he was a candidate for postmaster was when his commission was placed in his hand. The news broke in the New York City papers on April 27. As New Yorkers sent more telegrams of thanks to Grant, the press weighed in on the choice. The *Times* praised Jones as "a man of energy, integrity and practical experience." The *Evening Mail* noted that Jones had executive skills that well suited him for the post office. The *New York Dispatch* concurred and stated that good soldiers and consistent Republicans would find a friend and advocate in Jones, while his reputation for integrity and capacity would ensure an excellent administration. Greeley's *Tribune* congratulated the citizens on the selection. The *Irish-American* lauded Jones's appointment as one of the best made by the Grant administration, giving universal satisfaction to men of all shades of opinion.[11]

Not all of the papers praised the choice. Doubtless we could say that Jones is a very good fellow, stated the *Evening Express*, if we knew who he is. Without mentioning Jones specifically, the Democratic *Herald* took Grant to task for appointing to office "nobodies and nincompoops," "backwoods ignoramuses," "notorious drunkards," and "rogues and lobby jobbers." Days later, however, the *Herald* published an article praising Jones's record as a soldier and civil official.[12]

"Everybody pats Pat Jones on the back as Postmaster," the *Leader* observed, predicting Jones would be "cleverly popular" as postmaster. But in his political gossip column the Captain—who had berated Pecksniff Jones—voiced his displeasure at the replacement of his friend James Kelly. Kelly must have alienated Greeley and Fenton, who procured the office for "the little paper-manufactured hero" Jones. The Captain voiced sorrow for the conservative employees who had fed with Kelly from the post office crib. "Patrick will, no doubt, sweep all of these poor fellows out, and fill their places by importations from Pumpkin Plains and Squash Hollow," as he had stocked the register's office with rural "rag-tag." Jones was a "carpet-bagger" and an "obscure individual," the Captain charged, whose appointment was secured "when Grant had one of his animated spells on." Jones would repay Fenton and other supporters, the Captain asserted, with jobs for their family members.[13]

Jones's appointment was national news. The widely circulated *Harper's Weekly* and *Frank Leslie's Illustrated Newspaper* both ran biographical sketches and portraits of him. Cattaraugus County papers naturally carried the story. In far-off Vermillion, South Dakota, where Jones's mother was living with her daughter Mary Jones McHenry, the local paper proudly reprinted the *Harper's* account, "glad to see a representative of so worthy a family promoted to a position of so much trust and honor."[14]

Jones took an important step on April 29, when he filed bonds for a million dollars to protect the interests of the government during his term. His sureties were James B. Taylor for $800,000 and Horace Greeley and Samuel Sinclair for $100,000 each. Taylor was a millionaire real estate operator, a director of the *New York Times*, and a partner of Boss Tweed in a printing company that Tweed used to bilk the city. Sinclair was the publisher of Greeley's *Tribune*. That James Kelly had posted bonds for only $250,000 pointed to the vast increase in the post office's business in the seven years since his appointment. With his bonds filed, Jones was sworn in as New York City's postmaster.[15]

Accompanied by Addison Rice, Jones appeared at the main post office on Nassau Street, between Liberty and Cedar Streets, shortly before noon on May 1 and met with the outgoing postmaster. Contrary to custom, there was no formal ceremony or speeches made. Kelly offered to show the new postmaster around and make introductions. Jones initially demurred, saying he was unwell and not up to the task, perhaps troubled with a bout of malaria. He changed his mind, however, and followed Kelly through the entire building. Workers huddled in small groups and eyed their new boss uneasily, wondering if their jobs were safe. Some claimed they had served with him in the war and felt confident of retaining their posts. Knowing of his alliance with the liberals Greeley and Fenton, conservatives were downcast, certain they would be fired. Some speculated that Jones, realizing the value of experienced employees, would make few replacements. Others gossiped that he would "lay the axe about him very heavily." For his part Jones gave no hints about his inclinations regarding removals and appointments.[16]

Jones toiled for months before Grant formally nominated him to the Senate in December. In short order the Committee on Post Offices and Post Roads reported favorably on the nomination, and the Senate confirmed it. During his term as postmaster the firm of Rice, Wilson and Jones dissolved, and Jones formed a new partnership with his protégé, Michael Nolan, and a Chautauqua County man, George W. Palmer. Jones located his personal law office in quarters at 150 Nassau Street. It seems that Sarah and the boys were splitting their time between Manhattan and Cattaraugus County. The 1870 census recorded the family twice: in June at Edward Wilson's house at 91 West Eleventh Street, in July at the house in Randolph. City directories listed Jones at a succession of addresses: at Wilson's house, at 44 West Twelfth Street, and at the Irvine House hotel. He never seemed to settle on where to live in the city.[17]

Much of his time was spent on Nassau Street at the post office or his law office. An observer described the street—ten blocks long, crooked, poorly paved, and grimy—as more representative of the city than Broadway. Its labyrinthine buildings housed banks, newspapers (including Greeley's *Tribune*), hotels, and hundreds of other businesses, each with a garish sign to announce its presence. Peddlers hawked cheap wares from stands on the sidewalks. For ten or twelve hours every day Nassau Street bustled with men, women, and children going about their business. Bankers, journalists, government officials, capitalists, and artists mingled with newsboys, bootblacks, bartenders, rag collectors, and thieves. Everybody seemed to be in a hurry, intent on his or her own purpose, indifferent to others, and rude.[18]

As soon as Jones took the well-worn armchair inside the green door of the postmaster's office, he was besieged by office seekers, many of them veterans. The *Times*, which had earlier advised forbearance in making changes, now suggested that a large number of staunch Democrats be fired from their jobs and replaced by Republicans—patronage business as usual. But Jones retained a number of senior employees, among them John W. Norton, head of the money order department. A reporter lauded Norton's executive ability, business habits, and courtesy. Money order department business was booming, and Jones saw no reason to depose Norton.[19]

A month after assuming office, Jones announced his choice of superintendents of the twelve substations; seven were his appointees, five were holdovers. The onslaught of job seekers continued unabated. "Day after day," reported the *Times*, "throngs of this do-nothing class have dogged his footsteps, button-holed him in the street, and besieged the door of his private office." For every available job there were five hundred or six hundred applicants. A notice went up that no more would be considered. Three months later, however, the clamor continued. An average of seventy-five job hunters showed up daily. Many were refused admittance by the janitor on Jones's orders.[20]

A blizzard of recommendations inundated Jones. Many of them urged the retention of employees. Gen. Otis Howard wrote on behalf of Dr. Walter R. Gillette, an army surgeon during the war; Jones kept Gillette on as post office surgeon and made him his personal physician. Edwin Morgan wrote repeatedly to suggest friends; Jones showed proper deference to the powerbroker. Secretary of State Hamilton Fish stated that he did not wish to interfere or use any influence in Jones's appointments but recommended an old friend anyway. People begged Horace Greeley to use his influence with Jones on behalf of friends. Thurlow Weed recommended an elderly man for a job. Jones sent Weed a sample of the man's shaky handwriting and said he was afraid he would be compelled to reject him but would do the best he could. Roscoe Conkling's crony Chester A. Arthur pleaded with Jones to reinstate an employee who had been "removed under a misapprehension." Jones played both sides of the patronage game. When Bvt. Brig. Gen. Addison Farnsworth sought his aid in obtaining a position in the customhouse, Jones wrote a warm recommendatory letter to Moses Grinnell praising Farnsworth as a soldier and Republican, and Farnsworth got the job.[21]

When Jones's term as postmaster neared a close, the *Times* criticized the spoils system: "The Post-office, from top to bottom, is cursed with this evil of patronage." A large percentage of the employees were unskilled or inexperienced, hired solely for their politics, and the public had suffered from their blunders. "We do not lay the blame on the Postmaster" for the problems, emphasized the *Times*; "it belongs to the system." Jones had a finite number of positions to offer, which left many Republicans unhappy. They denounced him as inaccessible to office seekers, which led Jones to make some "hot and impatient" replies. The *Times* declared Jones to be in the right; the dissatisfied Republicans were being foolish.[22]

An article in *Harper's New Monthly Magazine* included an illustration of Jones in his office, besieged by job seekers, and related an anecdote regarding a problem appointee. This ward politician of some influence was assigned to a light job. On his first day he worked until noon, when he left his table and went to Jones's office. "Look here, gineral," he said, "I wanted an app'intment, not hard work; and ef this is the best thing you can do for me, I'll quit." Jones accepted his resignation, and the short-term employee departed to an uptown saloon.[23]

Not since his days commanding a brigade had Jones supervised so many men. The postal service had expanded rapidly in midcentury owing to reduced postage rates combined with advances in transportation, print technology, literacy, and a mobile population. The New York Post Office was one of the largest in the world and the most important in the United States, doing more business than any other three post offices in the country combined and contributing annual profits of $1.5 million to the federal Treasury. Every day its eight hundred employees handled between 120 and 150 tons of mail; the amount was increasing by 5 percent each year. Customers rented more than six thousand post office boxes and annually bought $2.6 million worth of stamps and other goods. The foreign business was growing rapidly; much of the mail traveling between the United States and other countries was funneled through New York. In just two days seventy thousand letters were sent to destinations as remote as Japan, Calcutta, and Madagascar. In a year the money order department sold roughly 21,000 orders worth more than a half-million dollars, and some 200,000 orders worth $3.25 million were paid. People were coming to appreciate this easy and safe way of sending money anywhere in the country. The department prided itself on its security; since it was established in 1864, it had made only four erroneous payments.[24]

While most observers praised the post office's efficiency, critics pointed to its flaws. The main office was housed in a decaying church that had been repeatedly enlarged but remained an inadequate embarrassment to the city. A switch from the old-fashioned box system to free delivery by carriers led to delays in receiving mail and gripes about inefficiency. Many complaints were made about lost mail. Hundreds of unstamped, misdirected, unsealed, or blank letters and packages accumulated daily. People complained about long lines at the stamp windows and the indifference and rudeness of postal clerks, who were said to be the hardest worked but poorest paid of public employees. Embezzlement at the post office, however, was believed to be next to impossible. Secret Service detectives kept a close watch on the operation and placed any suspected employees under surveillance. Postal workers were bonded for faithful performance of their duties, and cases of dishonesty or dereliction of duty were rare.[25]

As postmaster, Jones's concerns were wide-ranging. He regularly published announcements of shipments by rail or ship and reports on the volume of mail handled. He relocated the substations, making them more convenient for their patrons, and connected them with the main office by telegraph, enhancing communications and providing a benefit to the public, who had access to the service. He ordered the main office to open on Sundays and increased summer service to popular vacation spots. He reduced the number of boxes in the main office to concentrate on the free delivery service, which grew in public favor. He ordered extra clerks and sorters to work day and night to prevent delays. He represented his office in a court case regarding ambiguous postal laws. He did business with the operators of steamship lines, with whom he had become acquainted while working for the Commissioners of Emigration.[26]

Jones conferred in Washington, D.C., and New York with Grant's competent postmaster general, the Marylander John A. J. Creswell, presenting suggestions on a host of issues ranging from street mailboxes (which were plagued by vandalism) to franking privileges. On orders from Creswell, Jones refused to allow Alfred E. Beach, the editor-publisher of the *Scientific American*, to connect subterranean pneumatic tubes to the post office. Beach's plan called for a web of underground tubes to whisk mail beneath Manhattan and Brooklyn—but his ultimate purpose was to move carloads of people (a scheme that failed in the face of widespread opposition).[27]

A month after Jones took office, the *New York Evening Post* praised his performance. "He administers the duties with energy; he has already made several reforms and necessary improvements, and is sure to make more; and in other important respects he cannot be excelled." As time passed, the press continued to laud him. After two and a half years on the job, the *Times* complimented him for gradually bringing the post office to a high state of efficiency. In a letter to the editor a man writing to complain about slow delivery and rude clerks at his local substation nevertheless praised Jones's "good disposition." By all accounts Jones was a successful postmaster, a skilled administrator who won the loyalty of his employees and satisfied the wishes of the public at large.[28]

A constant source of frustration for Jones was the state of the main post office, housed since 1845 in a Dutch church dating to the seventeenth century, a structure the *Times* called "a hideous architectural fossil." Jones made an addition to the gallery, rearranged the furniture and partitions, and opened the entire interior into one great hall. Those steps improved light and ventilation, but the decaying, rat-infested structure was universally deemed inadequate to meet its needs.[29]

A *Herald* reporter described the place as a nondescript pile of stone and mortar surrounded by penny pie shops and peep shows. On a weekday noon it was as crowded and diverse as the Istanbul bazaar. Tourists from the country gawked at the rotting bell tower, the rickety rafters and leaky ceilings and fallen mortar, the dark recesses of the mailroom, the cramped, sweltering upstairs offices, the elevated terrace strewn with mailbags like sacks of corn on a barn floor. Every year about four thousand dollars worth of repairs was made to the old building, but every day it was becoming a less safe and satisfactory place of business. For all the detriments of their surroundings, the reporter noted, Jones and his employees "miraculously" carried on a worldwide business "with a completeness really wonderful under the circumstances."[30]

While Jones and his staff toiled in the old church, Congress appropriated $900,000 for the construction of a new main post office designed in the Second Empire style by Alfred B. Mullett, the Treasury Department's architect. To select a site for the building, Treasury secretary George S. Boutwell appointed a three-man commission including Horace Greeley and A. T. Stewart. Jones was intimately involved in the planning and construction of the new building. This was his first known connection to Stewart (although it is possible the two men had communicated regarding postal matters given that Stewart's department store did a vast mail-order business). Stewart threw the first stumbling block in the project's path, protesting the proposed site at the triangular southern tip of City Hall Park. Four months passed before Stewart was overruled, the City Hall Park site was secured, and contracts were let. Like Stewart, the refined diarist George Templeton Strong opposed placing the structure in City Hall Park. "This will destroy the best-known and most characteristic street view in New York," he complained.[31]

Jones devoted considerable time to the building project. He accompanied Mullett and superintendent of construction Calvin T. Hulburd to meetings with Boss Tweed's accomplice, Mayor A. Oakey Hall, in New York and with government officials in Washington; he consulted with Mullett regarding the building's design; he assisted Hulburd in supervising its construction; and he served as disbursing agent, paying the various contractors from funds appropriated by Congress. He appears to have impressed his federal colleagues. Mullett praised his "cordial cooperation and constant efforts to promote the success of the enterprise."[32]

Construction commenced with the excavation of an immense basement. A plank sidewalk for the public's convenience flanked the tall fence surrounding the site. Soon derricks spiked the sky, and hoisting engines groaned under their burdens as a hundred men labored. By the time the building began to take shape, however, Mullett had exhausted all but $170,000 of the original appropriation, and the congressional committee on post offices was investigating charges that he had overspent. When the committee convened in New York, Jones, Hulburd, and Stewart were among the witnesses examined. The committeemen returned to Washington, D.C., with more than five hundred pages of testimony.[33]

The new post office became a political football. After acrimonious debate, the investigating committee issued an inconclusive report. A further appropriation of $400,000 for the building was hotly debated before passing in the House of Representatives. The Senate refused to concur, and a House committee of conference was ordered. In the meantime, with funds running low, construction work crawled to a standstill. It was April 1870 before the conference committee agreed on an appropriation of $1 million to complete the project, which was agreed to after a harsh debate.[34]

Construction recommenced, only to be halted again at the end of 1870, when ambiguities in the appropriations bill and a consequent lack of funds caused the controller of the Treasury to stop disbursements. To date $1.5 million had been spent on the project. In his annual report for 1870 Mullett stated that the most difficult part of the work was done, but budgetary limitations would necessitate construction cutbacks. He sincerely hoped that Congress would appropriate funds to finish the building correctly. In response Congress appropriated $500,000.[35]

With construction stalled, newspapers continued to decry the inadequacies of the old post office. Commented *Harper's Weekly*, "It is a very ridiculous fact that the chief city upon this continent can not have a proper Post-office," comparing the old church to a cheese-monger's attic. Citing silence behind the fence enclosing the City Hall Park construction site, *Harper's* called the new post office "wholly a matter of faith" and closed with a wish—that "the delays and extravagances in the erection of the national building at the lower end of the Park will not rival the scandalous jobs of the municipal building at the upper end," where Boss Tweed's gang ruled and thieved at City Hall.[36]

The summer of 1871 brought a spurt of progress at the construction site. By autumn huge iron pillars and a stonework facade towered above the high perimeter fence, which was daily plastered with advertising handbills. In June 1872 Hulburd and architect Mullett altered the plans to allow for an underground railway to enter the building's basement. But by January 1873 the last congressional appropriation was depleted, and work again ground to a halt.[37]

So matters stood when Jones's term as postmaster ended. For four frustrating years he was entangled in the construction boondoggle as the old church rotted around him. The new building was continually delayed and did not open until 1875, two years after he left office. It did not have a lengthy or happy history. The overwrought architecture came to be considered an eyesore; wags dubbed the place "Mullett's Monstrosity" and "The Whale." As early as 1912, a congressional bill advocated demolishing the building, but it survived until it was razed in 1938–39. Jones never got to inhabit the suite of offices overlooking Broadway. Not only was he disappointed; he also received a financial blow.[38]

As the duly appointed disbursing agent for the post office construction project, Jones was entitled by law to compensation of three-eighths of 1 percent on all money spent on the building. But in 1877 he discovered that his compensation was set at one-quarter of 1 percent. Consequently, he sent a letter to Secretary of the Treasury John Sherman, General Sherman's brother, suggesting that he was entitled to the extra one-eighth of 1 percent. Sherman referred the matter to his department's solicitor, who ruled against the claim. Undeterred, Jones wrote again to Sherman to protest the decision. Sherman turned the letter over to his first comptroller, who reported that Jones had been compensated $11,649.28 for disbursements of more than $4.6 million. Frustrated, Jones wrote to Sherman a third time to plead his case yet again, pointing to discrepancies in the opinions of the solicitor and comptroller. Sherman remained unconvinced. He declared that the allowance made to Jones was legal and equitable and that "the question should not be opened." Rebuffed by the secretary of the Treasury, Jones turned to Congress. On March 25, 1878, Anson G. McCook, congressman from lower Manhattan, introduced a House bill calling for Sherman to pay Jones $5,805.82. Three days later Francis Kernan of New York introduced a similar bill in the Senate. Both bills were referred to the respective committees on buildings and grounds. Both committees reported adversely. It was a financial setback Jones could ill afford.[39]

One of Jones's duties as postmaster was fighting crime and corruption. Crooks perpetrated countless swindles through the mail, duping thousands of victims out of hundreds of thousands of dollars every year. "Dollar stores" and "gift enterprise men" offered goods from Bibles to banjos in mass-mailed flyers, but once paid, they never delivered. Sham lotteries, some pretending to benefit churches, promised instant riches to players. Shady druggists hawked quack patent medicines. Hucksters promoted all sorts of preposterous products, including a magic belt that made its wearer disappear. For fees the lovelorn were sent photographs of women and hollow promises of wedding dates.[40]

Jones went to war with the so-called sawdust swindlers. These criminals flooded the country with circulars offering counterfeit bills at a low price. Dupes who sent in money received in return small wooden boxes containing bits of cast iron embedded in sawdust (hence the name). The police were flooded with complaints from all parts of the country in regard to the scam. Jones made an effort to halt the crooks by confiscating their mail and firing accomplices among post office employees. He had some success, breaking up more than a dozen operations. One scammer had the nerve to charge Jones with detaining his mail illegally. The case was tried in federal district court. When the crook admitted to his fraud, Jones was acquitted.[41]

Jones tangled with one dishonest post office employee who was in cahoots with the sawdust swindlers. D. C. Ormsby was an Irish Protestant who impersonated a minister. He had been dismissed as a regimental chaplain during the war and fired for dishonesty as a customhouse clerk. Unabashed, he deceived influential New York City gentlemen into providing him with testimonials. Recommendations in hand, he had an audience with President Grant, who referred him to Postmaster Jones. Ormsby ingratiated himself with Jones; Jones gave him a job as a clerk and soon promoted him to superintendent of Station D. But a subordinate caught Ormsby tampering with the mail, and Jones preferred charges against him. After an examination, Ormsby was found guilty and removed from office.

Ormsby protested that he was the victim of religious prejudice on the part of two Roman Catholics: his whistle-blowing subordinate and Jones.

Accompanied by a lawyer, he returned to Washington, D.C., and convinced authorities that he was the victim of a conspiracy who should be vindicated and reinstated. On returning to New York, he snowed a special agent sent to investigate him by Postmaster General Creswell. Consequently, he was reinstalled as superintendent of Station D, and his subordinate accuser was transferred. Yet within days a visitor to Jones identified Ormsby as the former chaplain who had been fired from the customhouse. Evidence of his chicanery led Grant to order Creswell to conduct another investigation. For a second time, however, Ormsby was found innocent of wrongdoing.

A few months later Ormsby came to grief when it was revealed that he and two post office confederates were in cahoots with sawdust swindlers, clandestinely delivering hundreds of cash-stuffed letters to the crooks in midnight meetings and accepting kickbacks as reward. When Ormsby got greedy and began pilfering money and demanding a bigger take, the gang's leader ratted on him to police superintendent George W. Walling. A sting operation was set up, and Ormsby fell into the trap, ending his criminal career—for the time being, at least. For Ormsby somehow conned Grant to turn over his precious testimonials. When the *Times* broke the story a few years later, Ormsby was still using the recommendations, perhaps in other flimflams.[42]

Other post office employees were caught committing crimes while Jones was postmaster. A mail carrier was charged with embezzlement and secreting letters; witnesses testified that he was of unsound mind. The assistant superintendent of the foreign department was caught opening and stealing money from letters. A clerk with ten years of service was charged with pocketing letters and packages containing valuables. In another case Jones assigned Charles E. Bacon to meet the early-morning train in Hartford and sort the New York City–bound mail. Every morning, when the train pulled into New Haven at two o'clock, Bacon entered a hotel, got a drink at the bar, and went into the water closet before returning to the depot. The hotelkeeper thought nothing of it until some men told him they heard ripping noises coming from the water closet when Bacon occupied it. Suspicious, the innkeeper contacted the New York Post Office's special agent, who dispatched a detective to investigate. The detective staked out the water closet and observed Bacon open a letter, withdraw money from it, and stuff the cash in his vest pocket. The detective promptly arrested him. Bacon confessed to having robbed the mails for some months.[43] All of the crimes paled in comparison with one that struck the closest to Jones and hurt him the worst.

CHAPTER 6

Grant versus Greeley

Beyond doling out patronage as postmaster, Jones did a lot of politicking in a sphere that extended from state assembly districts in New York City all the way to the White House. Sometimes his obligations simply entailed appearing at certain events, such as the funeral of Henry Raymond, the congressman and editor of the *New York Times*. He joined other Republican notables to wish Senator Fenton bon voyage on a Europe-bound ship. He joined Thurlow Weed, Moses Grinnell, and other prominent men who called on George Boutwell during a visit of the Treasury secretary to New York. He was a distinguished guest at a banquet Grinnell hosted for a visiting senator. He hobnobbed with leaders of the state Republican committee at the elegant home of its chairman. He was a regular attendee at the annual balls of the Michael Cregan Association, a group of several hundred largely Irish American Republicans, where he rubbed shoulders with the likes of collector of the port and future president Chester Arthur.[1]

Politicking generated controversy. In June 1870 the Democratic *New York Sun* charged that post office workers had been solicited for contributions to buy a life insurance policy for President Grant. Party taxes on the wages of federal employees were routine in the spoils system, but this was something else altogether—the *Sun* called it "extortion." In the next day's issue an anonymous postal worker stated that employees expected to pay their regular political assessment but could not afford the extra solicitation. Jones immediately issued a statement expressing surprise at the assertion and denying the charge. The *Sun* continued the attack, however, claiming Jones himself had been taxed one thousand dollars toward the insurance policy. The imbroglio was typical of the opposition press's relentless attack against Grant administration corruption. Whether it was true or not is questionable. On one hand, Grant had an unfortunate penchant for accepting gifts from wealthy friends. On the other hand, opposition newspapers were not above leveling sensational but untrue charges.[2]

Within weeks after the life insurance flap, Jones accompanied George Boutwell to a cabinet meeting in Long Branch, New Jersey, where Grant had purchased a seaside cottage to escape Washington, D.C.'s constant pressure and wilting summer heat. Jones and Grant's relationship was intertwined with New York City and state politics, which were in a particularly volatile period. Jones had come to the president as a Greeley and Fenton man, but his two patrons were turning against Grant. Then the president made an appointment that brought matters to a head.[3]

The turning point occurred when Grant named the genial Irishman Thomas Murphy, Roscoe Conkling's advisor and henchman, to replace Fenton's man Moses Grinnell as collector of the port. Murphy was a city ward heeler, a notorious wartime shoddy contractor, and a business associate of Boss Tweed who shared the president's love of horses. He proved to be one of Grant's most controversial appointees. The move naturally alienated Fenton and Greeley, deepened the rift between the state party's Fenton and Conkling factions, and decisively linked Grant to Conkling. Murphy's leadership of what was soon dubbed the "Customhouse Gang" became a national scandal, criticized most vociferously by Greeley. Murphy resigned under fire in 1871. (Grant replaced him with Chester Arthur, who fine-tuned the customhouse as a political machine. "Chester Arthur," commented Greeley, "is Tom Murphy under another name.")[4]

Fenton and Greeley had guided Jones to political prominence. Would he remain true to them or switch his allegiance to Grant and Conkling? Greeley had soured on the president, thinking him incompetent. Grant was instrumental in effecting Greeley's loss of influence in New York State politics. This was evident at the September 1870 state Republican convention in Saratoga, where Jones was a delegate. There the Conkling faction—buttressed by a letter from Grant—nominated Stewart L. Woodford for governor over Greeley, who was backed by Fenton. It is uncertain whether Jones stood at this time with Greeley and Fenton or with the president and Conkling. In any case the balance of power within the state Republican Party had shifted securely to the Grant-Conkling faction. Diminished and embittered, Greeley turned from the party establishment to a group of liberal Republicans he had previously disdained.[5]

Following the election (which Woodford lost to the incumbent, Boss Tweed's man John T. Hoffman), the *New York Freeman's Journal and Catholic Register* charged that the city postal service had been "prostituted to partisan purposes" during the campaign, when letter carriers delivered spurious mail in an attempt to identify fraudulently registered voters. As a result, the paper alleged, the regular mail service was delayed, causing great inconvenience. Only a bumpkin such as Jones, it insinuated, would resort to such a feeble scheme. (Opposition city papers enjoyed poking fun at Jones's rural western New York roots.) In repeating the story, the *New York World* commented that popular indignation would be intense if it was discovered that Jones had misused his office for party or personal gain.[6]

The *Times* and the *Herald* leaped to Jones's defense, accusing the devoutly Democratic *World* of "a sort of insane vendetta" against him. "As a matter of fact," declared the *Times,* "the Postmaster has kept clear of all political complications." At its core, however, the story was true. The Republican general committee had sent so-called test-letters throughout the city and identified five thousand illegally registered voters. But Boss Tweed's puppet, Mayor Oakey Hall, had sent campaign circulars through the mail, it was noted, without interference from the postmaster. Jones showed no favor to either party, his defenders claimed, and in any case he had no authority to refuse to transmit either document. Undeterred, the *Freeman's Journal* damned the test-letters as "an outrage on the entire community."[7]

Grant had balanced his initial appointees to federal offices in New York State between adherents of Fenton and Conkling. Fenton's numerous supporters claimed him—congressman, governor, and now senator—as the state's truest representative of the Republican Party. Bowing to Fenton's wishes, Grant had appointed Jones and others to top offices, including Moses Grinnell as collector and Jones's law partner George Palmer as appraiser in the customhouse. Over time, however, Grant was repulsed by Fenton's megalomania. As the president wrote to a friend, "Fentonism in New York means simply a yielding of the Executive to Mr. Fenton for the punishment of all who do not agree that the Republican Party has no higher mission than to place him in control of it." Fenton, for his part, wrote to Grant regarding dissension within the party, defending his policies and exonerating himself. But Grant had soured on Fenton and many of the appointments he had made at Fenton's request.[8]

By 1870 Conkling—a renowned orator, brilliant organizer, and consummate party manager—was the favored advisor to the president, rewarded with all the federal patronage in New York State, where he firmly controlled an army of lieutenants and workers down to the county and district levels. The death knell to Fenton's ambition occurred in dramatic fashion during the debate on Tom Murphy's appointment as collector in the Senate. Conkling brandished a red-taped document at Fenton. Conkling did not reveal its contents, but Fenton knew exactly what it was—a record of his arrest as a young man on suspicion of theft. Conkling had blackmailed Fenton to checkmate. The Senate confirmed Murphy as collector, and Conkling toasted Reuben Fenton's political death. With Grinnell out and Murphy in, Grant removed other Fenton men from office and replaced them with Conkling supporters. Fenton's demise was confirmed at the 1871 Republican state convention, where the Conkling-Murphy machine crushed an attempted comeback by the Greeley-Fenton faction.[9]

Like the president, Jones grew disenchanted with Fenton and parted ways with him. William S. Hillyer, a New York City lawyer and brevet brigadier general who had served on Grant's staff during the war (and succeeded Jones as counsel to the Commissioners of Emigration), wrote to the president: "Jones is a sincere and sagacious friend of yours, who feels exceedingly grateful to you because he thinks you have stood by him in spite of a tremendous pressure against him. He is utterly disgusted with Fenton and is for Conkling as long as Conkling does not make your interest subservient to his." Jones now sided with the difficult Conkling, who was intolerant of any independent judgment by his lieutenants. Above Conkling, however, Jones's fealty was to Grant.[10]

While Reuben Fenton repelled the president, Jones's other patron, Horace Greeley, puzzled him. Grant described Greeley as "a genius without common sense." He acknowledged the journalist was "an honest, firm, untiring supporter" of the Republican Party. "But he is a free thinker," the president complained, prone to jumping to conclusions and misunderstanding the views of fellow Republicans. "I have long desired a free, full talk with Mr. Greeley because I have confidence in his intentions," Grant informed a friend in November 1870. "I have thought, at times, of inviting him to Washington for that purpose." The president's desire to communicate with the editor presented an opportunity to Jones, who was a friend of both men.[11]

Jones discussed the matter with Postmaster General Creswell in Washington and followed up with a private letter. Jones hoped that Creswell could get Greeley to meet with Grant for a free interchange of views, which would do "much good." Greeley had opinions about certain issues—including federal appointments in New York State—that might not fully accord with the president's, Jones admitted, but there would be "no clashing." Greeley was "easily satisfied and will not be found very factious." "Like all public men," Jones observed, "Mr. Greeley is often misrepresented by injudicious friends who assume to know his opinions when they do not." Greeley had repeatedly complained to Jones of such misrepresentations. Greeley especially deprecated efforts to estrange him from Grant's administration, which he warmly supported. He thought his written and printed statements should be considered reliable rather than reported conversations. Jones concurred. Greeley was uncertain who was trying to alienate him from Grant. Jones had a theory in that regard, but Greeley was "not yet prepared to believe it." Jones trusted that "no opportunity may be given to the lukewarm friends of the Administration to say to Mr. Greeley that his advice and influence are not sought for or considered at Head Quarters." This remarkable letter reveals that Jones was a conduit between Greeley and Grant during a time the two were drifting irrevocably apart. Within two years Jones's devotion to both men would present him with a dilemma.[12]

That Jones was close to Grant was illustrated by an incident of the president's misbegotten attempt to annex Santo Domingo. In Grant's annual message of December 1870 he urged Congress to authorize a special commission to report on conditions in the Caribbean nation. Despite the staunch opposition of Senator Charles Sumner, the Republican chairman of the foreign relations committee, the Senate approved the commission, and the House concurred. Grant appointed three commissioners, augmented by a staff that included a secretary, a military advisor, and a complement of scientists. At Grant's request Jones offered a place on the staff to the zoologist and geologist Louis Agassiz, professor at Harvard University. Agassiz was a personal friend of Senator Sumner, and he immediately understood that this friendship was the reason behind the offer—that the appointment was meant to appease Sumner. Consequently, Agassiz declined the appointment. Why Grant chose Jones to approach Agassiz is a mystery. In the end the commission reported favorably regarding annexation, but public opinion had turned against the idea. Grant submitted the commission's report to Congress without recommendation, and nothing came of the dream to annex Santo Domingo.[13]

While performing errands for President Grant, Jones continued to politick at the local level, serving, for example, as treasurer and delegate of the Seventh Assembly District's Republican association. But he had long since outgrown that scene. As the rift between Grant and Greeley widened, speculation arose regarding Jones's future. In a letter to Grant, Alfred Pleasanton, once Jones's rival for a federal appointment and now commissioner of Internal Revenue, urged Jones's removal as postmaster and suggested the German ethnic hero

Franz Sigel as a desirable replacement who would have Greeley's support. A Tennessee newspaper stated that Jones was the last Fenton man still in office in New York City and that his turn to be sacked by Grant "will probably come before long." Rumors said that Grant would remove Jones at the urging of Edwin Morgan or else because Greeley had recommended him for the job. If true, commented the *Brooklyn Daily Eagle,* it would be a mockery of the administration's professions for civil service reform. (Grant persuaded Congress to create the country's first civil service commission, but Congress neglected to appropriate or perpetuate it.) The *Eagle* noted that all of the Republican factions—and the Democrats to boot—admitted that Jones was a good postmaster: "His offence consists in having been recommended by Horace Greeley." Sacking Jones would only alienate Greeley further, declared the *Eagle,* adding sarcastically, "Every decapitated official makes *such* a zealous advocate of General Grant's renomination."[14]

Secretary of State Hamilton Fish visited New York in November 1871 to ask Jones that post office employees be allowed time off to vote in the election of local and state offices. A month later Jones wrote to Thurlow Weed about Fish. Jones had heard that the secretary could be taking an unfriendly attitude toward him. Jones's foes had accused him of being an inefficient postmaster. It was a legitimate subject of inquiry, he acknowledged, to which he had no objections. But he hoped Fish would not form an opinion without such an inquiry. He desired Fish's goodwill and confidence as an influential Republican and a representative of New York State in the cabinet. Jones hoped that Weed would write to Fish and give him as favorable a report of Jones's performance as was deserved. Whether Weed complied with Jones's request is uncertain.[15]

As the 1872 campaign approached, collector Thomas Murphy proposed to Grant that Jones, Pleasanton, and other federal officials in the city should pledge their support to the president, compel their subordinates to support him, and choose the delegates to attend the Republican state convention. But rifts tore the national Republican Party during Grant's first term, with the orthodox and conservative backers of Roscoe Conkling squaring off against the moderate reformers led by Speaker of the House James G. Blaine of Maine. More direly, some disaffected Republicans bolted the party entirely. Led by the former Eleventh Corps general and prominent German American Carl Schurz, the dissatisfied splinter group formed the Liberal Republican Party. Among its supporters, although detested as corrupt by many of them, was Reuben Fenton.[16]

The Liberal Republicans deplored Grant as a despot presiding over an administration marked by abysmal appointees and the inevitable resultant corruption. In speeches and in print they attacked the president's ethical, intellectual, military, and political abilities. They convened in Cincinnati in May and, to the surprise of many and the displeasure of some, nominated Horace Greeley for president. A month later the orthodox Republicans gathered in Philadelphia to nominate Grant for a second term. Another month went by before the Democrats convened in Baltimore, where they too nominated Greeley and endorsed the Liberal Republican platform. This coalition created a strained political muddle. Greeley was a longtime foe of the Democrats, and he was unacceptable to many Liberal Republicans as well. Now he was the presidential candidate of both parties. It was the only time in United States history that one of the two major parties endorsed a third-party candidate.[17]

Rumor had it that Jones privately favored Greeley in the 1872 election, but he came out publicly for Grant and stood by the president and the Conkling machine. Together with dozens of other prominent men, Jones was named honorary vice president of a massive campaign rally of five thousand Republicans at the Cooper Institute, at which Conking, as the main speaker, defended Grant and attacked Greeley. Jones routinely visited Republican Party headquarters in the Fifth Avenue Hotel. He also endorsed a call for the formation of "Veteran Clubs" to support the Republican ticket. He urged Thurlow Weed to attend a state convention of Republican veterans in Utica. He asked Weed to persuade William Seward "to give us one blast upon his bugle horn" during the campaign. Jones anticipated a tight race. "This is no 'walk over,'" he informed Weed. "Political quacks may tell you different but disbelieve them." Other New York Republican leaders shared Jones's concern. It proved to be exaggerated. While many Republican moderates found Grant undesirable, they remained faithful to the president out of party loyalty.[18]

During the campaign political assessments weighed heavily on Republican officeholders. Employees of the customhouse were taxed from 2 to 6 percent of their salaries to support the cause. While the Grant administration pointed proudly to new civil service rules instituted in the Chester Arthur–run customhouse, Greeley's supporters derided the successive changes in the collectorship from Grinnell to Murphy to Arthur. Jones came under Republican fire for expediting Greeley campaign documents through the mails. Grant's adherents were also peeved that Greeley and Fenton had used the franking privilege to mail for free hundreds of thousands of an issue of the *Tribune* attacking the president. Greeley was a millionaire, declared the *Times;* "he can at least afford to pay postage."[19]

Jones's prediction of a close presidential contest was wrong. The Democrats could not turn out the vote for their erstwhile enemy Greeley, while the Liberal Republicans could not unite behind him either. A clumsy alliance between traditional enemies and a temporary aberration, they made the worst showing in any nineteenth-century presidential election. Grant passed most of the campaign in silence at his Long Branch summer cottage, intentionally avoiding any political meetings. Greeley stumped the country from Maine to Texas, giving numerous speeches daily and wearing himself to exhaustion. For Greeley the campaign and its aftermath combined catastrophic political defeat and crushing personal tragedy.[20]

A campaign hagiography praised Greeley as a hard worker, scrupulously honest, and intellectually qualified for the presidency. But Greeley's old Republican friends, alienated by his Democratic nomination, savaged him with vile epithets and insulted him in pamphlets and the press. The editorial cartoonist Thomas Nast, whose pen had helped to topple Boss Tweed, skewered Greeley repeatedly in the pages of *Harper's Weekly.* A Republican campaign publication castigated him as an intellectual gadfly unfit to hold the nation's highest office. The author listed eleven reasons why Greeley should not be president. Number 5: "He is the worst judge of men. Instance his choice of political associates at home, and his almost daily experience in being duped by designing fellows, recommending rascals for office, etc." Although not mentioned by name, Jones was stained with this broad brush. Wounded by the criticism, Greeley commented that he never knew whether he was running for the presidency or the penitentiary. In a devastating blow his wife died a week before the election. Grant was reelected in a landslide, receiving approximately 3.6 million votes to Greeley's 2.8 million and garnering 286 electoral votes to Greeley's 66. Less than a month later, defeated, despondent, drained, and delirious, Greeley was placed in a private asylum near his home in Chappaqua, New York. There he died on November 29, 1872, twenty-four days after his defeat at the polls.[21]

The next day Greeley's corpse was brought by train to the city and displayed in an open casket at the home of *Tribune* publisher Samuel Sinclair. The sadness of his passing touched the nation; the ugliness of the campaign was forgotten in a sweeping tide of public sympathy for the deceased crusader. Crowds of mourners besieged Sinclair's house, hoping to gain admittance to pay their respects. Policemen kept them at bay; not one in fifty was permitted inside. In the evening several of Greeley's closest friends were invited to view his remains. Among them was Jones. Crowds of mourners filed by Greeley's coffin the next day in a public display at City Hall. At Greeley's funeral service on December 4 and in the following great procession down Fifth Avenue, Jones mourned his mentor in the company of President Grant, the entire cabinet, the vice president, the chief justice, governors, U.S. senators and representatives, mayors, and many other dignitaries. Four years later, when a monument to Greeley was dedicated at his grave in Brooklyn's Greenwood Cemetery, Jones was among the notables in attendance.[22]

Jones traveled to Washington in mid-March 1873 and held several meetings with President Grant. On March 15 he formally tendered his resignation as postmaster to the president, to take effect April 1. Did Grant request it? "The Silent Smoker," as the press called the taciturn, cigar-puffing president, remained characteristically mum regarding the matter. Jones's commission would not expire until May, but he chose the April date so his successor could take office at the start of a new accounting quarter. Grant promptly named that successor, Thomas L. James, deputy inspector in the customhouse, a devoted Conkling man. After his final meeting with the president, Jones returned to New York on a night train.[23]

Jones commended Thomas James without reservation and predicted he would satisfy everybody as postmaster. The *Times* noted that Jones had made slow progress in changing the culture at the post office. Many of the employees, long-tenured "fossils" whose notions were as antiquated as the old church in which they toiled, had persistently obstructed the introduction of modern methods. James would bring reform, the *Times* predicted. Such proved to be the case. A year and a half after taking office, James had made radical changes by reducing political influences and introducing reforms. James was less hampered by politicians than Jones had been, noted the *New York Republic,* so he could more readily effect change. Indeed, James's able leadership of the New York Post Office led to his appointment as postmaster general in the cabinet of President James A. Garfield.[24]

The news of Jones's resignation caused a stir in New York City. He had told his friends of his intention about four months earlier and expressed gratification that he would soon be relieved of the weight and care of the job. "The salary of the office [six thousand dollars a year] in no way compensates for the duties, responsibilities, and risks connected with it," observed the *New York Commercial Advertiser.* Political communities saluted Jones's service.

The Twelfth Assembly District Republican Association, for example, met and adopted a resolution tendering its thanks for many acts of courtesy he had shown them as postmaster.[25]

The post office employees, holding Jones in high regard, expressed much regret over the news of his leaving. A group of clerks began to solicit financial subscriptions from their coworkers to create a "testimonial" to present to their departing boss. Jones learned of the plan and firmly suppressed it. He explained that "the system of making presentations to all sorts of persons on all kinds of pretences" was "rapidly becoming a gross abuse." He added, "Many of the clerks, having families to support on small pay, cannot afford to subscribe, and yet dare not refuse." He was greatly pleased by the evidence of his employees' esteem. His precedent in refusing the testimonial only increased their positive opinion of him.[26]

A *Herald* reporter interviewed Jones at his Irvine House residence and asked why he had resigned. Jones replied that he had been considering the move for some time. The act had "no political significance whatever," he stated. "The President and myself are in perfect accord, and in my visit to Washington he treated me with great and kindly consideration. There has been no misunderstanding between us, and there was no reason in my resigning but that of my own volition." His performance in office had entirely satisfied Grant. He thought he had perfectly upheld the views of the Republican Party. Yet issues during his term had worried him exceedingly. He had been responsible for the good conduct of every post office employee and was personally liable for any mistakes or deficiencies they had made. He was frustrated by the inefficiencies of the main post office. Trying to conduct such a vast business in the old church was "like boring an auger hole with a gimlet, or like putting a bushel of corn into a quart measure." He was as well aware as anybody that the facility was inferior and that the public had reason to be dissatisfied. The press had been very kind to him in regard to the situation. He had done his best to make the place as efficient as possible but felt "it was of no use." He did not mention the ongoing delays in building the new post office. He stated that he had been offered a law partnership that would pay him more than anything the government could give him. He concluded by saying that he was glad once more to be able to get a night's rest.[27]

CHAPTER 7

Irishman and Veteran

Jones was naturally drawn to the activities and causes of two groups: Irish Americans and Civil War veterans. He linked those clannish and passionately political constituencies as few men could. He took leadership roles in their endeavors, chaired meetings, and sat on boards. But the depth of his devotion to their causes is difficult to gauge.

New York City's Irish Americans formed a diverse and sometimes fractious community, ranging from criminals and lowly laborers to leading businessmen such as A. T. Stewart. Fraternal and benevolent associations formed bonds between Irish American men. Jones, however, apparently did not join elite groups such as the Friendly Sons of St. Patrick or the Knights of St. Patrick; his name was never recorded in reports of their affairs. But from all appearances he was an Irish nationalist, seeking a republic of Ireland free of British domination. The nationalist movement was at the heart of Irish American communal life and identity, and New York City was the center of its parties and endeavors. The depth of Jones's support of Irish nationalism and the extent of his involvement in the movement are uncertain. Although publicly devoted to the cause, perhaps he was simply a figurehead.

In the days of Jones's grandfathers, the Act of Union in 1800 dissolved the Irish Parliament and created the United Kingdom of Great Britain and Ireland. In reaction, nationalism swept Ireland. The act rankled the Irish, filling them with hatred for England and a strong desire to be free of British rule. Religion complicated matters. Irish Catholics could vote, and they held other rights, but they could not sit in Parliament. They were second-class citizens in their own country, where a Protestant minority ruled.[1]

During the 1820s the gifted orator and organizer Daniel O'Connell led a mass political campaign that established Catholic civil rights and linked Irish identity to Catholicism. When he was elected to Parliament and that body abolished the last vestiges of discrimination, Catholic Emancipation was achieved, and Irish the world over celebrated, hailing O'Connell as the "Liberator." In 1840 he launched a campaign to repeal the Act of Union. Stoked by ethnic organizations and the press, America's Irish—poor, oppressed, Anglophobic—backed the crusade. When O'Connell died in 1847, however, the repeal campaign died with him.[2]

Jones took part during the 1870s in efforts to commemorate O'Connell. He served as secretary of a committee seeking to place a memorial to O'Connell in Central Park, which failed to achieve its goal. When the centennial of the Liberator's birth approached in 1875, Jones was secretary of a committee that planned a commemorative observance in New York. That effort met with success. At the resulting ceremony a standing room only crowd filled the great hall at Cooper Institute, and a mob outside clamored for admission. The stage was decorated with flags and a heroic-sized bust of O'Connell. The famous Sixty-Ninth New York was present in uniform, and its band played Celtic airs. Jones was named a vice president of the meeting. Before the audience settled in to hear the main oration, he and other dignitaries were introduced and applauded.[3]

As Daniel O'Connell's repeal movement faltered, frustrated activists formed the Young Ireland movement. They sought total independence rather than some type of home rule, and unlike O'Connell, they were willing to endorse armed revolution. Young Ireland advocates rose with the revolutionary fever that swept Europe in 1848 but were quelled for lack of support. Many became exiles in the United States, where they continued their crusade. In 1858 the Irish Republican Brotherhood (IRB) was formed in Dublin to foment an armed insurrection and overthrow British rule. That year an IRB branch was established in America and took the name Fenian Brotherhood, commemorating an ancient Irish warrior king.[4]

After a slow start the Fenians flourished in the United States, with as many as fifty thousand members by 1860 and many more supporters. Spurred by the Irish American press, Fenianism spread from New York City throughout the eastern states and westward. During and after the Civil War, Irish Union army veterans and the urban working class dramatically bolstered the organization's numbers. "Fenian Circles," as local chapters were known, multiplied, as did their treasuries. But after its sudden rise, the movement experienced a quick collapse. In 1866 and 1870 the Fenians invaded Canada, seeking to overthrow British rule there and consequently persuade Great Britain to relinquish rule over Ireland. (One of the plotters was Bernard Doran Killian, Jones's former employer at the *Buffalo Sentinel.*) In each instance the invaders were defeated by Canadian and British troops. The failures demoralized Irish American nationalists and doomed Fenianism. Fenian

Circles established in the Armies of the Potomac and the Cumberland offered Jones opportunities to become acquainted with the group and its goals. There is no evidence that he joined them, but actions he took in the postwar years indicate that they had his support. His relationship with Thomas J. Kelly offers an example.[5]

Kelly served as a captain in an Ohio regiment during the war. At its end he twice went to Ireland to assist the IRB cause. In January 1867 he traveled surreptitiously to England to join a group that sought to coordinate Fenian actions. At their direction Fenians attacked police barracks and other targets in Ireland, only to be broken up and hunted down. As a result, Kelly and a companion were arrested in Manchester. A week later, as a prison van carried the pair from the police court to prison, Fenians ambushed the vehicle to rescue their comrades. In the resulting melee a police sergeant was mortally wounded. The incident shocked and angered the British public. Five Fenians were captured and charged with the policeman's murder. Three of them—one a former Union army officer—were convicted and sentenced to death. Meanwhile, Kelly, freed by his rescuers, returned to America.[6]

The three Fenians were hanged at Manchester on the morning of November 23, 1867. On that "ever-memorable day in the history of the Irish race" they instantly became revered in folklore as the "Manchester Martyrs." Hours after the execution, Jones was among a crowd of Irish American Civil War veterans who filled Cooper Institute's great hall to react to the news. The meeting was solemn, without the music that usually enlivened such events. After several inflammatory speeches, resolutions were adopted, to deafening cheers, condemning the British for imprisoning American citizens without trial and calling on the United States government to demand their release. Jones, Charles Halpine, and a third man were appointed as a deputation to present the resolutions to President Andrew Johnson in Washington, D.C. While the execution of the Manchester Martyrs stimulated the Fenian cause, it also stoked British anger at Fenian terrorism and Irish American agitators.[7]

Irish American support for the Manchester Martyrs also drew the ire of native-born Americans such as the patrician George Templeton Strong, who habitually denigrated the Irish in terms such as "beastly Celtic bogtrotters." Strong considered the hanging of the Fenian trio as just and belittled the Cooper Institute rally as a "grand palaver." "Poor Ould Ireland is in low estate," he sneered, "because the majority of Irishmen are jackasses." Such was the prejudice that Irish Americans faced from certain quarters.[8]

In June 1869 Postmaster Jones appointed the notorious Thomas Kelly superintendent of one of the substations. Here was a public show of support for the Fenian leader and his cause—but it was also an instance of Jones's loyalty to Horace Greeley, who had requested it. Popular public opinion (molded in part by Greeley's influence) generally supported Irish nationalism. Tammany politicians as well as Grant Republicans such as Jones gave jobs to Irish nationalists as a show of support. When American supporters of an Irish republic held a national convention in Chicago on Independence Day 1869, Jones and Kelly were there to represent New York City. But Fenian extremism was another issue. When President Grant issued a proclamation warning against the second Fenian invasion of Canada, it was ignored, resulting in the fiasco of 1870. The administration was grappling with Great Britain over complex and thorny issues, which made the militant Fenians worrisome. In offering even symbolic support to the Fenian cause by hiring Kelly, Jones ran the risk of alienating moderate supporters of Irish nationalism.[9]

Jones was apparently familiar with another significant figure in American-Anglo-Irish relations, John Warren, one of the Americans held by the British over the protests of Irish Americans. Warren was arrested in Ireland in June 1867, tried and convicted of treason, and sentenced to fifteen years in the penitentiary. After serving two years he was discharged by an act of clemency by Queen Victoria. On returning to the United States, he sought damages against Great Britain. Failing that, Warren applied to Secretary of State Hamilton Fish for an appointment to a diplomatic post. He told Fish that he could obtain the influence of Jones, Thomas Murphy, Chester Arthur, and hundreds of others if necessary. Warren's name-dropping proved ineffective; he did not secure an appointment.[10]

Jones also engaged in Irish American cultural affairs. He was a member of a committee that greeted the celebrated Irish actor Barry Sullivan on his arrival from Liverpool. The committeemen invited Sullivan to a public reception at the theater where he was engaged for the season and a banquet at one of Lorenzo Delmonico's sumptuous restaurants. In 1875 Jones presided over large audiences in Cooper Institute's great hall at three lectures on Irish subjects. In introducing the speakers, Jones made brief public speeches, a rarity for him. One of the orators was John O'Connor Power, a member of Parliament for County Mayo, Ireland. Jones described Power as "one of the foremost of the 'advanced Irish nationalists.'" A polished speaker, Power was loudly cheered during his lecture on conditions in Ireland.[11]

One of Jones's endeavors combined Irish American and veteran interests. Although he had not served in Gen. Thomas Francis Meagher's Irish Brigade, Jones was an incorporator of the Irish Brigade Association. Chartered by the state legislature, the organization's purpose was to perpetuate the brigade's name and fame, to collect accounts and relics of its service and secure a city building to house them, and to erect a monument to Meagher.[12]

John McCloskey, archbishop of New York's Roman Catholic diocese and America's first cardinal, supported the efforts of a group of well-known and well-to-do Irish Americans to establish a bank in the city. A number of them met in June 1875 to elect temporary officers and take other steps toward establishing the Irish-American Savings Bank. Jones was elected president. He and the other trustees were said by the *Irish-American* "to constitute the wealthiest savings bank corporation of a similar nature on this Continent." A priest voiced the Catholic clergy's approval of the enterprise, believing it would be a blessing to the Irish American community. At another meeting a week later Jones and his fellow trustees formed a committee to ascertain their personal responsibility under a new state banking law, to estimate the cost of maintaining the bank for one year, and to recommend a suitable building to house it. But in the depression following the Panic of 1873, the Irish-American Savings Bank apparently never got beyond the planning stage.[13]

Jones lent his support throughout the 1870s to annual balls sponsored by the Catholic Young Men's Association to benefit the New York Roman Catholic Orphan Asylum. On these festive nights at the Academy of Music, he and Sarah joined "throngs of youth and beauty" dancing to the strains of a popular band, including many Irish airs. On a more sedate occasion Jones joined others at Archbishop McCloskey's Madison Avenue residence and heard the prelate deliver an appeal for funding to complete construction of the new St. Patrick's Cathedral on Fifth Avenue. McCloskey noted that the church's architect had waived his fees as a contribution and hoped his listeners would follow the example and give generously. Jones responded with a substantial five hundred–dollar donation.[14]

During his postpresidential world tour Ulysses Grant made a series of ceremonial visits in Ireland. When the Cork city council neglected to give Grant a public reception, Irish Americans were miffed. Jones chaired meetings of prominent compatriots to arrange for a mass protest of Cork's slight, to take place in Cooper Institute's great hall. In covering the planning sessions, the press noted that Jones had difficulties in smoothing dissension between Grant's supporters and his opponents, of which there were many. Apparently owing to that problem, the mass meeting never took place. The incident revealed how much partisan Irish American Democrats disliked Grant.[15]

Allied with Jones in the Cork protest was Michael Kerwin, like Thomas Kelly a radical Irish nationalist. A native of County Wexford, Ireland, Kerwin fought in the Civil War as colonel of a Pennsylvania cavalry regiment, serving under Sherman in 1865 and briefly commanding a brigade. During his army days he joined the Fenian movement. When he resigned his commission, he returned to Ireland, where the British government arrested and imprisoned him for six months. Returning to America, Kerwin settled in New York and in 1870 founded the *Tablet*, a weekly newspaper devoted to Catholic and Irish news, with a strong nationalist slant. Jones's wartime friend David Conyngham eventually became co-owner and editor of the paper. Kerwin supported the Clan na Gael (Family of the Irish), an organization that advocated violent revolution to overthrow British rule in Ireland. Founded in New York City in 1867, the group grew to include branches throughout the United States. By the late 1870s it had almost ten thousand members; at its peak it would number four times as many. As the Fenians declined, the Clan na Gael became the most extreme voice of Irish nationalism. In speeches, interviews, and the pages of the *Tablet*, Kerwin defended the Clan's advocacy of violence. Jones demonstrated his sympathy for the radical cause—as he had with Thomas Kelly—by giving both Kerwin and Conyngham jobs in the New York Post Office.[16]

Jones publicly indicated his approval of the recently deceased Irish revolutionary John Mitchel in 1875, when he made a fifty-dollar donation to a testimonial fund. During his tumultuous life Mitchel had been convicted of sedition in Ireland, transported to Australia, escaped to the United States, and supported slavery and the Confederacy, for which he was briefly jailed. (Jones's associate Bernard Doran Killian negotiated Mitchel's release.) Mitchel became editor of an Irish newspaper in New York and the acknowledged leader of Irish American nationalists. He then returned to Ireland and was elected to Parliament shortly before his death. To Jones, Mitchel's devotion to Irish nationalism apparently trumped his allegiance to the Confederacy.[17]

In 1880 Jones's friends Kerwin and Conyngham published an appeal in the *Tablet* calling for an Indianapolis convention of Irish Republicans to support the party's presidential nominee, James A. Garfield. Kerwin and Conyngham observed that the document told truths that Irish Americans would be wise to take to heart. It was unfortunate for the Irish both socially and politically to adhere so strongly to the Democratic Party, the two reflected. The Democrats took their support for granted and treated them unfairly when making up tickets and dispensing patronage. The Republican Party, on the other hand, had distributed patronage liberally to Irish Americans. Kerwin and Conyngham cited some prominent examples in New York City: Lincoln's postmaster, James Kelly, and Grant's appointees Thomas Murphy, Chester Arthur (albeit not a native Irishman), and Jones.[18]

That veterans' affairs and politics were closely entwined is well illustrated by Jones's involvement with the Soldiers' Business Messenger and Dispatch Company (SBMDC), one of several agencies founded in the postwar years to assist Union veterans seeking jobs. The New York State Legislature chartered the company in March 1867 with former Union general Alexander Shaler as president and Jones as secretary. The SBMDC's mission was to employ disabled veterans in a delivery service for packages and messages. The terms of incorporation permitted the SBMDC to erect booths on public streets, from which the veterans would run the service and also sell newspapers and sundries. The booth provision proved to be troublesome.[19]

The city board of health had regulatory power over street booths and for months exercised it in minute detail, creating a bureaucratic struggle. The board requested detailed plans from the SBMDC, it questioned the legality of street booths, and it initially refused the company's application to erect them. After months of controversy and haggling, the SBMDC received permission to place booths at steamboat landings, railroad depots, and hotels. Ten booths were erected on New Year's Day 1868. The company finally appeared to have established itself. There were plans to place eight hundred booths throughout New York City and Brooklyn. Some thirty-five hundred veterans applied for positions. By then Jones was no longer the organization's secretary; whether he remained connected to the group is unknown. The SBMDC had brief success, providing income to disabled veterans who could not find work elsewhere and becoming a popular and useful service. But poor management doomed the venture to failure, and it ceased operations in September 1868.[20]

Sometimes Jones's activities as a veteran were expressly political. During the 1866 election season he represented Cattaraugus County at the Southern

Tier Soldiers and Sailors Mass Convention in Elmira, where the delegates pledged support for the Republican nominees. In the Grant-Greeley presidential contest he endorsed the formation of assembly district "Veteran Clubs" and a state veterans' convention to support the orthodox Republican ticket. "No effort that we can properly make should be spared," a party call stated, "for upon the success of the Republican cause depends the perpetuity of all we have achieved during the last ten years." Republicans had saved the nation; only they could safely preserve it.[21]

The votes of veterans, like those of Irishmen in New York City, could swing elections. The greatest Union veteran association was the Grand Army of the Republic (GAR), founded in 1866 as a Republican Party political tool. Use of the organization for political purposes was banned in 1869, and by the 1880s, when membership boomed, partisanship faded from the agenda in favor of fraternization. Throughout those years GAR commanders in chief constantly denied partisan activities. Nevertheless, most members were Republicans; wags declared the group's acronym stood for "Generally All Republicans." By the end of the nineteenth century the GAR had grown to be one of the most potent lobbying forces in the country. Among other results one out of every three dollars collected by taxes went to Union soldiers' pension payments.[22]

Many Irish American veterans did not join the GAR. Native-born Protestants dominated the organization, and the Catholic Church discouraged its members from joining fraternal groups. Whether Jones joined is unknown. In 1872, on Memorial Day (a holiday promoted by the GAR), he attended the association's evening service at the Academy of Music as an honorary member of Governor John Hoffman's staff. In 1883 an African American GAR post in Brooklyn announced Jones and other dignitaries would speak at a flag presentation at its next meeting. When the ceremony was held, however, Jones apparently was absent.[23]

Jones made one of his rare speeches as an invited guest at an 1893 reunion of the Thirty-Third New Jersey, one of his old Second Brigade regiments. Around noon on an early September day, the local GAR post of Morristown, New Jersey, met three hundred arriving veterans at the town's railroad station and escorted them to the courthouse. There the former soldiers held a brief business meeting before a women's group served them a banquet. During the addresses and toasting that followed, Jones spoke briefly of the Thirty-Third's service in remarks that went unrecorded.[24]

It seems that Jones's busy life in the city prevented him from returning to Cattaraugus County for annual reunions of the 154th New York and Companies H and I of the Thirty-Seventh Regiment. He took an active interest, however, in the self-appointed effort of an Ellicottville lawyer to write a history of the 154th. Edwin D. Northrup announced his intention in a circular he sent to the regiment's veterans in 1878 requesting written records and reminiscences. Jones immediately responded by offering to share the regimental order book and other papers in his possession. "It is due to the gallant fellows & their families that I should do this," Jones notified Northrup, "if you desire to perpetuate the memory of these men."[25]

It seems unlikely the veterans of the 154th would have chosen Northrup to chronicle their deeds. Many of them, like Jones, were Republicans, whereas Northrup was a lifelong Democrat veering toward socialism and a devotee of various unorthodox causes. Most significantly to the old soldiers, Northrup had not served in the Civil War, although he was of age and had been drafted. Jones had an opportunity to size up the prospective historian in person in 1879, when Northrup made three visits to New York City, each time visiting Jones at his Nassau Street office. Jones apparently approved of the eccentric but dedicated Northrup, for he loaned him the regimental order book during one of his visits.[26]

Northrup worked on his manuscript in fits and starts and in 1894 rekindled his correspondence with Jones. Jones wrote about General Hooker's affection for the 154th and the regiment's role at Chancellorsville. He looked through his papers and found his 1863 diary. He wrote to acquaintances to locate information on Northrup's behalf. But his efforts—and those of scores of other 154th New York veterans—came to naught. After almost twenty years of work on his manuscript, Northrup had a dispute with a publisher, which led him to abandon the project. Jones was dead by the time Northrup lost many of his papers in a 1917 office fire and died two years later. His manuscript history of the 154th Regiment disappeared, but his notes and correspondence for the project survived. Among them was the largest single collection of Jones's correspondence, much of it dating from an obscure period of his life.[27]

The evening of April 4, 1866, found Jones attending a meeting of the Military Order of the Loyal Legion of the United States (MOLLUS), a veterans' association formed in May 1865. Unlike the GAR, MOLLUS was restricted to officers. The organization provided them an opportunity to continue their wartime associations and burnish their class status. Their exclusivity riled critics. MOLLUS companions professed belief in God and allegiance to the United States and, under penalty of a heavy fine, prohibited the discussion of sectarian or partisan topics within its commanderies. At the April meeting Jones was duly elected a Companion of the Order of the First Class of the State of New York's Commandery No. 1. Joining him as new legionnaires were Adm. David G. Farragut, Gen. Alfred Pleasanton (Jones's occasional political rival), Gen. William W. Averell, and others of lesser rank.[28]

With a low membership and poor administration, MOLLUS languished during its first dozen years. Regulations required companions-elect such as Jones to subscribe to the order's constitution and bylaws, pay an admission fee, and present himself at a commandery meeting within six months. If he neglected or refused to comply with those conditions, "his election may be declared null and void." Jones was one of more than a score of companions-elect of the New York commandery whose elections were declared null and void on December 1, 1869. Why he did not finalize his membership is unknown, but he was not alone—the elections of sixty-three other officers in the New York commandery were also voided.[29]

The earliest known portrait of Jones is this carte de visite by R. W. Addis of Washington, D.C., apparently taken while Jones was major of the Thirty-Seventh New York, the Irish Rifles. Author's collection.

Brigadier General Jones depicted in a carte de visite by J. Gurney & Son of New York. His promotions resulted from political backing as well as military prowess. Author's collection.

Jones was wounded at the Battle of Chancellorsville, Va., and injured at the Battle of Dug Gap on Rocky Face Ridge, Ga., depicted here in an engraving after Alfred R. Waud. Joseph M. Brown, *The Mountain Campaigns in Georgia; or, War Scenes on the W. & A. [Western & Atlantic Railroad]* (Buffalo: Matthews, Northrup & Co., 1886).

Reuben E. Fenton, congressman, governor, senator, Jones's political patron, friend, and foe. U.S. Army Military History Institute, Carlisle Barracks, Pa.

Jones's political mentor and friend, the celebrity newspaperman and presidential candidate Horace Greeley, in his later years. Carte de visite by an unknown photographer. Author's collection.

Jones in his office in the old post office, besieged by job seekers and other suppliants. The decrepit building, a former church, was a constant source of frustration to both postmaster and public. *Harper's New Monthly Magazine*, October 1871.

Jones as candidate for register, in his last known portrait. *Daily Graphic*, November 2, 1874, 1. Print Collection, Miriam and Ira D. Wallach Division of Art, Prints and Photographs, New York Public Library, Astor, Lenox and Tilden Foundations.

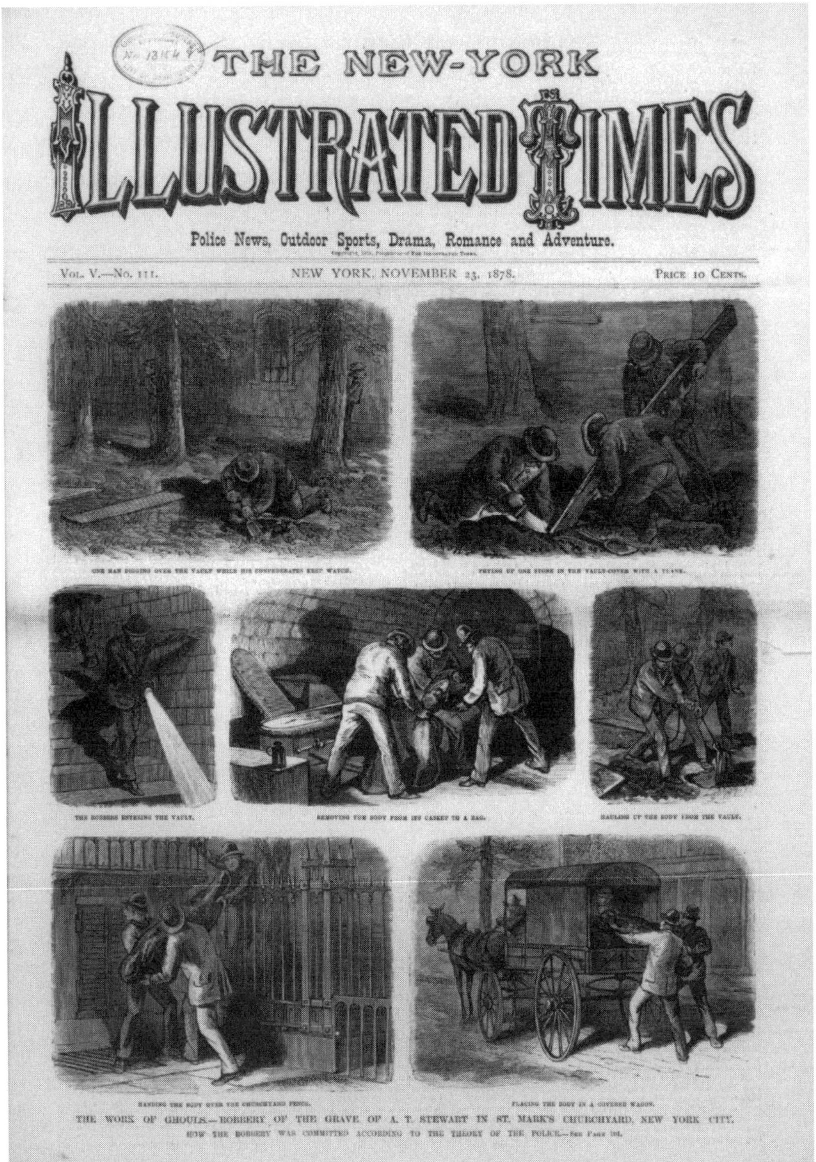

The A. T. Stewart grave robbery was front-page news in New York and beyond. This example features an artist's imaginary renderings of "The Work of Ghouls." *New York Illustrated Times*, November 23, 1878

A detail of the Otto Botticher print *Sherman at Savannah,* clearly showing the retouched portrait of Jones. Cattaraugus County Museum, Machias, N.Y.

CHAPTER 8
Miles O'Reilly's Halo

Irish Americans formed a strong current in the shifting postwar political tides. Veterans of homeland political crusades, familiar with their new country's forms of law and government, unhindered by a language barrier, the Irish took naturally to American politics and mobilized more quickly than other ethnic groups. They formed 21 percent of New York City's population in 1870, America's largest Irish community, most of them working-class inhabitants of ethnic enclaves in lower Manhattan. They generally voted as Democrats, viewing Republicans as nativists and class opponents. Democratic Party power was concentrated in Tammany Hall, which ruled the city from the 1850s to the 1930s. Boss Tweed, Tammany's "Grand Sachem," was neither Irish nor Catholic, but he made the Irish his own; his top two henchmen were native Irishmen. Tweed provided the Irish poor with food, fuel, and jobs, and they returned the favors with loyalty. But Tweed's ring, in cahoots with Mayor Abraham Oakey Hall, robbed the city over several years of an estimated forty-five million dollars (almost a billion in today's money). When the press exposed the ring, Tweed was toppled. But Tammany Hall survived and prospered.[1]

A new boss ruled the Wigwam. John Kelly, the son of immigrant parents, was the first ethnic Irishmen to be chosen Grand Sachem. Shrewd, forceful, personable, a devout Catholic, "Honest John" had served as an alderman, congressman, and sheriff of New York County. When he started as Grand Sachem, he faced turmoil in the wake of the Tweed disgrace. He cannily chose reformers as lieutenants, transforming Tammany in the public mind into a tribe cleansed of thieves. Organized at the ward, precinct, and block levels, Kelly's well-oiled machine turned out the voters from local headquarters in neighborhood saloons and churches, doled out patronage jobs, allied with business, and prospered. Part of the success was owing to the Panic of 1873 and the ensuing depression, when businesses went bankrupt, wages fell by up to 60 percent, and three million were unemployed. As the homeless crowded police stations on bitter nights and begging children swarmed the streets, the lower classes flocked to the Democrats in greater numbers than ever. Other voters defected from the ruling Republicans. The

Democrats also benefited from agitation about a third term for President Grant. Nevertheless, many Democrats deemed Kelly and his lieutenants to be one ring in place of another. One dissatisfied group broke from Tammany to form its own party. As his first election campaign as boss loomed in 1874, Kelly faced a ruptured party.[2]

Honest John Kelly personified Irish political power, but the Irish were still regarded as second-class citizens by many. Their reputation for violence was horribly confirmed in the New York City Draft Riots of July 1863 (which remains the most lethal riot in American history) and the Orange Day riots of 1870 and 1871, in which Irish Protestants and Catholics clashed. (Orange Day celebrated the Protestant victory over Catholics in the 1690 Battle of the Boyne.) In the aftermath of the riots, expressions of anti-Irish and anti-Catholic prejudice soared. Newspaper cartoonists—most famously, Thomas Nast in *Harper's Weekly*—skewered Paddy as an apelike creature, a "monstrous Celtic beast." Not until the 1880s and 1890s, when immigration from southern and eastern Europe brought increasing numbers of Italians, Jews, and Slavs to the United States, did Irish Americans, as Anglo-Saxons, come to be considered acceptable and begin to assimilate more seamlessly into American life. Before then, the general American public held few Irish Americans in high regard.[3]

For a year and a half after resigning as postmaster, Jones toiled at his law practice, refereed foreclosures (which mushroomed following the Panic of 1873), and handled other routine business. In the spring of 1874 a rumor circulated that New York City mayor William F. Havemeyer, like Jones a Democrat-turned-Republican, was going to nominate Jones as police commissioner. A state senator praised the idea as excellent, but nothing came of it. That summer Jones corresponded with a member of Governor John Dix's staff on party matters, consulted with city Republicans on Dix's behalf, and lobbied the governor on a bill. In the fall he was a delegate to the Republican state convention from the Seventh Assembly District; he also served the party's district association as treasurer. But such routine political matters were eclipsed by the excitement of an electoral campaign.[4]

As the 1874 election for mayor, register, and aldermen approached, Jones was the most prominent candidate mentioned by Republicans for the lucrative register's office, the post he had held briefly after the death of Charles Halpine. Jones's friends claimed he would garner a considerable amount of Democratic support as well as the full backing of Republicans. The anti-Tammany Independent Democrats were to convene ahead of the Republicans, who waited to see what the Independent Democrats would do. Many Republicans favored a coalition with the Independent Democrats, which included a strong German American element. If such a combination were formed, it was thought that the nomination for register might go to a German. The incumbent was one of that ethnic group's most prominent men, the Republican Franz Sigel, Jones's former commander in the Eleventh Army Corps.[5]

Many of the Independent Democrats who filled the large hall at Cooper Institute on the evening of October 20 were German. Scattered in the audience were Tammany loyalists, who occasionally disrupted the proceedings with catcalls. For mayor the delegates nominated Oswald Ottendorfer, the publisher of America's foremost German-language newspaper. The chairman of the nominating committee then announced Jones as the nominee for register. The hall erupted in cheers, although there were cries of "He is a Republican!" from the Tammany hecklers. Adding to the hubbub, the band struck up "The Bold Soldier Boy." The chairman then put the question to the audience, and Jones's nomination was unanimously accepted.[6]

"The Bold Soldier Boy" was a song Jones must have heard frequently. Irish folklorist Samuel Lover introduced his composition to American audiences in the 1830s, and it became a staple of Irish nationalist performances. Then the tune became Americanized. The jaunty melody was popular with bands. The lyrics told of a young soldier parading through a town full of female admirers. An "exuberant paean to the attractiveness of the marching Irish man," in the words of an analyst, the ditty "acquired a prominent place in the public symbolism of the Irish community in New York." Representing "the character of Irish fighting men in America," it was the perfect musical tribute to General Jones.[7]

Convention chairman Thomas J. Creamer closed the proceedings with a speech extolling Jones, the "modest retiring little gentleman" who as register had succored the widow of poor Miles O'Reilly. Jones had a claim upon the office and the citizens, especially as he was poor and his Tammany Hall opponent was rich. Creamer himself had proposed Jones's nomination, and he now called on the Independent Democrats to support him at the polls. As a final wave of cheering rocked the hall, Creamer adjourned the convention.[8]

Jones's nomination by the Independent Democrats stirred widespread commentary in the city press. It "will be very popular," declared the *Evening Mail.* The *Herald* emphasized the Halpine connection—"It seems almost poetic justice that the General should now be nominated for the office he once held for the sake of a dead friend"—and predicted Jones would wrest away much of Tammany's regular Irish constituency but might not win the support of apathetic Republicans. The *Tribune* praised him as a good soldier and a good postmaster who had become a poor man as a result of his honest public service. If there must be enriching offices such as register, it declared, Jones was the kind of man to hold them. The *Evening Post* and *Evening Telegram* saw his nomination as an effort to conciliate the Republicans and gain their endorsement. Jones stood little chance running against Tammany Hall, declared the *Daily Graphic.* The *Commercial Advertiser* played the nativist card: the Irish ruled Tammany Hall; the Germans ruled the Independent Democrats. If the native born took the same interest in politics that the immigrants did, railed the paper, "we would have better men in office." The *Times* observed that Jones was so well-known in the city that it was unnecessary to sketch his history.[9]

The same night that the Independent Democrats convened, county Republicans met to discuss a slate and appoint a nominating committee. Word leaked that Jones had support for the nomination as register but was no shoo-in. Chester Arthur, head of the powerful customhouse cadre, was said to back him, and no other candidate of any strength had been suggested. Jones was "very popular among the Republicans," the *Tribune* observed; he would be a formidable candidate. On the morning of October 22 the committee met in a secret session and, heeding the advice of Governor Dix, Edwin Morgan, and George Jones, publisher of the *Times,* agreed on a ticket. For mayor they chose Salem H. Wales, the wealthy former editor of *Scientific American* magazine and former president of the park commission. For register they named Jones. An honest and faithful public servant, Jones was "just the man for the place," commented the *New York Republic.* No candidate was more familiar with the register's duties, the paper noted, and no man was more deserving of the office.[10]

That night Thomas Murphy chaired the county convention at Republican Hall. As expected, Wales was nominated for mayor and Jones for register. The district attorney drew applause when he said that that everyone who loved honesty and trustworthiness in public affairs was glad to support Jones, whose character was stainless. The *Herald* reported that a volley of applause greeted Wales's nomination, but Jones's elicited an even greater response, bringing all the cheering delegates to their feet, waving their hats and handkerchiefs and transmitting their excitement to the crowd outside. It was a scene unsurpassed by Tammany Hall in its wildest days, thought the *Herald* reporter. Every mention of Jones's name caused an ovation.[11]

The newspapers weighed in on Jones's second nomination. The *Evening Mail* called it judicious. The *Commercial Advertiser* called him upright and deserving. "He has elements of popularity and many devoted friends," commented the *Daily Graphic*. The *Dispatch* took Jones to task for supporting a third term for President Grant, an avowed goal of Roscoe Conkling. "This is the only thing in his public career which is open to adverse criticism," the paper stated. "His honesty is beyond denial, and his honor above reproach. He is so immeasurably superior to his opponent for the office that no parallel can be drawn between them."[12]

Indeed, the city papers delighted in contrasting Jones with his Tammany Hall opponent, James Hayes. "It is enough for the honest voter's purpose to know that Gen. Jones is the superior man," declared the *Tribune*. Hayes was "a positively objectionable person," unfit for any public office. A city that would elect the corrupt Hayes instead of an honest gentleman such as Jones deserved mismanagement, opined the *Dispatch*. Between the two candidates, stated the *Republic*, "there can be no questions . . . where an honest voter's preference should be given."[13]

The object of the press's scorn was a half-year younger than Jones. A New York City native, Hayes had followed the lead of many—including Boss Tweed and Honest John Kelly—in moving from a job in a volunteer fire company to a role in politics. In 1866 he joined the board of supervisors, where he was a protégé of Tweed and an accomplice in perpetrating the Boss's robberies. As such, he amassed more than a half-million dollars in wealth. "'Jimmy' Hayes was one of the most fortunate, pecuniarily, of Tweed's understrappers and tools," observed the *Evening Mail*, which derided him as "the 'butt-cut' of Tweedism." In 1871 Hayes was elected to the state assembly; he had been reelected every year since.[14]

Hayes's political boss, John Morrissey, was vying with John Kelly for the leadership of Tammany Hall. A native Irishman and former convict, Morrissey got his political start in New York City by challenging any man in a

Tammany club to a fight. He worked as a runner preying on immigrants and a prizefighter before opening a taproom and faro parlor. He became an Irish folk hero when he was implicated in the murder of Bill "the Butcher" Poole, the American-born gang leader and nemesis of Irish immigrants. Having prospered, Morrissey sought a political career to legitimize his reputation and was elected to two terms in Congress. A cockfighting aficionado and professional gambler, by the 1870s he was operating lavish casinos in the city and in Saratoga, the popular summer resort, where he also held controlling interest in the racetrack. Morrissey led the "short hair," or lower-class, faction in Tammany Hall. He and Kelly split the 1874 ticket between their choices. Kelly chose a prominent diamond merchant, William H. Wickham, to run for mayor. Morrissey picked Hayes to vie for register. Kelly bitterly opposed Hayes's nomination. The Tammany-backed candidate for governor, Samuel J. Tilden, voiced grave reservations about its wisdom. It was said that both Kelly and Tilden would be satisfied if Hayes lost, as the defeat would hurt Morrissey. Democrats in general bemoaned being excluded from choosing candidates, who were, instead, dictated by the bosses. The inherent weakness of Hayes's candidacy was thus compounded by conflict in the Tammany Wigwam.[15]

Only two weeks separated the conventions and Election Day, making for a short campaign. Local party and reform associations met to endorse candidates. Jones naturally received the favor of the Republican assembly district organizations. He also earned the endorsement of certain Democratic clubs. In the Sixteenth Assembly District, Republicans and Democrats united to form a P. H. Jones Campaign Club and praised him for his "unimpeachable integrity and honesty," which deserved the support "of all intelligent citizens of every nationality and creed." Meanwhile, the newspapers mulled over election prospects. The *Herald* theorized that Jones would have to capture a sizable amount of orthodox Democratic votes in order to win, even if he received all the votes of the Independent Democrats and Republicans. The contest for register would be much closer than the mayor's race, the paper surmised, and—despite the Republicans' confidence in their ability to elect Jones—the chances favored Hayes.[16]

Ethnic political organizations overwhelmingly favored Jones over Hayes. His appeal to Irish voters was obvious, although diehard Irish Democrats vowed "no support for any Republican nominee, be he General Patrick H. Jones, or even a better man." Germans of all parties endorsed him. The publisher of the *Jewish Times* chaired a meeting that endorsed him. A convention of Polish voters pledged its support. The *Courrier des États-Unis* endorsed him in French. "Germany and Ireland strike hands for Jones," declared the *Commercial Advertiser.* "The American eagle screams for Jones, because he bore aloft the Stars and Stripes with Sherman in his march to the sea . . . Everybody is and everybody ought to be for Jones, for Jones is honest, worthy, and capable."[17]

Over and over newspapers reminded voters of Jones's previous service as register and his gracious and generous act of having donated his pay to Charles Halpine's family. The memory of Jones's charity "has become sentimental," the *New York Herald* declared, "and it may be called the poetry of the campaign." Jones's kindness to the Halpines shone like a star in the murky political sky. "There is not an Irishman in New York who does not or should not remember it. The memory of 'Miles O'Reilly' is the halo that surrounds the canvass of General Jones." To the *Herald* Jones's victory would be a triumph of generosity and kindness over machines and rings. "Irish hearts never lack warm appreciation of noble acts," declared the *Evening Mail,* "and every Irishman will vote for Jones." Jones left the register's office poor in purse, the *Republic* noted, "but rich in the possession of a character for patriotism, integrity and fidelity that no man has been able to tarnish." For his friendship to the unfortunate, declared the *Commercial Advertiser,* "no man has stronger claims on the public. No man is more deserving."[18]

The papers published biographical sketches of the candidates. The day before the election a lithographic portrait of Jones after a photograph by Mathew Brady's studio filled the front page of the *Daily Graphic.* The accompanying article concluded: "His chief characteristics as a civilian are great industry, cool judgment, and warm-hearted, open-handed liberality. The office of Register is one of vast importance to the city, and General Jones seems to be in every way qualified for it from his personal qualities and past experience."[19]

The press stressed the difference between Jones and Hayes's activities during the Civil War. Hayes remained in the city during the conflict, noted the *Times,* whitewashing corruption, robbing the city, and raking in Tweed ring money. Jones fought for his country on southern battlefields and won his way by bravery and wounds to the rank of general. Asked the *Times,* "Are citizens of any party so lost to decency, if not patriotism, as to vote for a man who was engaged, in 1863, in abetting corruption, as a sinecurist, at the very time when his opponent was facing death in the terrible battle of Chancellorsville?" The *Commercial Advertiser* made a direct appeal to veterans: "Now then, boys, all together, and give General Patrick H. Jones such a majority as will show that this City remembers the camp-fires of the rebellion, and can reward patriotism."[20]

The *Evening Express* reminded the public that the register's office, as a result of increased business, would yield an estimated $100,000 per annum to whoever was elected. The *Evening Post* termed such compensation "monstrous" and suggested that laws should limit the register's salary and require surplus income to be paid into the city treasury. In seeking the rich prize, the *Evening Express* noted, the candidates were as busy as bees. Both camps expressed confidence in the outcome. While Hayes's supporters worked quietly for him, Jones's people circulated twenty thousand copies of an Irish newspaper containing a flattering biographical sketch of their candidate.[21]

City Republicans gathered in the Cooper Institute's great hall on the night of October 29 to ratify their ticket. Jones's election "is now a foregone conclusion," declared the *Republic*. He would take the Republican vote, do well on the Independent Democratic ticket, and capture many Tammany votes "on his personal popularity alone." Questions arose about the Democrats. Did gubernatorial candidate Samuel Tilden support the Tammany Hall candidates or those of the Independent Democrats? His contribution of twenty-five thousand dollars to the Tammany campaign chest provided the answer. Why did John Kelly not attend the mass meetings in the various assembly districts? "Has the fact that 'Jimmy' Hayes's name (Morrissey's candidate) appears on the ticket anything to do with it?" the *Daily Graphic* wondered. Would the defeat of Hayes allow Tilden and Kelly to break with Morrissey, as the *Herald* speculated? While the public pondered such questions, they wagered bets on the election results.[22]

On election eve the papers issued their final predictions and urged their readers to support one or another ticket. The *Herald* foresaw a close contest for register, calling Tammany claims that Hayes would win by a large majority "all bombast." The *Evening Telegram* predicted Hayes would win but speculated that Jones would "make a splendid run nevertheless," noting, "He is working like a beaver, and though it is reported that he is personally poor, he is spending, or somebody is spending for him, quite a pile of money in the canvass." The *Republic* thought that Jones's "great personal popularity" would secure him victory. The *Evening Mail* asserted that Boss Tweed, were he not in jail, would vote for Hayes. The *Republic* warned its readers that Tammany Hall had distributed an immense number of Independent Democrat and Republican tickets containing Hayes's name instead of Jones's.[23]

The only paper that had a good word about Hayes could not bring itself to endorse him. Hayes was "an amiable man," declared the *Dispatch*, but he had been too amiable in aiding the thievery of the Tweed ring, and he was too amiable to hold office "in so ungodly a city as New York." Hayes would heed the thug Morrissey's commands and fill the register's office with gamblers and crooks. Jones, in contrast, "is known as a man who isn't amiable. He would refuse to fill the Register's office with 'check charmers' and 'bilks,' no matter who demanded the appointment." Hayes was a supple tool of the Tweed ring who had grown rich obeying the orders of his masters. Jones was an honest gentleman who had become poor because he was incapable of dishonesty. The *Dispatch* stood by Jones.[24]

Tuesday, November 3, 1874, dawned mild and sunny. The city wore a holiday appearance. Banks and exchanges were closed, giving their employees an opportunity to vote. Liquor stores also were closed, diminishing the usual Election Day drunkenness. The polls opened at six in the morning and were crowded with workingmen on the way to their labors. Rough wooden structures resembling sentry booths sat on the sidewalk near every polling place, adorned with posters. Each booth housed an election worker or two, who distributed ballots, called "tickets," printed and distributed at the expense of the candidate. A trail of dropped tickets littered the paths from the booths to the polling places, which were surrounded by ward heelers, policemen, and deputy marshals. Inside the polling places inspectors sat behind a row of glass jars, into which voters placed their folded tickets. For several hours the turnout was noticeably heavy. By noon many districts reported that two-thirds of registered voters had been to the polls.[25]

Throughout the city interest was greatest in the Jones-Hayes contest, which was expected to be the closest. Betting was lively at the poolrooms, in the hotels, and in private transactions. Hayes men eagerly snapped up the odds offered on Jones. At four in the afternoon, after the polls closed, the papers rushed their evening editions into print and onto the streets. Speculation had Jones beating Hayes in the uptown wards, where "every Democrat with a clean shirt," as the *Commercial Advertiser* put it, voted their party's straight ticket but scratched Hayes's name and substituted Jones's.

John Morrissey predicted Hayes would carry all but one district, but the *Advertiser* thought he was overconfident. "Jones is running unusually well for Register," the *Daily Graphic* reported. "It is estimated that more of his pasters are used than those of any other candidate."[26]

During the morning Jones stopped in briefly at Independent Democratic headquarters in Irving Hall to get the latest news. He was subdued, having heard that his supporters had deserted him in a downtown district, but those at party headquarters cheered him up by assuring him his election was foreordained. At Tammany Hall mayoral candidate William Wickham said the only contest in doubt was that for register, and he predicted a Hayes victory.[27]

With the exception of a murder in the Twenty-First Ward, the election passed quietly. Throughout the day the question could be heard, "How is Jones polling?" News that he was doing well and might be elected "went through the city like a telegram," the *Herald* reported, and brought many men who seldom voted to the polls. From seven in the evening to midnight crowds thronged bulletin boards to read the latest results. At Tammany Hall there were speeches, cheering, and fireworks. Gloom pervaded at Irving Hall, except for hopes for Jones's prospects. After a suspenseful night the morning papers carried the final results: a great Democratic victory throughout the eastern states and a Tammany Hall triumph in the city. Tilden was elected as governor; Wickham defeated Wales and Ottendorfer for the mayor's office. There was one exception to the Tammany sweep—Jones had defeated Hayes, 70,817 votes to 59,639. The number of votes cast far exceeded the average of recent years, indicating exceptional interest in the contest.[28]

In postelection analysis the press strove to explain Jones's anomalous win. In the opinion of the *Times* Hayes had been defeated because fellow Democrats considered him selfish and because Jones had taken the traditionally Democratic Irish vote. To the *Herald* Jones's victory—"a remarkable and gratifying event"—was a sign that voters disproved of Kelly and Morrissey and that "the Irishmen of New York have remembered Miles O'Reilly." The *Tribune* chided the Democrats for permitting the turbulent bruiser Morrissey to pick Hayes, an obvious throwback to the days of the Tweed ring, as the candidate for such an important office. The *Daily Graphic* likewise pointed to Hayes's Tammany ring ties as "sufficient to condemn him." The Democratic *World* judged Hayes's defeat to be a warning to Tammany Hall to choose its candidates more carefully. Jones had won the votes of about eight thousand Tammany Democrats, the *World* noted, a substantial portion of his margin of victory. The *Commercial Advertiser* detected a moral in the result that city politicians would be wise to study: "Nominate good men, nominate untainted candidates, above reproach, and the people will be with you." The *Evening Mail* saw Hayes's defeat as a blow to Tweed as well as Morrissey and judged Jones as "one of the best fellows in the world." The *Evening Telegram* thought that Jones's win showed "what can be done by the nomination of a gentleman and good officer." The *Irish World* contrasted Hayes—wealthy and backed by a powerful organization—with Jones, a poor man and a Republican, and concluded that Jones won because "Patrick Jones was an honest man."[29]

Reporters sought out Kelly and Morrissey to get their take on the results. Kelly denied that Hayes was solely Morrissey's candidate and complimented his opponents for their skill in promoting Jones's interests. He cited the contrast between Hayes's reported wealth and Jones's generosity to the Halpines. Morrissey attributed Hayes's defeat to the opposition of the press and the support of Jones by the Independent Democrats, traitors to their party. Some papers issued premature obituaries for Morrissey's political career. He should step down, the *Daily Graphic* suggested, as a Democratic leader. Kelly had demonstrated that his power exceeded Morrissey's, stated the *Dispatch;* Jones's win had laid Morrissey out. Kelly discounted the importance of the register's office from a political point of view. It was simply a plum. The register pocketed his fees and retired at the end of his term with a competence. There was very little patronage to be handed out in the office—just a few clerkships.[30]

Jones began his three-year term as register at noon on New Year's Day 1875, when he entered the Hall of Records and formally relieved his predecessor, Franz Sigel, who showed him through the office and introduced him to the employees. Jones decided not to hold a reception for his supporters. He also decided to hold off for two or three weeks on making any appointments. In the meantime he considered letting go some of the forty copying clerks; they were paid by the word, and there was scarcely enough work to provide all of them with remunerative employment. Jones doled out his meager patronage early in February, appointing an assistant deputy register, chattel mortgage clerk, collector, private secretary and messenger, and a number of clerks.[31]

If the patronage was puny compared to what he had wielded as postmaster, so was public interest in the register's office compared to the postal service. Rarely did the office make the news and then only for mundane matters. Political associates such as Edwin Morgan and collector Chester Arthur continued to write to Jones for the occasional favor, but overall, his term in the register's office had a neutral effect on his political prospects. On one hand, he finished his term unhampered by scandal, such as one that befell his predecessor, Franz Sigel, who was successfully sued for negligence in office. On the other hand, the job tended to isolate him from day-to-day politics.[32]

Jones did, however, join a group of city Republican delegates who traveled to Cincinnati for the party's 1876 national convention. That spring the state convention had voiced support for Roscoe Conkling for president, but the delegates remained unpledged. The race was wide open, with Conkling opposed by a half-dozen major candidates and favorite sons. A reporter interviewed Jones as the train steamed toward Ohio. "I am in favor of Mr. Conkling," Jones said, "but I will not vote this year for a man I know nothing about. I want a candidate, not a discovery." In Cincinnati, Chester Arthur led the New Yorkers as they tried with little success to drum up support for Conkling. Ohio's favorite son, Governor Rutherford B. Hayes, got the nod on the seventh ballot, with most of the New York bloc providing the margin of victory.[33]

During his three years as register, Jones continued his nomadic ways. He kept his law office at 150 Nassau Street, but he moved from 28 West Twelfth Street to 251 West Fourteenth Street to 62 West Forty-Sixth Street. During a rainy and chilly week in July 1877, he was a guest at a Long Branch hotel. His old friend President Grant was not at his seaside cottage, however, having left on the around-the-world tour that took him to the snub by the city of Cork.[34]

By the 1870s New York was well established as a theatrical center. Jones's friend Horace Greeley, once a rapturous enthusiast of the theater's "glory, and beauty, and splendor, and poetry," had come to dismiss the playhouse as "boards, and paint (coarsely laid on), and spangles, and general tawdriness." Jones seems to have shared Greeley's early love for the theater. In November 1877 he did a favor for General Sherman when he attended the New York debut of actress Mary Anderson at the Fifth Avenue Theater. (Sherman called on Jones for the occasional favor, once asking him to visit the Manassas battlefield to clarify certain aspects of the Second Bull Run battle.) Sherman was a devotee of the theater and loved to flirt with actresses. Anderson was one of his favorites; he described her as "young, handsome and reasonably attractive." After her performance Jones sent her a small basket of flowers accompanied by a note: "With compliments of self and the best wishes of our good friend Genl. Sherman." The next day Jones sent Sherman the reviews of

Anderson's performance from the city papers and offered his own critique. He planned to call on Anderson within a week. "My wife desires to know her," he added, "inasmuch as she is a friend of yours & mine."[35]

Jones's letter to Sherman offers a rare glimpse into his status as a celebrity and bon vivant. During those heady years he served on the finance committee for the Grand Opera Ball held at the Academy of Music, billed as "the only fashionable fancy dress ball of the season." In 1875 this extravaganza, which ran from ten at night to the wee hours of the morning, featured an orchestra of two hundred musicians, seventy-five dancers costumed as birds and insects, and other "fantastic," "eccentric," and "grotesque" dance acts with a French flavor. Taking in the spectacle, Pat and Sarah Jones must have reflected on how far they had come from sleepy Ellicottville. The Gilded Age good life, however, was not without its perils.[36]

CHAPTER 9

Fine Horses and Head Money

The story broke in New York's afternoon newspapers on September 13, 1871. The *Evening Telegram* summarized the main points. John Norton, the head of the city post office's money order department, had been caught embezzling more than $100,000. He reportedly had used the money in stock speculations on Wall Street. Norton had not been seen in the post office for days. His property in New Jersey was seized to reimburse the government for the defalcation. He was cooperating with the authorities.[1]

That evening's editions of the *Commercial Advertiser* described Norton as a thirteen-year employee who had "hitherto enjoyed an excellent reputation." He had been appointed superintendent of the money order department on its organization in 1864. It was uncertain when he had succumbed to lucre's temptation, but it was believed that he had been stealing for several years. In August 1871 it was revealed that Norton's departmental account did not jibe with the balances in the federal subtreasury in the city, where the funds were required to be deposited. Suspecting wrongdoing, Postmaster Jones had notified the authorities in Washington, D.C. A special agent was immediately sent to New York and discovered that while Norton's checkbook tallied with his own accounts, they differed from those of the subtreasury to the amount of $115,000. When Jones questioned Norton, he made a full confession, claiming he had intended to replace all the money he had taken but had gotten in deeper and deeper until he was unable to extricate himself. On September 1 Jones fired him.

As postmaster, Jones was responsible for the lost money. He called a meeting of his sureties, who were in turn responsible for Jones's loss. At the time Jones retained two of his original bondsmen, Horace Greeley and *Tribune* publisher Samuel Sinclair. Sheridan Shook and Abram Wakeman had joined them. Shook was proprietor of a theater and former collector of internal revenue. Wakeman was a former city postmaster and had also been a surveyor of the port. It was discovered that Norton and his wife owned property valued at $175,000, including an estate stocked with fine horses and one of the largest homes in Plainfield, New Jersey. Their extravagant lifestyle was inconsistent with Norton's $3,000 annual salary. When the bondsmen learned the Norton property was worth a sum sufficient to cover his thefts, it was all seized. But rather than sell it immediately, they agreed to hold it in trust and dispose of it at their convenience on the best possible terms. In the meantime it was reported that Abram Wakeman would pay $115,000 to the government to settle the account, with the understanding that he would receive the proceeds from the sale of the Norton property when it occurred.

Norton and his wife were highly respected in the Plainfield community. The childless couple remained in their home. While Norton was regarded as a temperate man of good habits and not a fast liver, rumors abounded that while speculating in the stock market on Wall Street, his repeated losses had dragged him ever deeper into criminal behavior.[2]

When the story broke, no successor to Norton had been named, and Jones was personally supervising the enormous business of the money order department. The *Commercial Advertiser* vouched for the system's safety; customers could trust their money to the department. The government stood to recoup its losses by the seizure of Norton's property. "Norton is the only loser," the paper assured its readers. The prediction would prove to be inaccurate.[3]

On September 14 the story was picked up by the major dailies. "Postmaster Jones has manifested an earnest desire from the outset to protect the Government from loss," the *Times* declared, "and his efforts will probably prove successful." Jones's sureties were good, and the government would not suffer a loss. Norton stood as an example of Republican fraud, remarked the *New York Star,* but his case showed "that these little incidents will occasionally happen amongst all parties," and the perpetrator of such an incident "cannot with justice be considered to reflect disgrace upon his party." The *Commercial Advertiser* recommended that Norton should be promptly punished. "This is no time for leniency with offenders against the law, and a few examples of public officers undergoing punishment would be salutary."[4]

The *New York Sun* covered the Norton story in its typical sensational style, dramatically depicting Jones as "much alarmed" by the discovery of the embezzlement, hastening to his "frightened" bondsmen and begging for their assistance, frantically telegraphing the postmaster general for official help. When the bondsmen learned of the worth of Norton's properties, Horace Greeley "beamed all over with quiet smiles," Abram Wakeman "was serenely happy," Samuel Sinclair "was overjoyed," and Sheridan Shook "could not contain himself, but went off incontinently in a convulsion of spasmodic laughs of gratification." The *Sun* portrayed Norton, stripped of his beautiful country home and his expensive horses, as a ruined man who had dragged his wife into the depths along with himself.[5]

Equally lurid was the account in the *Herald*, which used the opportunity to take some swipes at its perennial rival, Horace Greeley. When Jones met with his bondsmen and asked them "to pony up," the *Herald* alleged, Greeley was apoplectic. "He ripped out an appalling oath, and swore by all the hair on all the heads of the *Trombone* free lovers that he would have satisfaction." When Abram Wakeman agreed they should pay up, Greeley reportedly cried, "I'm damned if I do," and bolted from Jones's office, "spreading terror through the ranks of the astonished clerks of the Post Office by his frightful yells of rage and despair."

A *Herald* reporter interviewed Jones in his office. Norton had always "borne a good character," Jones said, and had been "exceedingly frank and straightforward" about his crime, adding, "I must confess that I was completely taken by surprise when the matter came to light, for he was the last man I would have suspected of such a thing." Asked if the government would lose anything by the transaction, Jones replied, "Certainly not, since I am responsible for the amount of any defalcation that occurs in the Post Office." His bondsmen had made arrangements to reimburse the government, and one of them had been appointed trustee of Norton's seized properties. After settling with the government, the bondsmen would reimburse themselves through the sale of the properties.

The intrigued reporter hurried from Jones's office to Plainfield. There he met locals, who took him to Norton's house. Mrs. Norton was present, but her husband was away. The reporter decided against intruding upon the afflicted lady's privacy, but he looked around the premises: a richly ornamented mansion, an exquisite garden, and stables that rivaled in magnificence those of Boss Tweed. The stalls, attended by three grooms, held six blooded horses worth an estimated twenty-five thousand dollars. Norton was an avid sportsman, running his horses on a nearby racetrack, where his stallion Black Crook was famous. Just lately, it was alleged, Norton had won twenty-eight hundred dollars betting on horse races.

His curiosity satisfied, the *Herald* reporter returned to Manhattan. He closed his story with some reflections on the case. Postmaster Jones was in no way responsible for the crime; "on the contrary, he showed admirable energy in ferreting out the particulars of the swindle when he was informed of its nature and extent." Jones now signed all the checks and exercised personal supervision over the money order department. There need be no hesitation in trusting the system: "Uncle Sam is a safe banker." A day later a *Herald* editorial further commended the postmaster: "General Jones has shown himself a model Postmaster in his prompt and unusual action in this case, and will receive much honor for the course he took to prevent loss to the government and to keep public confidence in the money order system from being impaired."[6]

The *New York World* also dispatched a reporter to interview Jones. "None at all," Jones replied when asked if he had ever suspected Norton's dishonesty. No steps had been taken to arrest Norton. "I have confined myself to getting the money back from him," Jones said, "but he is under surveillance now at Plainfield, and if the Treasury Department desire at any time to criminally prosecute him they can do so." Jones had been unaware that Norton was speculating in gold and stocks until Norton confessed to having lost forty thousand dollars in one week on Wall Street. The reporter got in a dig at President Grant. "Mr. Norton's little weakness," he wrote, "like another well-known office-holder, appears to have been his love for horseflesh." His herd included fit workhorses and splendid carriage horses in addition to the thoroughbred Black Crook.[7]

The Democratic *World* had several partisan observations to make about the Norton case. "A defalcation on the part of one of President Grant's office-holders is a matter of such common occurrence," the paper observed, that Norton's embezzlement "excites comment chiefly because it has occurred in our midst." Over the past few months the Republican *Times* had exposed the machinations of the Democratic Tweed ring. To the *World* Boss Tweed's wrongs were equaled by the likes of the corrupt Republican Norton. But Republican newspapers, so anxious to condemn dishonest Democratic officials, would probably pay little attention to this case of a Republican officeholder who had plundered the government.[8]

The deeds of Norton's properties were made over to Abram Wakeman in trust for his fellow bondsmen. The bondsmen would wait until a sale could be made most advantageously. In the meantime Wakeman's personal check for $115,311.85 was paid to the New York Post Office's treasurer, to be credited to the government in the office's returns at the end of the fiscal quarter. Whether that transaction occurred is uncertain, however, in light of subsequent events. In any case the Norton affair disappeared from the newspapers for a couple of months, until December 15, when Norton was arrested. Having surrendered his properties, he was under the impression he would not be prosecuted, and thus he was greatly surprised when he was seized.[9]

So the matter stood when the 1872 presidential campaign opened. With Grant administration corruption a major issue, the case inevitably drew political attention. At a large Republican rally for Grant at Cooper Institute, Roscoe Conkling passionately defended the president and assailed Greeley. With Jones looking on as a vice president of the meeting, Conkling discussed corruption, including the Norton case. Norton had begun his depredations prior to the Grant administration, Conkling noted, and once his crime was discovered, he was arrested. Moreover, Greeley was liable as bondsman for the loss, and if he lost the election, he would be obliged to pay up.[10]

A few days later Greeley's *Tribune* published a voluminous list of "public robberies and defalcations under the present Administration." In summarizing the Norton case, Greeley's name went unmentioned. The account closed by noting, "The bondsmen promptly made good the amount of the defalcation." A week later the *Times* refuted many of the *Tribune*'s allegations, deeming its account of the Norton case—which it quoted verbatim—as worthy of special mention. The *Times* denied that Jones's bondsmen had covered the loss: "Horace Greeley is one of them, and deserves a place in the list of defaulters with his name in conspicuous type. Every dollar will be recovered, but suits may be required, if not already ordered."[11]

Something had gone awry in the settlement of the Norton case. The particulars are unknown—the steps apparently went unreported by the press—but the agreement had fallen apart. A later judicial decision pinpointed the likely reason: no official had "the right to accept property in compromise of a crime." Consequently, the seized Norton properties could not be sold to reimburse Jones's bondsmen. What happened to Wakeman's payment is uncertain; perhaps his check was stopped and returned. In any case the onus fell back on Jones and his bondsmen, who found they still owed a vast sum to the government—plus interest.[12]

On October 15, 1872, Patrick and Sarah Jones sold their house and lot in Randolph—the only home they ever owned—for three thousand dollars. The transaction was a direct result of the financial crisis engendered by the Norton case. Jones needed the cash to relieve his bondsmen from having to pay the government the interest on the embezzled money.[13]

When Jones resigned as postmaster in March 1873, he cited the Norton case as a factor in his decision. "The fact is, I was growing afraid," he told a reporter. His personal responsibility for the defalcation was worrisome, "like sitting on a volcano." The constant, overwhelming bar to his peace of mind was the main reason for his resignation. Asked if the defalcation would affect him or his bondsmen, he answered no. Enough property had been seized to cover the amount of the embezzlement. But he painted a different picture for another reporter, saying that because of the defalcation, he now had to pay the government more money than he had made from it in salary.[14]

Acting as trustee for the federal government, Jones offered Norton's 105-acre Plainfield estate for sale in July 1873 through a broker. The land had been laid out in "villa plots" of ten to fifteen city lots each. Twenty-four plots had been sold, realizing $8,677.50, when Jones adjourned the sale because only two of his six bondsmen were present on the ground. It was rescheduled for two weeks later at the New York Real Estate Exchange. In the meantime Jones's broker sold another six plots for twenty-four hundred dollars. The results of the New York sale went unreported.[15]

The case against Norton came up in December 1873 before Judge Charles L. Benedict in the United States circuit court. Norton's counsel—Abram Wakeman, of all people—made a motion to quash the case and argued that Mrs. Norton had turned over all her property to the government with the understanding that no criminal proceedings would be continued against her husband. Wakeman read affidavits by both Nortons supporting the motion. The U.S. district attorney countered with affidavits declaring that no such promise had been made. After more maneuvering by both sides, Judge Benedict reserved his decision, and the court adjourned.[16]

A month later warrants were issued commanding Jones's bondsmen to appear before a United States district court judge in a suit to recover $150,000, the amount of Norton's defalcation plus interest. Jones's previous bond of a million dollars had been canceled on the deaths of his bondsmen James Taylor and two others who had been added over the years. Jones's bondsmen now included Abram Wakeman, Sheridan Shook, Samuel Sinclair, and seven other men, including two executors of Horace Greeley's estate. According to rumor, the bulk of the money the government was suing for would come from the estates of Greeley and Taylor. It was thought that the other bondsmen, with the exception of Shook (who expected to pay $1,000) and Wakeman, would escape having to pay under some provision of the law.

The suit was expected to furnish an important precedent regarding the legal liability of principals for the defalcation of subordinates. At an unknown date a second suit was brought against Jones's bond to recover other, much lesser amounts of money embezzled while he was postmaster.[17]

The *New York Sun* observed that Horace Greeley and Samuel Sinclair had been greatly annoyed during the 1872 presidential campaign by Jones's bond issue. The paper also stated that Jones had not publicly supported Greeley over Grant in the campaign "for fear of imperiling the property of all his bondsmen." The *Sun* noted that the Norton defalcation had caused Jones much suffering, compelling him to resign as postmaster and to sell his Randolph homestead. "He has striven indefatigably for two years to extricate his bondsmen from any responsibility, but has encountered difficulties which he could not overcome." It had been suggested that Congress pass an act relieving him; a similar case had established precedent for such a measure. The *Sun* closed its story with a surprising fact—until just a few weeks earlier, Norton had continued to occupy his Plainfield mansion, until Jones had him ejected.[18]

Norton was indicted for embezzlement in February 1874. When requested to plead at the circuit court's June 1874 term, his counsel stated that two years had passed between the alleged offense and the indictment, exceeding the statute of limitations set by an 1790 law and thereby precluding a trial. The government disagreed with that notion, which resulted in a hearing on June 30 in Judge Benedict's courtroom. That day Abram Wakeman argued the 1790 statute of limitations before Judge Benedict. The assistant district attorney contended that a later law of 1804 had fixed the limitation at five years instead of two. Judge Benedict deferred making a decision for the time being, but in the end he and other circuit court judges were divided in opinion, and the Norton case eventually wound up in the U.S. Supreme Court.[19]

In the meantime Jones made his successful run for register in 1874. A speechmaker at the Republican nominating convention was applauded by the delegates when he praised Jones for stripping himself of his own property and leaving the office of postmaster an honest man, albeit a poor one, his character unstained. During the campaign the press lauded Jones for honorable behavior in the Norton scandal, which had reduced him to poverty. After pledging all of his property to make good the defalcation, the *Tribune* declared, Jones had been impoverished "solely by reason of his honest public service." "He did not attempt to squirm out of his responsibility," echoed the

Dispatch, contending that Jones was "a poor man because he was incapable of dishonesty." His election as register gave Jones the opportunity to replenish his purse, but in the end he was unable to mass a fortune.[20]

Two years elapsed before the U.S. Supreme Court rendered a decision in July 1876 in the case of the *United States v. John W. Norton*. The justices decided that the 1804 law stipulating a five-year statute of limitations was not applicable in Norton's case. Therefore, they applied the 1790 act to his case and decided that Norton could not be prosecuted, tried, or punished. With that Norton's legal woes ended—but Jones's were yet to be resolved.[21]

In May 1876 Jones traveled to Washington, D.C., to lobby for the passage of a congressional bill to indemnify him from his losses as postmaster. But that August the Committee on Claims refused to relieve Jones's bonds. The *National Republican*, a paper published in the capital, called the decision "one of the greatest outrages of the session." A compromise was reached in December by the postmaster general and the sureties of Jones and his predecessor, James Kelly. It was determined that Norton had embezzled $35,000 while Kelly was postmaster and $80,428.71 during Jones's term.[22]

The two suits against Jones's bonds were merged into one by the U.S. district court in May 1877. The *Tribune* predicted the suit would "probably be dropped eventually." This was incorrect. Within two weeks not one but four suits pending in the court against Jones's sureties—all relating to embezzlements by post office employees, including Norton—were settled in the compromise authorized by the government the previous December. Judgments of eighty-five hundred dollars, plus costs, were rendered in each of the four cases against Jones, making a total of approximately forty-five thousand dollars. The *Times* reported that the fines had nearly all been paid, but by whom it did not say.[23]

In her later years Sarah Jones blamed the Norton embezzlement for her poverty. "I have no property or means of any character whatsoever," she swore in a deposition after Patrick died. "My husband left nothing in the way of property or means for me. There was a defalcation in the New York Post Office while he was the Postmaster and it took all his means to make it good, hence he died penniless." If Jones paid the forty-five thousand–dollar settlement—or reimbursed his bondsmen for that amount—it could indeed have impoverished him even after his years of earning a large salary as postmaster and raking in huge sums as register. Other factors may have been at play, however. On Jones's death an Ellicottville newspaper commented, "General

Jones died, as he lived, comparatively poor, for he never could withstand the appeal of a friend in need, and never enriched himself at the expense of a human being."[24]

During his flush years as postmaster and register, Jones knew many less fortunate people who no doubt made appeals to his largesse. He was celebrated for his generosity, made famous by his kindness to Charles Halpine's family. But any assessment of Jones's financial status is speculation. He and Sarah certainly lived modestly in their later years, far from the heady days of dinners at Delmonico's and balls at the Academy of Music. What is certain is that the Joneses' finances were hurt badly by two setbacks that evolved over the same period: the failure of Congress to adjust Jones's disburser's fee in the construction of the new post office; and the long, expensive legal process culminating in a substantial judgment against him in the Norton defalcation case.

In July 1875, while the Norton-related suits against Jones were still ongoing, a New York State Assembly Committee of Investigation began an inquiry into the affairs of the Commissioners of Emigration and Quarantine, for which Jones had served as counsel from 1867 to 1870. The committee met at Castle Garden, the commission's immigration center at the southern tip of Manhattan, where Jones had camped with the Irish Rifles during the war and worked in more recent years on commission legal issues. Part of the investigation centered on past activities of New York County assistant district attorney Michael Nolan, Jones's former protégé, assistant, and partner. At issue was Nolan's lobbying work in Albany for the Steamship Conference, a cartel of New York City steamship lines. As a result of his efforts, in 1871 the state legislature had passed legislation reducing head money, the per immigrant tax that the steamship companies paid to finance the commission's work. Steamship Conference members in turn paid Nolan for each immigrant who landed in New York. In all he had received tens of thousands of dollars from the cartel. But investigators found that he had kept less than 10 percent of the money. A large amount of cash was unaccounted for. Had some of it gone to bribe legislators? Had some gone to pay confederates who were merely using Nolan for their own ends? Was Nolan in cahoots with his mentor Patrick Henry Jones?[25]

Three years before the 1875 investigation, there were inklings of what was to come. In February 1872 the state legislature's Committee on Commerce and Navigation began an investigation of the Commissioners of Emigration.

It became evident the commissioners were active in lobbying the legislature on matters pertaining to their work. Testimony revealed that Jones had received three thousand dollars in commission funds for work in Albany. Jones's successor as counsel, William Hillyer, had been paid six thousand dollars to lobby in Washington, D.C.[26]

When the legislative committee met at Castle Garden in March 1872, Commissioners of Emigration president Richard O'Gorman promised cooperation. A Dublin native, O'Gorman had fled the failure of the Young Ireland uprising in 1848 for New York City, where he opened a law office, became president of the Friendly Sons of St. Patrick and the Irish Emigration Society, and won renown as a popular public speaker and an outspoken Copperhead. The committee called a number of witnesses, among them an agent for a steamship line, who testified that his company had profited from the 1871 reduction in head money. A lawyer named Nolan had lobbied the head money reduction law through the legislature. Nolan had reportedly persuaded lawmakers that the reduction would increase the number of immigrants and reduce fares.[27]

When released in April 1872, the committee report caused a bit of a stir. *Harper's Weekly* praised the Commissioners of Emigration for the agency's valuable services in welcoming, protecting, and providing for immigrants. But the investigation had revealed problems. Recently, the board had been controlled by "unworthy influences," its funds had been mismanaged, its resources wasted, and its reputation impaired. The commission was in need of thorough reform.[28]

The 1872 flap proved to be minor compared with the sensational revelations of 1875. As the legislative committee began its mid-July investigation at Castle Garden, Jones's name came up repeatedly. The treasurer of the Commissioners of Emigration reported that the firm of Rice, Wilson and Jones had continued to do commission work after Jones resigned as counsel, earning more than forty-seven hundred dollars in 1871 and 1872 by copying laws and representing the commission in Washington and in a lawsuit brought by Alfred Beach of pneumatic tube notoriety. But these were transparent and legal acts. The investigators soon turned their attention to the shadier and secretive activities of Michael Nolan, who was called to testify on July 24.[29]

The legislators grilled Nolan for four hours. A reporter for the *Herald* described the thirty-year-old as "the most excitable, uncomfortable, nervous witness that probably was ever seen in the witness chair." Nolan related having met his patron Jones during the war and their subsequent close business relationship. During Jones's tenure as counsel to the Commissioners of Emigration, Nolan had familiarized himself with the business and attended to it on a regular basis in Jones's stead. When Jones resigned as counsel, Nolan also ceased working for the commission. Nolan dated Jones's resignation to 1869, after his appointment as postmaster—one of many instances in which Nolan's admittedly poor memory failed him.[30]

After Jones resigned as counsel, Nolan recalled, the Commissioners of Emigration passed a resolution calling for a head money reduction from $2.50 to $1.50. When the assembly dragged its heels in passing the necessary legislation, the Steamship Conference hired Nolan to go to Albany and get the bill passed. He spent about five days in the capital in March 1871, he testified, but his memory of the events was hazy. He drafted a bill, had someone introduce it—he did not remember whom—and it sailed through the Committee on Commerce and Navigation and passed unanimously in both houses. He denied bribing legislators to pass the bill. According to his agreement with the Steamship Conference, for six months after passage of the bill, he was to be paid twenty-five cents for each immigrant arriving in New York. He thought he had received "something over $30,000," although he declined to be specific. "I think it was a very large compensation for the service I rendered," he cheerfully admitted, "and a very lucky hit, and that is about the end of it." His inquisitors questioned him repeatedly about his role in the bill's passage. As often as he was asked, Nolan refused to answer when he was paid and by whom and in which bank he had deposited the money. He insisted, "That is my private affair."[31]

The questioning turned to Nolan's relationship with Edward Wilson, formerly of the firm Rice, Wilson and Jones and Nolan's law partner since 1871. Nolan put thirty-five hundred dollars of his head money take into the firm of Wilson and Nolan and split it with his partner, 60 percent to Nolan, the rest to Wilson. Jones "had not the slightest interest" in the firm of Wilson and Nolan, Nolan stated; he had had never acted as counsel to it and never received a penny from it. As for the duration of Nolan and Jones's partnership, Nolan's memory was foggy. "I don't remember," he stated; "I can tell by looking at my books."[32]

The whole head money business had become an "annoyance" to him,

Nolan complained. He had been agitated since the 1872 investigating committee had caused a scandal. He blamed his faulty memory on "a bad head for details." His recollection was especially poor regarding the head money case. Beyond the thirty-five hundred dollars paid to Wilson and Nolan, he refused to state what had happened to the rest of the money. When asked if certain individuals—including Jones—had received loot from him, Nolan answered in each case, "I decline to answer that."[33]

The *Herald* described Nolan's testimony as "the spiciest and most exciting that has taken place here for many a day." The reporter was amused by Nolan's constant fidgeting, drumming on the table, nervous laughter, and smug and defiant answers. Nolan's contradictory and hesitant testimony belied any oratorical eloquence on his part, a *Herald* editorial slyly noted, but he had had no trouble talking the legislature into passing the head money bill.[34]

Nolan was recalled on July 26. He admitted to the committee that he had been "somewhat a petulant witness," but he continued to refuse to answer certain questions. As he and the committeemen engaged in a back-and-forth, he repeatedly denied bribing legislators and declared his lobbying efforts were not unusual. He had heard—from Jones, he thought—that another law firm had a similar arrangement with the Steamship Conference. When told that commission records showed that Jones drew a salary as counsel up to January 1, 1871, Nolan expressed surprise and reasserted that Jones's official duties had ended in 1869. He continued to insist that because he had done no work for the commission since 1869, he believed Jones had not done any either. Jones would have to explain the discrepancy.[35]

Dogged questioning dug deeper into the Nolan-Jones relationship. Did Nolan consult with Jones in 1871 regarding passage of the head money reduction bill in the legislature? Nolan thought he might have; it was likely. Was it then that Jones had told him about another law firm's arrangement with the Steamship Conference? Nolan could not remember; he thought it was Jones who told him about it, to relieve him of worry about his own arrangement. Then the committee struck at the heart of the matter. "Did General Jones and other persons, or General Jones individually, procure for you this employment as counsel for the steamship companies in 1871, and didn't General Jones share with you in the profits of that transaction?" Nolan declined to answer. He admitted that he did not know what had steered the job his way—he had had no previous experience as a lobbyist. The committee chairman remarked that Nolan's hiring by the Steamship Conference, so closely following Jones's resignation as counsel, was a remarkable coincidence. Asked again if he had agreed to pay a portion of the head money cash to Jones, Nolan again declined to answer, "without making implications at all upon anybody." His refusal to answer, of course, left the implication wide open.[36]

Confronted with a receipt for salary received from the commission signed by Jones and dated December 1870, Nolan continued to insist—to the exasperation of the committeemen—that Jones had resigned as counsel in 1869. Nolan was vague about the law partnership of Palmer, Jones and Nolan. He admitted that Jones merely lent his name to the firm as "a sort of quasi partner" out of friendship, "which undoubtedly did me some good in acquiring business." Nolan also refused to say whether he had shared head money profits with George Palmer. Then he changed his tune and said that Jones and Palmer had never received any of the money. Both men were earning a great deal at the time, he observed, Jones as postmaster and Palmer as appraiser. They knew all about his deal with the Steamship Conference and his trip to Albany, but they did not assist or advise him.[37]

The *Herald* found the day's revelations—or lack thereof—"again of the most exciting interest." Nolan was misplaced in his mundane occupation as assistant district attorney, the paper declared; he should work as a Washington lobbyist. On a more serious note the *Herald* called for Nolan's resignation. It noted that Nolan had portrayed himself as a reformer—but so had Boss Tweed, whose legislature had passed the head money reduction bill. There was "more than ten cents' worth of promptitude" about the bill's rapid passage, the *Tribune* observed—and Tweed's legislatures "were not in the habit of doing many ten-cent jobs." Nolan's stubborn refusal to admit he had bribed legislators and to name them, the *Tribune* fumed, was "another instance of the fidelity of rogue to rogue." The *Evening Post* doubted that Nolan's "fat purse" had not been divided among "men of real power who worked with him." Jones was not named, but he certainly fit that description. Nolan's denial of a conspiracy would not stifle inquiry, the paper added. "If true, it only narrows the investigation; if false, it will only plunge him into greater difficulties."[38]

Nolan was not the only witness to testify regarding his case. A string of Steamship Conference representatives described their relationships with the lobbyist and enumerated the large fees they had paid him. Some of the steamship company agents related that they knew Jones, not from his work as counsel to the Commissioners of Emigration but as postmaster—their ships carried overseas mail as well as immigrants.[39]

The day after he finished testifying, Michael Nolan submitted his resignation as assistant district attorney, citing the "unfortunate prominence" of his case. A reporter for the *Evening Telegram* interviewed Nolan while he was writing his letter of resignation. "They have got all out of me that they are going to," Nolan said of the investigative committee. He vowed to bring the committee to an accounting, to subpoena former legislators to testify on his behalf, and to issue a statement on the matter that had hung over him "like a pall" for the past several years. He closed the interview on an optimistic note: "I think the matter will blow over pretty quickly, and I don't think as many people will be hurt as is imagined."[40]

The press naturally weighed in on Nolan's resignation. The *World* excused his lobbying efforts as business as usual and condemned the investigative committee for "prying into what did not concern them." The *Commercial Advertiser* likewise dismissed the case as much ado about nothing. There was no evidence that Nolan had bribed legislators, and his lobbying for the Steamship Conference was not unordinary. To the *Dispatch*, if Nolan had not bribed legislators, he was guilty of no moral turpitude in pocketing his immense fees.[41]

July 1875 ended with more testimony, but in Nolan's absence it failed to excite the press. At the close of proceedings on July 29, the investigative committee adjourned until August 10. When it reconvened, Nolan—who had promised to appear and make a full statement—was absent. The committee's sergeant at arms reported that he had tried without success to serve Jones with a subpoena to appear and testify. Edward Wilson took the stand on August 11 and testified that Jones had introduced him to Nolan; that following his partnership with Jones and Addison Rice he had formed a firm with Nolan; that he knew that the Steamship Conference had employed Nolan but was unaware of the details of the deal; and that all he had received from the head money was the thirty-five hundred dollars Nolan had mentioned in his testimony. Wilson claimed he knew nothing about Nolan's huge windfall until he read about it in the newspapers. Nolan then appeared and presented a printed statement summarizing the case and pleading his ignorance of wrongdoing. The investigators questioned Nolan yet again about his dealings with Jones over the years. Then a letter from Jones was read into the record, in which he expressed surprise at reading in the newspapers of the sergeant at arms' search for him and offered to appear before the committee if it desired.[42]

On August 12, 1875, Jones appeared before the investigative committee to tell his side of the story. He described his employment as counsel to the Commissioners of Emigration as primarily advisory. He had attended the agency's meetings only when requested to comment on some legal matter and had written an occasional legal opinion, but Nolan or Palmer had transacted the everyday business. He had let those quasi-partners use his name and take the salary. He had paid the rent for Nolan's workplace and had bought the law library and supplies, but he stressed that he "never drew a dollar out of the partnership at all in my life for any purpose."[43]

Jones stated that he might have introduced Nolan to the steamship operators because he knew nearly all of them and would encounter them in the street. But he knew nothing about Nolan's arrangement with the Steamship Conference until it was revealed by the 1872 investigation. He had never consulted with Nolan about the head money issue, nor did he ever receive a single dollar from Nolan, except in repayment of loans. "He owes me now $1,000," Jones exclaimed; "I loaned him $1,000 not more than three months ago." He never received any money from Nolan through a third party. He had heard rumors that Steamship Conference money had been used to bribe legislators, but, he said, "such rumors are always afloat."[44]

Nolan had discussed the head money issue with Jones after the 1872 investigative committee revelations, but Jones had told his protégé that it was none of his business and that he did not want to know anything about it: "I like to avoid trouble as much as possible." He had not been surprised to learn of Nolan's arrangement with the Steamship Conference because it was not unusual. He did not offer Nolan any advice regarding the matter. He simply did not want to get involved in Nolan's business. Perhaps alluding to the Norton imbroglio, he added, "I had business enough of my own at the time to bother me."[45]

As the interrogation continued, a committeeman repeated the main question: did Jones arrange for Nolan to obtain the Steamship Conference lobbying job or have anything to do with it? Jones reiterated that he knew nothing about it. He had loaned Nolan money on occasion but otherwise knew little about his financial status. Jones closed by stating that what he knew of Nolan's head money arrangement he had learned from testimony before the committee, which was widely reported in the press. With that Jones was dismissed.[46]

When Jones had left the hearing room, a committeeman remarked, "It looked very queer that Pat Jones, who was like a father to this young man Nolan, did not know his business." Another committeeman said that Jones had "practically contradicted a portion of Nolan's testimony." A third stated that it was evident that Nolan did not care whom he implicated and had been very careless in his statements.[47]

Nolan was recalled and continued to refuse to cooperate fully. Questioned repeatedly, he said he thought Jones knew nothing about the Steamship Conference deal until it was disclosed. But he hemmed and hawed about whether Jones had given him advice on getting the head money legislation passed, blaming his faulty memory. When pressed yet again on whether Jones had helped him secure the lobbying job, however, Nolan unequivocally stated that he alone had made the deal. The day's questioning completed, the committee held a lengthy executive session.[48]

Commenting on the day's testimony, the *Tribune* stated, "No one supposed that Gen. P. H. Jones could be implicated in the head-money lobbying, or in any other disreputable transaction at Albany . . . Still, there will be a sense of hearty satisfaction at the explicit nature of his testimony." In a lengthy and scornful editorial the *Tribune* attacked Nolan for refusing to answer questions regarding his head money bonanza, describing him as a "pettifogging lobbyist" who had bribed legislators. The *Herald* observed that Nolan was "getting into deeper and more troubled water every day. The testimony in his case yesterday bore very heavily upon him."[49]

Jones's bondsman when he was postmaster, Abram Wakeman, testified before the investigative committee the next day as counsel for a steamship line. According to Wakeman, a few years back the company had approached him with a concern: if it resisted paying Nolan for his lobbying services, would the news reach Jones, who as postmaster determined which steamship companies held the lucrative mail-carrying services? Wakeman quietly investigated and concluded that Jones had no connection to the lobbying scheme and had never received a penny of the head money loot.[50]

Two days later Richard O'Gorman testified. The former president of the Commissioners of Emigration initially stated that he knew nothing of Jones's connection with Nolan but then recalled Nolan had assisted Jones when Jones was commission counsel. George Palmer testified regarding the partnership of Palmer, Jones and Nolan, claiming he had no knowledge of Nolan's lobbying work until the story broke in the newspapers. Days later the investigative committee adjourned for several weeks.[51]

The committee reconvened on November 9, 1875, in a secret executive session at Castle Garden. Jones, O'Gorman, and Wilson were subpoenaed and questioned individually in a private room, from which reporters were barred. O'Gorman was examined first, Wilson next, followed by Jones, whereupon O'Gorman was recalled and questioned again. After testifying, Jones told a reporter that the questioning was simply about the Nolan affair. A committeeman told the assembled reporters that they need not wait: the proceedings would not be made public. The next day Jones was interrogated again in another secret session. He again refused to make any statement to the press regarding his testimony other than to say it concerned the Nolan matter.[52]

In January 1876 the investigative committee announced the imminent release of its report. The *Times* predicted "a very full and somewhat startling report" that would show that Nolan had bribed legislators—findings that would be "very damaging to a number of men who held high positions during the Legislative session of 1871."[53]

The Committee of Investigation's final report stated that Nolan's contract with the Steamship Conference was made in the fall of 1870. The contract stipulated that Nolan would procure the head money reduction and thereby receive twenty-five cents for each immigrant landed for one year—not for six months, as Nolan had testified. Nolan was not qualified, either by his knowledge of the legislative process or his stature as a lawyer, to undertake such important work for the steamship companies. The investigative committee was convinced that he was merely used to bribe legislators on behalf of his cartel clients. He refused to state how much he had been paid, in which banks he had made deposits, and other dispositions of the money he had gained. After considerable difficulty, the committee determined that Nolan had received $77,518.25 from the steamship companies. Nolan's contract with them was only meant to last one year, but when the Commissioners of Emigration recommended to the legislature in 1872 an increase in head money, some steamship companies renewed his contract to fight the measure.

Unable to ascertain how Nolan had disposed of the money, the committeemen had hired an experienced investigator to look into the matter.

The facts he uncovered led them to question in secret sessions "certain persons"—Jones, O'Gorman, and Wilson went unnamed. The committee came to no conclusive judgment in regard to the complicity of any of the three in Nolan's scheme, while "some" of them "were completely exonerated from even mere suspicion." Jones, O'Gorman, and Wilson had all been linked by widely publicized innuendo to the Nolan case. Now, anonymously, the three were exonerated to a degree from complicity, and "some" were regarded as completely innocent—but remained unnamed. After all the questionable publicity Jones had been subjected to during the Nolan scandal, to be exonerated anonymously in the final report—which received little if any coverage in the newspapers—must have been small solace. The report closed by recommending a further investigation of the Nolan scandal by an appropriate legislative committee, a suggestion that apparently was never adopted.[54]

As in the Norton case, Jones had been waylaid by the malfeasance of a close associate. It appears, however, that he was publicly unperturbed by the Nolan case. During the weeks of suggestive testimony and sensational headlines, he attended to his official duties as register and maintained his usual round of activities. Throughout the scandal he maintained his innocence and refrained from publicly castigating his wayward protégé, letting Nolan's demeanor and testimony speak for itself. The stench of the Nolan scandal soon dissipated in the fetid air of Gilded Age chicanery. Within three years, however, Jones was fouled by the greater stink of a horrible crime that clung to him mercilessly for the rest of his life.

A macabre coda to the Nolan case occurred a few months after the release of the investigative committee's report. Shortly before midnight on April 15, 1876, a gray-bearded man wearing dark clothes and carrying a cane brushed past a lame watchman on the wharf at the foot of East Twenty-Third Street. When the watchman asked him where he was going, the man—apparently intoxicated—told him to mind his own business. Seconds later, the watchman heard a splash. On scrabbling to the end of the dock, he spotted the fellow in the East River. He extended his crutch to the drowning man, who did not attempt to grasp it. The police later found a black hat and malacca cane floating in the slip. The cane bore a silver plate inscribed with the monogram "E.J.W." Several days later the victim was tentatively identified as Edward Wilson. He had left his house at 91 West Eleventh Street on the evening of the drowning and had not been seen since. A month later, on May 13, two policemen found a corpse floating in the river at the foot of Nineteenth Street. Recovered and taken to the morgue, it was positively identified as Wilson. Wilson's sole surviving relative—a brother—and his intimate friends did not believe he had committed suicide, but the newspapers reported it as such and offered a possible explanation. The bachelor had accumulated real estate reported to be worth $300,000. When that fortune was diminished following the Panic of 1873, Wilson had attempted unsuccessfully to sell his property. That setback was said to have greatly depressed him and led to his demise. The papers made no mention of his involvement in the Nolan case.[55]

CHAPTER 10

Ghoul's Errand

The Norton embezzlement broke Jones financially, and the Nolan scandal sullied his reputation. Those two blows were followed by a third that befell him on a January morning in 1879, when he arrived at his office to find a letter and package. On examining their contents, he immediately knew that he had been dragged into one of the most shocking crimes of the era. His role in the case remained secret until seven months later, when it was revealed in a series of sensational newspaper reports. Jones's connection to the case stuck with him for the rest of his days. When the press reported his death more than twenty years later, the Norton and Nolan cases went unmentioned, but the great crime was dredged up once again. It struck his identity a blow from which he never recovered. He was a diminished man in its wake.

The crime had occurred two months before Jones became involved. At some point during the night spanning November 6 and 7, 1878, thieves stole the body of the multimillionaire merchant Alexander T. Stewart from its temporary crypt in the cemetery of St. Mark's Church, at the intersection of East Tenth Street and Second Avenue. Marble slabs marking subterranean burial vaults dotted the lawns on both sides of the church. An eight-foot iron fence surrounded the property. Gas street lamps lit the graveyard. Passersby had a clear view of the plot.

Unbeknownst to the public, the Stewart vault had been tampered with a month earlier. On October 9, 1878, the church's sexton, George W. Hammill, and his assistant, Francis Parker, discovered the slab to the Stewart vault had been moved the previous night. They reported the incident to Judge Henry Hilton. Hilton was a lawyer of little prominence and a court of common pleas judge of short term until his association with A. T. Stewart. Stewart's wife, Cornelia Clinch Stewart, was second cousin to Hilton's wife, and the familial relationship evolved into an unofficial partnership. Hilton became Stewart's intimate friend and trusted counselor. He was treated like a son by the childless magnate and his wife and gained much control over Stewart's affairs. This boosted Hilton's status in the community, but his relationship with the Stewarts was fraught. Onlookers cringed at his highhanded treatment of the couple. George Templeton Strong considered Hilton's reputation for honesty "shabby and threadbare."

After inspecting the cemetery in October, Hilton took steps to increase security, including moving the Stewart slab to a new location and covering its old spot with sod. He kept the incident secret, not wanting press accounts to inspire other ghouls to disturb the corpse of his benefactor. And he ordered Hammill to hire a private watchman to guard the graveyard at night. Hammill hired Michael Bruton, night watchman for a nearby livery stable. Bruton attended to his duties until November 1, when he was discharged on Hilton's orders, the judge having decided that his services were no longer needed.

When Assistant Sexton Parker opened the graveyard gates on the morning of November 7, he immediately noticed a pile of dirt by the Stewart vault. He hurried to Sexton Hammill's house with the news. The two rushed back to St. Mark's, moved the flat stone covering the vault's stairs, and Hammill descended. A quick look told him that Stewart's body had been stolen. Hammill then hurried to Henry Hilton's house and informed the judge of the theft. Hilton immediately drove to police headquarters and reported the crime. An alarm was issued ordering a diligent search of every precinct for the stolen remains.

Hilton, the police brass, a team of detectives, and the coroner descended on St. Mark's churchyard. The men were astonished that the thieves had successfully located the vault given that its identification slab had been moved the previous month. The thieves had dug down precisely to the vault's stone cover; a small shovel caked with soil had been left behind. Having removed the cover stone, the thieves had descended the stairs into the arched-ceilinged brick vault using a cheap tin lantern—which they also left behind—to find their way. Along the vault's sides ran stone shelves holding five coffins, four of them worm eaten and decayed. Stewart's coffin was enclosed in a thick cedar box with an engraved copper nameplate. The robbers unscrewed and removed the box top. They cut through a lining of hermetically sealed lead and peeled it back to reveal a magnificent oak casket covered in black velvet adorned with heavy gold fringe and tassels. The ghouls forced the coffin open, breaking the lock and hinges and knocking off some of the ornamental screw caps. They wrenched the heavy silver nameplate from the casket's inner lid and cut out a pentagonal-shaped piece of the velvet, evidently intending to use both for identification purposes.

Police theorized that the robbers had lifted the corpse from the casket and placed it in a bag before leaving the vault, but they wondered what sort of shape the body was in. The vault emitted a dreadful stench that sickened men standing outside its mouth. How the robbers had removed their burden from the cemetery was a mystery. Climbing the daunting fence seemed doubtful; the ground yielded no footprints. In addition to the shovel and lantern, the thieves had left behind an old issue of the *New York Herald*, a piece of board, and a narrow strip of a woman's stocking, sewed together at the ends.

The authorities surmised that the theft was carried out to secure a ransom for the corpse. Judge Hilton refused to offer a reward for its recovery, but people felt that Cornelia Stewart would use any means to recover it. She had never intended for her husband to rest permanently at St. Mark's. An ornate mausoleum was under construction in the cathedral at Garden City, the planned community Stewart had developed on Long Island. Stewart had died too early to be buried in Garden City, hence his temporary resting place at St. Mark's.

By the afternoon of November 7 police determined that the shovel and lantern had been purchased at a downtown hardware store, but the clerk could not identify the buyer. George Hammill, Francis Parker, and night watchman Michael Bruton were all interrogated. As the sensational story swept the city, shocked and horrified crowds surrounded the graveyard. The curious onlookers buzzed with theories about the crime. Hilton's arrival caused a hubbub, with someone in the crowd pointing him out as "the man who had got all old Stewart's money." The police declared that the theft was the first case of body snatching in the city; it was thought to be exceedingly strange that it would involve such an extraordinary man as Stewart.

A crowd of friends called at Judge Hilton's house that evening to express their indignation at the crime and offer sympathy for Mrs. Stewart. Hilton issued a statement reporting the October tampering case and his horror on hearing the news of the theft. He described breaking the news to the ailing seventy-five-year-old Cornelia Stewart. That afternoon, when newsboys began hawking their papers outside of her Fifth Avenue mansion, she had wondered what the fuss was about. When Hilton gently broke the news to her, she "bore the shock with wonderful heroism," he said, before "she sank perceptibly under the blow."[1]

The newspapers published column after lurid column on the crime. The *Herald* struck a typical note: "Fiendish ingenuity in devising ways to make money can scarcely go to viler extremes than that it has touched in dragging from its sepulcher the body of the late Mr. Stewart." The illustrated newspapers added pictorial coverage; the *Daily Graphic* and the *New York Illustrated Times* covered their front pages with imagery. The first of many theories arose to explain the crime. Detectives speculated that Stewart's body had actually been stolen in October, for example, or that the robbers were medical men or undertakers, with the requisite knowledge to handle decomposing remains and the stomach to do the horrible work. The police were generally tightlipped to the press on the investigation's progress. Ever greater throngs crowded the usually quiet neighborhood of St. Mark's Church.[2]

After consulting with top police brass on November 8, Judge Hilton agreed to stop talking to reporters. With police approval, and at the insistence of Cornelia Stewart, he issued a $25,000 reward "for the return of the body and information which will convict the parties who were engaged in the outrage." Police scoffed at the offer, theorizing that the thieves considered Mrs. Stewart a soft touch who would pay up to $500,000 for the return of her husband's remains. Meanwhile, officers followed a multitude of leads. Although the police continued to suspect Hammill or Parker of complicity, St. Mark's rector, the Reverend Dr. J. H. Rylance, vouched for their trustworthiness. Curious crowds peered through the graveyard fence all day long.[3]

Combing the cemetery yet again on November 9, police officers, aided by a bloodhound, discovered several putrid blotches. The freshness of the stains put to rest the theory that the crime had occurred in October. Acting on tips from witnesses, the police investigated tales of suspicious wagons in the vicinity on the night of the crime. People offering information and theories overwhelmed the authorities. The entire detective force was engaged in following up leads, most of which proved to be untrustworthy. Judge Hilton twice visited police headquarters; both he and superintendent George W. Walling told journalists there was nothing new to report. Detectives poked around in Newark, exploring the first of many leads that the body had been taken to New Jersey.[4]

November 10 was a Sunday. At St. Mark's thousands of spectators crowded the church and its grounds as Reverend Rylance gave a sermon on "Epidemics of Crime." That night a rumor reached police headquarters that Stewart's body had been found and was in the possession of Judge Hilton. Interviewed the next morning, Hilton at first denied the tale, before refusing to say anything more, having pledged to the police his silence. A police captain opined that a successful reward would be restricted to the return of the remains, not the apprehension of the criminals. The police otherwise remained mum about the case, but despite their reticence, reporters managed to spin lengthy columns of speculation about the crime. Suspicions were cast on one George A. Christian, who had been arrested four years earlier for grave robbery. His photograph was found in the police department's rogues' gallery, but his whereabouts were unknown.[5]

On Monday the *Herald* published an editorial highly critical of the police. "Graves are despoiled in the very heart of the city," the paper fumed, "and yet no arrests are made. It is about time this state of affairs was changed." Policemen remained busy chasing down hundreds of false leads, while crowds continued to surround the churchyard. Judge Hilton and Superintendent Walling were bombarded with letters propounding theories from amateur detectives across the country. The two men met privately for two hours, but Hilton had nothing to say to the press when he emerged from the confab.[6]

Police wore glum looks on November 12, but Hilton promised the press a "big sensation" within days. He reportedly had forty private detectives working independently of the police. Meanwhile, another search petered out in New Jersey, and new rumors sprouted of mysterious wagons and vindictive enemies of Stewart. Shoppers streamed from Stewart's store to join the crowds gawking at the desecrated grave. People had taken to joking about the case. In an interesting twist the assistant district attorney assigned to direct the investigation turned out to be one Horace Russell, Judge Hilton's son-in-law.[7]

The police exuded renewed confidence on November 13. In an interview Judge Hilton voiced amazement at people's belief in spiritualism, clairvoyance, dreams, "and such like trash." A week had passed since the crime, the *Herald* noted, and contrary to all expectations the whereabouts of Stewart's corpse remained unknown. Reporters grasped at straws, spilling ink over unfounded rumors, false alarms, and inconsequential tidbits.[8]

Jacob A. Riis, a police reporter at the time for the *Tribune*, stated in his autobiography that the Stewart grave robbery was an "epoch-making" crime that had "made a sensation such as New York has not known since." He added: "The police, most of the time, were as much in the dark as the rest of us, and nothing was to be got from that source. Heaven knows I tried." One night, as Judge Hilton left police headquarters accompanied by two detectives, Riis jumped into a carriage with them, only to be unceremoniously thrown out moments later. "It truly was the dawn of yellow journalism," Riis wrote. "I slept little or none during that month of intense work and excitement, but spent my days as my nights sifting every scrap of evidence."[9]

With "official permission from the highest authorities," the *Times* reported on November 15 that Stewart's body had been found and the perpetrators discovered. When the full story emerged, an official stated, "it will raise the hair on the heads of the people of New York." Judge Hilton was evasive when interviewed by a reporter. He repeated his insistence that the case would not be completed without the apprehension of the robbers. He released for publication a sampling of the thousands of letters he had received in the week since the crime, most of them offering to reveal valuable information for a fee or suggesting all sorts of hiding places for the remains. Many were from clairvoyants, spiritualists, and dreamers. The next day the *National Police Gazette,* the sensational weekly tabloid most often read in "barrooms and bagnios, gambling saloons and rat-pits," published two lengthy illustrated articles on the case. The daily papers reported arrests had been made, but the authorities refused to confirm the allegations.[10]

A day later police officials and Judge Hilton remained tight-lipped regarding developments, although rumors swirled that the body had been found and arrests of the perpetrators were imminent. Indeed, two men—William Burke and Henry Vreeland (alias Hank Whelan), both ex-convicts and residents of a dingy boardinghouse on East Twelfth Street—had already been arrested, but they were believed to be accessories, not the principal thieves. Hauled before a judge, they were remanded until the next afternoon.[11]

An editorial in the *Herald* castigated body snatchers as the lowest class of the criminal underworld, declaring them inhuman professionals who went about their grisly business as unconcernedly as a cobbler half-soled a pair of shoes. A subsequent editorial observed that as the search continued to fail, clues diminished. Police officials again stated that Hilton had made a mistake by including the apprehension of the criminals as a stipulation of the reward. Only if an unfettered reward were offered for the return of the remains would the grave robbers be tempted to surrender "their unholy booty."[12]

The *Times* reported a rumor on November 19 that five socially respectable men had conspired to steal Stewart's body, using Burke and Vreeland and others to carry out the actual theft. That day Burke and Vreeland were arraigned in a police court. After a police captain testified that the pair had confessed to involvement in the crime, the prisoners were held for the next day's proceedings, when they were formally charged with helping to steal Stewart's body. The judge set bail at five thousand dollars each and sent the two back to their cells. The public was divided about their guilt or innocence.[13]

By this time the increasingly outlandish stories had fallen to the back pages of the papers. Judge Hilton was now ducking the press, but it was announced that he had doubled the reward, upping it to fifty thousand dollars. The clause stipulating that the reward would be paid only after the thieves were convicted was retained. The police claimed to be on the track of the well-known "resurrectionist" George Christian. Suspicions also were cast on a manufacturer of soda water, William H. May, who had reportedly bragged of the possibility of stealing Stewart's body and storing it in a portable, airtight soda water tank.[14]

Sensational reports and wild rumors continued to sprout. Lingering investigations in New Jersey continued to be fruitless. William Burke was arraigned on a charge unrelated to the Stewart case; he pleaded not guilty and was remanded. The police continued to search for William May. A hack driver named Michael "Bull" Kelly came under suspicion because of his odd doings on the night of the crime. The case garnered more national publicity in an illustrated article in *Harper's Weekly*, which deemed it a "daring and shocking sacrilege." A new horror had been added to death, declared the *New York Illustrated Times*, adding wryly, "A safe deposit burial company may be one of the business enterprises of the near future."[15]

The *Times* stated on November 24 that there was nothing new to report on the grave robbery. "Unless something is unearthed within a day or two the case will likely pass into history," declared the *Herald* the next day. The papers continued to receive countless letters promising to reveal the hiding place of the remains or to implicate suspects. Superintendent Walling reported that a man suspected of being the sought-after George Christian was actually a patent medicine salesman in Pittsburgh. Neither May the soda water manufacturer nor Bull Kelly the hack man were to be found. Red herrings continued to spawn. Acting on a tip, two city detectives traveled to the cellar of a New Jersey beer saloon, where they found a freshly slaughtered hog stretched on a board and covered by a sheet. With no progress being made, a number of detectives were taken off the case.[16]

As November closed, the *National Police Gazette* observed that Judge

Hilton and the police had both admitted their utter inability to obtain a genuine clue. December passed with few mentions of the case in the press. A city undertaker again implicated hack driver Bull Kelly, but a police inspector doubted his story and dismissed Kelly as too stupid to have committed the crime. Two private detectives followed a false lead from the city to Fredericksburg, Virginia.[17]

A month passed with no new reports on the case. Then, on January 16, 1879, the *New York Sun* reported that Mrs. Stewart had told friends her husband's remains had been recovered and were secured in a well-guarded vault, awaiting the completion of the Garden City crypt. Judge Hilton had arranged to ransom the remains for fifty thousand dollars in cash. Hilton refused to comment on the report; Superintendent Walling and other police officials denied it. The *Tribune* and the *Herald* both condemned the story as spurious, but the *Sun* continued to stand by it, adding vague details supplied by unnamed informants. As the month ended, the *Tribune* published a significant detail. Early on the morning of January 28 a police detective, having obtained permission from Henry Hilton, had the Stewart crypt reopened in order to inspect the empty coffin. He had with him a pentagonal piece of brown paper. When he placed the paper over the hole cut from the velvet coffin cover, it proved to be an exact fit.[18]

Two days before the detective's visit to St. Mark's churchyard, on the morning of January 26, 1879, a letter carrier delivered a missive to Jones's law office at 150 Nassau Street. It was postmarked Montreal and addressed in an odd hand. When Jones opened the envelope, a one hundred dollar bill fluttered to the floor. The accompanying letter, which was dated January 24 and addressed from Montreal, was written in a mix of upper- and lowercase letters to disguise the writer's true hand. It opened: "Surprising as it may seem that such a being exists, nevertheless friends in your city assure me that you are an honest lawyer. Your public career and private character strengthen that belief to such an extent that I remit herewith a retainer of $100. Having thus established the relation of counsel and client, I request your professional assistance in the following matter."[19]

The matter, of course, was the Stewart grave robbery. The writer stated that he had remained silent until Judge Hilton was convinced of the futility of finding Stewart's remains. "The press, the people and the police have been beaten from the start," he bragged—he had followed their ineffectual efforts in the New York papers. Stewart's remains were stolen before midnight on November 6, 1878, he revealed, and carried in a grocer's wagon to a house near 116th Street, where they were encased in a zinc-lined trunk, which was shipped from the city on a morning train to Plattsburg, New York, and thence to Canada, where it was buried. Various proofs, the writer stated, were being delivered in a separate package. If more evidence was needed, Jones was to insert a personal advertisement in the *Herald*—"Canada, send P. Counsel"—whereupon the silver coffin plate would be sent. If Jones declined to act, someone would call on him to retrieve the retainer. If he accepted the proposal, he should confer with Reverend Rylance, Judge Hilton, and Mrs. Stewart, and when they were ready to "talk business," Jones should insert another personal in the *Herald:* "Canada—Will do business. Counsel." The writer declared that attempts to trace him would be unavailing; he was free from extradition and was the only man on earth who held the evidence or knew where the remains were buried—"they never can get to me." He signed himself Henry G. Romaine.[20]

Thunderstruck, Jones called his office boy and asked whether a package had arrived that morning. The lad went into the outer office and returned with a small parcel delivered earlier by the American Express Company. Jones opened it and found a screw, four silver screw caps, a small strip of black velvet, and a pentagonal piece of brown paper. He doubted the value of the screw and caps as evidence—"they might have been duplicated"—but the piece of brown paper and the fabric sample seemed conclusive. He had no doubt that Romaine was either one of the thieves or their agent.[21]

After puzzling over what to do, Jones decided to deliver the items the next day to the district attorney's office, where Henry Hilton's son-in-law Horace Russell was employed. On his way there he ran into his own trusted counsel and friend Freeman J. Fithian, a former Reuben Fenton appointee to the state supreme court. Fithian told Jones that it was customary to take such evidence to police headquarters. Jones consequently carried the articles to 300 Mulberry Street, where he presented them to his old acquaintance Superintendent George Walling.[22]

Walling was briefly stunned speechless by Jones's revelation. He wrote Jones a receipt and kept the items as evidence. Hoping to trap the robbers, he decided that Jones should request the coffin plate as stipulated. Jones sat down and wrote out the personal. Walling had it and the requisite fee delivered to the *Herald* office. It was published on January 29. Three days later

Jones received a letter by mail and a package by express. Both came from Boston. The package contained the inscribed silver coffin plate. In the letter, dated January 31, Romaine explained that on seeing Jones's personal in the *Herald,* he had decided to express the plate from Boston rather than have it discovered by Canadian customs officers. He ordered Jones to show the plate to Mrs. Stewart's representatives. When they were convinced it was genuine, Jones was to insert the "Will do business" personal in the *Herald.* "You are specially requested to maintain the strictest secrecy," Romaine instructed, "and you can assure Judge Hilton that any business done with me will never be known by mortal man." Jones immediately showed the letter and coffin plate to Walling, who kept the plate and wrote another receipt for it. At the superintendent's request Jones wrote the requested personal, and Walling sent it to the *Herald,* which published it on February 5.[23]

After the publication of the second personal, Walling informed Jones that Henry Hilton wanted to see him. Hilton had heard from so many crackpots concerning the case that he was initially reluctant to deal with Jones, but the coffin plate and other evidence had convinced him otherwise. Hilton had approved of the "Will do business" message, Jones was told. The two men met on February 5 or 6. Jones found Hilton to be haughty and offensive. The judge decided he had no choice in the matter but to accept Jones as negotiator. Consequently, Jones wrote to Romaine on February 7, acknowledging receipt of the letters and packages and retaining fee, informing him that the coffin plate and other items were in either Walling's or Hilton's hands and asking him to state his terms for the return of Stewart's corpse. Jones would present Romaine's demands to Hilton and let Romaine know the result.[24]

Romaine responded from Boston on February 11. He fully approved of Jones's actions to date, except for his visits to police headquarters—he had a spy following Jones. He wanted Jones to negotiate solely with Hilton, in absolute secrecy, and "to maintain forever an unbroken silence in regard to the transaction." The robbers had decided they wanted $200,000 for the return of Stewart's corpse, with Jones to deliver the ransom to Romaine's representative, an unnamed prominent merchant in New York, who would in turn deliver it to an eminent but unnamed Canadian lawyer, who would give it to Romaine, who would distribute it to the robbers. Stewart's remains would be returned to Jones and Hilton within twenty-five miles of Montreal. Jones was to relay Hilton's agreement with another personal in the *Herald:*

"Canada—Terms accepted. Counsel." Until it appeared, Jones would not hear from Romaine again. He added a postscript: if the $200,000 ransom was deemed extravagant, it was insignificant considering Stewart's estate amounted to fifty million dollars. He closed with emphasis, "*And nothing less will ever be accepted.*"[25]

Jones again met with Walling. The superintendent threw Romaine's letter down and exclaimed: "I can't deal with this man for money. I'm trying to find the culprits." He sent Jones to Hilton. Their second meeting was even more unpleasant than their first. "Preposterous!" blurted Hilton on reading the letter. "I'll not give a cent for the body. I care not for that. I want the robbers themselves." All he was authorized to do, Jones told the judge, was present Romaine's demands; by paying the ransom, Hilton would recover the remains. "I will not listen to it any longer," exclaimed Hilton. He asked if Jones knew the robbers. "All I can say as their lawyer," Jones replied, "is that these men will carry out the contract they propose to make with you through me." "I'll have nothing to do with it," Hilton angrily replied. He ordered Jones to insert a reply in the *Herald:* "Canada—Parties refuse to consider the terms proposed, and decline any negotiations through personals. Counsel." Jones left the irate Hilton's office, according to a report in the *Times*, "feeling that I had been thrust into a false position by my mysterious correspondent, and wishing heartily that I was out of the whole business." Hilton, suspecting Jones of complicity in the crime, hired two former police detectives to tail him and record his contacts.[26]

Jones addressed another letter to Romaine on February 16. "I do not care to have much more to do with this business," he wrote. "It is not in my line, and the sooner it is closed the better I will like it." Detectives annoyed him, and his business and comforts were being disrupted. He admitted to having visited police headquarters and turning over the evidence to Walling. If Romaine was dissatisfied with his actions, their correspondence could cease. He explained that Hilton had dictated the negative *Herald* personal. While Jones, the police, and Hilton all believed that Romaine held Stewart's remains, Jones did not think Hilton truly wanted them. "At least," he wrote, "he does not evince much anxiety in the business—not so much as he appeared to at first."[27]

Romaine responded from Montreal on February 19, enclosing $250 as a second retainer. He wrote that he admired Hilton's promptness but could not commend his prudence. If Hilton's motives were mercenary, he was an ingrate—"the vilest of human reptiles"—because Stewart's fortune was "more than sufficient to secure the prosperity of the living and the peace of the dead." If Hilton was stalling in the hope that stupid detectives might stumble on success, he was deluded. He never would succeed in discovering the robbers. If he refused to negotiate through personals, how did he propose to settle the matter? "He declines our plan," Romaine observed; "we await his." Romaine ordered Jones to communicate with Hilton immediately, ascertain his purpose, and relate the results. "We have decided upon a definite course of action in this matter," he closed, "and do not intend to be easily diverted from it."[28]

Jones took Romaine's latest letter to Hilton, who "was even more offensive" than in their previous encounter. An acrimonious discussion ensued. Jones finally said to Hilton: "Judge, I think the best thing that I can do is to close this whole business. I am getting tired of it." Hilton answered: "If these scoundrels imagine that they are going to get any money from me to compromise their crime they will get tired of the business, too. I will hunt them down if it costs a fortune. Here, let me write a personal." He picked up a pen and scrawled, "Canada—Terms not accepted. Counsel." It was published in the *Herald* the next morning. Jones left Hilton's office for what proved to be the final time.[29]

Jones reported on his meeting with Hilton in a letter to Romaine written February 25. The judge seemed unwilling to reopen negotiations, Jones related; he still appeared to be less interested in recovering the remains than in capturing the criminals. "He says that he wants the body in New York," wrote Jones, "and that he does not care to go to Canada." Hilton had casually mentioned that he might consider a five thousand–dollar ransom. Jones advised Romaine to keep himself and Stewart's corpse out of New York, "for I will not be answering for the action of Judge Hilton in case you are found here." Jones desired to do his duty to Romaine, but if his actions displeased his client, "I would willingly be relieved."[30]

Romaine responded from Montreal three days later. "It is labor lost to continue this correspondence," he wrote. He ordered Jones to have no more communication with Hilton but to give copies of their entire correspondence to Mrs. Stewart. If she wanted it, she could have her husband's corpse within two days after paying a "paltry pittance." Jones should then report promptly the success or failure of his mission.[31]

Jones had transcripts of his correspondence with Romaine prepared and pasted into a scrapbook. The originals he stored in a safe. He asked a friend of Cornelia Stewart, a prominent lawyer, to deliver the scrapbook to the widow. The lawyer did not take the scrapbook to Mrs. Stewart, however—he brought it to Henry Hilton, who was outraged that Jones had tried to circumvent him. More mistrustful of Jones than ever, Hilton sent Dr. Sidney H. Carney, a medical examiner for the New York Life Insurance Company who had worked on the case as an amateur detective, to Jones with a new offer: twenty-five thousand dollars for Stewart's body, irrespective of the capture of the robbers. Jones wrote to Romaine on March 14 and 24 to relay the Carney offer and awaited a reply.[32]

Meanwhile, a former captain of the city police detectives, James Irving, who had been dismissed from the force because of his involvement in a forgery case, began investigating the Stewart case on his own. In Nassau Street, Irving happened upon some former colleagues who were surveilling Jones. When they revealed that Hilton had hired them, the detective realized that Jones was somehow involved in the case and sought him out. The two men met and conferred for a couple of hours, deciding that they would continue negotiations with Romaine without consulting Hilton. If they did need to consult the judge, they would use his son-in-law Horace Russell as an intermediary.[33]

Romaine wrote again from Montreal on March 30. He rejected Carney's "munificent offer" on Hilton's behalf of twenty-five thousand dollars for the return of the remains and pegged Carney as a detective hoping to collect a sizable reward. Whenever Hilton was ready to pay a ransom "worthy of the position and fortune of Mr. Stewart," he would obtain the remains. Until then Romaine refused to consider any more propositions from Hilton. "This letter closes our correspondence on this subject," he concluded. "We are engaged upon a matter that promises to be profitable, and cannot longer occupy our time with this affair."[34]

Jones replied on April 2. He acknowledged Romaine's rejection of the twenty-five thousand–dollar offer and his refusal to deal with Carney. "In this you err, I think," Jones informed his client. "It should be a matter of indifference to you through what source the money is received. I hope that you will reconsider your decision, and advise me." Romaine responded from Montreal three days later. The thieves had reconsidered the matter and agreed to deal with Carney, for as Jones had stated, it was inconsequential who paid for or received the remains. On that inconclusive note the Romaine-Jones correspondence closed—at least for the time being.[35]

The negotiations between Romaine, Jones, and Hilton remained secret for months. Early in August 1879 newspapers reported—and questioned—rumors that Stewart's body had been recovered. Then, on August 13, the *New York Herald* published a four-column article boldly headlined "Unrecovered." It recapitulated the crime, stated that the remains were still in the hands of the thieves, and revealed the story of Romaine's negotiations with a Nassau Street lawyer without mentioning Jones by name. It included an interview with Hilton, who condemned the grave robbers and their lawyer as "a pack of rascals and scoundrels and thieves." The lawyer knew "all about the robbers," Hilton claimed, "knows their haunts, meets them right here in New York." The lawyer "knew all about" the crime. He doubted that the lawyer was actually the thieves' legal representative. The correspondence between Romaine and the lawyer was "all made up for a purpose." He reiterated, "I deny that this lawyer, who hides himself under this cloak of legal adviser, is the representative of these men in a manner where he can be shielded by his professional oath. I don't believe it. He knows more about them than an ordinary lawyer." Hilton cast doubt on the lawyer's claim of having received retainers, insinuated that Romaine's original letters and the lawyer's copies were written on the same paper, and denied hiring detectives to shadow the lawyer.[36]

The *Herald*'s scoop created a sensation, and other newspapers—including one in Montreal—immediately picked up the story. One of the evening dailies lauded Hilton's actions in the affair; another chastised him for misleading the public—and Cornelia Stewart—to believe the remains had been recovered. By the next day, August 14, all of the New York City journals had weighed in on the revelations.[37]

That day the *Times* revealed the Nassau Street lawyer to be Jones. In an interview Jones emphasized, "My practice is not the kind which seeks grave-robbers for clients." He denied having quarreled with Hilton. The judge had been discourteous to him, he stated, but had not insulted him or evinced any lack of faith in his honor. Reflecting on Hilton's *Herald* interview, he supposed that Hilton "was under the impression all the time that I was simply an agent of the robbers." Hilton had never hinted that to Jones; if he had, Jones would "have promptly resented the imputation in the manner that it deserved." "I find that I have been abused and misrepresented in this business throughout," Jones complained. "I am very sorry that this story has been made public at all, but as it has been I mean to see that justice is done to me in my share of the business." If Hilton attempted to impugn his motives, he would make public the entire correspondence "and leave my friends to judge whether I have done right or wrong in the course which I have taken."[38]

The *Herald* of August 14 published an interview with Jones in which he remained anonymous. He confirmed the correctness of the previous day's account, stated the robbers had managed their work with "a most wonderful tact," and described Romaine as "an exceedingly smart man." What had so riled Judge Hilton was a comment by Romaine, which Jones paraphrased: "Romaine holds Stewart's body, and Judge Hilton holds his property." He observed that it was "hard, very hard" for Hilton or anyone else to acknowledge that the thieves had "made such a clean job of it." He showed the reporter his scrapbook of the Romaine correspondence, noting that he had been "exceedingly careful" in documenting the case. He closed the interview by declaring: "The entire matter disgusts me and annoys me, but I am not going to be blackguarded by Mr. Hilton or anybody else, and feel that I have discharged my duty as a lawyer. It remains for the other side to say whether they will listen to what this Romaine proposes or not. That is their business."[39]

Jones told a reporter from the *Tribune* that he had not negotiated with Romaine since the spring and that while he had shared all of his information on the case with the district attorney and other officials and discussed it with his friends, he had always been cautious to avoid any publicity that could have halted the process. The *Tribune* reported that Hilton, seeking to reopen negotiations with the thieves, had inserted a personal in the July 24 issue of the *Herald:* "Canada. Counsel desires to communicate." But Jones had heard nothing further from Romaine.[40]

Jones spoke to a reporter from the *Commercial Advertiser,* telling him that he had withdrawn from the case and believed that Stewart's remains had not been recovered. "General Jones is not particularly gratified at the notoriety the case has given him," the writer observed, "and declines to have anything more to do with it." As in the aftermath of the crime, press coverage of the latest development veered in different directions. A reporter for the *Evening Mail* heard that Jones's story had been an open secret for some time but that investigations had failed to confirm it, hence its late appearance in print. The *Sun* stuck by its allegation that Stewart's remains had been recovered. Papers in Montreal scoffed at reports of the city's connection to the crime.

The *Evening Express* suggested that the knowledgeable and skilled thieves should be invited back to New York and appointed police commissioners. The *Brooklyn Daily Eagle* lampooned the city police as "uninformed blockheads and numbskulls." The *Daily Graphic* imagined a future "rich men's body market," with the corpses of wealthy celebrities offered for high prices. On a more sober note an editorial in the *Tribune* stated, "There should be no compromise with the thieves." Not a dollar should be paid for Stewart's remains; better that the magnificent mausoleum and cathedral in Garden City stand as his memorial.[41]

Two significant publications appeared on August 17. The *Herald* published a long recapitulation of the Romaine-Jones negotiations, illustrated with facsimiles of an envelope and letter sent by Romaine. It included an interview with Jones. Responding to Hilton's remarks published in the *Herald* four days earlier, Jones stated: "I will not allow Judge Hilton to throw any reflections upon me . . . My transactions from first to last have been honorable toward Judge Hilton, but I cannot say as much for him . . . I wish him to understand that, even if he is a rich man, I will not allow him to defame me . . . To have him tell the truth is the main thing I seek, and I shall try hard, now that he has acted in this way, to make him speak." Jones denied threatening Hilton with publication of the matter in the press, he refuted Hilton's charge that Romaine's original letters and the copies were written on the same paper by showing them to be different, and he cited his experience as postmaster to confirm that the letters had been mailed and postmarked as stated. Finally, he released for publication a stern letter he had sent to Hilton the previous day: "In regard to the Stewart matter, which has occupied the attention of some readers of the newspapers, I understand from a reported interview that you state that I know more of the matter and the personnel of the thieves than has been printed. Be kind enough to assert squarely what you mean. It may lead to a judicial investigation. If so I say that I will not commence any civil action against you for defamation, and will not seek any other redress than to make you tell the truth if I can. This is an open letter."[42]

Coincidentally, the *Sun* of August 17 published the entire Romaine-Jones correspondence, transcribed from Jones's scrapbook. While other newspapers had published certain of the letters, the *Sun* made a significant contribution to posterity by printing them all. It included Jones's open letter to Hilton, which was also picked up by other papers.[43]

In the wake of these revelations some newspapers criticized Jones's role in the case. The *World* dismissed his story as resting "entirely upon his own word," which the paper deemed untrustworthy when compared to that of Hilton, "a gentleman long trained as an able advocate to estimate evidence." (That Jones—"a local politician invented by Horace Greeley and the late Miles O'Reilly"—was a Republican and Hilton a Democrat went unsaid by the Democratic *World*.) In a scathing and dismissive summary of the Romaine-Jones correspondence, the *World* asserted that the style of both writers "seems to be one and the same"—insinuating that Jones wrote all the letters himself. In a letter to the *Tribune* Cornelia Stewart's physician charged Jones and the thieves with a "cruel and fiendish plot to extort money from her." A Buffalo newspaper editorialized: "Patrick H. Jones has no objection to acting as counsel for grave-robbers, but when Judge Hilton questions his motives or his method in doing so he feels that his honor demands a suit for libel. Mr. Jones is trying to compromise a crime, against the law he professes to serve; but he feels that as a lawyer his acts ought to be beyond criticism. Is it the law that has fallen so low, or is it merely Mr. Jones?"[44]

Jones granted an interview to an *Evening Express* reporter on August 19. Beyond the Romaine correspondence, he said, he had nothing else to put before the public. He had reason to believe that Hilton's statements implicating him in the crime had been misquoted. He had yet to hear from Hilton in response to his open letter, but he believed the judge would respond in a day or two. As counsel, he could not and would not do anything to implicate the thieves or assist in their arrest, even if it was in his power to do so. He was convinced that Romaine knew what he was doing and was unlikely to be caught in a trap. He theorized that Romaine might actually be some prominent person who was acting on behalf of the thieves. He doubted the ransom would be paid because Hilton was still optimistic that the culprits would be caught. He closed by saying he had no theories about future developments in the case.[45]

A Cattaraugus County newspaper expressed amazement at the way other papers had reported Jones's part in the story. That he had promptly communicated with the police and Judge Hilton "entirely clears him of any wrong doing." The writer was personally acquainted with Jones and considered him "utterly incapable of doing so outrageous a wrong against society, or any wrong. In all the communications between him and the agent of the criminals, there is not a sentence or a word that could implicate him in any wrong." They were heartfelt words in Jones's defense, but they were uttered far away from the media maelstrom in New York City.[46]

Interest in the Stewart grave robbery was intense but brief that August 1879. Other headlines vied for the public's attention, like those trumpeting a Roscoe Conkling sex scandal. After the revelation of Jones's involvement, the Stewart case disappeared from the press until June 1881. That month the *New York Star* ran a lurid four-part series that purported to give the true story of the crime as related by an anonymous New York City "special detective." It was a convoluted pastiche of the 1878 and 1879 news accounts that skewed the sequence and details of events into a fantastic fiction. The detective portrayed Jones in an unflattering light, depicting him as fearing for his life and describing his "queer tactics" in the case. He introduced a new character into the tale, identifying the prominent attorney whom Jones had solicited to approach Mrs. Stewart as congressman and former Union general Benjamin F. Butler. The *Star* claimed its series was the talk of the town, that the Stewart mystery had been solved, and that its narrative of the case was "a relation of actual facts from a well-informed and authentic quarter." In reality the series—which appears to have been a hoax—went unremarked by other city papers, although the shooting of President James Garfield on July 2, 1881, would have eclipsed any commentary they wished to make. Jones apparently did not comment on it.[47]

That summer saw another false lead in the case. Under the direction of New York City detectives, workmen began digging up a plot in Brooklyn's Cypress Hills Cemetery. The search commenced after a painting was delivered to a private detective. It depicted a landscape within the cemetery with the inscription "Stewart is buried here." Judge Hilton sent an emissary to observe the search. When the spot was located and digging commenced, hundreds of people gathered to gawk at the excavation and debate the issue. After a few days the head detective called off the search, admitting he had been fooled.[48]

The marble mausoleum in the Cathedral of the Incarnation in Garden City was completed in February 1883. The public wondered: would Cornelia Stewart see her husband's remains buried in the crypt, or would she eventually occupy it alone? Was the corpse in the possession of Hilton or the thieves? Nobody knew. When the church was consecrated in June 1885, the question of whether it held Stewart's remains was still unanswered. Visitors crowded the mausoleum and whispered and wondered if the crypt was occupied or empty.[49]

Cornelia Stewart died in October 1886 in her Manhattan mansion. Her funeral service was held at the Cathedral of the Incarnation, with burial in the crypt. Her obituary in the *Times* lauded her sponsorship of the cathedral and her keen business sense. It was observed that after her husband died, she had lived very quietly and "always dreaded publicity or display." No mention was made of the grave robbery. Less circumspect was the *World*, which accompanied its obituary with a summary of the case, declaring that only the ghouls knew the location of Stewart's body.[50]

Henry Hilton—described by one chronicler as "a greedy, self-important, soulless tyrant"—died in August 1899 after a long illness. A. T. Stewart had bequeathed Hilton one million dollars, and Cornelia Stewart had turned over all of her assets to him; estimates of their worth ranged from thirty-five million to sixty million dollars. But Hilton was a poor businessman; he alienated Jewish and women customers, his ventures failed repeatedly, lawsuits drained millions, and the worth of the enterprise plummeted. Over roughly twenty years Hilton and his family squandered the immense Stewart fortune. Hilton's obituary in the *Times* referred to the grave robbery case in ambiguous terms. Hilton had never admitted that Stewart's remains had been recovered, it noted, but many people believed they had been found and buried secretly. Hilton's obituary in the *Brooklyn Daily Eagle*, however, observed that a conclusion to the case had been reported more than a decade earlier.[51]

During the blizzard of publicity surrounding the revelation of his role in the Stewart case, Jones stated that he would have nothing further to do in the matter. If the account presented in police superintendent George Walling's memoirs is accurate, Jones changed his mind. Walling was the only participant to record a conclusion to the case. In it Jones was a key player in the ransom and return of Stewart's remains.[52]

Walling's book appeared to great fanfare in 1887. It covered the most prominent and sensational crimes of his forty years on the police force, including "the complete story" of the Stewart case. But Walling's account of the case's denouement was admittedly secondhand. "The authentic story of the recovery of Stewart's body has not yet been publicly told," he wrote, "but a gentleman who is in a position to know the exact facts recently rehearsed the narrative, and for the first time it is given here." Who the gentleman was went unsaid, but Walling's friend Jones is certainly a strong possibility.[53]

Walling inexplicably presented two versions of Jones's initial involvement in the case. The first was brief, vague, and fanciful. In it Walling said Jones had identified Romaine as "a man who formerly served under me in the army." A certain Henry C. Romaine had served in the Second New York Infantry, which was assigned to the Third Corps after the Battle of Fair Oaks. It is possible but unlikely Jones had encountered him then; he was never under Jones's command. Romaine was absent without leave from the Second for months and subsequently deserted from a New York heavy artillery regiment, never to return. There is no evidence or indication, however, that he was the grave robbers' representative. After all, it seems unlikely that the writer of the Romaine letters had used his real name in the correspondence. Perhaps he simply borrowed the deserter's name, getting the middle initial wrong. In any case Henry G. Romaine was never identified.[54]

Walling's second version generally adhered to the press reports. He attributed the breakdown of the Jones-Romaine negotiations to Hilton's intransigence in opposing Cornelia Stewart's desire to make a deal with the thieves. In Walling's opinion Hilton had trampled Mrs. Stewart's affections under his foot. "Her nights were almost sleepless," he wrote. "She was well nigh driven insane." Finally, in the spring of 1881 Cornelia Stewart opened negotiations on her own account, without Hilton's consent. Correspondence with the robbers resumed, once again conducted by Jones: "The lawyer was still the medium of communication with the ghouls." Presumably, Jones had again swapped letters with Romaine. The thieves stated they were willing to accept a $100,000 ransom, half of their initial demand. Jones made a counteroffer of $20,000, which the crooks accepted.[55]

The thieves gave instructions for the exchange. A young relative of Cornelia Stewart undertook the mission. He left New York City alone at ten o'clock at night in a one-horse buggy and drove into Westchester County along a lonely road. At three the next morning a masked horseman rode up, gave an agreed-upon signal, and turned the buggy up a deserted lane. A mile farther, the emissary found a wagon blocking his way. A masked man carrying a bag appeared. "Here 'tis," he said. "Where's the money?" "Where is the proof of identity?" asked the young man. "Here!" said the masked man, shining a lantern on a pentagonal piece of velvet. The fabric was compared with a piece of paper the young man had brought with him; they matched. The robber placed the bag in the wagon; the young man handed over the ransom. The thieves counted the loot by lantern light and departed in their wagon. The young man turned homeward, "glad to escape from such company." The next night a freight car traveled from Manhattan to Garden City. In it was a trunk, on which sat the young Stewart relative. At the Cathedral of the Incarnation two men transferred Stewart's bones from the trunk to a coffin, which was placed in the mausoleum. It was said the vault was rigged with a device that would ring the bells in the church's tower and send an instant alarm should the resting place of A. T. Stewart ever again be disturbed.[56]

Neither Jones nor Hilton is known to have commented on Walling's account. Had they confirmed it, the mystery would have been put to rest. But such was not the case, and critics then and since have cast doubt on Walling's version of the Stewart case. In its review of his book the *Times* accused Walling of presenting the facts "with the imagination necessary to form a proper literary conclusion," in an account that "cannot be relied on as entirely authentic." Walling's tale had the "black and gloomy style" of penny horrible literature. "The whole story, considering the non-committal attitude of the parties who know best the actual facts, savors slightly of the queer . . . As to whether the remains were or were not actually returned, those in possession of the facts still refuse to say." The *Times* did not identify who possessed the facts; presumably, the newspaper was referring to Jones and Hilton. An evening paper reported that high officials at police headquarters had laughed at Walling's account.[57]

Later writers have differed on Walling's reliability. Herbert Asbury adapted it without comment in his popular book *The Gangs of New York*. In an article in the *New Yorker* Marquis James observed, "It lacks satisfactory corroboration or successful contradiction." James found no "documentary confirmation" that Stewart's remains were in the Cathedral of the Incarnation. Stewart's biographer, Stephen N. Elias, noted that Walling's account "has an ending that differs from the facts available through any other source" and rests on "no foundation—other than Walling's reminiscences." The author of an unpublished Stewart biography, Harry E. Resseguie, judged Walling's account as "highly circumstantial, not to say fantastic."[58]

Two recent books are devoted to the Stewart grave robbery. In *The Missing Corpse* Wayne Fanebust neither endorses nor refutes Walling's account but concludes that "the weight of the evidence" suggests that Stewart's body was not recovered. Fanebust comments positively about Jones's role in the case: "In selecting Jones, a man with a good reputation and a degree of prominence, the plotters displayed good sense. Seeking a less reputable man to act as their agent would have probably caused the authorities and Hilton to dismiss the proposition summarily." He cites Jones's "hard work" on the case: "Jones was persistent, perhaps clinging to some hope that he might yet be able to successfully conclude the negotiations and assume the lofty role as the man who solved the greatest grave robbery mystery in America. Wouldn't that set New York abuzz?" In the end, however, Fanebust notes, "it was a connection with history he could live without after all."[59]

In *Bag of Bones* J. North Conway accepts Walling's account at face value: "There was no reason to believe he wasn't telling the truth as he knew it in his book." Like Fanebust, Conway is equivocal about the fate of Stewart's remains. "There is no doubt that the remains of *someone* were carefully placed in the crypt at the Cathedral of the Incarnation sometime in late 1880 or early 1881," he states, but "no one knows for certain whose bones are buried in the cathedral vault." Conway assesses Jones's part in the story with a striking metaphor: "Jones's role in the Stewart case was not one he sought or desired, and it became an albatross around his good name chiefly because of the actions of Henry Hilton."[60]

As Fanebust and Conway indicate, uncertainty about the mysterious, never-solved Stewart case lingers to this day. Did Jones negotiate the return of A. T. Stewart's remains? If we accept George Walling's account, he did. Do Stewart's remains lay in the Cathedral of the Incarnation crypt? If Walling is correct, they do. One fact seems certain—the ambiguities of Jones's involvement in the Stewart case indelibly stained his reputation. In 1883 the *Tribune* ran a short article quoting an anonymous gentleman said to be familiar with the case. In commenting on the Jones-Romaine negotiations, he said: "Nothing came of them except the ruin of poor Jones. He often says that connection with the case did him irretrievable damage." When asked if Jones was suspected of complicity with the robbers, he stated, "Oh! no; but really valuable clients fight shy of lawyers who touch such cases." Certain criminal cases saddled lawyers with "malodorous" and "evil" reputations. Criminals themselves ranked grave robbers the lowest of the low. Jones's association with the Stewart ghouls ruined his once-respectable career. The taint from his involvement in the crime would follow him to his own grave.[61]

CHAPTER 11

Decline

When Jones finished his term as register in 1877, his name was bandied about as a potential candidate for reelection to the office. But it was not to be. The register traditionally held the office for one term only, and that practice continued long after Jones held the position. Honest John Kelly described the post as a plum to be plucked, whereupon the register retired with a competence. By the 1890s the *Irish-American* described the office as a "political grave." So it proved to be for Jones. After his term as register, he floundered politically.[1]

When the November 1878 elections approached, the *Times* listed Jones as the Greenback-Labor Party candidate for Congress in New York's Ninth District. This was a mistake—another man ran instead—but it is possible that Jones had declined to accept the nomination, as did several other potential Greenback-Labor candidates. In any case mere mention of Jones in connection with the new party indicates he was dissatisfied with the Republicans and attracted to a third party that was growing in popularity, particularly among the urban Irish working class. Perhaps he was offended by the Republican Party's abandoning of Reconstruction in the wake of the 1876 presidential election or by its attempts to stir anti-Catholic prejudice with attacks on the pope and parochial schools. Years of striving by various labor reform and farmers' groups culminated in a strong Greenback-Labor Party showing in the election; nationwide, it garnered more than a million votes and sent fourteen representatives to Congress. Had Jones run on the Greenback-Labor ticket—with his cross-party popularity and appeal to the large Irish vote (and before his involvement in the Stewart case)—he might well have toppled the legendary incumbent, Democrat Fernando Wood, who had long enjoyed the support of the Irish.[2]

Jones was one of a number of prominent politicians present when the Republican Party's state committee met at a Fifth Avenue hotel in July 1879. But the Republicans no longer had his unswerving loyalty. In that year's fractured political scene, six parties—Republican, Tammany Democrat, Anti-Tammany Democrat, Greenback-Labor, Socialist, and Prohibition—fielded candidates for state offices. Shortly before the November election, Jones attended a meeting of veteran soldiers that endorsed the Anti-Tammany Democratic candidate for county sheriff.[3]

By 1880 Jones had reportedly rejoined the Democratic Party. In July he released a letter to the press announcing his support of Gen. Winfield S. Hancock, the Democrat running for president against Republican James A. Garfield. Democratic newspapers gleefully pointed out that Jones had "moved with great distinction" and "been influential in the councils" of the Republican Party. That August a reporter from the *Times* met Jones in the hotel rooms of the Democratic State Committee. The mayor and two of his cronies were also present, smoking cigars and seeming to ignore Jones's presence. "General, tell me something new," said the reporter. Jones "almost groaned," as he replied, "Go into the streets and ask the bootblacks. They can give you more information than you will get here." Tammany Hall and Anti-Tammany Democrats were squabbling. Weeks later the two groups thronged a hotel and strived to heal their breach. Jones was again present. In the interim he was one of a number of visitors who greeted General Hancock at a reception on Governor's Island. But reports of Jones's return to the Democratic Party were belied by his election as vice president of the National Association of Conservative Republicans and Independent Voters that September. In light of his chameleonic politics at the time, Jones was probably best described as an independent.[4]

Another two years passed before Jones was mentioned in newspaper political coverage. This time he sat on the platform with other dignitaries at a June 1882 meeting of the New York County Anti-Monopoly League in Cooper Institute's great hall. The hall was only half-full when the meeting was called to order. With Jones onstage were a number of Tammany ward politicians and other leaders in the movement. During the evening the hall was just two-thirds full.[5]

Jones's involvement with the Anti-Monopolists is as obscure as his connections to the Greenback-Labor and Democratic Parties. The New York City branch of the Anti-Monopoly League formally organized in January 1881. It sought to restrict the powers of the gigantic railroad and telegraph monopolies that were ruining old-fashioned businessmen. Its members included men of all political persuasions, including former Greenback-Labor Party members, women suffragists, and a small contingent of black men. As Election Day neared in 1882, the Anti-Monopolists deliberated which of the two major parties to support. In the end they backed the Democrats as the lesser of two evils.[6]

Jones's fleeting alliances with the Greenback-Labor Party, the Anti-Monopoly League, and the Democrats never delivered the political promise he had experienced with the Republican Party. He never again ran for or was appointed to an office. His old crony Chester Arthur became president in 1881 after the assassination and death of James Garfield. Had Jones remained a staunch orthodox Republican, he might have benefited by a favor from the Arthur administration, but that was not meant to be.[7]

Another factor worked against Jones's political future: He was Irish. "The Irish-American community of the late nineteenth century was undergoing a process of change in which individual achievement loomed larger than social unity," observed historian Seymour Mandelbaum. "Getting ahead in politics, like success in business, was a sign of individual achievement and ethnic glory. It had very little to do with public policy." Jones had enjoyed political success, albeit the aberrant success of an Irish Republican, but other than in patronage dispensed, it had not generally redounded to the greater good of the Irish American community. Nor had it ensured his future success. As Mandelbaum noted, "The Irish came to power but could not command respect."[8]

In the mid-1880s two of Jones's best-known political associates died within a month of each other. Ulysses Grant succumbed to throat cancer in July 1885. Grant eventually was given a hero's funeral and entombment in New York City. Some eighteen thousand Union veterans marched in the funeral procession before an estimated one and a half million onlookers, but Jones was not among the many old soldiers or other dignitaries listed in the press. That day Reuben Fenton—characterized by one historian as "the old wirepuller and bribe-taker"—made his last public appearance at his mansion in Jamestown, New York, in a memorial service for Grant. In the years after his political career, Fenton presided over a Jamestown bank and won renown as an expert on monetary matters. He was appointed by President Rutherford B. Hayes to chair the United States delegation to an 1878 international monetary conference in Paris. It was his last public service. Fenton died at his bank in August 1885.[9]

Jones lost a favorite former commander when Joseph Hooker died in 1879. For five years the general had enjoyed living on Long Island in A. T. Stewart's planned community, Garden City. He died there just two months after Jones's role in the Stewart grave robbery case was revealed. Services for Hooker were held in Garden City prior to a massive tribute in New York City and his eventual burial in Cincinnati. There is no evidence that Jones attended Hooker's funeral or that of General Sherman, who died in New York in 1891 and was likewise commemorated with a ceremony by vast crowds in the city, including tens of thousands of veterans, before being buried in St. Louis. By the time Sherman died, Jones had left Manhattan and largely disappeared from public life.[10]

The year of the Stewart grave robbery sensation—1879—was the last time Jones was listed in city directories as a resident at 62 West Forty-Sixth Street. In 1880 the Joneses were living at 56 East Twenty-Fifth Street. By the next year they were residing on Staten Island. Jones kept his office at 150 Nassau Street until around 1883, when he moved to one on Exchange Place in Manhattan. At some point he gave up a Manhattan office altogether and conducted business from his Staten Island home. In 1883 and 1884 his residence was listed on Burgher Avenue and Water Street in West New Brighton. In approximately 1885 the Joneses rented a small house on Ann Street in Port Richmond; it was there that he lived the rest of his days. Eldest son Thomas Jones, a bookkeeper for a lumber company, reportedly left the family in 1897. It seems the estrangement occurred under strained circumstances; Thomas was not seen or heard from again. His younger brother, James Jones, worked as a salesman and stayed in his parents' cottage.[11]

"Barring the mosquitoes, all New-Yorkers have a fond feeling for Staten Island," stated an 1890 article in the *Times*. The island abounded in "inviting rural retreats," but it was rapidly becoming urbanized. In four years, from 1886—when the Staten Island Railroad inaugurated rapid transit train service—to 1890, the number of residents on the island increased fifty-fold. An unpleasant aspect of commuter life was the crowded morning and evening rush hour ferryboats, which steamed every half hour between the foot of Whitehall Street in Manhattan and St. George on the island. Returning home from the city, Jones paid a dime at St. George and took the train along the Kill von Kull through New Brighton, Snug Harbor, Livingston, and West New Brighton to Port Richmond and his Ann Street home. But his trips to Manhattan gradually diminished as the years passed.[12]

A federal act of 1862 provided for invalid pensions to be paid to wounded, injured, and disabled Union veterans. Although Jones qualified, he did not fill out a pension application until the autumn of 1881 and did not submit it to the Pension Office in Washington until 1884. It is reasonable to assume he was finally driven to apply from financial necessity. His application stated that he was greatly disabled from the effects of malarial fever contracted during the Peninsular campaign and the gunshot wound of his right hip suffered at Chancellorsville. With it he submitted a deposition in his own hand and certificates and affidavits attesting to his disabilities from his personal physician, Dr. Walter Gillette, from Dr. William O'Meagher, former surgeon of the Thirty-Seventh New York, and from Henry Van Aernam, former surgeon of the 154th New York. O'Meagher added that Jones had hearing loss stemming from artillery and musketry firing during the war.[13]

On the receipt of Jones's application, the Pension Office ordered him to appear before a board of medical examiners in New York. A doctor reported he suffered from pain from the gunshot wound (symptoms that were aggravated by stormy weather and prolonged exercise) and the effects of malaria for a week or two every spring and fall. During those attacks he huddled by the stove in the morning, wrapped in a blanket, shivering with the chills; afternoons he burned with fever. He weighed 125 pounds and appeared malnourished. A Pension Office legal reviewer approved his claim for the gunshot wound but rejected his claim for malarial poisoning. In September 1885 a medical reviewer approved the wound claim, classifying it as a one-quarter disability, and granted him an invalid pension of $7.50 per month.[14]

Soon after receiving it, Jones filed for an increase, seeking to have his malarial maladies recognized in addition to the gunshot wound. A Pension Office deputy commissioner and former distinguished brigadier general and division commander in the Army of the Potomac, Joseph Jackson Bartlett, put in a good word for his friend, citing Jones's "high character." A reviewer did not doubt the merit of Jones's claim but requested more evidence. Once again, a doctor examined him, stating that the gunshot wound and malarial effects amounted to a total disability. As a result, Jones was granted an increase to twenty dollars per month, upped to twenty-seven dollars per month in October 1886.[15]

As the nineteenth century closed, social trends, including criticism of liberal pension policies, served to diminish the status of aging Civil War veterans in the eyes of the public. "Veterans remained very prominent at all levels of politics and society throughout the 1870s and 1880s," historian James Marten observed. "But their wave crested soon thereafter, and despite the continuation of much of the admiring rhetoric [extolling their service], veterans remained isolated from the rest of society." Old soldiers faded away to stereotype in the new concerns of the Gilded Age, viewed by other Americans as patriotic heroes on one hand and on the other hand, in Marten's words, as " dangerous tramps, helpless drunks, and institutional amputees." Jones apparently fit both stereotypes.[16]

The doctor who examined Jones in 1886 noted that he was somewhat emaciated, his conjunctivas were yellowish, his skin looked anemic, and his liver and spleen were markedly enlarged—signs of alcoholism. In 1872 Jones made a fifty-dollar donation toward a proposed statue in New York of Theobald Mathew, the Irish priest internationally renowned as a temperance advocate. But Jones did not adhere to Father Mathew's total abstinence pledge or heed the warnings of Catholic clergy about alcoholism. "He was a man of good habits," insisted his son James. "He would drink some but not to excess." But alcohol abuse was apparently a long-standing problem for Jones, as it was for many of his fellow former soldiers. As James Marten has noted, "Alcoholism and alcohol abuse were among the major disabilities suffered by [Civil War] veterans." They often drank to excess to alleviate physical or psychological torment, subjecting themselves in the process to socially unacceptable and unlawful behavior, a wide range of health issues, and a sullied reputation as a class.[17]

Whiskey had certainly been available at Jones's headquarters during the Civil War. Michael Kerwin, the Clan na Gael supporter and post office employee, knew Jones well during his Manhattan years and described him as a "hard drinker" who nevertheless appeared to be in good health. By the time Jones moved to Staten Island, his problem reportedly had worsened. In an 1888 letter to a fellow former officer of the 154th New York, Henry Van Aernam wrote: "I am sorry to say that Genl. P. H. Jones is a moral and physical wreck. Whiskey has destroyed him! Generous, kind hearted, and gentle and brave, he was a noble specimen of a true man—whiskey destroyed him prematurely. He is *staying* about New York and New Brighton completely demoralized and not much better than a tramp. Truly a very sad ending of his career!" This damning testimony came from a friend whom Jones called "a very careful chronicler not given to balderdash." A former officer of the 154th Regiment who moved to Port Richmond in 1892 and visited his old commander on a regular basis noticed the general had the shakes. A doctor who treated Jones during his last years stated, "I have heard that he was a drinking man but have no personal knowledge of it." A Pension Office special examiner, making inquiries around the Joneses' Port Richmond neighborhood, was told that Jones drank "to some extent" and that Sarah Jones—who was widely regarded as "queer"—drank "a great deal." As a consequence, the couple had few visitors and appeared to have few friends. Sarah Jones would later admit, "We never had any neighbors on Staten Island that we were intimate with."[18]

Van Aernam's characterization of Jones as a tramp on the streets appears to have been an exaggeration. Although at one point Jones admitted, "I am so uncertain about my movements that I can hardly say one day what I am to do the next," he continued to do law work in New York and as far away as Albany until about 1895, when declining health forced him to forsake it. He conducted an extensive correspondence with E. D. Northrup regarding the history of the 154th Regiment. He ended one letter to Northrup: "In the Irish way of opening a letter I will close thus—'We are all well & prosperous thanks be to God for the same and hope this will find you also enjoying the same blessing.'" He still had his papers, which he rummaged through to find materials for Northrup. He followed events in the newspapers. A veteran of the 154th visited the Joneses at Port Richmond in 1895 and made no mention of squalor; Sarah Jones's mother was living with the family at the time. Jones attended the Manhattan funeral of a former post office employee in 1897. Together with the other living former postmasters, he attended a mass meeting in 1898 to protest threatened cuts in the city's postal facilities. That year he also served on the executive committee of the Anti-British Alliance Association, an organization opposed to the ratification of a proposed arbitration treaty with Great Britain.[19]

By then his health was failing. "He seems to be all broken up," a doctor noted. Malnourished, emaciated, and weak, Jones tottered around Port Richmond with a cane, stopping in for brief visits in stores and offices. Around 1898 he suffered a stroke that left him, in his own words, "much enfeebled." E. D. Northrup visited Jones at his Ann Street home on July 6, 1900, and later described the scene: "I . . . cannot put out of mind his last brave words (so like his heroic spirit) as I gave him my last handshake, said scarcely above a whisper: 'Goodbye, Northrup: D—n it, it might just as well be today as tomorrow, it [is] all right!' He, of course, referred to his dying; and he was the same cool, nervy man as when he *stood* at Chancellorsville, and faced death there, as long before he had at Williamsburg, &c."[20]

The New York area stifled in an enervating heat wave during Jones's last days. For months Sarah and James had carried him from his bed to a chair. Now he was bedridden, yellow with jaundice, his feet swollen with dropsy, unable to control his bladder or bowels. He was dosed with calomel, citrate of magnesia, and a patent medicine pitched as an Indian remedy. His only nourishment was scalded milk and brandy. His only visitors were a doctor and the priest from Port Richmond's St. Mary's Church. Jones was not a regular parishioner; the priest had first met him eight months earlier. The general received the cleric lying on a sofa, swathed in blankets, scarcely speaking above a whisper. Their discussions went unrecorded.[21]

Jones died of heart failure at his Ann Street home about 4:30 p.m. on July 23, 1900. The indirect cause of death was gastroenteritis. On July 25, following a morning funeral service at St. Mary's Church at which a Requiem Mass was said for the repose of his soul, he was buried in St. Peter's Cemetery in Port Richmond, where a simple marble headstone marks his grave. That day the first obituaries appeared in the New York City newspapers. They quickly spread to papers upstate and elsewhere in the country, to Catholic and Irish American journals, and into a historical review and a biographical directory. Each sketched his life in brief, concentrating on his Civil War service and political career. Despite his later political vagaries, he was described as he was remembered, a staunch Republican. The *Staten Islander* called him "a man of good appearance and a favorite of the community and all who knew him." Not a word was mentioned of the Norton and Nolan scandals or of the Stewart grave robbery.[22]

Personal tributes appeared in western New York newspapers. Jones was "a gallant and able officer," stated a Jamestown paper, "devoted to the interests of his soldiers and was rewarded by their friendship and affection." "Pat Jones was well known here as a dashing and capable soldier, trusted by his superiors and respected by his men," reported a Little Valley paper, which quoted a veteran of the Thirty-Seventh New York: "We consider 'Pat' Jones, as we always called him, as good a soldier as was ever made and they made some good ones." The Ellicottville paper printed a warmhearted tribute: "It is not fulsome flattery to say of General Jones, that no man excelled him in any of the qualities that make up a genuine nature's nobleman. His generosity, self-abnegation, gentility and affability were unsurpassed. Withal, he possessed a conscious, unassuming pride that impressed all with whom he came in contact. He had a host of true, admiring friends and he was always sincerely true to them. He loved and served his country with devotion . . . The moist eyes of so many, far and wide, as they learn that General Jones has answered 'the last roll call,' are an eloquent tribute to his worth, valor and character."[23]

Jones's old army comrades took other steps to revere his memory. When the veterans of the 154th New York held their annual reunion in the fall, they passed resolutions commemorating their former commander. Writing to E. D. Northrup, a former officer described the "brave and gallant" Jones as "one of the best, and one of the most loyal men that ever stood in line." When Ellicottville's Grand Army of the Republic post organized a Sons of Veterans camp in 1902, they named it after the general.[24]

Thus, tributes were heaped upon the deceased. But even in his grave, Jones could not escape the specter of A. T. Stewart's moldering corpse. A scant three days after he died, the *New York Sun* dredged up the story. Old-time detectives at police headquarters, on seeing Jones's obituary, had recalled his role in the negotiations for the return of Stewart's remains. Now the *Sun* recapitulated the Romaine-Jones correspondence and Jones's open letter to Henry Hilton in a story reprinted as far away as Fort Worth, Texas.[25]

In January 1901 Sarah Jones filed an application for a widow's pension. She was living in Manhattan at the East Sixty-Seventh Street home of George Colyer, a family friend. Her husband had died a poor man, she testified in an affidavit, leaving her almost penniless. For the last two years of his life they had lived on his pension, a little money she made sewing, "and help as kind and indulgent friends could give to us." Any articles of monetary value had long since been sold for their support. Her few remaining household goods were worth little. Her husband had no life insurance, and his funeral expenses remained unpaid. A Pension Office special examiner described her as "a most elegant woman" who had been reduced to absolute want. She had pawned all of her possessions. But she initially hinged her application on the claim that her husband's death was caused by war-related maladies. As a result, she was not immediately granted a pension.[26]

The Colyer family had moved to Whitestone, Queens, by February 1902; Sarah accompanied them. By May of that year she had moved to the Philadelphia home of her sister, Mary Hannah Morris. In August 1904 she was living with her niece Helen E. Hoopes in the Philadelphia suburb of Ambler. Hoopes had made her home with the Jones family from 1873 (when she was three years old) to 1896, when she married and moved to Pennsylvania. Now she took in her aged and impoverished aunt, providing her with room and board. "She has always been like a mother to me," Hoopes said, "and I always treat her as such." James Jones also moved to Philadelphia but no longer lived with his mother. He was there in 1904, but his whereabouts after that date are unknown—as is whether he or his brother Thomas ever married or had children.[27]

Sarah Jones was granted a pension of $8 per month in 1904, retroactive to three years earlier. In 1908 a special act of Congress granted her an increase to $30 a month. She died in Philadelphia on December 17, 1912, at age seventy-five. The cause was anemia, "from nervous throat trouble." She was buried in Greenwood Cemetery (also known as Knights of Pythias Cemetery) in Philadelphia. Her niece Helen Hoopes paid the undertaker's $100 funeral bill, which included a dress for the deceased. Sarah left a $90 life insurance policy; the beneficiary was her sister Mary Morris, who was paid premiums of $125.85.[28]

Tangible reminders of Patrick Henry Jones are few. In 1897 New York City postmaster Charles W. Dayton presented the office with a composite image incorporating portraits of all the city's postmasters to date. Dayton had spent two and a half years gathering the paintings, engravings, and photographs of his predecessors, including Jones. The current location of the montage is unknown. Post office officials are uncertain whether it was put in storage or destroyed.[29]

Most of Jones's belongings have vanished, but bits of his legacy have surfaced in the century-plus since his death: carte de visite wartime portraits, various documents, and his Colt Police revolver, Model 1862. Jones is as uncommon in the world of Civil War memorabilia as he is in Irish American history.[30]

In 1923 an Ellicottville man donated to the Cattaraugus County Memorial and Historical Building in Little Valley the saddle and equipment that the 154th New York had presented to Jones during the Civil War. The saddle, with its presentation escutcheon on the pommel, sat in the museum's basement for many years. After the institution moved to Machias in 2004, it was awarded a grant to conserve the saddle and exhibit it in a custom-built case. It has been on display since 2005.[31]

The saddle's donor might have been the same person who gave the museum an unusual tribute to Jones. It was a hand-tinted 1865 lithograph after the painting *Sherman at Savannah, Ga.* by the soldier-artist Otto Botticher. The image depicted Sherman and his generals on horseback, galloping across

Savannah's parade ground. Nineteen officers were portrayed and identified in fine script in the print's bottom margin. Jones, however, was not included. To rectify that matter, an artistic admirer skillfully retouched one officer's portrait to appear as Jones and added Jones's name to the line of captions. The result was a one-of-a-kind image and tribute to a local hero. Posterity had neglected Jones, but someone had seen fit to remember him.[32]

Horace Greeley once ruminated, "Fame is a vapor; popularity an accident; riches take wings; the only earthly certainty is oblivion." Greeley's words were apt when applied to his friend Patrick Henry Jones. Jones deserved to be remembered as a leading nineteenth-century Irish American. He rose from obscurity to a place of prominence, traveling a long way from his humble roots in Ireland and Cattaraugus County to the podium at the Cooper Institute and visits to President Grant's Long Branch summer cottage. But after the rise came a fall. When the end came, his proud days were long behind him, and he was a sad shadow of his former self.[33]

Like most Irish Americans, Jones struggled under twin disadvantages: being a poor immigrant and being despised for it. From humble beginnings on a hardscrabble farm, he rose through ability, ambition, and hard work to a respectable position in his adopted community. Along the way he overcame the nativist discrimination that drove the rest of his Irish immigrant family from western New York to the western frontier. His brief career in journalism exposed him to a wider world, city life in Buffalo and an opportunity to see the West. But he returned to Cattaraugus County, where he found his true profession, the law, and made a wise choice of teacher and partner in Addison Rice. He defied a social taboo with a religiously mixed marriage that lasted his lifetime. His pleasant personality endeared him to his contemporaries regardless of political persuasion. In his first three decades he rose from impoverished youth to the life of a well-respected professional in the village he made his home. There he well might have remained, if not for the Civil War.

Jones's military career spanned the entire conflict and was marked by meritorious service. He was an able and brave soldier and a beloved officer. He earned consecutive promotions. At each level he was highly regarded by his superiors and the men under his command. His military career amply demonstrates how tightly politics permeated promotions and shaped the officer corps. He was politically astute, switching allegiance from the

Democratic to the Republican Party and finding powerful patrons in Reuben Fenton and Horace Greeley.

As one of the most prominent Irish American politicians in postwar New York City, Jones was widely considered honest and trustworthy during an era known for corruption and scandal. He appealed to members of both major parties. As a spoils system officeholder, he was praised for his integrity and competence, in stark contrast to certain of his crooked contemporaries. By all accounts he was a good man, which makes his ultimate decline all the sadder. Stripped of his fortune by the Norton embezzlement, he fell into poverty. Smeared by the Nolan scandal, he stood on his good name but was nevertheless diminished. His involvement in the Stewart grave robbery, however, was the major factor in hastening his downfall. Before the Stewart crime, Jones stood poised to carry his political career to new heights. After his involvement in the case became known, he began a steady slide into oblivion. His fine legacy as an Irish American soldier and political leader was overshadowed. Patrick Henry Jones's name is seldom if ever found in histories of the Civil War or the Irish in America—but it is certain to turn up in books about the infamous crime.

ACKNOWLEDGMENTS

My interest in Patrick Henry Jones dates back decades and runs parallel to my study of the regiment he led as colonel, the 154th New York. This biography completes a sextet of books on various aspects of the 154th's history. I posed by Jones's headstone circa 1980 for the author's photo on the jacket of my first book, a pose I saw fit to strike again thirty years later for this one. For years, as Jones made fleeting appearances in my other books, I daydreamed about the possibility of a biography. It was while preparing for a presentation on Jones at the Twenty-Third Annual Reunion of Descendants of the 154th New York, held in 2008 in his adopted hometown of Ellicottville, New York, that I finally expanded my research and determined to write a full biography. My thanks to Town of Ellicottville Historian Mary Elizabeth Dunbar for making the arrangements for the reunion that provided the impetus behind this book.

I am eternally grateful to the hundreds of descendants of members of the 154th New York who have shared material on their ancestors with me over the years and to friends who have likewise shared regimental sources. Space prevents me from listing them individually here, but my special thanks goes to those named in the bibliography. My sincere thanks also goes to the many helpful and dedicated staffers at the repositories listed, who eased my task in person or through correspondence.

Certain individuals deserve personal recognition. Joan N. Popyack of San Diego, California, granddaughter of Jones's brother Thomas B. Jones, provided valuable family information and toured Jones sites in Cattaraugus County with me when she attended our 2008 reunion. Thomas O'Hare of Williamsville, New York, descendant of Jones's uncle Edward Jones, shared copies of the Jones listings from the Clonmellon church records, solving the mystery of the Jones family's specific roots in Ireland. Genealogical researcher Mary Wallace Bridges of Amherst, New York, identified Jones's daughter, Anna, by locating her grave in Randolph, New York.

During research trips to New York City I enjoyed staying in Astoria, Queens, with my niece Jennifer Gambino and her husband, Frank, and my nephew Jake Rowland and his wife, Allison, and daughter, Mia. Wayne Fanebust of Sioux Falls, South Dakota, author of a book about the Stewart grave robbery, shared with me items from his files. Andrea Ignazio of the New York State Court of Appeals provided me with publications on the court's history. Marilyn Marcus, executive director of the Historical Society of the Courts of the State of New York in White Plains, notified me of a document relating to Jones's clerkship at the court of appeals. Bill Watkins, trustee at the Cattaraugus County Museum in Machias, New York, provided me with the newspaper reminiscences of a veteran of the Thirty-Seventh New York. Terry A. Johnston Jr. of Margate, New Jersey, informed me of several Thirty-Seventh New York sources. Paul K. McCutcheon of the National Postal Museum Library in Washington provided some obscure sources. When I asked for help to determine why Jones's election to the Military Order of the Loyal Legion of the United States was voided, Dr. Richard J. Sommers, Senior Historian at the U.S. Army Heritage and Education Center at Carlisle Barracks, Pennsylvania, searched records there and turned to Roger D. Hunt of Gettysburg, Pennsylvania, who found the answer.

While most of my research was conducted in New York City and Washington, two trips took my wife, Annette, and I further afield. Gary Sides of Dakota City, Nebraska, gave us a thorough tour of Dakota County's Jones family sites and shared Jones family information from his extensive collection of county historical materials. Annette's second cousin John Hannah, of Ruddington, Nottinghamshire, England, and his wife, Sandy, conducted us on a pleasant tour of England, Wales, and Ireland, where we visited the Jones family's ancestral sites in County Westmeath. Damien Shiels of Cork, Ireland, author of the "Irish in the American Civil War" weblog, dug up sources for me, suggested others, permitted me to guest post on my Jones project, critiqued my chapter on the Joneses' Irish years, and with his girlfriend, Sara Nylund, joined our party for a festive evening in Cork.

This is the fourth of my books that T. Michael Parrish has guided to publication as editor of the series Conflicting Worlds: New Dimensions of the American Civil War. I am deeply grateful to Mike for his support of my work and unerring advice over the past decade.

Three historians kindly reviewed the manuscript and made suggestions for its improvement. My thanks to James Marten of Marquette University; Robert C. Williams of Center Lovell, Maine; and Barnet Schecter of New York City for the time and effort they put into critiquing my work. The result of their recommendations is a much better book. Responsibility for any errors of fact or interpretation, however, is mine alone.

Our son, Karl Dunkelman, is now a married man, and Megan Dunkelman is a delightful addition to our family. The happy couple lives in Winter Park, Florida, a pleasant destination for occasional breaks from the routine in Rhode Island.

My wife, Annette, and I have been together since we were students in the class of 1969 at the Rhode Island School of Design. I simply could not have accomplished what I have been able to do in Civil War history and other endeavors without her love and support over the decades. Ours—like Patrick and Sarah Jones's—is a lifetime bond. I am grateful to dedicate this book to the love of my life.

NOTES

INTRODUCTION

1. James Marten, *Sing Not War: The Lives of Union and Confederate Veterans in Gilded Age America* (Chapel Hill: University of North Carolina Press, 2011), 2, 9–10, 243.

2. Christian B. Keller, "New Perspectives in Civil War Ethnic History and Their Implications for Twenty-First-Century Scholarship," in *This Distracted and Anarchical People: New Answers for Old Questions about the Civil War–Era North*, edited by Andrew L. Slap and Michael Thomas Smith (New York: Fordham University Press, 2013), 123–25, 128–29, 131–33, 138.

3. Michael A. Gordon, *The Orange Riots: Irish Political Violence in New York City, 1870 and 1871* (Ithaca: Cornell University Press, 2009), 6; Seymour J. Mandelbaum, *Boss Tweed's New York* (Chicago: Ivan R. Dee, 1990), 132–33.

4. Ezra J. Warner, *Generals in Blue: Lives of the Union Commanders* (Baton Rouge: Louisiana State University Press, 1964), 59–60, 87–88, 93–94, 165–66, 249–50, 254–55, 265–56, 276–77, 317–18, 444–45, 465–66, 491–92, 603; Damian Shiels, *The Irish in the American Civil War* (Dublin: History Press Ireland, 2013), 105–14.

5. "General Patrick H. Jones," *Ellicottville Post*, August 15, 1900, 3; Shiels, *Irish in the American Civil War*, 7, 8. Jones did merit a brief mention as one of some five hundred influential Irish Americans in John D. Crimmins, *Irish-American Historical Miscellany* (New York: Published by the author, 1905), 371, 414.

6. Sarah Morris Jones affidavit, January 30, 1903, Patrick Henry Jones pension records, National Archives, Washington, D.C. (hereafter cited as PHJ PR, NA).

1. FROM COUNTY WESTMEATH TO CATTARAUGUS COUNTY

1. Jay P. Dolan, *The Irish Americans: A History* (New York: Bloomsbury Press, 2008), 17, 58–59, 108; Thomas Keneally, *The Great Shame: and the Triumph of the Irish in the English-Speaking World* (New York: Nan A. Talese, Doubleday, 1999), 21; Maire O'Brien and Conor Cruise O'Brien, *Ireland: A Concise History* (London: Thames & Hudson, 1999), 27, 61; Samuel Lewis, *A Topographical Dictionary of Ireland* (London: S. Lewis & Co., 1837), 2:695; *An Introduction to the Architectural Heritage of County Westmeath* (Dublin: National Inventory of Architectural Heritage, 2007), 5, 7.

2. Lewis, *Topographical Dictionary of Ireland*, 2:695–99; Michael Herity, ed., *Ordnance Survey Letters: County Longford and Westmeath* (Dublin: Fourmasters Press, 2011), 118; *Introduction to the Architectural Heritage of County Westmeath*, 7, 33; Sister Mary Gilbert Kelly, *Catholic Immigrant Colonization Projects in the United States, 1815–1860* (New York: United States Catholic Historical Society, 1939), 212; Tom Hunt, "Mullingar Sport in the 1890s: Communities at Play," in *Mullingar: Essays on the History of a Midlands Town in the 19th Century*, edited by Mary Farrell (Mullingar, Ireland: Westmeath County Library, 2002), 4–6; Seamus O'Brien, "Mullingar in Mid-Century—Famine, Execution and an Attempted Uprising by the People," in Farrell,

Mullingar, 94, 99–103; Ruth Illingworth, "Transport 1806–1905," in Farrell, *Mullingar,* 154–56; Micheal O'Conlain and Ruth Illingworth, "Mullingar Town Commission," in Farrell, *Mullingar,* 178–80; Eugene Sheridan, *The Parish of Clonmellon/Killallon: Including the Medieval Parishes of Killua, Clonamey and Killallon: Faith, History, Folklore and Memories of Our Parish* (Published by the author, 2001), 65, 76, 77–78.

3. Clonmellon Roman Catholic Parish records, courtesy of Thomas O'Hare, Williamsville, N.Y.; Lewis, *A Topographical Dictionary of Ireland,* 1:371, 2:121–22, 155, 411–12; *Introduction to the Architectural Heritage of County Westmeath,* 36, 39, 43, 49; Paul Connell, "Bishop John Cantwell," in Farrell, *Mullingar,* 41–42; Illingworth, "Transport 1806–1905," in Farrell, *Mullingar,* 126–37; O'Conlain and Illingworth, "Mullingar Town Commission," in Farrell, *Mullingar,* 167, 180–81.

4. "Westmeath Voters 1832," *Irish Genealogist* 5, no. 2 (1975): 234–49; 5, no. 6 (1979): 772–89; 6, no. 1 (1980): 77–98; Sheridan, *Parish of Clonmellon/Killallon,* 65; William Adams, ed., *The Historical Gazetteer and Biographical Memorial of Cattaraugus County, New York* (Syracuse: Lyman, Horton & Co., 1893), 359; S. R. Harlow and H. H. Boone, *Life Sketches of the State Officers, Senators, and Members of the Assembly of the State of New York, in 1867* (Albany: Weed, Parsons & Co., 1867), 46; Patrick Henry Jones (hereafter cited as PHJ) to Brig. Gen. L. Thomas, May 22, 1865, Letters Received by the Commission Branch of the Adjutant General's Office, 1863–1870, National Archives; Clonmellon Roman Catholic Parish records.

5. O'Brien and O'Brien, *Ireland,* 102–3, 105–6; Sheridan, *Parish of Clonmellon/Killallon,* 65–66, 74; Dolan, *Irish Americans,* 28–29, 35–36, 68; Dale T. Knobel, *Paddy and the Republic: Ethnicity and Nationality in Antebellum America* (Middletown, Conn.: Wesleyan University Press, 1986), 24, 45.

6. Dolan, *Irish Americans,* 36–39, 76–77; Illingworth, "Transport 1806–1905," in Farrell, *Mullingar,* 132.

7. "The Death of Grandma Jones," *North Nebraska Eagle* (Dakota City), October 18, 1888; "Obituary [Edward C. Jones]," *North Nebraska Eagle,* May 7, 1880; M. M. Warner, *Warner's History of Dakota County, Nebraska* (Dakota City, Neb.: Lyons Mirror Job Office, 1893), 144, 177; "The Story of Catherine Jones Twohig," in "An Epic of Early Iowa: Father Trecey's Colonization Scheme," *Iowa Catholic Historical Review* 3 (1931): 8; John M. Clemens to author, August 23, 2001; Joseph M. Clemens to author, April 25, 2002; Adams, *Historical Gazetteer,* 359; Harlow and Boone, *Life Sketches,* 46.

8. Passenger Lists of Vessels Arriving at New York, 1820–1897, M-237, Roll 42, National Archives; "Commercial Line of Packets for New York," *Boston Pilot,* June 6, 1840, 160; Dolan, *Irish Americans,* 37–38.

9. "Commercial Line of Packets for New York," *Boston Pilot,* June 6, 1840, 160; Dolan, *Irish Americans,* 37–38; Friedrich Kapp, *Immigration and the Commissioners of Emigration of the State of New York* (New York: Nation Press, 1870), 24–27, 33; Passenger Lists of Vessels Arriving at New York, 1820–1897, M-237, Roll 42, National Archives.

10. "Story of Catherine Jones Twohig," 8; Franklin Ellis, ed., *History of Cattaraugus County, New York* (Philadelphia: L. H. Everts, 1879), 52–56; Dolan, *Irish Americans,* 42–46. Catherine Jones Twohig mistakenly stated that her father worked on the Erie Canal, which was completed more than a decade before the family's arrival in America.

11. 1840 U.S. Census, Hinsdale, Cattaraugus County, New York; "Story of Catherine Jones Twohig," 8; James Brown Scott, ed., *Cases on Quasi-Contracts* (New York: Baker, Voorhis & Co.,

1905), 641; Joel Tiffany, *Condensed Digest of the Court of Appeals Reports of the State of New York* (Albany: Weare C. Little, 1866), 56, 110, 240, 241; Dolan, *Irish Americans*, 46. The Genesee Valley Canal never lived up to expectations and was closed and abandoned by New York State in 1878. Ellis, *History of Cattaraugus County*, 55.

12. 1850 U.S. Census, Little Valley, Cattaraugus County, N.Y.; Adams, *Historical Gazetteer*, 573, 580; Kelly, *Catholic Immigrant Colonization Projects*, 14–15; "Fish Hill Residents Do Not Want to Lose Name," *Ellicottville Post*, February 23, 1938.

13. "Story of Catherine Jones Twohig," 8–9. Catherine incorrectly identified the circus as Barnum and Bailey's, which was not organized until decades later.

14. Adams, *Historical Gazetteer*, 359; Harlow and Boone, *Life Sketches*, 46; "Ellicottville Union School," *Cattaraugus Republican*, September 4, 1850, 3; "Gen. P. H. Jones," *Cattaraugus Freeman*, September 27, 1865; "Buffalo Sentinel," *Cattaraugus Republican*, June 9, 1853, 2.

15. Walter A. McDougall, *Throes of Democracy: The American Civil War Era 1829–1877* (New York: Harper, 2008), 104–6; Arthur M. Schlesinger Jr., ed., *The Almanac of American History* (New York: Bramhall House, 1983), 148–50, 239, 240; James M. McPherson, *Battle Cry of Freedom: The Civil War Era* (New York: Oxford University Press, 1988), 26–30; Florence E. Gibson, *The Attitudes of the New York Irish toward State and National Affairs, 1848–1892* (New York: Columbia University Press, 1951), 14.

16. Harlow and Boone, *Life Sketches*, 46; Dolan, *Irish Americans*, 55; "Buffalo Sentinel," *Cattaraugus Republican*, June 9, 1853, 2.

17. Harlow and Boone, *Life Sketches*, 46; Frank H. Severance, comp., "The Periodical Press of Buffalo," *Publication of the Buffalo Historical Society* 19 (1915): 259–60, 264–65; "Buffalo Sentinel," *Cattaraugus Republican*, June 9, 1853, 2; "McGee Goes to New York," *Boston Pilot*, May 28, 1853, 4; "Buffalo Sentinel," *Boston Pilot*, June 11, 1853: 5; "Bernard Killian Dies," *New York Times*, November 9, 1914, 9; Jack Morgan, *Through American and Irish Wars: The Life and Times of General Thomas W. Sweeney 1820–1892* (Dublin: Irish Academic Press, 2006), 56, 129. Killian subsequently moved west and edited a Catholic newspaper in St. Louis. He served in the Civil War as a captain in a Missouri regiment, played an active role in Fenian affairs, and edited the *New York Tablet* (David Power Conyngham's paper). He practiced law in New York City, wrote poetry, and lived for some years on Staten Island.

18. Harlow and Boone, *Life Sketches*, 46; Adams, *Historical Gazetteer*, 329, 359; Ellis, *History of Cattaraugus County*, opposite 255; "Business Cards," *Cattaraugus Freeman*, August 14, 1856: 3; McPherson, *Battle Cry of Freedom*, 27–31; Gibson, *Attitudes of the New York Irish*, 89–90.

19. Dolan, *Irish Americans*, 55, 58–59, 60, 62; Knobel, *Paddy and the Republic*, 30, 36, 46, 60–63, 70, 81–85, 88, 90–128, 132–43, 148–49, 181.

20. Dolan, *Irish Americans*, 82, 85–86, 96–98; Tyler Anbinder, *Nativism and Slavery: The Northern Know Nothings and the Politics of the 1850s* (New York: Oxford University Press, 1992), ix; Kelly, *Catholic Immigrant Colonization Projects*, 213; Steven P. Erie, *Rainbow's End: Irish-Americans and the Dilemmas of Urban Machine Politics, 1840–1985* (Berkeley: University of California Press, 1988), 25; Susannah Ural Bruce, *The Harp and the Eagle: Irish-American Volunteers and the Union Army, 1861–1865* (New York: New York University Press, 2006), 30; Lawrence J. McCaffrey, "Forging Forward and Looking Back," in *The New York Irish*, edited by Ronald H. Bayor and Timothy J. Meagher (Baltimore: Johns Hopkins University Press, 1996), 214; Gibson, *Attitudes of the New York Irish*, 12, 78.

21. Anbinder, *Nativism and Slavery*, 3–7, 9–33; Kelly, *Catholic Immigrant Colonization Projects*, 213–16; Mitchell Snay, *Horace Greeley and the Politics of Reform in Nineteenth-Century America* (Lanham, Md.: Rowman & Littlefield, 2011), 122–23; Gibson, *Attitudes of the New York Irish*, 70–85.

22. Anbinder, *Nativism and Slavery*, 36–37, 43–53, 75, 76, 84–86, 104–20, 166, 183–85, 194–245; Adams, *Historical Gazetteer*, 91.

23. "Only Spring and Trees Now Mark Place of Father Trecy's Settlement at St. John's, 70 Years Ago," *North Nebraska Eagle*, October 22, 1925; "Story of Father Trecy Colony and Ill-Fated Settlement of St. John's," *Sioux City (Iowa) Journal*, July 25, 1954, 9; James P. Shannon, *Catholic Colonization on the Western Frontier* (New Haven: Yale University Press, 1957), 19, 37–39; "A Message from the 'Pioneer,'" *Boston Pilot*, September 7, 1850, 1; "The West," *Boston Pilot*, November 2, 1850, 4; "Letter from the Bishop of Dubuque," *Boston Pilot*, October 5, 1850, 5; "The West," *Boston Pilot*, May 10, 1851, 4; "Emigrants, Attention!" *Boston Pilot*, July 17, 1852, 4; "Things in Dubuque," *Boston Pilot*, April 23, 1853, 6; "Iowa Correspondence," *Boston Pilot*, May 21, 1853, 3; "Iowa Correspondence," *Boston Pilot*, July 3, 1853, 6; "An Irish Settlement in Iowa," *Boston Pilot*, November 20, 1852, 2; Interview of Ellen Jones Boler by Edna B. Pearson, October 31, 1938, courtesy of Gary Sides, Dakota City, Neb. (hereafter cited as Ellen Jones Boler interview); "Story of Catherine Jones Twohig," 9; McDougall, *Throes of Democracy*, 289–93.

24. Kelly, *Catholic Immigrant Colonization Projects*, 1–4, 143–63; Shannon, *Catholic Colonization*, 32–37.

25. "Story of Catherine Jones Twohig," 9–10; "Only Spring and Trees," *North Nebraska Eagle*, October 22, 1925; Ellen Jones Boler interview.

26. "Story of Catherine Jones Twohig," 10; "Only Spring and Trees," *North Nebraska Eagle*, October 22, 1925; Ellen Jones Boler interview; Trecy biography by David P. Conyngham in an unpublished manuscript, "The Chaplains of the Federal and Confederate Armies," David Power Conyngham Papers, University of Notre Dame Archives, Notre Dame, Ind.; John Fitch, *Annals of the Army of the Cumberland* (Philadelphia: J. B. Lippincott, 1864), 326–30; "The Rt. Rev. Bishop of Dubuque at Council Bluff," *Boston Pilot*, July 15, 1854, 4; "Homes in the West," *Boston Pilot*, September 9, 1854, 5; "Diocese of Dubuque," *Boston Pilot*, October 7, 1854, 3; Kelly, *Catholic Immigrant Colonization Projects*, 150, 239–40.

27. "Only Spring and Trees," *North Nebraska Eagle*, October 22, 1925; "Story of Catherine Jones Twohig," 10–11; Warner, *Warner's History of Dakota County*, 177; "Obituary [Edward C. Jones]," *North Nebraska Eagle*, May 7, 1880; "Great Grandmother of Ten Presents Claim to Title of Earliest Living S.C. Pioneer," *North Nebraska Eagle*, December 27, 1923; Kelly, *Catholic Immigrant Colonization Projects*, 238–40.

28. "Things in Dubuque," *Boston Pilot*, March 15, 1856, 4; "The Bishops and the Buffalo Convention," *Boston Pilot*, April 26, 1856, 5; "Piopolis," *Boston Pilot*, April 26, 1856, 5; Shannon, *Catholic Colonization*, 37; Kelly, *Catholic Immigrant Colonization Projects*, 217–38, 240, 248.

29. "Only Spring and Trees," *North Nebraska Eagle*, October 22, 1925; "Story of Catherine Jones Twohig," 11; Gertrude Henderson, "The Expedition and the Colony," in "An Epic of Early Iowa: Father Trecey's Colonization Scheme," *Iowa Catholic Historical Review* 3 (1931): 4–5; "St. John's 1856," Nebraska Historical Marker, Jackson; Ellen Jones Boler interview; "Obituary [Edward C. Jones]," *North Nebraska Eagle*, May 7, 1880; Warner, *Warner's History of Dakota County*, 144, 177, 198; Kelly, *Catholic Immigrant Colonization Projects*, 248–49; "Gertrude Henderson Furnished the Following Writeup of J. F. Duggan's Journey to Dakota County," *North*

Nebraska Eagle, June 24, 1924; "Great Grandmother of Ten Presents Claim to Title of Earliest Living S.C. Pioneer," *North Nebraska Eagle,* December 27, 1923; "Sioux City's First Thanksgiving Day Feast Described by Only Woman Survivor of Those Who Attended Dinner," *Sioux City (Iowa) Journal,* November 25, 1926; "Almost Half a Century Ago," *North Nebraska Eagle,* May 30, 1901; "History of Colony," *North Nebraska Eagle,* July 26, 1906; "Descending the Missouri River," *Boston Pilot,* July 26, 1856, 3.

30. "Gertrude Henderson Furnished the Following Writeup," *North Nebraska Eagle,* June 24, 1924; Henderson, "Expedition and the Colony," 5–7; Kelly, *Catholic Immigrant Colonization Projects,* 249–50.

31. "St. Patrick's Colony, Nebraska," *Boston Pilot,* February 14, 1857, 3; Kelly, *Catholic Immigrant Colonization Projects,* 253.

32. "Questions for the St. Patrick's Colonists," *Boston Pilot,* March 7, 1857, 3; "Emigration," *Boston Pilot,* July 11, 1857, 5; "Emigration," *Boston Pilot,* July 11, 1857, 5; "Western Emigration—Nebraska," *Boston Pilot,* July 25, 1857, 4; "Notice to All," *Boston Pilot,* July 25, 1857, 4; "Emigration to the West," *Boston Pilot,* August 1, 1857, 4; "St. Patrick's Settlement," *Boston Pilot,* August 29, 1857, 2; "Western Emigration," *Boston Pilot,* September 5, 1857, 6; "St. Patrick's Settlement, N.T.," *Boston Pilot,* September 5, 1857, 6; "More about St. Patrick's Settlement," *Boston Pilot,* September 12, 1857, 2; Kelly, *Catholic Immigrant Colonization Projects,* 253–55.

33. Kelly, *Catholic Immigrant Colonization Projects,* 251–53; Shannon, *Catholic Colonization,* 37–38.

34. "Only Spring and Trees," *North Nebraska Eagle,* October 22, 1925; Henderson, "Expedition and the Colony," 7; "Gertrude Henderson Furnished the Following Writeup," *North Nebraska Eagle,* June 24, 1924; Warner, *Warner's History of Dakota County,* 45, 53–54, 79; "Descending the Missouri River," *Boston Pilot,* July 26, 1856, 3; "St. John's 1856," Nebraska Historical Marker; Kelly, *Catholic Immigrant Colonization Projects,* 256–57.

35. Kelly, *Catholic Immigrant Colonization Projects,* 256–57; Shannon, *Catholic Colonization,* 38–39; "The Rev. Jeremiah F. Trecy," in "An Epic of Early Iowa: Father Trecey's Colonization Scheme," *Iowa Catholic Historical Review* 3 (1931): 4.

36. Ellen Jones Boler interview; "Obituary [Edward C. Jones]," *North Nebraska Eagle,* May 7, 1880; Warner, *Warner's History of Dakota County,* 144, 177; "Hon. Edward Jones," *Cattaraugus Freeman,* December 31, 1857: 2; "Hon. Edward S. Jones," *Cattaraugus Freeman,* January 28, 1858, 3.

37. "The Death of Grandma Jones," *North Nebraska Eagle,* October 18, 1888; "[Thomas B. Jones] Died on Friday Morning," *North Nebraska Eagle,* November 27, 1914; "The Remains of Mrs. James McHenry," *North Nebraska Eagle,* September 21, 1922; Headstones, St. John's Cemetery, Dakota County, Neb.

38. "Lyceum," *Cattaraugus Freeman,* November 20, 1856, 2; "The Citizens of Ellicottville," *American Union,* November 21, 1856, 2; Ellis, *History of Cattaraugus County,* 72, 166, 257; William King Laidlaw, *St. John's Church of Ellicottville* (Ellicottville, N.Y.: Published by the author, 1977), 4, 14.

39. Sarah Morris Jones affidavit, April 1, 1901, PHJ PR, NA; "Married," *Cattaraugus Freeman,* December 22, 1859, 3; "Married," *American Union,* December 23, 1859, 3; Schlesinger, *Almanac of American History,* 149.

40. Adams, *Historical Gazetteer,* 87–88, 89–90, 91–92.

41. "Democratic Club," *American Union* (Ellicottville), January 20, 1860, 2; "Democratic Club," *American Union,* February 3, 1860, 2; "The Soft Clique," *American Union,* March 30, 1860, 2.

42. Adams, *Historical Gazetteer*, 359, 363–64, 370.

43. 1860 U.S. Census, Ellicottville, Cattaraugus County, N.Y.; Liber 50, pp. 521–22, and Liber 59, pp. 342–43, Deed Books, Cattaraugus County Clerk's Office, Little Valley, N.Y.

44. Schlesinger, *Almanac of American History*, 275–77.

45. "Business Cards," *Cattaraugus Freeman*, December 20, 1860, 3.

2. THE IRISH RIFLES

1. "Our Esteemed and Patriotic Friend P. H. Jones," *Cattaraugus Freeman*, April 25, 1861, 2.

2. "Enthusiastic Rally for the Union!" *Cattaraugus Freeman*, April 25, 1861, 2.

3. "Our Town," *Cattaraugus Freeman*, May 16, 1861, 2; "Company K," *Cattaraugus Freeman*, April 25, 1861, 2; PHJ to John Manley, May 10, 1861, quoted in Ellis, *History of Cattaraugus County*, 100.

4. Ellis, *History of Cattaraugus County*, 280–82.

5. Ellis, *History of Cattaraugus County*, 100; Adams, *Historical Gazetteer*, 208; "Company K," *American Union*, September 3, 1858, 2; "Patriotic Meeting at Allegany," *Olean Times*, May 4, 1861, 2.

6. Patrick Henry Jones military records, National Archives (hereafter cited as PHJ MR, NA); "Patrick H. Jones," *Cattaraugus Freeman*, May 16, 1861, 2; "Off for Elmira," *Cattaraugus Freeman*, May 23, 1861, 2; Adams, *Historical Gazetteer*, 1159.

7. Ellis, *History of Cattaraugus County*, 100; William Bird Jr. to his father, May 20 and 24, 1861; "Off for Elmira," *Cattaraugus Freeman*, May 23, 1861, 2; "Another Company Gone," *Olean Times*, May 25, 1861, 2; "From Our Volunteers!" *Cattaraugus Freeman*, May 30, 1861, 2. Quotes from unpublished letters and diaries have been rendered with standardized spelling, punctuation, and case.

8. Ellis, *History of Cattaraugus County*, 100; "The War," *American Union*, May 31, 1861, 2; "From Our Volunteers!" *Cattaraugus Freeman*, June 6, 1861, 1; "Simon," *Cattaraugus Freeman*, June 13, 1861, 2; Nelson Loomis diary, May 26 and June 2, 1861, U.S. Army Military History Institute, U.S. Army Heritage and Education Center, Carlisle, Pa.

9. "From Our Volunteers!" *Cattaraugus Freeman*, June 6, 1861, 1.

10. Bird to his father, May 30, 1861; "From Our Volunteers!" *Cattaraugus Freeman*, June 6, 1861, 2; "The 75th 'Irish Rifles,'" *Irish-American*, June 1, 1861, 2; Frederick Phisterer, *New York in the War of the Rebellion, 1861 to 1865* (Albany: Weed, Parsons & Co., 1890), 400–401.

11. Dolan, *Irish Americans*, 98; Shiels, *Irish in the American Civil War*, 12, 45, 74; Bruce, *Harp and the Eagle*, 2, 6, 50–52, 54, 55, 59, 60; Susannah J. Ural, "Ye Sons of Green Erin Assemble: Northern Irish American Catholics and the Union War Effort, 1861–1865," in *Civil War Citizens: Race, Ethnicity, and Identity in America's Bloodiest Conflict*, edited by Susannah J. Ural (New York: New York University Press, 2010), 99–101, 103; Edward K. Spann, "Union Green: The Irish Community and the Civil War," in *The New York Irish*, edited by Ronald H. Bayor and Timothy J. Meagher (Baltimore: Johns Hopkins University Press, 1996), 193, 195, 203.

12. Bird to his father, May 30, 1861; "From Our Volunteers!" *Cattaraugus Freeman*, June 6, 1861: 2; "Judge John H. McCunn," *New York Times*, July 7, 1872: 1; Ellis, *History of Cattaraugus County*, 100–101; Frank A. Boyle, *A Party of Mad Fellows: The Story of the Irish Regiments in the Army of the Potomac* (Dayton, Ohio: Morningside, 1996), 31–33; Denis Tilden Lynch, *The Wild Seventies* (New York: D. Appleton-Century, 1941), 18, 20; Gibson, *Attitudes of the New York Irish*, 123; William Clark interview notes, December 7, 1894, Edwin Dwight Northrup Papers, #4190,

Department of Manuscripts and University Archives, Cornell University, Ithaca, N.Y. (hereafter cited as EDN Papers).

13. "The Thirty-Seventh Regiment at the Battery," *New York Times*, June 7, 1861, 8; Bird to his parents, June 7, 1861; "From Our Volunteers!" *Cattaraugus Freeman*, June 13, 1861, 2; "Col. M'Cunn's Regiment," *New York Times*, June 8, 1861, 9; *Irish-American*, June 15, 1861: 2; "New York Correspondence," *American Union*, June 14, 1861, 2; "New York Correspondence," *American Union*, June 21, 1861, 2; PHJ MR, NA; Edwin G. Burroughs and Mike Wallace, *Gotham: A History of New York City to 1898* (New York: Oxford University Press, 1999), 456, 711, 738.

14. "Our New York Correspondence," and "The Letter Which We Publish To-day," *Cattaraugus Freeman*, June 13, 1861, 2; Adams, *Historical Gazetteer*, 326–27.

15. PHJ MR, NA; "Thirty-Seventh Regiment—Battery," *New York Times*, June 12, 1861, 8; "Camp Weed," *Cattaraugus Freeman*, June 13, 1861, 2; "The New-York Medical Association" and "Col. McCunn's Regiment," *New York Times*, June 13, 1861, 9; Jerome Andrews to his father, June 14, 1861 New York State Library, Albany; "Personal," *Cattaraugus Freeman*, June 20, 1861, 2; "Correspondence," *Cattaraugus Freeman*, June 20, 1861: 2; "From Our Volunteers!" *Cattaraugus Freeman*, June 27, 1861, 2; "Our New York Correspondence" *Cattaraugus Freeman*, June 27, 1861, 2; Loomis diary, June 15, 1861.

16. "Col. J. H. M'Cunn's Regiment," *New York Times*, June 23, 1861, 8; "Departure of the 37th Regiment," *Irish-American*, June 29, 1861, 2; "The following extract from a letter," *American Union*, July 6, 1861, 3; Andrews, no salutation, June 25, 1861; Bird to his father, June 26, 1861; "From Our Volunteers!" *Cattaraugus Freeman*, July 4, 1861, 2; "Through Baltimore to Washington!" *Cattaraugus Freeman*, July 11, 1861, 2; Reverend Peter Tissot, "Year with the Army of the Potomac," United States Catholic Historical Society, *Historical Records and Studies* 3, pt. 1 (January 1903): 43; Conyngham, "Chaplains of the Federal and Confederate Armies"; Boyle, *Party of Mad Fellows*, 34; Loomis diary, June 23–24, 1862.

17. Tissot, "Year with the Army of the Potomac," 43; "From Washington," *Cattaraugus Freeman*, July 4, 1861, 2; Andrews, no salutation, June 25, 1861; Bird to his father, June 26 and July 3, 1861; "Review of the Thirty-Seventh," *New York Times*, June 27, 1861, 1; "Visit of the President and Mrs. Lincoln to Col. M'Cunn's Regiment," *New York Times*, June 28, 1861, 1; "From Our Volunteers!" *Cattaraugus Freeman*, July 11, 1861, 1; "The Thirty-Seventh Regiment," *American Union*, July 19, 1861, 2; "From a 'Bold Soldier Boy' from Cattaraugus," *American Union*, September 6, 1861, 2.

18. "Personal," *Cattaraugus Freeman*, June 27, 1861, 3; PHJ MR, NA; "From Our Volunteers!" *Cattaraugus Freeman*, July 18, 1861, 1; Marvin S. Cole, "With the 37th N.Y.V. Inf.: Bull Run Battle," *Ellicottville Post*, July 26, 1911, 6.

19. Bird to his father, July 17, 1861; "From Our Volunteers!" *Cattaraugus Freeman*, July 25, 1861, 2; Ellis, *History of Cattaraugus County*, 101; Loomis diary, July 4, 1861.

20. James A. Rawley, *Edwin D. Morgan, 1811–1883: Merchant in Politics* (New York: Columbia University Press, 1955), 4–9, 12, 16, 18 20–24, 33, 37, 47, 49, 57–58, 77, 82, 107, 113, 118–19, 152.

21. Butler F. Dilley, *Biographical and Portrait Cyclopedia of Chautauqua County, New York* (Philadelphia: John M. Gresham, 1891), 326–27; James G. Wilson and John Fiske, *Appleton's Cyclopedia of American Biography* (New York: D. Appleton, 1887), 2:430; *The National Cyclopedia of American Biography* (New York: James T. White, 1893), 3:51–52; Allen Johnson and Dumas Malone, *Dictionary of American Biography* (New York: Charles Scribner's Sons, 1931), 6:326.

22. Tissot, "Year with the Army of the Potomac," 45; Bird to his father, July 17, 1861; "From Our Volunteers!" *Cattaraugus Freeman*, July 25, 1861, 2; "Dispatch to the Associated Press," *New York Times*, July 22, 1861, 1; "Our Volunteers!" *Cattaraugus Freeman*, July 25, 1861, 2; "The Cattaraugus Guards," *American Union*, July 26, 1861, 2; Ellis, *History of Cattaraugus County*, 100; Loomis diary, July 14, 1861.

23. William C. Davis, *Battle at Bull Run: A History of the First Major Campaign of the Civil War* (Garden City, N.Y.: Doubleday, 1977), 76; Bird to his father, July 17, 1861; "Dispatch to the Associated Press," *New York Times*, July 22, 1861, 1; Tissot, "Year with the Army of the Potomac," 45; "Our Volunteers!" *Cattaraugus Freeman*, July 25, 1861, 2; Loomis diary, July 17–21, 1861.

24. Cole, "With the 37th N.Y.V. Inf.: Bull Run Battle," *Ellicottville Post*, July 26, 1911; William Clark interview notes, December 7, 1894, EDN; Davis, *Battle at Bull Run*, 242.

25. Tissot, "Year with the Army of the Potomac," 45–46; U.S. War Department, *The War of the Rebellion: A Compilation of the Official Records of the Union and Confederate Armies* (Washington, D.C.: Government Printing Office, 1880–1901), ser. 1, 2:748, 753, 754 (hereafter cited as *OR*); "From Our Volunteers!" *Cattaraugus Freeman*, August 1, 1861, 2; Cole, "With the 37th N.Y.V. Inf.: Bull Run Battle," *Ellicottville Post*, July 26, 1911.

26. Tissot, "Year with the Army of the Potomac," 46; Bird to his father, July 23 and 25, 1861; Andrews, no salutation, July 25, 1861; "From Our Volunteers!" *Cattaraugus Freeman*, August 1, 1861, 2; Cole, "With the 37th N.Y.V. Inf.: Bull Run Battle," *Ellicottville Post*, July 26, 1911; Loomis diary, July 21–24, 1861; "Washington Correspondence," *Irish-American*, August 10, 1861, 2.

27. Loomis diary, July 24, 1861; Bird to his father, July 25, 1861; Andrews, no salutation, July 25, 1861; "From Our Volunteers!" *Cattaraugus Freeman*, August 1, 1861, 2.

28. Tissot, "Year with the Army of the Potomac," 46–7; Bird to his father, August 1, 1861; "From Our Volunteers!" *Cattaraugus Freeman*, August 8, 1861, 2; "Washington Correspondence," *Irish-American*, August 10, 1861, 2; Loomis diary, July 30–31, 1861.

29. "The Body of Col. Cameron," *New York Times*, August 21, 1861, 3.

30. PHJ MR, NA; Ellis, *History of Cattaraugus County*, 101; "From Our Volunteers!" *Cattaraugus Freeman*, August 15, 1861, 2; "From Washington," *Cattaraugus Freeman*, August 15, 1861, 2; Loomis diary, August 5, 1861.

31. Bird to his brother, August 7, 1861; Marvin S. Cole, "The Thirty-Seventh: Long Bridge and Fort Washington," *Ellicottville Post*, August 23, 1911, 7; Loomis diary, August 23 and 30, 1861.

32. "From Our Volunteers!" *Cattaraugus Freeman*, August 15, 1861, 2; "One of the Cattaraugus soldiers," *American Union*, August 9, 1861, 2; Cole, "With the 37th N.Y.V. Inf.: Bull Run Battle," *Ellicottville Post*, July 26, 1911.

33. "From Washington," *Cattaraugus Freeman*, August 15, 1861, 2; Ellis, *History of Cattaraugus County*, 281; "Letters," *American Union*, August 16, 1861, 2.

34. "Col. McCunn in Difficulty," *New York Times*, August 16, 1861, 1; "Reports from Alexandria," *New York Times*, August 17, 1861, 9; "From Washington," *Cattaraugus Freeman*, August 22, 1861, 2; "The Sentence of Col. McCunn," *New York Times*, August 31, 1861, 1; "The Case of Col. McCunn," *New York Times*, September 2, 1861, 3; "We Regret to Learn," *Irish-American*, September 7, 1861, 2.

35. "Special Dispatch from Washington," *New York Times*, September 4, 1861, 1; "We Regret to Learn," 2; "The Thirty-Seventh New-York," *New York Times*, September 11, 1861, 1;

"Dismissed," *New York Times,* September 14, 1861, 1; "Col. M'Cunn Sent from Washington," *New York Times,* September 20, 1861, 1; "From Our Volunteers!" *Cattaraugus Freeman,* September 26, 1861, 2; "Colonel McCunn," *American Union,* September 27, 1861, 2; "Affairs of the New-York Thirty-Seventh," *New York Times,* September 29, 1861, 1; "The 37th Regiment," *Irish-American,* September 14, 1861, 2; "The 37th Regiment," *Irish-American,* September 28, 1861, 2; "The Court Martial," *Irish-American,* October 5, 1861, 2; Tissot, "Year with the Army of the Potomac," 50–51.

36. "A Note from City Judge McCunn," *New York Times,* April 21, 1862, 2; "Judge John H. McCunn," *New York Times,* July 7, 1872, 1; Lynch, *Wild Seventies,* 240–42, 245.

37. Capt. L. G. Harmon to Gen. L. Thomas, September 9, 1861, PHJ MR, NA; "From Our Volunteers!" *Cattaraugus Freeman,* September 26, 1861, 2; Bird to James Bird, September 26, 1861; "Lieutenant Patrick H. Jones," *Cattaraugus Freeman,* September 26, 1861, 3; Loomis diary, September 20, 1861.

38. "We call attention," *Cattaraugus Freeman,* October 3, 1861, 3; "Departure of More Volunteers," *American Union,* October 11, 1861, 3; "From Washington," *Cattaraugus Freeman,* October 17, 1861, 2; "Recruits for the Cattaraugus Companies at Fort Washington," *Cattaraugus Freeman,* October 17, 1861, 2; "Recruits Wanted," *Cattaraugus Freeman,* October 17, 1861, 3; "Enlisting," *American Union,* October 18, 1861, 2; "Lieut. P. H. Jones," *Cattaraugus Freeman,* October 31, 1861, 2; "More Volunteers," *American Union,* November 1, 1861, 2; "Recruiting," *Cattaraugus Freeman* November 7, 1861, 2; Loomis diary, October 11 and 30, November 28 and 29, 1861.

39. Andrews to his sister, September 25, 1861; Bird to James Bird, September 26, 1861; "From Fort Washington," *American Union,* October 25, 1861, 2; Tissot, "Year with the Army of the Potomac," 54; Cole, "Thirty-Seventh: Long Bridge and Fort Washington"; Marvin S. Cole, "The Thirty-Seventh: All Quiet along the Potomac," *Ellicottville Post,* September 20, 1911.

40. Ellis, *History of Cattaraugus County,* 101; "Colonel of the Thirty-Seventh," *New York Times,* October 7, 1861, 1; "Col. McCunn's Successor," *American Union,* October 11, 1861, 2; Roger D. Hunt and Jack R. Brown, *Brevet Brigadier Generals in Blue* (Gaithersburg, Md.: Olde Soldier Books, 1990), 274; "The 'Irish Rifles,' 37th Regiment, N.Y. Volunteers," *Irish-American,* November 23, 1861, 4; Tissot, "Year with the Army of the Potomac," 51, 57, 58; Bird to his father, November 23, 1861; Cole, "With the 37th N.Y.V. Inf.: Bull Run Battle," *Ellicottville Post,* July 26, 1911.

41. "The 'Irish Rifles,' 37th Regiment, N.Y. Volunteers," *Irish-American,* November 23, 1861, 4; "The 'Irish Rifles,' 37th Regiment, N.Y. Volunteers," *Irish-American,* December 28, 1861, 4; PHJ MR, NA; Bird to his father, December 4, 1861; "Promoted," *Cattaraugus Freeman,* December 5, 1861, 3. Jones's commission was dated December 2, 1861, with rank from November 4.

42. PHJ MR, NA; Sarah Jones, deposition of August 1, 1904, PHJ PR, NA. Jones's commission as major was dated February 17, 1862, with rank from the date of his muster.

43. "Promoted," *Cattaraugus Freeman,* March 6, 1862, 2; "Major P. H. Jones," *Cattaraugus Freeman,* March 20, 1862, 2.

44. "A Correction," *Cattaraugus Freeman,* March 27, 1862, 1.

45. Bird to his father, February 9, 1862; Bryce D. Benedict, *Jayhawkers: The Civil War Brigade of James Henry Lane* (Norman: University of Oklahoma Press, 2009), 3–21, 33–36.

46. Benedict, *Jayhawkers,* 130–31, 186–89, 200–201, 219–38.

47. Tissot, "Year with the Army of the Potomac," 59–67; Bird to his father, April 13 and 24,

1862; Ellis, *History of Cattaraugus County,* 101; William C. Green to Fannie Green, April 18 and 21, 1862; Andrews to his father, April 28 and May 1, 1862; Marvin S. Cole, "With the 37th Regt.," *Ellicottville Post,* April 17, 1912, 7.

48. Green to Fannie Green, May 4, 1862; Tissot, "Year with the Army of the Potomac," 67–69; "The Battle before Richmond," *New York Times,* June 8, 1861, 8; "Letter from Young Cole," *Cattaraugus Freeman,* May 22, 1862, 2; Bird to his father, May 7, 1862; "Letter from Lieut. Baillet," *Cattaraugus Freeman,* May 22, 1862, 1; Andrews to unknown recipient, May 11, 1862; "From Washington," *Cattaraugus Freeman,* May 15, 1862, 2; "37th N.Y.V. ('Irish Rifles')," *Irish-American,* May 24, 1862, 2; "The Battle of Williamsburg," *Irish-American,* June 7, 1862, 1; "Return of Capt. Clarke and Lieut. Harmon," *Cattaraugus Union,* May 30, 1862, 3; Stephen Sears, *To the Gates of Richmond: The Peninsula Campaign* (New York: Ticknor & Fields, 1992), 68–78.

49. "The Irish Rifles at Williamsburg," *Irish-American,* May 16, 1863, 4; "Letter from Young Cole," *Cattaraugus Freeman,* May 22, 1862, 2; "Letter from Lieut. Baillet," *Cattaraugus Freeman,* May 22, 1862, 1; Tissot, "Year with the Army of the Potomac," 70; Phisterer, *New York in the War of the Rebellion,* 401; Boyle, *Party of Mad Fellows,* 91; Bird to his father, May 7, 1862; "From Washington," *Cattaraugus Freeman,* May 15, 1862, 2; Green to Fannie Green, May 14, 1862; "The Bravery of New-Yorkers," *New York Times,* July 13, 1862, 3; "Our Boys in Battle," *Cattaraugus Union,* May 16, 1862, 3.

50. Tissot, "Year with the Army of the Potomac," 70–71; Bird to his father, May 11, 16, and 22, 1862; Bird to his brother, May 29, 1862; "Letter from Lieut. Baillet," *Cattaraugus Union,* May 30, 1862, 2; Green to Fannie Green, May 14, 1862; Green to his mother, May 18, 1862; Andrews, no salutation, May 22, 1862.

51. Tissot, "Year with the Army of the Potomac," 71–72; Sears, *To the Gates of Richmond,* 124–28.

52. *OR,* ser. 1, vol. 11, pt. 1, 870–71; Boyle, *Party of Mad Fellows,* 100–101; Andrews, no salutation, June 8, 1862.

53. "Our Boys at Richmond," *Cattaraugus Union,* June 13, 1862, 3; Andrews to his sister, June 8, 1862; Phisterer, *New York in the War of the Rebellion,* 401; "Letter from Maj. P. H. Jones," *Cattaraugus Freeman,* June 19, 1862, 2.

54. "Letter from Maj. P. H. Jones," *Cattaraugus Freeman,* June 19, 1862, 2; SMJ Deposition, August 1, 1904, PHJ PR, NA; Andrew McIlwaine Bell, *Mosquito Soldiers: Malaria, Yellow Fever, and the Cause of the American Civil War* (Baton Rouge: Louisiana State University Press, 2010), 2, 6, 10, 11, 29, 72, 73, 76, 118.

55. "Letter from Maj. P. H. Jones," *Cattaraugus Freeman,* June 19, 1862: 2; "Obituary [Edward C. Jones]," *North Nebraska Eagle,* May 7, 1880; Warner, *Warner's History of Dakota County,* 144, 177; 1860 U.S. Census, St. John's, Dakota County, Neb.; Ellen Jones Boler interview; Miscellaneous notes and Henry Van Aernam interview notes, October 17, 1893, EDN Papers; Marten, *Sing Not War,* 64–65. In his later years, Edward Jones returned to the South in ill health. He died of pneumonia at age 48 on April 13, 1880, at Neblett's Landing, Bolivar County, Miss.

56. Mississippi Department of Archives and History, to author, June 9, 2008.

57. *OR,* ser. 1, vol. 11, pt. 1, 871.

58. Tissot, "Year with the Army of the Potomac," 73–82; Sears, *To the Gates of Richmond,* 257, 299–304, 344–48; Phisterer, *New York in the War of the Rebellion,* 401; Andrews to his sister, July 20, 1862.

59. Ellis, *History of Cattaraugus County,* 101; Bird to his brother, August 21, 1862; Bird to his father, September 4, 1862; Andrews, no salutation, September 4, 1862.

60. Andrews, no salutation, September 4, 1862; Tissot, "Year with the Army of the Potomac," 84; Bird to his father, September 18, 1862.

61. "The 37th New York 'Irish Rifles,'" *Irish-American,* August 30, 1862, 4; "Major P. H. Jones," *Cattaraugus Freeman,* October 2, 1862, 3; Special Orders No. 283, Adjutant General's Office, War Department, Washington, PHJ MR, NA. The Latin phrase is a quotation by the Italian Jesuit priest Claudio Acquaviva (1543–1615)

3. COLONEL AND BRIGADIER GENERAL

1. Phisterer, *New York in the War of the Rebellion,* 21–22; Mark H. Dunkelman and Michael J. Winey, *The Hardtack Regiment: An Illustrated History of the 154th Regiment, New York State Infantry Volunteers* (East Brunswick, N.J.: Fairleigh Dickinson University Press, 1981), 21–23; George W. Patterson to Thomas Hillhouse, July 12, 1862, Correspondence and Petitions, 1821–1896, New York State Adjutant General's Office, B0462, New York State Archives, Albany (hereafter cited as NYSAGO); "The Mayville Convention!" *Cattaraugus Freeman,* July 17, 1862; "War Meeting at Mayville!" *Cattaraugus Freeman,* July 17, 1862.

2. "From Washington," *Cattaraugus Freeman,* July 17, 1862; Addison G. Rice to Thomas Hillhouse, July 21, 1862, NYSAGO; "From Washington," *Cattaraugus Freeman,* October 17, 1861.

3. "The Colonelcy," *Jamestown Journal,* August 8, 1862; "Important War Bulletin," *Cattaraugus Freeman,* August 21, 1862.

4. "Important War Bulletin," *Cattaraugus Freeman,* August 21, 1862; Dunkelman and Winey, *Hardtack Regiment,* 22.

5. "Local Military Matters," *Jamestown Journal,* September 5, 1862; "The Cattaraugus County Regiment," *Cattaraugus Union,* September 5, 1862; "Uneasy," *Cattaraugus Union,* September 5, 1862; "Local Column," *Mayville Sentinel,* September 10, 1862; "Uneasy," *Jamestown Journal,* September 12, 1862; Adams, *Historical Gazetteer,* 195.

6. "Major P. H. Jones," *Cattaraugus Freeman,* September 18, 1862; Dunkelman and Winey, *Hardtack Regiment,* 22.

7. Dunkelman and Winey, *Hardtack Regiment,* 25–31; Charles W. Abell to his family, undated fragment. Henry Loomis was the brother of Nelson Loomis of the 37th New York.

8. Addison G. Rice to Thomas Hillhouse, October 31, 1862, NYSAGO; 154th New York muster-out roll, June 11, 1865, PHJ MR, NA; "Ten Days with the Army," *Cattaraugus Freeman,* April 23, 1863.

9. "From the 154th Regiment," *Cattaraugus Freeman,* November 6, 1862; "Col. A. G. Rice," *Cattaraugus Freeman,* November 6, 1862; "Ten Days with the Army," *Cattaraugus Freeman,* April 23, 1863; Dunkelman and Winey, *Hardtack Regiment,* 34–36.

10. Orders found in the back of the Regimental Descriptive Books (hereafter cited as DBO), National Archives, Washington, D.C., microfilm exposure numbers 218–20; Dunkelman and Winey, *Hardtack Regiment,* 36; PHJ to Capt. J. Alexander, Assistant Adjutant General, 2nd Division, 11th Corps, November 29, 1862, Regimental Letter Book, Ellicottville (N.Y.) Historical Society (hereafter cited as ELL).

11. Richard J. McCadden to his brother, December 7, 1862; George Eugene Graves to Celia Smith, November 23, 1862; George W. Newcomb to his wife, December 4, 1862.

12. Joel M. Bouton to Stephen E. Hoyt, December 7, 1862.

13. Sidney David Brummer, *Political History of New York State during the Period of the Civil War* (New York: AMS Press, 1967), 213–18; Jerome Mushkat, *The Reconstruction of the New York Democracy, 1861–1874* (East Brunswick, N.J.: Fairleigh Dickinson University Press, 1981), 34; Rawley, *Edwin D. Morgan*, 182, 186–88.

14. Brummer, *Political History of New York State*, 18, 64, 201–4, 218; Mushkat, *Reconstruction of the New York Democracy*, 27, 30; Chauncey M. Depew, *My Memories of Eighty Years* (New York: Charles Scribner's Sons, 1922), 19, 23; Homer A. Stebbins, *A Political History of the State of New York, 1865–1869* (New York: Columbia University Press, 1913), 24; Edwin A. Merritt, *Recollections, 1828–1911* (Albany: J. B. Lyon, 1911), 19–20.

15. Brummer, *Political History of New York State*, 218–21, 224–26; Mushkat, *Reconstruction of the New York Democracy*, 35.

16. Brummer, *Political History of New York State*, 227–35, 238–48; Mushkat, *Reconstruction of the New York Democracy*, 36

17. Brummer, *Political History of New York State*, 252; "Military Advice and Dictation," *Cattaraugus Union*, November 21, 1862.

18. "Military Advice and Dictation," *Cattaraugus Freeman*, November 27, 1862; "Passage by the Senate of the Soldiers' Suffrage Bill," *Cattaraugus Freeman*, April 9, 1863; Arthur Hotchkiss to his father, March 29, 1864; Mushkat, *Reconstruction of the New York Democracy*, 37; Bruce, *Harp and the Eagle*, 136–40; Ural, "Ye Sons of Green Erin Assemble," 114–15.

19. Dunkelman and Winey, *Hardtack Regiment*, 39–40; Stephen R. Green to his wife, December 12, 1862; Bruce, *Harp and the Eagle*, 141–42.

20. "From the 154th Regiment," *Cattaraugus Freeman*, December 18, 1862; Barzilla Merrill to his wife, April 11, 1863; Alansing Wyant to his family, February 24, 1863; Richard J. McCadden to his sister, February 15, 1863; First Lieutenant and Acting Adjutant Cooley A. Murdock to Capt. J. Alexander, January 12, 1863, 154th New York Returns, National Archives; "The Weather—The Army," *Cattaraugus Freeman*, January 22, 1863; Dunkelman and Winey, *Hardtack Regiment*, 43–44; PHJ to New York State Adjutant General John T. Sprague, January 23, 1863; Emory Sweetland to his wife, January 26, 1863; "Promotions," *Cattaraugus Union*, January 30, 1863.

21. Dunkelman and Winey, *Hardtack Regiment*, 44; Hiram Vincent to his wife, February 9, 1863; Marshall O. Bond diary, February 14 and 16, 1863; Thaddeus L. Reynolds to his family, February 15, 1863; George A. Taylor to his wife, March 6, 1863; William Charles to his wife, March 9 and 23, 1863; Barzilla Merrill to his wife, March 24, 1863; James W. Clements to his wife, March 10, 1863; Edwin R. Osgood to his brother, March 12, 1863; PHJ to Horatio Seymour, March 13, 1863, ELL; PHJ to John T. Sprague, March 13 and 16, 1863, NYSAGO; James D. Emmons to his sister, February 27, 1863.

22. DBO 282, 291; PHJ MR, NA; Marshall O. Bond diary, February 19 and 27, March 7, 1863; George A. Taylor to his wife, March 6, 1863; Dunkelman and Winey, *Hardtack Regiment*, 45–46; James D. Quilliam to his wife, March 17, 1863; "Ten Days with the Army," *Cattaraugus Freeman*, April 16, 1863.

23. "Ten Days with the Army," *Cattaraugus Freeman*, April 16, 1863; Boyle, *Party of Mad Fellows*, 236–38; Keneally, *Great Shame*, 380.

24. DBO 294; PHJ MR, NA; James W. Clements to his wife, April 1, 1863; Stephen Welch diary, April 8, 1863; Dunkelman and Winey, *Hardtack Regiment,* 50; "Letter from the 154th!" *Cattaraugus Freeman,* April 9, 1863.

25. Dunkelman and Winey, *Hardtack Regiment,* 50–51; William A. Farlee to E. D. Northrup, January 28, 1879, EDN Papers.

26. Dunkelman and Winey, *Hardtack Regiment,* 51–63; PHJ MR, NA; Lewis D. Warner diary, May 2, 1863; Stephen Welch diary, May 2, 1863; Horace Smith diary, May 2, 1863.

27. Dunkelman and Winey, *Hardtack Regiment,* 65; Henry Van Aernam to his wife, May 7, 1863; George J. Mason to his sister, May 7, 1863; George W. Newcomb to his wife, May 8, 1863; Hiram Vincent to his wife, May 8, 1863; John N. Porter to his brother-in-law, May 9, 1863; James G. Macomber to his mother, May 12, 1863; James W. Washburn to his parents, May 12, 1863; Devillo Wheeler to his parents, May 12, 1863.

28. Samuel D. Woodford to his wife, circa May 10, 1863; Oscar M. Taylor to his cousin, May 9, 1863; "The Battle of Chancellorsville," *Cattaraugus Freeman,* May 28, 1863.

29. George Eugene Graves to Celia Smith, May 14, 1863; "Memorandum from Prisoner of War Records," PHJ MR, NA; George W. Newcomb to his wife, May 15, 1863; Emory Sweetland to his wife, May 15, 1863; Henry Van Aernam to his wife, May 15, 1863; "Examining Surgeon's Certificate," Dr. William O. McDonald, August 20, 1884, and "Surgeon's Certificate" issued by a board of examiners, October 13, 1886, both with diagrams, PHJ PR, NA; Henry Van Aernam interview notes, October 17, 1893, EDN Papers; William Charles to his wife, May 17, 1863; Thaddeus L. Reynolds to his family, May 20, 1863; Truman Harkness to Andrew, May 16, 1863.

30. "The Killed and Wounded from Cattaraugus," *Cattaraugus Union,* May 15, 1863; Francis Strickland to his wife, May 17, 1863; Thaddeus L. Reynolds to his family, May 20, 1863; PHJ PR, NA; Medical certificate of Surgeon William Moss, U.S. Volunteers, May 19, 1863, PHJ MR, NA; Special Orders No. 225, Adjutant General's Office, War Department, Washington, May 20, 1863; "The 154th Regiment," *Cattaraugus Union,* May 29, 1863; Laidlaw, *St. John's Church of Ellicottville,* 4, 14.

31. James W. Washburn to his parents, May 24, 1863; Letter of "D. K.," June 2, 1863, published in undated issue of the *Gowanda [N.Y.] Reporter.*

32. Henry Van Aernam to his wife, May 15, 1863.

33. "From Washington," *Cattaraugus Freeman,* May 14, 1863; "From Washington," *Cattaraugus Freeman,* May 21, 1863; "The Battle of Chancellorsville," *Cattaraugus Freeman,* May 28, 1863.

34. Charles W. Sanders Jr., *While in the Hands of the Enemy: Military Prisons of the Civil War* (Baton Rouge: Louisiana State University Press, 2005), 116; PHJ to General John T. Sprague, New York State Adjutant General, June 9 and 10, 1863, ELL; PHJ to Sprague, June 11, 1863, NYSAGO; Adams, *Historical Gazetteer,* 370.

35. "Letter from Col. Jones," *Cattaraugus Freeman,* June 18, 1863; PHJ PR, NA; Medical Certificate of Surgeon W. R. DeWitt Jr., U.S. Army, July 2, 1863, PHJ MR, NA; PHJ Medical Records, National Archives; July 16: "Personal," *Cattaraugus Freeman,* July 16, 1863; "Letter from Capt. C. P. Vedder," *Cattaraugus Freeman,* July 23, 1863; "Col. Jones," *Cattaraugus Union,* July 17, 1863; "Funeral of Capt. Fuller," *Cattaraugus Union,* July 24, 1863; "Returned," *Cattaraugus Union,* July 24, 1863.

36. PHJ PR, NA; "Memorandum from Prisoner of War Records," PHJ MR, NA; R. Rebecca

Morris, *A Low and Dirty Place: The Parole Camps of Annapolis, MD, 1862–1865* (Linthicum, Md.: Ann Arrundell County Historical Society, 2012), v, 10, 19, 23, 26, 27, 47, 48, 49, 50–51, 53, 61.

37. PHJ PR, NA; "Memorandum from Prisoner of War Records," PHJ MR, NA; PHJ Medical Records, National Archives; Franklin T. Saunders to George Saunders, August 29, 1863; "Memorandum from Prisoner of War Records" and Returns, PHJ MR, NA; "From Washington," *Cattaraugus Freeman,* November 25, 1863.

38. "From Washington," *Cattaraugus Freeman,* November 25, 1863; "Letter from Major L. D. Warner," dated October 22, 1862, undated clipping from the *Olean Times;* Dunkelman and Winey, *Hardtack Regiment,* 91–95.

39. Stephen R. Green to his wife, November 21, 1863; Stephen R. Green diary, November 21, 1863; Dunkelman and Winey, *Hardtack Regiment,* 95–96; *OR,* ser. 1, vol. 31, pt. 2, 366–67.

40. Stephen R. Green, Co. E, to his wife, December 28, 1863; Emory Sweetland to his wife, January 14, 1864; William Charles to his wife, November 27, 1863.

41. Dunkelman and Winey, *Hardtack Regiment,* 96–98; Lewis D. Warner diary, December 6, 1863.

42. PHJ to John T. Sprague, New York State Adjutant General, December 18, 1863, January 4, 8, and 22, 1864, ELL; PHJ to Edwin M. Stanton, December 19, 1863, ELL; PHJ to Capt. C. C. Brown, Assistant Adjutant General, First Brigade, December 21, 1863; PHJ to Col. J. B. Fry, Provost Marshal General, Washington, January 12, 1864, ELL; PHJ to Col. E. D. Townsend, Assistant Adjutant General, Washington, January 14, 1864, ELL; PHJ to Brig. Gen. Lorenzo Thomas, Adjutant General, Washington, January 14, 1864, and endorsements by O. O. Howard and Joseph Hooker, Letters Received by the Commission Branch of the Adjutant General's Office, 1863–1870, National Archives.

43. Dunkelman and Winey, *Hardtack Regiment,* 98–99; Alonzo A. Casler to Cinderella Casler, January 29, 1864; Martin D. Bushnell to his parents, January 29, 1864; PHJ to E. D. Northrup, January 16, 1894, EDN Papers.

44. *OR,* ser. 1, vol. 31, pt. 1, 138; Alonzo A. Casler to Cinderella Casler, January 29, 1864.

45. PHJ to Lt. Robert E. Beecher, Acting Assistant Adjutant General, Second Division, Eleventh Corps, January 30, 1864, PHJ MR, NA; Arthur Hotchkiss to his father, February 1 and 22, 1864, March 6, 1864.

46. Bruce, *Harp and the Eagle,* 219; Ural, "Ye Sons of Green Erin Assemble," 111, 113–15, 117 119–20, 125; "Coming!" *Cattaraugus Freeman,* February 3, 1864; PHJ to Col. E. D. Townsend, Assistant Adjutant General, Washington, February 6, 1864, ELL; DBO 323; Stephen R. Green to his wife, February 18, 1864; Lewis D. Warner diary, February 25 and March 22, 1864; "Col. P. H. Jones," *Cattaraugus Freeman,* March 24, 1864; "Letter of Maj. L. D. Warner," March 26, 1864, in undated clipping, *Olean Times;* William Charles diary, March 22, 1864.

47. Abraham Lincoln to Edwin M. Stanton, March 17, 1864, John Hay Library, Brown University, Providence, R.I.

48. Dunkelman and Winey, *Hardtack Regiment,* 100; Bradford Rowland and Clark E. Oyer interview notes, undated, EDN Papers; Homer A. "Dell" Ames to his parents, April 17, 1864.

49. Dunkelman and Winey, *Hardtack Regiment,* 101; PHJ to General John T. Sprague, New York State Adjutant General, April 16, 1864; Emory Sweetland to his wife, April 8, 1864.

50. Dunkelman and Winey, *Hardtack Regiment,* 103–9; *OR,* ser. 1, vol. 38, pt. 2, 246, 247; Charles Harry Matteson interview notes, October 6, 1893, EDN Papers; Henry Van Aernam

interview notes, October 17, 1893, EDN Papers; "Letter of Maj. L. D. Warner," May 21, 1864, in an undated clipping from the *Olean Times*.

51. PHJ MR, NA; PHJ PR, NA; *OR*, ser. 1, vol. 38, pt. 2, 247; Charles W. Hall interview notes, May 22, 1895, EDN Papers; Richard J. McCadden to his mother and brother, May 9, 1864; Lewis D. Warner diary, May 9, 1864; Emory Sweetland to his wife, May 20, 1864; "Letter of Maj. L. D. Warner," May 21, 1864, in an undated clipping from the *Olean Times; Cattaraugus Freeman*, May 26, 1864, quoting letter of John Manley.

52. PHJ Medical Records, National Archives; PHJ to Capt. C. C. Brown, Acting Assistant Adjutant General, Second Brigade, Second Division, Twentieth Corps, June 7, 1864, PHJ MR, NA; Lewis D. Warner diary, June 7, 1864; *OR*, ser. 1, vol. 38, pt. 2, 208; Samuel D. Woodford to his wife, May 30 and June 3, 1864.

53. *OR*, ser. 1, vol. 38, pt. 2, 208–10, 214.

54. Rev. W. Hickey, "Major David Power Conyngham," *Irish Book Lover* 5, no. 6 (1914): 7–8; Michael Fitzgerald, "From Ballingarry to Fredericksburg: David Power Conyngham (1825–1883)," *Tipperary Historical Journal* (1988): 192–200; George W. Pepper, *Personal Recollections of Sherman's Campaigns in Georgia and the Carolinas* (Zanesville, Ohio: Hugh Dunne, 1866), 209–11; "Major David Power Conyngham, LL. D." *New York Herald*, April 2, 1883, 10; David P. Conyngham, *Sherman's March through the South* (New York: Sheldon & Co., 1865), 114.

55. *OR*, ser. 1, vol. 38, pt. 2, 210–12; Conyngham, *Sherman's March through the South*, 130–31; William Charles diary, June 26, 1864; "Letter from Col. P. H. Jones," *Cattaraugus Freeman*, July 7, 1864, quoting letter of June 24, 1864.

56. *OR*, ser. 1, vol. 38, pt. 2, 212; Fergus Elliott diary, July 19, 1864, Civil War Times Illustrated Collection, U.S. Army Military History Institute, Carlisle Barracks, Pa.; Lewis D. Warner diary, July 19, 1864; William Clark interview notes, September 9, 1891, EDN Papers.

57. *OR*, ser. 1, vol. 38, pt. 2, 212–14; July 28, near Atlanta, "Letter from Maj. Lewis D. Warner," undated clipping from the *Olean Times;* Conyngham, *Sherman's March through the South*, 160–61; Charles Harry Matteson interview notes, October 6, 1893, EDN Papers; Bradford Rowland, Clark E. Oyer, and Esley Groat interview notes, EDN Papers; "From the 154th Regiment," *Cattaraugus Freeman*, August 11, 1864, quoting PHJ's letter of July 23, 1864.

58. *OR*, ser. 1, vol. 38, pt. 2, 214.

59. PHJ Medical Records, National Archives; Lewis D. Warner diary, August 2 and 8, 1864; Arthur Hotchkiss to his father, August 2, 1864; Special Orders No. 39, Headquarters, Second Division, Twentieth Corps, August 8, 1864, PHJ MR, NA; PHJ to Gen. John T. Sprague, New York State Adjutant General, August 14, 1864, NYSAGO; PHJ Medical Records, National Archives; PHJ to E. M. Stanton, May 21, 1865, Letters Sent, 20th Corps, April 1864–May 1865, Vol. 20, RG 393, Part 2, Entry 5377, National Archives; Horace Smith diary, August 31, 1864; Special Orders No. 59, Headquarters, Second Division, Twentieth Corps, September 17, 1864, PHJ MR, NA; *OR*, ser. 1, vol. 44, 295.

60. Brummer, *Political History of New York State*, 254, 274, 278–83, 291–92, 294, 299, 348–49, 395–97; Mushkat, *Reconstruction of the New York Democracy*, 51–51; Depew, *My Memories of Eighty Years*, 34.

61. Brummer, *Political History of New York State*, 415–18; Mushkat, *Reconstruction of the New York Democracy*, 52; Schlesinger, *Almanac of American History*, 290–91; McDougall, *Throes of Democracy*, 486–87; McPherson, *Battle Cry of Freedom*, 713–18, 770–76, 788–91.

62. R. E. Fenton to Secretary of War, September 14, 1864, Register of Letters Received by the Office of the Secretary of War, M22, National Archives; R. E. Fenton to unnamed recipient, undated, and endorsements by W. T. Sherman (September 22, 1864), G. H. Thomas (September 23, 1864), J. W. Geary (September 26, 1864), and H. W. Slocum (September 28, 1864), Letters Received by the Commission Branch of the Adjutant General's Office, 1863–1870, National Archives; "From the 154th Regiment," *Cattaraugus Freeman*, October 6, 1864; R. E. Fenton to Abraham Lincoln, October 11, 1864, PHJ MR, NA; PHJ to Brig. Gen. William D. Whipple, Assistant Adjutant General, Department of the Cumberland, October 15, 1864, PHJ MR, NA.

63. Bruce, *Harp and the Eagle*, 221–32; Ural, "Ye Sons of Green Erin Assemble," 126; Spann, "Union Green," 208–9; Arthur Hotchkiss to his father, March 29, 1864, November 22, 1864; Dunkelman and Winey, *Hardtack Regiment*, 122; Emory Sweetland to his wife, October 30, 1864.

64. Horace Smith diary, November 14, 1864; *OR*, ser. 1, vol. 44, 295–97; Henry Van Aernam to John Manley, November 22, 1864, author's collection; U.S. Congress, *Senate Exec. Journal*, 38th Cong., 1st sess., 12 December 1864, 14:40–41.

65. Certificate of Second Brigade Chief Surgeon J. G. Dunn, December 25, 1864, PHJ MR, NA; PHJ to Lt. Col. H. W. Perkins, Assistant Adjutant General, Twentieth Corps, December 26, 1864, PHJ MR, NA; DBO 258; Lewis D. Warner diary, January 4, 5, and 14, 1865; Reuben E. Fenton to Senator Edwin D. Morgan, January 4, 1865, and Morgan to Fenton, January 9, 1865, both in Edwin D. Morgan Papers, New York State Library, Albany; Francis M. Bowen diary, January 5, 1865; Emory Sweetland to his wife, January 20, 1865; "Deserved Promotion," *Cattaraugus Freeman*, January 26, 1865.

66. Certificate of Amos P. Jones, M.D., January 30, 1865, PHJ MR, NA; U.S. Congress, *Senate Exec. Journal*. 38th Cong., 2nd sess., 1 February 1865, 14:125; "Promoted," *Fredonia Censor*, February 1, 1865; "Local and Miscellaneous," *Cattaraugus Freeman*, February 9, 1865; U.S. Congress, *Senate Exec. Journal*, 38th Cong., 2nd sess., February 14, 1865, Vol. 14, 163; "Confirmations," *New York Times*, February 15, 1865; PHJ to Brig. Gen. E. D. Townsend, Assistant Adjutant General, Washington, February 17, 1865, PHJ MR, NA; Certificate of Nelson Saunders, M.D., February 17, 1865; SMJ Deposition, August 1, 1904, PHJ PR, NA.

67. M. T. McMahon to unidentified colonel, February 27, 1864, Letters Received by the Commission Branch of the Adjutant General's Office, 1863–1870, National Archives.

68. Dunkelman and Winey, *Hardtack Regiment*, 133–39; Alexander Bird diary, March 24, 1865; Lewis D. Warner diary, March 24, 25, and 30, 1865; Richard J. McCadden to his mother and brother, March 29, 1865; Marcellus W. Darling to his family, March 27, 1865.

69. PHJ MR, NA; Lewis D. Warner diary, March 30 and April 20, 1865; "Mr. D. P. Conyngham's Despatch," *New York Herald*, April 15, 1865; Winfield S. Cameron to Dana P. Horton, April 23, 1865; Edgar Shannon to Francelia Hunt, April 7, 1865; Mervin P. Barber diary, April 16, 1865; Endorsement by Secretary of War, December 6, 1864, Letters Received by the Commission Branch of the Adjutant General's Office, 1863–1870, National Archives; PHJ to Gov. Reuben E. Fenton, April 20, 1865, NYSAGO; Arthur Hotchkiss to his father, April 29, 1865.

70. Charles W. McKay, "'Three Years or During the War,' With the Crescent and Star," *National Tribune Scrap Book*, n.p., n.d., 156; Dunkelman and Winey, *Hardtack Regiment*, 140–45; PHJ MR, NA; PHJ PR, NA; Joshua R. Pettit diary, May 26, 1865; Lewis D. Warner diary, May 26, 1865.

71. Henry Van Aernam to Brig. Gen. L. Thomas, May 8, 1865, Letters Received by the Commission Branch of the Adjutant General's Office, 1863–1870, National Archives; PHJ to

Brig. Gen. L. Thomas, May 20, 22, and 26 (with endorsements by J. W. Geary and R. E. Fenton), 1865, and Oath of Office, May 20, 1865, Letters Received by the Commission Branch of the Adjutant General's Office, 1863–1870, National Archives; PHJ, acknowledgment of receipt of his commission, May 24, 1865, Register of Letters Received and Endorsements Sent, Second Brigade, Second Division, Twentieth Army Corps, RG 393, pt. 2, National Archives; Union Staff Officers Files, 1861–1866, box 56, entry 518, National Archives.

72. Dunkelman and Winey, *Hardtack Regiment*, 145; PHJ, certificate of June 11, 1865, James L. Harding Papers, courtesy of Ken Ursin, Mechanicsburg, Pa.; PHJ to Brig. Gen. L. Thomas, June 17, 1865, Letters Received by the Commission Branch of the Adjutant General's Office, 1863–1870, National Archives. Jones's staff at the end of the war included Acting Assistant Inspector General James L. Harding, Provost Marshal Commodore Perry Vedder, Chief of Pioneers Byron A. Johnston, and Chief of the Ambulance Corps Warren Onan, all of the 154th New York, and Acting Assistant Adjutant General James T. Joslin of the 134th New York; PHJ PR, NA.

73. Chief of Bureau of Military Record, *Presentation of Flags of New York Volunteer Regiments and Other Organizations, to His Excellency, Governor Fenton, in Accordance with a Resolution of the Legislature, July 4, 1865* (Albany: Weed, Parsons & Co., 1865), 15; Merritt, *Recollections*, 37–38.

74. "Brigadier-General P. H. Jones," *Cattaraugus Freeman*, July 12, 1865; "Brigadier General Jones," *Cattaraugus Union*, July 13, 1865; Marten, *Sing Not War*, 35–37.

4. POLITICS BECKON

1. Harlow and Boone, *Life Sketches*, 48; Arthur Hotchkiss to his father, July 29, 1865; Dilley, *Biographical and Portrait Cyclopedia of Chautauqua County*, 327, 328; Johnson and Malone, *Dictionary of American Biography*, 6:326; Depew, *My Memories of Eighty Years*, 35.

2. "Union State Convention," *New York Times*, September 21, 1865, 1; "Union State Convention," *Albany Evening Journal*, September 21, 1865, 2; "The Union Nominations," *Albany Evening Journal*, September 22, 1865, 2; "New York Union State Ticket," *Cattaraugus Freeman*, September 27, 1865; "Union Nominations!" *Cattaraugus Freeman*, November 1, 1865; Stebbins, *Political History of the State of New York*, 55–59; Mushkat, *Reconstruction of the New York Democracy*, 75; Junius Henri Browne, *The Great Metropolis: A Mirror of New York* (1869; repr., New York: Arno Press, 1975), 365–71.

3. Hiram Calkins and De Witt Van Buren, *Biographical Sketches of John T. Hoffman and Allen C. Beach, the Democratic Nominees for Governor and Lieutenant-Governor of the State of New York* (New York: New York Printing Co., 1868), 110–11; "Correspondence of the Freeman," *Cattaraugus Freeman*, February 18, 1858, 2.

4. Stebbins, *Political History of the State of New York, 1865–1869*, 69, 74; "New York Union State Ticket," *Cattaraugus Freeman*, September 27, 1865; "Gen. Jones," *Fredonia Censor*, October 4, 1865.

5. "The Coming Election," *Irish-American*, November 4, 1865, 2; "General Patrick H. Jones," *Albany Evening Journal*, November 6, 1865, 2; "The Argus Publishes 'Henry Jones,'" *Albany Evening Journal*, September 21, 1865, 2.

6. *The Union State Ticket: Personal Character and Military Services* (New York: Baker & Godwin, 1865), 19–21.

7. PHJ to R. E. Fenton, August 8, 1865, NYSAGO; PHJ to unnamed general, October 22,

1865, NYSAGO; Phisterer, *New York in the War of the Rebellion*, 36, 157, 427; Conyngham, *Sherman's March through the South*, 1, 6; Hickey, "Major David Power Conyngham," 7–8; Fitzgerald, "From Ballingarry to Fredericksburg," 196–97. The state later awarded Conyngham the brevet rank of major.

8. Stebbins, *Political History of the State of New York, 1865–1869*, 76–77; Mushkat, *Reconstruction of the New York Democracy*, 79; Rawley, *Edwin D. Morgan*, 215; "The Late Elections," *New York Times*, November 9, 1865, 1; "The Past and Coming Elections," *Irish-American*, November 18, 1865, 2; "A Mistake Made in Printing the Democratic State Ticket," *New York Times*, November 8, 1865, 8. The results from several counties were reported in "The Victory," *Albany Evening Journal*, November 15, 1865, 2.

9. "Gen. Jones," *Albany Evening Journal*, December 22, 1865, 2; "Deputy Clerk of the Court of Appeals," *Albany Evening Journal*, December 29, 1865, 2; Adams, *Historical Gazetteer*, 360; Harlow and Boone, *Life Sketches*, 48; "General P. H. Jones," *Cattaraugus Freeman*, January 6, 1866: 3; Francis Bergan, *The History of the New York Court of Appeals, 1847–1932* (New York: Columbia University Press, 1985), 3, 8, 15–19, 24, 33, 36–37, 43, 44–45, 48, 90–91; *Court of Appeals State of New York* (n.p., n.d.), 2, 4, 19; *"There shall be a Court of Appeals . . .": 150th Anniversary of the Court of Appeals of the State of New York* (n.p., n.d), 13, 15, 110; Stebbins, *Political History of the State of New York, 1865–1869*, 368, 392. Today the Court of Appeals is housed in the Greek Revival State Hall at 20 Eagle Street.

10. Francis A. Lord, *They Fought for the Union* (New York: Bonanza Books, 1960) 123; Bergan, *History of the New York Court of Appeals*, 45; "Notes of the City Canvass," *New York Times*, November 2, 1874, 5; "Report of the Clerk of the Court of Appeals," in *Documents of the Assembly of the State of New York Eighty-Ninth Session—1866*, vol. 6, no. 124 (Albany: C. Wendell, 1866), 1–19; "General Patrick H. Jones," *Ellicottville Post*, August 15, 1900, 3.

11. Harlow and Boone, *Life Sketches*, 48.

12. Adams, *Historical Gazetteer*, 350–52; David McAdam, ed., *History of the Bench and Bar of New York* (New York: New York History Co., 1897), 186–88; Browne, *Great Metropolis*, 390; PHJ PR, NA; Anna Jones headstone, Randolph Cemetery, Randolph, N.Y.; Liber 75, p. 164, Deed Books, Cattaraugus County Clerk's Office, Little Valley, N.Y.; *Atlas of Cattaraugus County, New York* (New York: D. G. Beers & Co., 1869), 24; Harold M. Williams to author, April 29, 1984; *The Albany Directory, for the Year 1866* (Albany: Sampson, Davenport & Co., 1866), 90; *The Albany Directory, for the Year 1867* (Albany: Sampson, Davenport & Co., 1867), 90; *The Albany Directory, for the Year 1868* (Albany: Sampson, Davenport & Co., 1868), 93; U.S. Census, Randolph, Cattaraugus County, New York, July 30, 1870; "Court of Appeals," *New York Times*, October 9, 1866, 2; "Court of Appeals," *New York Times*, September 23, 1867, 5. The Jones house still stands at 65 Jamestown Street in Randolph.

13. Adams, *Historical Gazetteer*, 360; *Trow's New York City Directory* (New York: John F. Trow, 1868), 532; H. Wilson, comp., *Trow's New York City Directory* (New York: John F. Trow, 1869), 558; Harlow and Boone, *Life Sketches*, 48; "A Supposed Suicide," *New York Times*, April 24, 1876, 8; "Reported Suicide of a Lawyer," *New York Evening Post*, April 24, 1876, 1; Dolan, *Irish Americans*, 34–35; Browne, *Great Metropolis*, 397; Burroughs and Wallace, *Gotham*, 672, 968.

14. "The Commissioners of Emigration," *New York Evening Post*, March 1, 1867, 2; "Commissioners of Emigration," *New York Times*, January 31, 1872, 2; Kapp, *Immigration and the*

Commissioners of Emigration, 62–63, 65, 69; Browne, *Great Metropolis*, 238–40; Burroughs and Wallace, *Gotham*, 737.

15. "Commissioners of Emigration," *New York Times*, January 31, 1872, 2; Kapp, *Immigration and the Commissioners of Emigration*, 86, 89–90, 95, 97–99, 101–2; Rawley, *Edwin D. Morgan*, 21–22; Burroughs and Wallace, *Gotham*, 737–38.

16. Kapp, *Immigration and the Commissioners of Emigration*, 107–9, 111–18, 124, 126; Browne, *Great Metropolis*, 238–39; Burroughs and Wallace, *Gotham*, 738–39.

17. Kapp, *Immigration and the Commissioners of Emigration*, 106, 120; "The Ship James Foster," *New York Times*, March 26, 1869, 5; "Report of the Committee of Investigation into the Affairs of the Commissioners of Emigration and Quarantine," in *Documents of the Assembly of the State of New York Ninety-Ninth Session—1876*, vol. 4, no. 33 (Albany: Weed, Parsons & Co., 1876), 267–69, 515 (hereafter cited as Committee of Investigation). Nolan claimed to have known Jones since 1862, which seems unlikely. Prior to joining Geary's staff, he was a captain in the Sixtieth New York and served as acting assistant adjutant general of the Third Brigade, Second Division, Twelfth Corps. *OR*, ser. 1, vol. 31, pt. 2, 440, 442, 447.

18. Adams, *Historical Gazetteer*, 360; "The Presidency," *New York Times*, May 19, 1868, 2; Stebbins, *Political History of the State of New York, 1865–1869*, 303, 306–11, 313; Mushkat, *Reconstruction of the New York Democracy*, 82; Merritt, *Recollections*, 44–45.

19. Schlesinger, *Almanac of American History*, 311–12; McDougall, *Throes of Democracy*, 524–25; Gibson, *Attitudes of the New York Irish*, 219–23.

20. William Hanchett, *Irish: Charles G. Halpine in Civil War America* (Syracuse: Syracuse University Press), 1970), xiii, 3, 5–6, 21, 24, 30, 33, 34, 55, 75, 77, 79–80, 83, 94, 103, 130, 136; Browne, *Great Metropolis*, 302–5, 313–14.

21. Hanchett, *Irish*, 1, 157–60, 178.

22. "The Late General Halpine," *Irish Citizen*, August 15, 1868, 5; "General Sheridan's Letter," *Soldier's Friend*, August 22, 1868, 2; "Gov. Fenton Has Appointed Gen. Patrick H. Jones," *New York Tribune*, August 14, 1868, 4; "It Is Credible," *New York Sun*, August 15, 1868, 2; Glyndon G. Van Deusen, *Horace Greeley: Nineteenth-Century Crusader* (Philadelphia: University of Pennsylvania Press, 1953), 311–12, 365; Hanchett, *Irish*, 176.

23. "Minor Topics," *New York Times*, August 6, 1868, 4; "A Letter from General Sheridan," *Irish-American* (N.Y.), August 15, 1868, 2; Edwin D. Morgan to Reuben E. Fenton, August 7, 1868, Edwin D. Morgan Papers, New York State Library, Albany; "Maj. Gen. C. G. Halpine," *Boston Pilot*, September 5, 1868, 2; Robert C. Williams, *Horace Greeley: Champion of American Freedom* (New York: New York University Press, 2006), 139–42; Snay, *Horace Greeley and the Politics of Reform in Nineteenth-Century America*, 94–96, 98, 123, 148–49, 166.

24. Williams, *Horace Greeley*, xvi, 9–25, 44–46, 56–58, 61, 86–113, 118–24, 130, 139–42, 161, 165–66, 168–69, 178, 267, 282–83, 289; Horace Greeley, *Recollections of a Busy Life* (New York: J. B. Ford & Co., 1868), 64, 76–80, 98–105, 136–43, 311–22; Van Deusen, *Horace Greeley*, 10–11, 64–66, 36–39, 98–100, 184–92, 268–69, 365; Jeter Allen Isely, *Horace Greeley and the Republican Party, 1853–1861: A Study of the New York Tribune* (Princeton, N.J.: Princeton University Press, 1947), vii, 10–11, 15, 70–75, 80, 89–98, 103–11; Snay, *Horace Greeley and the Politics of Reform in Nineteenth-Century America*, 19, 22, 43–46, 49–50, 131; Ellis, *History of Cattaraugus County*, 252–53, following 256; Browne, *Great Metropolis*, 214–19, 306–7, 368.

25. "Gov. Fenton Has Appointed Gen. Patrick H. Jones," *New York Tribune*, August 14, 1868, 4; "General Halpine's Successor," *New York Evening Post*, August 14, 1868, 3.

26. "Appointment of Register of the City of New-York in Place of the Late Gen. Halpine," *New York Times*, August 14, 1868, 1; "Patrick H. Jones," *New York Herald*, August 14, 1868, 4; "City Intelligence," *New York Commercial Advertiser*, August 14, 1868, 3; "Halpine's Successor," *New York Evening Mail*, August 14, 1868, 3; "The City Register," *New York World*, August 14, 1868, 5; "Yesterday Morning," *New York Evening Telegram*, August 15, 1868, 4; "Appointment of Gen. P. H. Jones as Register of New York City," *Cattaraugus Republican* (Little Valley, N.Y.), August 20, 1868, 3; "Gen. Patrick H. Jones," *Irish-American* (New York), August 22, 1868, 1; "The Late General Halpine," *New York Commercial Advertiser*, January 11, 1869, 4; "Personal," *New York Evening Post*, June 11, 1869, 2. According to a later report, the funds Jones provided to the Halpine family "were all placed in the hands of a trustee who went to Europe some time ago with these and other funds in his possession, and Mrs. Halpine was bereft of all." "A Monument to Miles O'Reilly," *New York Herald*, June 14, 1881, 5.

27. "The New Register," *New York Dispatch*, August 16, 1868, 4; "Note from Register Jones," *New York Evening Post*, August 22, 1868, 4; "Appointments in the Register's Office," *New York Times*, August 23, 1868, 6; "Robert B. Roosevelt," *Harper's Weekly*, September 23, 1873, 885; "Miscellaneous," *New York Herald*, August 23, 1868, 4; Lynch, *Wild Seventies*, 108.

28. "The Guillotine at Work," *New York Herald*, August 27, 1868, 8; "Removals from the Register's Office," *New York Evening Post*, August 31, 1868, 4; "Radical Rapacity," *Albany Argus*, September 15, 1868, 2, quoting *New York Mercury*.

29. "The Captain's Political Gossip," *New York Leader*, August 29, 1868, 5; Charles Dickens, *Martin Chuzzlewit* (New York: Dodd, Mead, 1944), 27, 28, 49, 53, 434, 436, 613.

30. "The Captain's Political Gossip," *New York Leader*, August 29, 1868, 5.

31. Margaret G. Halpine to Horace Greeley, New York, August 29, 1868, Horace Greeley Papers, 1831–1873, New York Public Library (hereafter cited as Greeley Papers, NYPL); "The Captain's Political Gossip," *New York Leader*, September 5, 1868, 5.

32. Josiah Bunting III, *Ulysses S. Grant* (New York: Times Books, 2004), 122–26; Charles W. Calhoun, *From Bloody Shirt to Full Dinner Pail: The Transformation of Politics and Governance in the Gilded Age* (New York: Hill & Wang, 2010), 7.

33. Hanchett, *Irish*, 157, 179; "General Patrick Henry Jones," *Harper's Weekly*, May 15, 1869, 315.

34. "Commissioners of Emigration," *New York Times*, December 23, 1870, 3; "The Commissioners of Emigration Arrivals during the Year," *New York Tribune*, December 23, 1870, 2.

5. POSTMASTER

1. Joan Waugh, *U. S. Grant: American Hero, American Myth* (Chapel Hill: University of North Carolina Press, 2009), 104, 125–27; William S. McFeely, *Grant: A Biography* (New York: Norton, 1981), 286, 289–303; Jean Edward Smith, *Grant* (New York: Simon & Schuster, 2001), 462–66, 468–75; Matthew Josephson, *The Politicos: 1865–1896* (New York: Harcourt, Brace & Co., 1938), 80–83, 119; Allan Nevins, *Hamilton Fish: The Inner History of the Grant Administration* (New York: Dodd, Mead, 1936), 109, 280; Bunting, *Ulysses S. Grant*, 87, 90–94, 122.

2. Stephen N. Elias, *Alexander T. Stewart: The Forgotten Merchant Prince* (Westport, Conn.: Praeger, 1992), xii–xiii, 2–5, 11, 18–23, 26–29, 32–33, 39–40, 45, 49, 54, 60–61, 69, 72, 74;

Thomas Kessner, *Capital City: New York City and the Men behind America's Rise to Economic Dominance, 1860–1900* (New York: Simon & Schuster, 2003), 12–16, 36–37, 86–87; Browne, *Great Metropolis*, 289–94.

3. Josephson, *Politicos*, 80–83; Bunting, *Ulysses S. Grant*, 90–94; McFeely, *Grant*, 291–94.

4. Josephson, *Politicos*, 81; George S. Boutwell to Horace Greeley, March 8, 1869, Greeley Papers, NYPL; Horace Greeley to Hamilton Fish, March 22, 1869, Hamilton Fish Papers, vol. 58, Library of Congress; Snay, *Horace Greeley and the Politics of Reform in Nineteenth-Century America*, 116; William T. Sherman to Horace Greeley, March 14, 1869, Greeley Papers, NYPL; Adams, *Historical Gazetteer*, 360.

5. Van Deusen, *Horace Greeley*, 366–68, 372–74, 384–85, 388; Snay, *Horace Greeley and the Politics of Reform in Nineteenth-Century America*, 175–76; Nevins, *Hamilton Fish*, 121; David M. Jordan, *Roscoe Conkling of New York: Voice in the Senate* (Ithaca, N.Y.: Cornell University Press, 1971), 35, 49, 94.

6. Jordan, *Roscoe Conkling*, 127; Nevins, *Hamilton Fish*, 118, 120; Johnson and Malone, *Dictionary of American Biography*, 6:326; Depew, *My Memories of Eighty Years*, 77, 84; "Washington," *New York Tribune*, March 26, 1869, 1; "Washington," *New York Tribune*, March 25, 1869, 1; "Washington," *New York Tribune*, March 27, 1869, 3; "Washington," *New York Tribune*, April 9, 1869, 1; "Washington," *New York Tribune*, April 12, 1869, 3.

7. "Washington," *New York Tribune*, April 14, 1869, 1; Reuben E. Fenton to Ulysses S. Grant, April 12, 1869, in *The Papers of Ulysses S. Grant*, edited by John Y. Simon (Carbondale: Southern Illinois University Press, 1967–2010), 21:15 (hereafter cited as Simon, Papers of USG); Mushkat, *Reconstruction of the New York Democracy*, 148–49.

8. Adams, *Historical Gazetteer*, 361; "The Wild Hunt for Office," *New York Herald*, April 13, 1869, 8; Nevins, *Hamilton Fish*, 130.

9. "Washington," *New York Tribune*, April 16, 1869, 1; "Moses H. Grinnell," *New York Times*, November 25, 1877; Browne, *Great Metropolis*, 667; Burroughs and Wallace, *Gotham*, 713, 860, 861.

10. "The New-York Post Office," *New York Times*, August 27, 1875, 2; "Washington," *New York Tribune*, March 10, 1869, 1; "Mr. William B. Taylor," *New York Tribune*, March 10, 1869, 4; "Washington," *New York Tribune*, March 26, 1869, 1; "Washington," *New York Tribune*, April 1, 1869, 1; Josephson, *Politicos*, 92, 96; "Washington," *New York Tribune*, April 21, 1869, 1; "Washington," *New York Tribune*, April 23, 1869, 1; "Washington," *New York Times*, April 23, 1869, 1; Horace Greeley to Ulysses S. Grant, April 24, 1869, Simon, Papers of USG, 20:232; "The New York Postmastership," *New York Commercial Advertiser*, April 29, 1869, 4; Waugh, *U. S. Grant*, 185.

11. Adams, *Historical Gazetteer*, 360–61; "Washington," *New York Tribune*, April 26, 1869: 1; Record of Appointment of Postmasters, 1832–September 30, 1971, M 841, Roll 88, National Archives; "Rumored Removal of Postmaster Kelley," *New York Evening Telegram*, April 27, 1869, 1; "Rumored Removal of Postmaster Kelly," *New York Herald*, April 28, 1869, 5; "The City," *New York Herald*, April 28, 1869, 8; "Gen. Patrick Henry Jones Appointed Postmaster for New-York City," *New York Tribune*, April 28, 1869, 1; "The New Postmaster," *New York Commercial Advertiser*, April 28, 1869, 2; "Postmaster Kelly to Be Set Adrift," *New York Sun*, April 28, 1869, 1; "New York City Postmastership," *New York World*, April 28, 1869, 1; "The New Postmaster," *New York Spectator and Weekly Commercial Advertiser*, April 29, 1869, 2; James B. Taylor to Ulysses S. Grant, April 24 and 28, 1869, Simon, Papers of USG, 20:231–32; "The City Post Office," *New*

York Times, April 28, 1869, 6; "The Postoffice," *New York Evening Mail*, April 28, 1869, 2; "The New Postmaster," *New York Dispatch*, May 2, 1869, 4; "It Is Reported from Washington," *New York Tribune*, April 28, 1869, 4; "One of the Best Appointments," *Irish-American* (New York), May 8, 1869, 4.

12. "The City Postmaster," *New York Evening Express*, April 28, 1869, 2; "General Grant's Appointments," *New York Herald*, April 27, 1869, 8; "The New Postmaster," *New York Herald*, April 30, 1869, 7.

13. "Everybody Pats Pat Jones," *New York Leader*, May 8, 1869, 4; "The Captain's Political Gossip," *New York Leader*, May 8, 1869, 5.

14. "General Patrick Henry Jones," *Harper's Weekly*, May 15, 1869, 315; "General Patrick H. Jones," *Frank Leslie's Illustrated Newspaper*, May 15, 1869, 135; "Gen. P. H. Jones," *Cattaraugus Republican* (Little Valley, N.Y.), April 29, 1869, 2; "General Patrick Henry Jones," *Dakota Republican* (Vermillion, S.D.), May 15, 1869, 2.

15. "The New Postmaster," *New York Evening Post*, April 29, 1869, 4; "Patrick H. Jones Our New Postmaster," *New York Sun*, April 29, 1869, 1; "The New Postmaster," *New York Herald*, April 30, 1869, 7; "General Patrick H. Jones," *New York Tribune*, April 30, 1869, 4; "Local Intelligence," *New York Evening Express*, April 30, 1869, 3; Lynch, *Wild Seventies*, 37; "The Last Ruin in Wall Street," *New York Sun*, September 14, 1871, 1; Williams, *Horace Greeley*, 167, 310; "Mr. Greeley's Estate in Peril," *New York Sun*, January 27, 1874, 2.

16. "The New Postmaster," *New York Evening Telegram*, May 1, 1869, 1; "Local Intelligence," *New York Evening Express*, May 1, 1869, 4; "The New Postmaster," *New York Times*, May 2, 1869, 8; "The New Postmaster," *New York Herald*, May 2, 1869, 5; "The New Postmaster," *New York Sunday Mercury*, May 2, 1869, 4; "The New Postmaster," *New York Spectator and Weekly Commercial Advertiser*, May 6, 1869, 3; Browne, *Great Metropolis*, 416. According to "Ex-Postmaster Kelly," *New York Herald*, January 14, 1871, 9, Jones served as a pallbearer at Kelly's funeral.

17. U.S. Congress, *Senate Exec. Journal*, 41st Cong., 2nd sess., December 6, 1869, 19:272; December 13, 1869, 19:313, 326; "The Public Service," *New York Times*, December 22, 1869, 1; Adams, *Historical Gazetteer*, 360–61; U.S. Census, 9th Election District, 9th Ward, New York City, June 27, 1870; U.S. Census, Randolph, N.Y., July 30, 1870; *Trow's New York City Directory* (New York: John F. Trow, 1870–72), [1870] 567, [1871] 614, [1872], 583; Burroughs and Wallace, *Gotham*, 815. Palmer had nominated Jones for the court of appeals clerkship in 1865.

18. Browne, *Great Metropolis*, 381–89; Williams, *Horace Greeley*, 168.

19. "The New Postmaster," *New York Evening Express*, May 4, 1869, 4; "The City Post Office," *New York Times*, April 28, 1869, 6; "New-York Post Office," *New York Times*, September 12, 1869, 5; "Official Changes," *New York Times*, May 3, 1869, 4; "Gen. Patrick H. Jones assumed the duties of Postmaster," *New York Tribune*, May 3, 1869, 4; "The New York Post Office," *New York Evening Post*, May 3, 1869, 4; "City Post Office," *New York Evening Express*, May 3, 1869, 3.

20. "Post Office Appointments," *New York Herald*, June 3, 1869, 5; "Appointments at the Post Office," *New York Times*, June 4, 1869, 2; "The Post Office," *New York Herald*, June 23, 1869, 5; "New-York Post Office," *New York Times*, September 12, 1869, 5; "Applicants for Positions in the Post Office," *New York Times*, January 5, 1870, 2.

21. Oliver Otis Howard to PHJ, May 18, 1869, Oliver Otis Howard Papers, Bowdoin College Library, Brunswick, Me.; "Dr. Gillette in Hospital," *New York Times*, October 30, 1908, 16; PHJ PR, NA; Edwin D. Morgan to PHJ, November 29 and December 4, 1869; March 28, June 6,

and December 23, 1871; August 17 and December 7, 1872; March 14, 1873, Edwin D. Morgan Papers, New York State Library, Albany; Hamilton Fish to PHJ, June 22, 1869, September 19, 1870, November 2, 1872, Hamilton Fish Papers, Library of Congress; Caroline D. Roberts to Horace Greeley, May 10, 1869; E. H. Chapin to Greeley, May 10, 1869 (two letters), Horace Greeley Papers, 1831–1873, New York Public Library; PHJ to Thurlow Weed, August 30, 1872, Rush Rhees Library, University of Rochester, Rochester, N.Y.; Josephson, *Politicos*, 91; Chester A. Arthur to PHJ, October 18, 1871, Chester Alan Arthur letter press books, New-York Historical Society; Joshua M. Van Cott to PHJ, April 15, 1871, New-York Historical Society; PHJ to Moses H. Grinnell, August 23, 1869, author's collection; "Gen. Addison Farnsworth," *New York Times*, April 3, 1877; Hunt and Brown, *Brevet Brigadier Generals in Blue*, 200.

22. "What Patronage Does in This City," *New York Times*, February 23, 1873, 4; "Reform in the Post-Office," *New York Times*, February 16, 1873, 4; "Hints to Our City Republicans," *New York Times*, June 16, 1869, 4.

23. T. B. Thorpe, "New York City Post-Office," *Harper's New Monthly Magazine* 43, issue 257 (October 1871): 660–61.

24. David M. Henkin, *The Postal Age: The Emergence of Modern Communications in Nineteenth-Century America* (Chicago: University of Chicago Press, 2006), 17, 22, 27; "The New-York Post-Office," *New York Times*, December 16, 1870, 2; "Business of the New-York Post Office for 1869," *New York Times*, January 1, 1870, 5; "New-York," *New York Times*, December 19, 1869, 8; "The Post-Office," *New York Times*, February 4, 1871, 6; Elias, *Alexander T. Stewart*, 27–28; Browne, *Great Metropolis*, 382, 385, 416–17.

25. Browne, *Great Metropolis*, 415–22; "The New-York Post-Office," *New York Times*, December 16, 1870, 2; "New York Postal City Delivery," *New York Herald*, May 4, 1869, 8–9; "Washington," *New York Times*, November 5, 1869, 1; "Local News In Brief," *New York Times*, June 7, 1871, 8; Thorpe, "New York City Post-Office," 661–62; Howard Wallace Connelly, *Fifty-six Years in the New York Post Office* (New York: C. J. O'Brien, 1931), 8.

26. "Departure of Foreign Mails," *New York Times*, May 8, 1869, 8; "The Post Office," *New York Times*, May 16, 1869, 8; "The Post-Office Stations," *New York Times*, March 10, 1870, 5; "The Post Office," *New York Herald*, June 23, 1869, 5; "Local News in Brief, New York," *New York Times*, June 11, 1870, 8; "Local News in Brief. New York City," *New York Times*, June 15, 1871, 8; "The Mail Delivery," *New York Times*, December 28, 1872, 8; "A Defect in the Postage Laws," *New York Times*, December 8, 1872, 4; "Trouble with the Mail Steamers," *New York Times*, December 28, 1869, 5; "The Foreign Mail Service," *New York Times*, December 29, 1869, 1; "The Mails," *New York Times*, December 31, 1869, 2; "The Ocean Mail Service," *New York Times*, January 3, 1870, 1; "Ocean Mail Service," *New York Times*, January 1, 1872, 5; "The Postal Service," *New York Times*, January 19, 1870, 1.

27. "Who Owns Broadway?" *New York Times*, January 29, 1870, 2; "A Tubular Post," *New York Times*, April 25, 1871, 4; Burroughs and Wallace, *Gotham*, 932; "Personal," *New York Herald*, September 28, 1870, 10; "Washington," *New York Times*, March 27, 1871, 5; "The City Letter Boxes," *New York Evening Post*, February 14, 1873, 2; John A. J. Creswell to PHJ, December 18, 1871, Records of the Office of the Postmaster General, RG 28, Entry 2, Letters Sent, October 3, 1789–December 31, 1910, 81:234; Nevins, *Hamilton Fish*, 110, 139–40, 580, 589, 719.

28. "Personal," *New York Evening Post*, June 11, 1869, 2; "The Work of the Post-Office," *New York Times*, September 3, 1871, 3; "Post Office D," *New York Times*, July 20, 1872, 5.

29. "The Post Office," *New York Herald,* June 23, 1869, 5; "The Old Post Office," *New York Times,* August 16, 1869, 5; "The New-York Post-Office," *New York Times,* April 26, 1871, 4; Thorpe, "New York City Post-Office," 655–57; Burroughs and Wallace, *Gotham,* 942; "The New City Post-Office," *Harper's Weekly,* November 12, 1870, 727; Browne, *Great Metropolis,* 415–16.

30. "The Post Office," *New York Herald,* June 23, 1869, 5; "The New-York Post-Office," *New York Times,* December 6, 1870, 4. See also Browne, *Great Metropolis,* 418–22.

31. "Washington," *New York Tribune,* April 2, 1869, 1; Alexander T. Stewart to Horace Greeley, April 3, 1869, Horace Greeley to George S. Boutwell, April 4, 1869, A. Oakey Hall to Horace Greeley, April 6, 1869, all in Horace Greeley Papers, 1831–1873, New York Public Library; PHJ to H. A. Nelson, May 21, 1869, Eldridge Collection, Henry E. Huntington Library and Art Gallery, San Marino, Calif.; "The New-York Post Office," *New York Times,* May 24, 1869, 1; "Minor Topics," *New York Times,* June 16, 1869, 4; "The Captain's Political Gossip," *New York Leader,* July 24, 1869, 5; "The New New-York Post Office," *New York Times,* July 27, 1869, 1; "The New-York Post Office," *New York Times,* July 31, 1869, 1; "The New-York Post Office," *New York Times,* August 3, 1869, 1; "The New-York Post Office," *New York Times,* August 4, 1869, 4; "The New-York Post Office," *New York Times,* August 5, 1869, 1; Allan Nevins and Milton Halsey Thomas, eds., *The Diary of George Templeton Strong: Post-War Years 1865–1875* (New York: Macmillan, 1952), 251.

32. "The New Post Office," *New York Times,* August 6, 1869, 2; "The New Post-Office Building, New York," *Harper's Weekly,* October 23, 1869, 679; "Interior of the New Post Office," *New York Times,* November 23, 1869, 2; "Architect Mullet's Report on Public Buildings," *New York Herald,* December 3, 1869, 6; "Washington," *New York Times,* November 29, 1869, 1; "Treasury Architecture," *New York Times,* December 2, 1869, 3.

33. "The New Post-Office Building, New York," *Harper's Weekly,* October 23, 1869, 676, 679; "The New City Post-Office," *Harper's Weekly,* November 12, 1870, 727; "New-York," *New York Times,* December 4, 1869, 5; "New-York," *New York Times,* December 10, 1869, 8; "New-York," *New York Times,* December 18, 1869, 5; "The New-York Post Office," *New York Times,* December 22, 1869, 2; "The New-York Post Office and its Architect," *New York Times,* December 24, 1869, 4; "The New Post Office," *New York Times,* December 31, 1869, 2; "The New-York Post Office," *New York Times,* January 6, 1870, 1.

34. "The Post-Office Investigation," *New York Times,* April 20, 1870, 1; "The New-York Post Office," *New York Times,* March 16, 1870, 1; "Washington," *New York Times,* April 10, 1870, 1; "New-York," *New York Times,* January 7, 1870, 8; "The New-York Post Office," *New York Times,* January 31, 1870, 1; "The New-York Post Office," *New York Times,* February 10, 1870, 5; "The New Post-Offices," *New York Times,* April 16, 1870, 1.

35. "The New Post-Office," *New York Times,* May 27, 1870, 2; "The New-York Post-Office and Court-House," *New York Times,* June 10, 1870, 1; "The Civil Expenses," *New York Times,* July 31, 1870, 8; "Work on the New Post-Offices to Be Stopped," *New York Times,* September 10, 1870, 5; "Washington," *New York Times,* November 17, 1870, 5; "The New-York Post-Office," *New York Times,* December 6, 1870, 4; "Washington," *New York Times,* February 23, 1871, 5.

36. "The New-York Post-Office," *New York Times,* April 26, 1871, 4; "The New York Post-Office," *Harper's Weekly,* March 4, 1871, 187.

37. "Local New in Brief, New York," *New York Times,* June 5, 1871, 8; "The New Post-Office—Rapid Progress," *New York Times,* June 28, 1871, 3; "Local News in Brief, New York," *New*

York Times, September 23, 1871, 10; "Work on the New Post-Office," *New York Times,* January 12, 1873, 3; "The New Post-Office Building in New-York," *New York Times,* January 13, 1873, 1; Nevins and Thomas, *Diary of George Templeton Strong,* 376, 380.

38. Henkin, *Postal Age,* 68; "The Mullett Post Office Site," April 28, 1912; Burroughs and Wallace, *Gotham,* 941–42.

39. "Senate," *New York Times,* March 29, 1878, 2; *Congressional Record,* 45th Cong., 2nd sess., 1878, 7, pt. 3, 2009, 2097, 3960, 4581; *A Bill for the Relief of Patrick H. Jones,* 45th Cong., 2nd sess., S. 1005; U.S. House of Representatives, *Report of the Committee on Public Buildings and Grounds,* 45th Cong., 2nd sess., 1878, H. Doc. 890, 1–8; Hunt and Brown, *Brevet Brigadier Generals in Blue,* 395.

40. "Mail-Bag Mysteries," *New York Times,* June 11, 1871, 6; "A Card from Wm. R. Roberts," *New York Times,* May 3, 1873, 2; Edward Crapsey, *The Nether Side of New York; or, the Vice, Crime and Poverty of the Great Metropolis* (New York: Sheldon & Co., 1872), 69–70; Browne, *Great Metropolis,* 574–79; Henkin, *Postal Age,* 155–58.

41. "The Story of Station 'D,'" *New York Times,* February 22, 1875, 2; "New York Swindles," *New York Times,* November 29, 1871, 2; "The Sawdust Swindle," *New York Times,* January 22, 1873, 8; Crapsey, *Nether Side of New York,* 63–73; "Application Has Been Made," *Dakota Republican* (Vermillion, S.D.), March 24, 1870, 2; "Local News in Brief: New-York," *New York Times,* April 7, 1870, 8; "The Charge against the Postmaster of Illegally Detaining Letters," *New York Herald,* April 7, 1870, 5; "Postmaster Jones' Fight with Swindlers," *New York Herald,* April 14, 1870, 5; "United States Commissioners' Office," *New York Times,* April 22, 1870, 3; "United States Commissioners' Office," *New York Herald,* April 22, 1870, 4.

42. "Story of Station 'D,'" 2.

43. "New-York," *New York Times,* December 14, 1869, 8; "The Charge against Mr. Riley," *New York Times,* January 20, 1872, 6; "Post-Office Embezzlements," *New York Times,* May 12, 1872, 3; "A Letter Thief," *New York Times,* February 16, 1871, 3.

6. GRANT VERSUS GREELEY

1. "The Late Henry J. Raymond," *New York Times,* June 22, 1869, 1; Browne, *Great Metropolis,* 230–35; Burroughs and Wallace, *Gotham,* 679; "Departure of Senator Fenton for Europe," *New York Times,* July 25, 1869, 6; "Departure of Secretary Boutwell," *New York Times,* September 18, 1869, 2; "Banquet to Senator Williams, of Oregon," *New York Times,* January 27, 1870, 8; "Republican State Committee," *New York Times,* March 10, 1871, 8; "Balls Last Night," *New York Times,* March 21, 1872, 5; "Reception of the M. Cregan Association," *New York Times,* February 6, 1875, 8; "An East Side Festival," *New York Times,* August 27, 1874: 5; "Captain Cregan Deposed," *New York Times,* July 2, 1887, 1.

2. "The Gift of a Fifty Thousand Dollar Life Insurance Policy to General Grant," *New York Sun,* June 21, 1870, 2; "Can It Be True?" *New York Sun,* June 21, 1870, 2; "A Post Office Clerk's Opinion of Gen. Grant's Life Insurance Policy," *New York Sun,* June 22, 1870, 2; "Gen. Grant's Presents and Relations," *New York Sun,* June 22, 1870: 2; "A Card from Postmaster Jones," *New York Times,* June 23, 1870: 8; "Grant's Life Insurance Policy," *New York Herald,* June 23, 1870: 7; "Gen. Grant's Life Insurance," *New York Sun,* June 24, 1870: 2; "Light on Life Insurance," *New York Sun,* June 25, 1870: 2; Josephson, *Politicos,* 61; Waugh, *U. S. Grant,* 126–27; Kessner, *Capital City,* 115.

3. "Long Branch," *New York Times*, August 2, 1870: 5; "The President's Cottage at Long Branch," *Harper's Weekly*, August 13, 1870, 525.

4. Rawley, *Edwin D. Morgan*, 239; Josephson, *Politicos*, 94–96, 120; Johnson and Malone, *Dictionary of American Biography*, 6:327; Jordan, *Roscoe Conkling*, 133–35; Lynch, *Wild Seventies*, 65–67, 70–72, 84, 164–66, 187–88; Mushkat, *Reconstruction of the New York Democracy*, 165; Van Deusen, *Horace Greeley*, 387–88, 390–97; Nevins, *Hamilton Fish*, 368, 593–95; Gibson, *Attitudes of the New York Irish*, 277–81.

5. "Political," *New York Times*, September 7, 1870,5; Van Deusen, *Horace Greeley*, 388–92; Mushkat, *Reconstruction of the New York Democracy*, 165.

6. "The New York Post Office as a Party Tool in Politics," *New York Freeman's Journal and Catholic Register*, November 12, 1870, 4; "Politics in the Post-Office," *New York World*, November 11, 1870, 4.

7. "Minor Topics," *New York Times*, November 12, 1870, 4; "The Postmaster of New-York," *New York Tribune*, November 12, 1870, 4; "The New York Post-Office as a Political 'Stool-Pigeon,'" *New York Freeman's Journal and Catholic Register*, November 19, 1870, 4; Browne, *Great Metropolis*, 307–8.

8. "Divisions among Republicans—Fenton vs. Conkling," *New York Times*, August 21, 1871, 6; Ulysses S. Grant to John Russell Young, November 15, 1870, Simon, Papers of USG, 21:8–9; Reuben E. Fenton to Ulysses S. Grant, April 12, 1869, Simon, Papers of USG, 21:13–14; U. S. Grant to Roscoe Conkling, November 18, 1870, Roscoe Conkling Papers, Library of Congress; Josephson, *Politicos*, 89, 92–94, 97; Lynch, *Wild Seventies*, 67–68, 114–21; Jordan, *Roscoe Conkling*, 136–37; Van Deusen, *Horace Greeley*, 394–96.

9. Josephson, *Politicos*, 89, 92–94, 97; Lynch, *Wild Seventies*, 67–68, 114–21; Jordan, *Roscoe Conkling*, 136–37; Van Deusen, *Horace Greeley*, 394–96; Mushkat, *Reconstruction of the New York Democracy*, 186.

10. William S. Hillyer to Ulysses S. Grant, October 27, 1871, Simon, Papers of USG, 22:243–44; Hunt and Brown, *Brevet Brigadier Generals in Blue*, 285; Depew, *My Memories of Eighty Years*, 85; Lynch, *Wild Seventies*, 40.

11. Waugh, *U. S. Grant*, 143; Ulysses S. Grant to John Russell Young, November 15, 1870, Simon, Papers of USG, 21:8; Van Deusen, *Horace Greeley*, 392.

12. PHJ to John A. J. Creswell, December 27, 1870, New York State Library, Albany.

13. Bunting, *Ulysses S. Grant*, 103–5; McFeely, *Grant*, 336–45; Smith, *Grant*, 499–506; Nevins, *Hamilton Fish*, 249–78, 309–34, 363–71, 453–54, 497–501; Charles Sumner to Francis W. Bird, April 25, 1871, Simon, Papers of USG, 21:132–34; Josephson, *Politicos*, 142–46; Waugh, *U. S. Grant*, 135–38; Lynch, *Wild Seventies*, 172–74, 176–77, 180–81.

14. "Republican Reorganization," *New York Times*, July 12, 1871, 5; "New York City News," *New York Times*, October 12, 1872, 10; William Evarts Benjamin, Catalogue No. 42, March 1892: 18, cited in Simon, Papers of USG, 22:244; "Grant is making a vigorous war upon Senator Fenton," *Nashville (Tenn.) Union and American*, April 15, 1871, 2; "This Morning's Report," *Watertown Daily Times*, March 21, 1870, 3; "Summary of News," *Irish-American*, May 20, 1871, 5; "If the Report That Patrick H. Jones," *Brooklyn Daily Eagle*, September 4, 1871, 2; Bunting, *Ulysses S. Grant*, 123–26; Smith, *Grant*, 587–89.

15. Hamilton Fish to Ulysses S. Grant, November 6, 1871, Simon, Papers of USG, vol. 22,

202–3; PHJ to Thurlow Weed, December 15, 1871, Rush Rhees Library, University of Rochester, Rochester, N.Y.; Josephson, *Politicos*, 43.

16. "The Custom-House," *New York Times*, March 27, 1872, 1; U. S. Grant to Roscoe Conkling, July 9, 1872, Roscoe Conkling Papers, Library of Congress; Waugh, *U. S. Grant*, 142–43; Josephson, *Politicos*, 90, 137–38, 159–64, 179–80; Nevins, *Hamilton Fish*, 597–98; Williams, *Horace Greeley*, 301–305; Lynch, *Wild Seventies*, 189–93, 203, 212–15; Andrew L. Slap, *The Doom of Reconstruction: The Liberal Republicans in the Civil War Era* (New York: Fordham University Press, 2006), 31, 40–42, 46–62, 90–99, 107, 113, 120–25 134–35, 141–46, 159–63.

17. Slap, *Doom of Reconstruction*, 41–42, 120–23, 155–63, 182, 185, 191–92, 209–15.

18. "Mr. Greeley's Estate in Peril," *New York Sun*, January 27, 1874, 2; "Issues of the Day," *New York Times*, July 24, 1872, 1–2; "At the Grant Headquarters," *New York Herald*, August 2, 1872, 5; "The Republican Headquarters," *New York Herald*, October 5, 1872: 3; "The Boys in Blue," *New York Times*, August 10, 1872, 5; PHJ to Thurlow Weed, August 15, 1872, Rush Rhees Library, University of Rochester, Rochester, N.Y.; Josephson, *Politicos*, 164; Jordan, *Roscoe Conkling*, 181–82; Lynch, *Wild Seventies*, 216–17; Slap, *Doom of Reconstruction*, 131, 145; Nevins, *Hamilton Fish*, 607.

19. Josephson, *Politicos*, 168; Everett Chamberlin, *The Struggle of '72* (Chicago: Union Publishing Co., 1872), 229, 312–13; "We Submit a Question," *New York Times*, June 22, 1872, 4; "Gross Abuse of the Post-Office," *New York Times*, June 25, 1872, 5; "Two of the Reformers," *New York Times*, June 25, 1872, 4.

20. Smith, *Grant*, 551; Williams, *Horace Greeley*, 300–306; Van Deusen, *Horace Greeley*, 408–25; William M. Cornell, *The Life and Public Career of Hon. Horace Greeley* (Boston: Lee & Shepard, 1872), 268–98; U. S. Grant to Roscoe Conkling, July 15, 1872, Roscoe Conkling Papers, Library of Congress; Chamberlin, *Struggle of '72*, 498–506.

21. Cornell, *Life and Public Career of Hon. Horace Greeley*, 268–98; Williams, *Horace Greeley*, 300–306; Josephson, *Politicos*, 162–63; Chamberlin, *Struggle of '72*, 498–506; Lynch, *Wild Seventies*, 228–39; Slap, *Doom of Reconstruction*, 164–82, 188, 197–98; Schlesinger, *Almanac of American History*, 322.

22. Williams, *Horace Greeley*, xii–xv; Smith, *Grant*, 551; Van Deusen, *Horace Greeley*, 424–25; "Horace Greeley," *New York Times*, December 3, 1872, 8; "Distinguished Mourners," *New York Tribune*, December 5, 1872, 5; "The Greeley Monument," *Irish-American*, December 16, 1876, 8.

23. "The Postmaster of New York Resigns," *New York Times*, March 16, 1873, 1; "The Postmaster of New York Resigns," *New York Herald*, March 16, 1873, 9; "Postmaster Jones's Probable Successor," *New York Tribune*, March 17, 1873, 1; "Deputy Collector James to Succeed General Jones in the Post Office," *New York Herald*, March 17, 1873, 10; "The New-York Postmaster," *New York Times*, March 17, 1873, 1; Jordan, *Roscoe Conkling*, 151; Waugh, *U. S. Grant*, 128.

24. "Resignation of Postmaster Jones," *New York Times*, March 17, 1873, 8; "The Post Office," *New York Republic*, October 23, 1874, 3; Henry Clews, *Twenty-Eight Years in Wall Street* (New York: Irving Publishing Co., 1887), 682; Stephen Fiske, *Off-Hand Portraits of Prominent New Yorkers* (New York: George R. Lockwood & Son, 1884), 191–97.

25. "Resignation of Postmaster Jones," *New York Times*, March 17, 1873, 8; "Postmaster of New York," *New York Commercial Advertiser*, March 17, 1873, 2; "The Twelfth Assembly District Republican Association," *New York Times*, May 1, 1873, 5.

26. "Gen. Patrick H. Jones," *New York Times,* March 29, 1873, 12; "The Retirement of Postmaster Jones," *New York Evening Post,* March 28, 1873, 4.

27. "A New Postmaster," *New York Herald,* March 17, 1873, 8.

7. IRISHMAN AND VETERAN

1. Stephen Rohs, *Eccentric Nation: Irish Performance in Nineteenth-Century New York City* (Madison, N.J.: Fairleigh Dickinson University Press, 2009), 27, 52, 62; Dolan, *Irish Americans,* 50–51, 109; O'Brien and O'Brien, *Ireland,* 92, 98–101; Hasia R. Diner, "'The Most Irish City in the Union': The Era of the Great Migration, 1844–1877," in *The New York Irish,* edited by Ronald H. Bayor and Timothy J. Meagher (Baltimore: Johns Hopkins University Press, 1996), 104–5; Crimmins, *Irish-American Historical Miscellany,* 298–301, 332–34, 342–43.

2. O'Brien and O'Brien, *Ireland,* 101–2; Dolan, *Irish Americans,* 51–52, 187–88; Keneally, *Great Shame,* 7–8.

3. "Telegrams," *Memphis (Tenn.) Daily Appeal,* May 25, 1873, 2; "City and Suburban News," *New York Times,* March 24, 1875, 12; "The Observances in This City," *New York Times,* August 7, 1875, 2; Burroughs and Wallace, *Gotham,* 436–47, 599, 723–24, 879, 948.

4. O'Brien and O'Brien, *Ireland,* 102, 107–8; Dolan, *Irish Americans,* 183–85; Keneally, *Great Shame,* 317; W. S. Neidhardt, *Fenianism in North America* (University Park: Pennsylvania State University Press, 1975), 1–7; Brian Jenkins, *Fenians and Anglo-American Relations during Reconstruction* (Ithaca: Cornell University Press, 1969), 23–27.

5. Dolan, *Irish Americans,* 185–87; Neidhardt, *Fenianism in North America,* 10–15, 28–35, 43–52, 58–82; Keneally, *Great Shame,* 437–43, 500–505; Jenkins, *Fenians and Anglo-American Relations,* 25–39, 215–16, 318–20; Morgan, *Through American and Irish Wars,* 56–58, 109–13, 118–22, 122–24, 128–35, 144–45; McCaffrey, "Forging Forward and Looking Back," 223; Gibson, *Attitudes of the New York Irish,* 174–206.

6. Keneally, *Great Shame,* 415, 459–62; Neidhardt, *Fenianism in North America,* 92; Jenkins, *Fenians and Anglo-American Relations,* 71–72, 218, 231, 241–42, 244–46, 249.

7. "Mass Meeting of Irish Soldiers," *Irish Citizen,* November 30, 1867, 5; Keneally, *Great Shame,* 462; Jenkins, *Fenians and Anglo-American Relations,* 246–47, 254, 255.

8. Nevins and Thomas, *Diary of George Templeton Strong,* 167–69, 295, 352.

9. "Local News in Brief," *New York Times,* June 9, 1869, 8; George B. Van Brunt to Horace Greeley, May 31, 1869, Horace Greeley Papers, Library of Congress; "Irish Republican National Convention," *New York Times,* June 26, 1869, 8; "Irish Republican National Convention," *New York Herald,* June 26, 1869, 7; Burroughs and Wallace, *Gotham,* 1005; Nevins, *Hamilton Fish,* 388–95.

10. Jenkins, *Fenians and Anglo-American Relations,* 237–44, 247, 249, 250, 268, 273, 284, 295; John Warren to Hamilton Fish, March 4, 1875, Simon, Papers of USG, 21:227–28.

11. "Amusements," *New York Times,* August 8, 1875, 6; "Welcome to Barry Sullivan," *New York Tribune,* August 11, 1875, 8; "Lectures," *Irish-American,* February 1, 1873, 8; "Robert Emmet," *Irish-American,* January 2, 1875, 1–2; "Rev. J. V. McNamara," *Irish-American,* January 30, 1875, 4; "Ireland and the Irish," *New York Times,* October 8, 1875, 8; "The Condition of Ireland," *New York Herald,* October 8, 1875, 7; "O'Connor Power," *Irish-American,* October 16, 1875, 1, 8.

12. "The State Capital," *New York Herald,* January 30, 1869, 10; "The State Capital," *New York Herald,* March 10, 1869, 7; "Irish Brigade Officers' Club," *Irish-American,* July 17, 1869: 4.

13. "The 'Irish-American Savings Bank,'" *Irish-American* June 19, 1875, 5; "The 'Irish-American Savings Bank,'" *Irish-American* June 26, 1875, 1.

14. "The Ball Season," *Irish-American*, January 22, 1870, 5; "Ball Season," *Irish-American*, January 25, 1873, 5; "The Ball Season," *Irish-American*, December 27, 1873, 5; "The 'Orphans' Ball,'" *Irish-American*, January 29, 1876, 4; "The Church in New York," *Irish-American*, March 18, 1871, 6. According to "The Orphans' Fair," *New York Evening Post*, December 27, 1870, 4, Jones, together with President Grant and Generals Sherman, Hooker, McClellan, McDowell, and others, were among the candidates voted for in a "sword contest" at a fair to benefit the Union Home and School for orphans.

15. McFeely, *Grant*, 471; Rohs, *Eccentric Nation*, 202, 207; "Cork's Discourtesy," *New York Herald*, January 9, 1879, 4; "Cork's Insult," *New York Herald*, January 10, 1879, 8; "The War against Cork," *Trenton Daily State Gazette*, January 10, 1879, 2; "Cork's Treatment of Grant," *New York Herald*, January 11, 1879, 5; "Grant and the Corkonians," *New York Morning Telegraph*, January 12, 1879, 8.

16. "The War against Cork," *Trenton Daily State Gazette*, January 10, 1879, 2; "Gen. Michael Kerwin Dead," *New York Times*, June 21, 1912, 13; *OR*, vol. 47, pt. 1, 55; "Michael Kerwin," *Journal of the American-Irish Historical Society* 12 (1913): 276–77; "McClane Out, Kerwin In," *New York Times*, July 17, 1894, 1; "Kerwin and the Clan-na-Gael," *New York Tines*, July 17, 1894, 2; "Gen. Kerwin Reappointed," *New York Times*, April 16, 1902, 8; Hickey, "Major David Power Conyngham," 7–8; Fitzgerald, "From Ballingarry to Fredericksburg: David Power Conyngham (1825–1883)," 192–200; "Major David Power Conyngham, LL. D." *New York Herald*, April 2, 1883, 10; Charles William Heckethorn, *The Secret Societies of All Ages and Countries* (London: George Redway, 1897), 282; Dolan, *Irish Americans*, 189; Keneally, *Great Shame*, 513, 521; Jenkins, *Fenians and Anglo-American Relations*, 320–21; McCaffrey, "Forging Forward and Looking Back," 223–24.

17. "The 'Mitchel Testimonial,'" *Irish-American*, August 21, 1875, 1; Keneally, *Great Shame*, 209–11, 261–70, 300–302, 528–29; Morgan, *Through American and Irish Wars*, 56.

18. "Irish Republican Convention," *New York Times*, July 6, 1880, 2; "An Address to Irishmen," *New York Times*, June 22, 1880, 5.

19. "Abstract of Bills in the New-York Legislature," *New York Times*, March 10, 1867: 5; "The State Legislature," *New York Times*, March 15, 1867, 1; "Soldiers' Messenger Corps," *New York Times*, May 21, 1867, 8; Warner, *Generals in Blue*, 434–35; "Employment for Discharged Soldiers," *New York Times*, July 23, 1867, 8; Marten, *Sing Not War*, 56–58.

20. "Board of Health," *New York Times*, August 7, 1867, 2; "Board of Health," *New York Times*, August 15, 1867, 8; "Board of Health," *New York Times*, August 23, 1867, 8; "Board of Health," *New York Times*, September 20, 1867, 2; "Board of Health," *New York Times*, October 4, 1867, 8; "The Board of Health and Street Incumbrances," *New York Times*, November 17, 1867, 4; "Our Disabled Soldiers," *New York Times*, January 2, 1868, 3; "We Are Sorry for the Failure," *New York Times*, September 16, 1868, 4.

21. "Southern Tier Soldiers and Sailors Mass Convention," *Fredonia Censor*, October 17, 1866; "The Boys in Blue," *New York Times*, August 10, 1872, 5.

22. Stuart McConnell, *Glorious Contentment: The Grand Army of the Republic, 1865–1900* (Chapel Hill: University of North Carolina Press, 1992), 15, 25–27, 103, 149, 212, 258–59 n. 43.

23. Bruce, *Harp and the Eagle*, 234–36; "Our Dead Soldiers," *New York Times*, May 31, 1872,

5; "News of the Grand Army," *New York Times*, January 14, 1883, 5; "Presentation of a Flag," *Brooklyn Daily Eagle*, January 19, 1883, 2.

24. "Re-union of the 33d Regiment," *Jerseyman*, Morristown, N.J., September 8, 1893, 3; "M. R. Dennison Attended the 3d Annual Reunion," *Middletown (N.Y.) Daily Times*, September 8, 1893.

25. "Soldiers' Re-Union," *Cattaraugus Republican* (Salamanca, N.Y.), October 7, 1869; PHJ to E. D. Northrup, June 13, 1878, EDN Papers; Mark H. Dunkelman, *Brothers One and All: Esprit de Corps in a Civil War Regiment* (Baton Rouge: Louisiana State University Press, 2004), 269–70.

26. E. D. Northrup diary, January 18 and 20, 1879, August 14 and 16, 1879, October 30, 1879, EDN Papers; Dunkelman, *Brothers One and All*, 270–71.

27. PHJ to E. D. Northrup, January 14 and 16, February 8, 20, 23, 24, and 26, 1894, September 25, 1894, EDN Papers; Joseph W. Dickinson to PHJ, February 6 and 13, 1894, EDN Papers; EDN diary, July 6, 1900, EDN Papers; Dunkelman, *Brothers One and All*, 271–75.

28. "The Military Order of the Loyal Legion of the United States," *New York Times*, April 8, 1866, 8; Robert G. Carroon and Dana B. Shoaf, *Union Blue: The History of the Military Order of the Loyal Legion of the United States* (Shippensburg, Pa.: White Mane Books, 2001), 3–8, 14.

29. Carroon and Shoaf, *Union Blue*, 8; MOLLUS records, Civil War Library and Museum, Philadelphia, Pa.; "Roster of New York Commandery, MOLLUS, 1885," Archives of Commandery in Chief, Military Order of the Loyal Legion of the United States, U. S. Army Military History Institute, U.S. Army Heritage and Education Center, Carlisle, Pa. MOLLUS memberships of lower status were available to members' firstborn sons and direct male descendants and civilians of influence during the war.

8. MILES O'REILLY'S HALO

1. Dolan, *Irish Americans*, 135–40; Lynch, *Wild Seventies*, 22, 34–37, 111–12, 132–33, 142–46, 151; Burroughs and Wallace, *Gotham*, 927–28, 930–31, 1008–11; Kessner, *Capital City*, 136–49; Gordon, *Orange Riots*, 7–13, 182; Mandelbaum, *Boss Tweed's New York*, 66–86; Erie, *Rainbow's End*, 28, 31, 33, 36–38, 43. 57; Diner, "The Most Irish City in the Union," 87, 91–94, 102; McCaffrey, "Forging Forward and Looking Back," 216; Gibson, *Attitudes of the New York Irish*, 240.

2. Dolan, *Irish Americans*, 140–41; Fiske, *Off-Hand Portraits of Prominent New Yorkers*, 217–21; J. Fairfax McLaughlin, *The Life and Times of John Kelly, Tribune of the People* (New York: American News Co., 1885), 9–10, 13–15, 17, 19–20, 34–44, 94, 142, 211, 244, 249, 275–76, 278–85; Lynch, *Wild Seventies*, 249, 251, 261–72; Burroughs and Wallace, *Gotham*, 1020–25, 1027–28, 1030; Mandelbaum, *Boss Tweed's New York*, 92–93; Gibson, *Attitudes of the New York Irish*, 259–60; Gustavus Myers, *The History of Tammany Hall* (New York: Boni & Liveright, 1917), 250, 252–53, 255–56; Josephson, *Politicos*, 186–87; Kessner, *Capital City*, 155, 158–62, 191–97; Mushkat, *Reconstruction of the New York Democracy*, 226–27, 236; Erie, *Rainbow's End*, 39.

3. Dolan, *Irish Americans*, 101–4, 108; Lynch, *Wild Seventies*, 101–5; Burroughs and Wallace, *Gotham*, 888–96, 1003–1008; Barnet Schecter, *The Devil's Own Work: The Civil War Draft Riots and the Fight to Reconstruct America* (New York: Walker, 2005), 7, 136, 173, 209–10, 233–38, 242, 247, 251, 339–41; Gordon, *Orange Riots*, 9, 21–22, 27–49, 104–48, 163–67; Bruce, *Harp and the Eagle*, 173–89; Ural, "Ye Sons of Green Erin Assemble," 121–25; McCaffrey, "Forging Forward and Looking Back," 218; Gibson, *Attitudes of the New York Irish*, 245–50.

4. "Real Estate Transactions," *New York Times*, May 29, 1873: 6; Burroughs and Wallace,

Gotham, 1022–23; "The Police Commissionership," *New York Herald,* March 5, 1874: 3; "New York Legislature," *New York Evening Post,* March 5, 1874, 3; PHJ to Sidney DeKay, undated, July 11, 1874, box 6, John A. Dix Papers, Rare Book and Manuscript Library, Columbia University, New York, N.Y.; "Sidney DeKay," *New York Times,* August 31, 1890, 5; "The Delegates," *New York Times,* September 23, 1874, 1.

5. "The Republican Primaries," *New York Times,* December 9, 1874: 5; "City Politics," *New York Tribune,* October 20, 1874, 8; "The Reform Movement," *New York Herald,* October 21, 1874, 6; Lynch, *Wild Seventies,* 134–35, 138; Stephen D. Engle, *Yankee Dutchman: The Life of Franz Sigel* (Fayetteville: University of Arkansas Press, 1993), 219–20.

6. "Opposition to Tammany," *New York Times,* October 21, 1874, 1; "An Anti-Tammany Ticket," *New York Tribune,* October 21, 1874, 5; "The Coming Election," *New York World,* October 21, 1874: 5; Burrows and Wallace, *Gotham,* 739.

7. Rohs, *Eccentric Nation,* 24–25, 28, 35, 39–41, 49, 68–69, 72, 210.

8. "Anti-Tammany," *New York Herald,* October 21, 1874, 4.

9. "A Great Meeting," *New York Evening Mail,* October 21, 1874, 2; "The Reform Movement," *New York Herald,* October 21, 1874, 6; "Municipal Nominations," *New York Tribune,* October 21, 1874, 4; "Can Tammany Be Beaten?" *New York Evening Post,* October 21, 1874, 2; "City Politics," *New York Evening Telegram,* October 21, 1874, 1; "Local Politics," *Daily Graphic,* October 21, 1874, 804; "Anti-Tammany Democrats," *New York Commercial Advertiser,* October 21, 1874, 2; "Opposition to Tammany," *New York Times,* October 21, 1874, 1.

10. "General Political News," *New York Tribune,* October 21, 1874, 1; "City Politics," *New York Evening Telegram,* October 21, 1874, 1; "Republican County Convention," *New York Republic,* October 21, 1874, 4; "The City Political Contest," *New York Evening Express,* October 21, 1874, 3; "The Republican Programme," *New York Tribune,* October 22, 1874, 10; "The Republicans," *New York Commercial Advertiser,* October 22, 1874, 3; "The Regular Republican Candidates," *Daily Graphic,* October 22, 1874, 816; "We Understand That the Nomination," *New York Republic,* October 22, 1874, 4; "Sketches of the Republican Candidates on the County Ticket," *New York Evening Express,* October 22, 1874, 4; "Local Nominations," *New York Tribune,* October 23, 1874, 1.

11. "Republican Convention," *New York Times,* October 23, 1874, 5; "Republican Convention," *New York Herald,* October 23, 1874, 10; "Local Nominations," *New York Tribune,* October 23, 1874, 1.

12. "First-Rate Nominations," *New York Evening Mail,* October 23, 1874, 2; "Municipal Nominations," *New York Commercial Advertiser,* October 23, 1874, 2; "General Patrick H. Jones," *Daily Graphic,* October 23, 1874, 820; "Too Precipitate," *New York Dispatch,* October 18, 1874, 4; "An Admirable Ticket," *New York Dispatch,* October 25, 1874, 4; Waugh, *U. S. Grant,* 160; Lynch, *Wild Seventies,* 253–54; Nevins, *Hamilton Fish,* 896.

13. "The Last Municipal Ticket," *New York Tribune,* October 23, 1874, 4; "The City Ticket," *New York Tribune,* October 30, 1874, 4; "All the Candidates for the Mayoralty," *New York Tribune,* November 2, 1874, 6; "An Admirable Ticket," *New York Dispatch,* October 25, 1874, 4; "The Democratic Candidate," *New York Republic,* October 26, 1874, 4.

14. "Candidates for Register," *New York Herald,* October 26, 1874, 4; "The Democratic Candidate," *New York Republic,* October 26, 1874, 4; "James Hayes and William M. Tweed," *New York Evening Express,* October 31, 1874, 3; "The Contest for the Registership," *New York Times,* October 30, 1874, 5; "The Death of James Hayes," *New York Times,* March 16, 1897, 9; "And It

Now Appears," *New York Evening Mail,* October 30, 1874, 2; "Morrissey's Man, Hayes," *New York Evening Mail,* November 2, 1874, 2; Lynch, *Wild Seventies,* 322; Myers, *History of Tammany Hall,* 257; Mandelbaum, *Boss Tweed's New York,* 112.

15. "Late Tweed and Sweeny," *Harper's Weekly,* October 31, 1874, 891; Burrows and Wallace, *Gotham,* 823–24, 827, 879, 955, 1027; Lynch, *Wild Seventies,* 26–28, 48–50, 251, 317; Herbert Asbury, *The Gangs of New York: An Informal History of the Underworld* (Garden City, N.Y.: Garden City Publishing Co., 1928), 90–100; Matthew P. Breen, *Thirty Years of New York Politics Up-to-Date* (Published by the author, 1899), 525–31; "Is There Treason in the Wigwam?" *New York Herald,* November 1, 1874, 7; "Mayor and Register," *New York Evening Post,* November 2, 1874, 2; "Morrissey's Man, Hayes," *New York Evening Mail,* November 2, 1874, 2; "Morrissey's Candidate," *New York Dispatch,* November 1, 1874, 4; Rohs, *Eccentric Nation,* 42–48, 66–67; Mandelbaum, *Boss Tweed's New York,* 112; Erie, *Rainbow's End,* 48; Gibson, *Attitudes of the New York Irish,* 82, 236.

16. "Enthusiastic Meeting of the Republicans of the Eighteenth Assembly District," *New York Times,* October 24, 1874, 2; "The Tilden-Dorsheimer Club," *New York Tribune,* October 23, 1874, 5; "The Fox Rebellion," *New York Herald,* October 25, 1874, 6; "P. H. Jones Campaign Club of the Sixteenth Assembly District," *New York Times,* October 30, 1874, 5; "Eighteenth Ward Council of Political Reform," *New York Times,* October 25, 1874, 7; "Political Notes," *New York Times,* November 1, 1874, 7; "The Local Campaign," *New York Herald,* October 24, 1874, 5; "The Prospect in the City," *New York Herald,* October 25, 1874, 6; "The Republican Canvass," *New York Herald,* October 25, 1874, 6.

17. "The Duty of the Hour," *Irish-American,* October 31, 1874, 5; "Mr. Ottendorfer's Position," *New York Tribune,* October 22, 1874, 10; "German Indorsement of the Republican County Ticket," *New York Times,* October 29, 1874, 8; "German Mass-Meeting," *New York Times,* October 31, 1874, 2; "The Republican Convention," *New York Times,* October 16, 1875, 7; "Ottendorfer's Constituents Active," *New York Tribune,* October 31, 1874, 7; "Notes of the City Canvass," *New York Times,* November 2, 1874, 5; "Closing Incidents of the Canvass," *New York Tribune,* November 2, 1874, 1; "Les Elections," *Courrier des États-Unis,* October 27, 1874, 1; "Jones for Register," *New York Commercial Advertiser,* October 28, 1874, 2.

18. "A 'Miles O'Reilly' Canvass," *New York Herald,* November 1, 1874, 10; "The 'Miles O'Reilly Canvass,'" *New York Herald,* November 2, 1874, 6; "Sketches of the Republican Candidates on the County Ticket," *New York Evening Express,* October 22, 1874, 4; "Irishmen Will Remember," *New York Evening Mail,* November 2, 1874, 2; "The City and County Ticket," *New York Republic,* October 23, 1874, 4; "Our City Ticket," *New York Commercial Advertiser,* October 26, 1874, 2; Hanchett, *Irish,* 24.

19. "Candidates for Register," *New York Herald,* October 26, 1874, 4; "General Patrick H. Jones," *Daily Graphic,* November 2, 1874, 1; "General Patrick Henry Jones," *Daily Graphic,* November 2, 1874, 2.

20. "The Contest for the Registership," *New York Times,* October 30, 1874, 5; "Our Next Register," *New York Commercial Advertiser,* October 30, 1874, 2; "The Registership," *New York Times,* November 1, 1874, 2; "Political Notes," *New York Commercial Advertiser,* November 2, 1874, 3.

21. "The Registership or $100,000 a Year," *New York Evening Express,* October 28, 1874, 4; "The Register's Compensation," *New York Evening Post,* November 2, 1874, 2; "The Battle Eve," *New York Evening Telegram,* November 2, 1874, 1.

22. "The Meeting To-night," *New York Commercial Advertiser,* October 29, 1874, 2; "A Rally

for Good Municipal Government," *New York Evening Mail*, October 29, 1874, 2; "A Republican Rally," *New York Times*, October 30, 1874, 1; "Vote for Wales," *New York Commercial Advertiser*, October 29, 1874, 2; "The Election of Gen. Patrick H. Jones," *New York Republic*, October 29, 1874, 4; "Not Yet Answered," *New York Commercial Advertiser*, October 29, 1874, 2; "City Political Gossip," *Daily Graphic*, October 30, 1874, 873; "Is There Treason in the Wigwam?" *New York Herald*, November 1, 1874, 7; "Pool-Selling on the Election," *Daily Graphic*, October 30, 1874, 876.

23. "A Close Combat for Register," *New York Herald*, November 1, 1874, 7; "The City Election," *New York Herald*, November 1, 1874, 10; "Before the Battle," *New York Herald*, November 2, 1874, 6; "If Hayes," *New York Herald*, November 2, 1874, 6; "Throw Away No Vote," *New York Dispatch*, November 1, 1874, 4; "The Battle Eve," *New York Evening Telegram*, November 2, 1874, 1; "A Full Republican Vote," *New York Republic*, November 2, 1874, 4; "Who Would Tweed Vote For," *New York Evening Mail*, November 2, 1874, 2; "As the Last Resort," *New York Republic*, November 3, 1874, 4.

24. "Morrissey's Candidate," *New York Dispatch*, November 1, 1874, 4.

25. "The Die Cast," *New York Evening Telegram*, November 3, 1874, 1; "City Election," *New York Commercial Advertiser*, November 3, 1874, 4; "A Talk with Sachem Kelly, *New York Herald*, November 5, 1874, 3; "The Elections," *Daily Graphic*, November 3, 1874, 14; Lynch, *Wild Seventies*, 328.

26. "Pools at the Astor House," *Daily Graphic*, November 3, 1874, 14; "The people of this city," *Daily Graphic*, November 4, 1874, 18; "The City Vote," *New York Herald*, November 4, 1874, 4; "Political Surmises and Wagers," *New York Tribune*, November 4, 1874, 2; "The City Vote," *New York World*, November 4, 1874, 1; "City Election," *New York Commercial Advertiser*, November 3, 1874, 4.

27. "The Elections," *Daily Graphic*, November 3, 1874, 14.

28. "The City Vote," *New York Herald*, November 4, 1874, 4; "Democratic Victory," *New York Times*, November 4, 1874, 1; "At Irving Hall," *New York Herald*, November 4, 1874, 5; "Recapitulation of the Vote for Register," *New York Herald*, November 4, 1874, 7; "The Local Vote," *New York Evening Telegram*, November 4, 1874, 1; Gibson, *Attitudes of the New York Irish*, 266–68.

29. "The Result in the City," *New York Times*, November 4, 1874, 4; "The Ring Frauds," *New York Times*, January 13, 1875, 6; "The City Election," *New York Herald*, November 4, 1874, 6; "The Irishmen," *New York Herald*, November 4, 1874, 6; "The Registership and Mr. Morrissey," *New York Herald*, November 5, 1874, 6; "Morrissey's Man," *New York Tribune*, November 4, 1874, 4; "The City Returns," *New York Tribune*, November 4, 1874, 1; "The People of This City," *Daily Graphic*, November 4, 1874, 18; "The election of Mr. Wickham," *New York World*, November 4, 1874, 4; "The Returns of the Election," *New York World*, November 5, 1874, 4; "General Jones's Triumph," *New York Commercial Advertiser*, November 4, 1874, 2; "What Does It Mean and Amount To?" *New York Evening Mail*, November 4, 1874, 2; "Editorial Spinnings," *New York Evening Mail*, November 4, 1874, 2; "General Jones' Election," *New York Evening Telegram*, November 4, 1874, 2; "It is astonishing," *New York Evening Mail*, November 5, 1874, 2; *Irish World*, November 14, 1874, quoted in Gibson, *Attitudes of the New York Irish*, 265–66.

30. "A Talk with Sachem Kelly, *New York Herald*, November 5, 1874, 3; "The Opinion of John Morrissey," *New York Herald*, November 5, 1874, 3; "A Talk with the Tammany Chief," *New York Tribune*, November 5, 1874, 1–2; "John Morrissey," *Daily Graphic*, November 5, 1874, 26; "Morrissey Laid Out," *New York Dispatch*, November 8, 1874, 4.

31. Adams, *Historical Gazetteer*, 361; "The Municipal Levees," *New York Times*, January 2,

1875, 8; "The New Register," *New York Herald*, January 2, 1875, 3; "The City's New Year," *New York Tribune*, January 2, 1875, 2; "The Register's Office," *New York Times*, January 3, 1875, 12; "City and Suburban News. New-York," *New York Times*, February 2, 1875, 8; "Municipal Notes," *New York Herald*, February 2, 1875, 8; "City and Suburban News. New-York," *New York Times*, April 4, 1875, 2.

32. "Applying the Touchstone of Common Sense," *New York Times*, March 18, 1875, 2; "Alleged Forged Records," *New York Times*, January 18, 1877, 3; "A Possible Fire in the Register's Office," *New York Times*, September 27, 1877, 2; "The Stewart Estate," *New York Times*, April 17, 1876, 5; "Conveyances by Mrs. A. T. Stewart," *New York Times*, March 17, 1877, 5; Edwin D. Morgan to PHJ, August 25 and October 1, 1875, January 5, 1876, Edwin D. Morgan Papers, New York State Library, Albany; Chester A. Arthur to PHJ, January 19, 1876, Chester Alan Arthur letter press books, New-York Historical Society; Engle, *Yankee Dutchman*, 224.

33. "What the Politicians Say," *Daily Graphic*, June 9, 1876, 3; Jordan, *Roscoe Conkling*, 229–47.

34. *Trow's New York City Directory* (New York: Trow City Directory Co., 1875), 659 (1876), 672 (1877), 692 (1878), 710; Browne, *Great Metropolis*, 25; "The Life at Long Branch," *New York Times*, July 22, 1877, 1; Smith, *Grant*, 606.

35. Greeley, *Recollections of a Busy Life*, 200–206; PHJ to William T. Sherman, November 13, 1877, William T. Sherman Papers, Manuscript Division, Library of Congress; "Fifth-Avenue Theatre," *New York Times*, November 13, 1877, 5; Michael Fellman, *Citizen Sherman: A Life of William Tecumseh Sherman* (New York: Random House, 1995), 354; John F. Marszalek, *Sherman: A Soldier's Passion for Order* (New York: Free Press, 1993), 480–81; Mary Anderson, *A Few Memories* (New York: Harper & Brothers, 1896), 12, 79–81, 82, 116; "Gossip of the Day," *New York Commercial Advertiser*, December 24, 1874, 1.

36. "Amusements," *New York Herald*, February 14, 1875, 16.

9. FINE HORSES AND HEAD MONEY

1. "What's Wrong with the Post Office?" *New York Evening Telegram*, September 13, 1871, 1.

2. "The Post Office Defalcation," *New York Commercial Advertiser*, September 13, 1871, 3; "Post Office Defalcation," 4.

3. "Post Office Defalcation," 3; "Money Orders," *New York Commercial Advertiser*, September 13, 1871, 3; "Post Office Defalcation," 4.

4. "Washington News," *New York Times*, September 14, 1871, 1; "The Government Fleeced," *New York Star*, September 14, 1871, 1; "Post-Office Defalcation," *New York Star*, September 14, 1871, 2; "The Postoffice Defalcation," *New York Evening Post*, September 14, 1871, 4; "Postoffice Defalcation," *New York Evening Telegram*, September 14, 1871, 4; "Two Defaulters," *New York Commercial Advertiser*, September 14, 1871, 2.

5. "The Last Ruin in Wall Street," *New York Sun*, September 14, 1871, 1; Burroughs and Wallace, *Gotham*, 523–25, 640.

6. "A Federal Defalcation," *New York Herald*, September 14, 1871, 7; "Commendable Conduct of Officials," *New York Herald*, September 15, 1871, 7.

7. "Another Defalcation, *New York World*, September 14, 1871, 1.

8. "Post-Office Defalcation," *New York World*, September 14, 1871, 6.

9. "Another Defalcation, *New York World*, September 14, 1871, 1; "The New-York Money-

Order Case," *New York Times,* September 26, 1871, 5; "Arrest of Norton of the Post-Office," *New York Times,* December 16, 1871, 1.

10. John A. J. Creswell to U. S. Grant, June 8, 1872, Records of the Office of the Postmaster General, RG 28, Entry 2, Letters Sent, October 3, 1789–December 31, 1910, 81:135–36; "Issues of the Day," *New York Times,* July 24, 1872, 1–2.

11. "Defaulters Under Grant," *New York Tribune,* July 27, 1872, 1–2.

12. "A Sequel to the Norton Case," *New York Tribune,* January 27, 1874, 8.

13. Liber 87, p. 503, Deed Books, Cattaraugus County Clerk's Office, Little Valley, N.Y.; "Mr. Greeley's Estate in Peril," *New York Sun,* January 27, 1874, 2.

14. "A New Postmaster," *New York Herald,* March 17, 1873, 8; "Resignation of Postmaster Jones," *New York Times,* March 17, 1873, 8.

15. "Real Estate Matters," *New York Herald,* July 12, 1873, 8; "The Real Estate Market," *New York Evening Post,* July 12, 1873, 4; "Real Estate Matters," *New York Herald,* July 16, 1873, 9; "Real Estate Matters," *New York Herald,* July 17, 1873, 8; "The Real Estate Market," *New York Evening Post,* July 18, 1873, 4; "Real Estate Affairs," *New York Herald,* July 29, 1873, 9.

16. "The Post Office Defaulter," *New York Times,* December 24, 1873, 8.

17. "The Post Office Defalcation," *New York Commercial Advertiser,* January 26, 1874, 4; "Suit against Ex-Postmaster Jones," *New York Times,* January 27, 1874, 2; "Business in the Other Courts," *New York Herald,* January 27, 1874, 9; "A Sequel to the Norton Case," *New York Tribune,* January 27, 1874, 8; "Mr. Greeley's Estate in Peril," *New York Sun,* January 27, 1874, 2; "The Postoffice Defalcation," *New York Evening Mail,* January 27, 1874, 4; "The Norton Post-Office Defalcation," *New York World,* January 27, 1874, 2; "New-York," *New York Times,* May 23, 1874, 8; "A Suit," *Daily State Journal* (Alexandria, Va.), January 30, 1874, 2; "Summary of Law Cases," *New York Herald,* May 3, 1877, 8.

18. "Mr. Greeley's Estate in Peril," 2.

19. "Law Reports," *New York Times,* July 25, 1876, 3; "United States Circuit Court Business," *New York Times,* June 26, 1874, 2; "The Norton Embezzlement Case," *Brooklyn Daily Eagle,* July 1, 1874, 4.

20. "Republican Convention," *New York Times,* October 23, 1874, 5; "Local Nominations," *New York Tribune,* October 23, 1874, 1; "Municipal Nominations," *New York Tribune,* October 21, 1874, 4; "Morrissey's Candidate," *New York Dispatch,* November 1, 1874, 4; "We Understand That the Nomination," *New York Republic,* October 22, 1874, 4; "The City and County Ticket," *New York Republic,* October 23, 1874, 4; "The City Ticket," *New York Tribune,* October 30, 1874, 4.

21. "Law Reports," *New York Times,* July 25, 1876, 3.

22. "Personal," *National Republican,* May 19, 1876, 1; "Current Capital Topics," *National Republican,* August 7, 1876, 1; U.S. House of Representatives, *Report of the Postmaster General of the United States,* 45th Cong., 2nd sess., 1877, Ex. Doc. 1, pt. 4, 18.

23. "The Suits against Ex-Postmasters," *New York Times,* May 15, 1877, 3; "Summary of Law Cases," *New York Herald,* May 3, 1877, 8; "The Courts," *New York Tribune,* May 3, 1877, 2. The *Herald* reported three suits and a total payment of twenty-five thousand dollars.

24. Sarah Morris Jones (hereafter cited as SMJ) Deposition, August 1, 1904, PHJ PR, NA; "General Patrick H. Jones," *Ellicottville Post,* August 15, 1900, 3.

25. Committee of Investigation.

26. "A Balky Team," *New York Times*, February 13, 1872, 2; "Another Legislative Committee," *New York Times*, February 23, 1872, 4.

27. "Castle Garden," *New York Times*, March 3, 1872, 3; Committee of Investigation, 88; "Richard O'Gorman Dead," *New York Times*, March 2, 1895; Rohs, *Eccentric Nation*, 105; Bruce, *Harp and the Eagle*, 56, 155, 216; Spann, "Union Green," 208.

28. "The Emigrant Commission," *New York Times*, April 11, 1872, 8; "Emigration and the Emigrant Commission," *Harper's Weekly*, May 31, 1872, 453.

29. Committee of Investigation, 53, 56, 57–58, 85–86, 100, 106–9, 114, 119, 121, 200, 208, 213, 216–18, 250–55, 255–60, 261–62, 265–66, 267; "The Emigration Board," *New York Times*, July 21, 1875, 8; "The Emigration Inquiry," *New York Times*, July 24, 1875, 5.

30. "Nolan's Testimony," *New York Times*, July 25, 1875, 2; "Nolan on the Rack," *New York Herald*, July 25, 1875, 5; Committee of Investigation, 267–70, 284.

31. Committee of Investigation, 271–89, 311.

32. Committee of Investigation, 299–300, 310. Wilson was also a former partner of commission president Richard O'Gorman.

33. Committee of Investigation, 302, 324–26.

34. "Nolan on the Rack," *New York Herald*, July 25, 1875, 5; "Mr. Michael Nolan as an Orator," *New York Herald*, July 25, 1875, 6.

35. Committee of Investigation, 329–41; "Nolan Reappears," *New York Commercial Advertiser*, July 26, 1875, 3; "Nolan Cross-Examined," *New York Times*, July 27, 1875, 1; "The Head-Money Payments," *New York Tribune*, July 27, 1875, 8.

36. Committee of Investigation, 341–44.

37. Committee of Investigation, 344–47, 351, 363–67.

38. "The Hobby of Reform," *New York Herald*, July 26, 1875, 4; "Nolan the Reformer," *New York Herald*, July 27, 1875, 8; "Nolan's Spoils," *New York Tribune*, July 26, 1875, 7; "Crime in New-York—and Albany," *New York Tribune*, July 27, 1875, 4; "The Investigation at Castle Garden," *New York Evening Post*, July 27, 1875, 2.

39. Committee of Investigation, 88–89, 100–101, 106–9, 114, 200–208, 213, 216–18, 250–66, 397–426; "Nolan's Fee," *New York Times*, July 28, 1875, 2.

40. "Resignation of Nolan," *New York Times*, July 28, 1875, 2; "Nolan Resigns," *New York Evening Telegram*, July 27, 1875, 1.

41. "There Will Be No Dissent," *New York World*, July 28, 1875, 4; "Moral Turpitude," *New York Commercial Advertiser*, July 29, 1875, 2; "Moral Turpitude," *New York Dispatch*, August 1, 1875, 4.

42. Committee of Investigation, 434, 455, 469–88; "Investigating Nolan," *New York Herald*, July 28, 1875, 5; "The Emigration Board," *New York Times*, July 29, 1875, 5; "Nolan's Little Fee," *New York Herald*, July 29, 1875, 8; "Not the Least of the Causes," *New York Tribune*, August 12, 1875, 4; "The Assembly Committee," *New York Tribune*, July 29, 1875, 4; "Witnesses Concerning Emigration Affairs Hard to Find," *New York Tribune*, August 11, 1875, 8; "The Emigration Inquiry," *New York Times*, August 12, 1875, 2; "Nolan's Head Money Fees," *New York Tribune*, August 12, 1875, 2; "Nolan's Volens," *New York Herald*, August 12, 1875, 10; "Nolan Has Made a Statement," *New York Herald*, August 12, 1875, 4; "Mr. Michael Nolan's 'Statement,'" *New York Evening Post*, August 12, 1875, 2.

43. Committee of Investigation, 514–15.

44. Committee of Investigation, 515–16, 519; "Head Money and Ship-Owners," *New York*

Times, May 3, 1867, 2; "The Emigration Investigation," *New York Evening Post*, August 12, 1875, 3; "The Emigration Inquiry," *New York Commercial Advertiser*, August 12, 1875, 4; "The Emigration Investigation," *New York Evening Telegram*, August 12, 1875, 1; "Nolan's Head Money," *New York Herald*, August 13, 1875, 6; "Nolan Still Defiant," *New York Tribune*, August 13, 1875, 2; "The Quarantine Investigation," *New York Evening Mail*, August 13, 1875, 4.

45. Committee of Investigation, 516–22.

46. Committee of Investigation, 522–26.

47. "Emigrant Head-Money," *New York Times*, August 13, 1875, 3.

48. Committee of Investigation, 526–32; "Nolan's Head Money," *New York Herald*, August 13, 1875, 6.

49. "No One Supposed," *New York Tribune*, August 13, 1875, 4; "Michael Nolan's Professional Privilege," *New York Tribune*, August 13, 1875, 4; "Nolan," *New York Herald*, August 13, 1875, 4.

50. Committee of Investigation, 532–39; "The Emigration Inquiry," *New York Times*, August 14, 1875, 3.

51. Committee of Investigation, 607–10, 756.

52. "Secret Meeting of the Emigration Committee," *New York Times*, November 10, 1875, 8; "The Emigration Investigation," *New York Herald*, November 10, 1875, 4; "The Emigration Investigation Committee," *New York Evening Telegram*, November 10, 1875, 4; "The Legislative Committee," *New York Evening Mail*, November 10, 1875, 4; "The Emigration Investigation," *New York Tribune*, November 11, 1875, 2.

53. "Quarantine and Emigration," *New York Times*, January 13, 1876, 1.

54. Committee of Investigation, iv–vi.

55. "An Unknown Man Drowned," *New York Times*, April 17, 1876, 2; "A Supposed Suicide," *New York Times*, April 24, 1876, 8; "Two Recent Suicides," *New York Tribune*, April 24, 1876, 5; "Reported Suicide of a Lawyer," *New York Evening Post*, April 24, 1876, 1; "Stories of Suicide," *New York Times*, May 14, 1876, 12; "A Supposed Suicide," *Irish-American*, May 6, 1876, 7.

10. GHOUL'S ERRAND

1. "Ghouls in New-York City," *New York Times*, November 8, 1878, 1; "Ghouls at Work," *New York Herald*, November 8, 1878, 3–4; "A. T. Stewart's Body Stolen," *New York Tribune*, November 8, 1878, 1; "Henry Hilton Is Dead," *New York Times*, August 25, 1899, 1, 3; Browne, *Great Metropolis*, 293; Nevins and Thomas, *Diary of George Templeton Strong*, 388.

2. "Desecration of the Grave," *New York Herald*, November 8, 1878, 6; "The Robbery of the Grave of A. T. Stewart," *Daily Graphic*, November 8, 1878, 49; "No Trace of the Ghouls," *Daily Graphic*, November 8, 1878, 54; "The Work of Ghouls," *New York Illustrated Times*, November 23, 1878, 97, 98, 101–2.

3. "The Cemetery Robbery," *New York Times*, November 9, 1878, 1; "Stewart's Body," *New York Herald*, November 9, 1878, 3; "The Theft of a Corpse," *New York Herald*, November 9, 1878, 4; "The Robbery of the Grave," *New York Tribune*, November 9, 1878, 1.

4. "The Grave Desecrators," *New York Times*, November 10, 1878, 1; "The Stewart Outrage," *New York Herald*, November 10, 1878, 3.

5. "The Robbers of the Tomb," *New York Times*, November 11, 1878, 1; "Wrapped in Mystery," *New York Herald*, November 11, 1878, 3.

6. "The Hounds Balked," *New York Herald*, November 11, 1878, 6; "Seeking for the Ghouls," *New York Times*, November 12, 1878, 1; "The Profaned Tomb," *New York Herald*, November 12, 1878, 4; "A Game of Blind Man's Bluff," *New York Herald*, November 12, 1878, 6.

7. "Is Stewart's Body Found?" *New York Times*, November 13, 1878, 1; "Despairing Police," *New York Herald*, November 13, 1878, 4.

8. "Stewart's Stolen Body," *New York Times*, November 14, 1878, 1; "Not Found," *New York Herald*, November 14, 1878, 4.

9. Jacob A. Riis, *The Making of an American* (New York: Macmillan, 1919), 217–21.

10. "A. T. Stewart's Body Found," *New York Times*, November 15, 1878, 1–2; "Mr. Walling's Trip to New-Jersey," *New York Times*, November 15, 1878, 2; "Light on the Mystery," *New York Herald*, November 15, 1878, 4; "The Cemetery Robbery," *New York Times*, November 16, 1878, 1; "Working Up a Fine Clue," *New York Times*, November 18, 1878, 5; "The Great Search," *New York Herald*, November 16, 1878, 3; "Hunting the Body Snatchers," *New York Herald*, November 16, 1878, 4; "The Desecration of Mr. Stewart's Tomb," *National Police Gazette*, November 16, 1878, 2; "Human Hyenas," *National Police Gazette*, November 16, 1878, 3; Browne, *Great Metropolis*, 314–15.

11. "Closing on the Ghouls," *New York Times*, November 17, 1878, 1; "Under Lock and Key," *New York Herald*, November 17, 1878, 6.

12. "Mr. Stewart's Body," *New York Herald*, November 17, 1878, 8; "The A. T. Stewart Outrage," *New York Times*, November 18, 1878, 1; "Undiscovered," *New York Herald*, November 18, 1878, 3; "The St. Mark's Churchyard Mystery," *New York Herald*, November 18, 1878, 6.

13. "Stewart's Stolen Body," *New York Times*, November 19, 1878, 1; "Stewart's Stolen Body," *New York Times*, November 19, 1878, 1; "The Body Said to Be Under Guard," *New York Times*, November 19, 1878, 2; "Two Prisoners in Court," *New York Times*, November 19, 1878, 2; "Puzzled," *New York Herald*, November 19, 1878, 4; "Why Not?" *New York Herald*, November 19, 1878, 6; "Stewart's Grave Robbers," *New York Times*, November 20, 1878, 1; "The Village of Chatham Excited," *New York Times*, November 20, 1878, 2; "Vreeland and Burke Committed," *New York Times*, November 20, 1878, 2; "The Clare Mystery," *New York Times*, November 20, 1878, 2.

14. "The Stolen Body," *New York Herald*, November 20, 1878, 5; "The New Reward," *New York Herald*, November 22, 1878, 6; "Grave-Robber Christian," *New York Times*, November 21, 1878, 1.

15. "Not Yet Run Down," *New York Herald*, November 21, 1878, 4; "Search for the Robbers," *New York Times*, November 22, 1878, 5; "Still a Mystery," *New York Herald*, November 22, 1878, 4; "The Grave-Yard Robbers," *New York Times*, November 23, 1878, 2; "A Revolting Outrage," *Harper's Weekly*, November 23, 1878, 937–38; "If the Burglars of St. Mark's Succeed," *New York Illustrated Times*, November 23, 1878, 98.

16. "No Further Arrests Made," *New York Times*, November 24, 1878, 2; "Dr. Douglass Not Dr. Christian," *New York Times*, November 24, 1878, 2; "The Discouraging Search," *New York Herald*, November 24, 1878, 6; "The Stewart Outrage," *New York Herald*, November 25, 1878, 10; "The Stewart Grave-Robbery," *New York Times*, November 26, 1878, 2.

17. "The Search for Stewart's Remains," *National Police Gazette*, November 30, 1878, 3; "Mr. Alexander T. Stewart," *New York Times*, December 3, 1878, 3; "The Search for Stewart's Body," *New York Times*, December 12, 1878, 2.

18. "The Body of A. T. Stewart," *New York Sun*, January 16, 1879, 1; "The Recovery of Stewart's Body," *Brooklyn Daily Eagle*, January 16, 1879, 2; "A. T. Stewart," *Brooklyn Daily Eagle*, January 16, 1879, 4; "The Body of A. T. Stewart," *New York Sun*, January 17, 1879, 1; "The Grave

Robbery," *New York Tribune*, January 17, 1879, 2; "The Body of A. T. Stewart," *New York Sun*, January 18, 1879, 1; "Mr. A. T. Stewart's Body," *New York Sun*, January 19, 1879, 1; "The Stewart Grave Robbery," *New York Tribune*, January 30, 1879, 1; "Was Mr. Stewart's Body in That Box?" *New York Sun*, March 3, 1879, 3; "The Stolen Body," *New York Herald*, August 14, 1879, 3.

19. "Unrecovered," *New York Herald*, August 13, 1879, 3; "The Body of A. T. Stewart," *New York Times*, August 14, 1879, 2; "A. T. Stewart's Body," *New York Herald*, August 17, 1879, 5; "Mr. A. T. Stewart's Body," *New York Sun*, August 17, 1879, 5; "Mrs. Stewart Deceived," *New York Tribune*, August 16, 1879, 5.

20. "Mr. A. T. Stewart's Body," *New York Sun*, August 17, 1879, 5.

21. "The Body of A. T. Stewart," *New York Times*, August 14, 1879, 2; "Unrecovered," 3; "Mr. A. T. Stewart's Body," *New York Sun*, August 17, 1879, 5.

22. "Unrecovered," 3; "The Body of A. T. Stewart," *New York Times*, August 14, 1879, 2; "Mr. A. T. Stewart's Body," *New York Sun*, August 17, 1879, 5; "Mrs. Stewart Deceived," *New York Tribune*, August 16, 1879, 5; "The Stolen Body," *New York Herald*, August 14, 1879, 3; Nevins and Thomas, *Diary of George Templeton Strong*, 237.

23. "The Body of A. T. Stewart," *New York Times*, August 14, 1879, 2; "Stewart's Body Not Found," *New York Tribune*, August 14, 1879, 1; "A. T. Stewart's Body," *New York Herald*, August 17, 1879, 5; "Mr. A. T. Stewart's Body," *New York Sun*, August 17, 1879, 5.

24. "Mr. A. T. Stewart's Body," *New York Sun*, August 17, 1879, 5.

25. "Mr. A. T. Stewart's Body," 5.

26. "The Body of A. T. Stewart," *New York Times*, August 14, 1879, 2; "Mr. A. T. Stewart's Body," *New York Sun*, August 17, 1879, 5; "Unrecovered," *New York Herald*, August 13, 1879, 3; "Mrs. Stewart Deceived," *New York Tribune*, August 16, 1879, 5.

27. "Mr. A. T. Stewart's Body," *New York Sun*, August 17, 1879, 5.

28. "Mr. A. T. Stewart's Body," *New York Sun*, August 17, 1879, 5; "The Body of A. T. Stewart," *New York Times*, August 14, 1879, 2.

29. "The Body of A. T. Stewart," *New York Times*, August 14, 1879, 2.

30. "Mr. A. T. Stewart's Body," 5.

31. "Mr. A. T. Stewart's Body," 5.

32. "Unrecovered," *New York Herald*, August 13, 1879, 3; "The Body of A. T. Stewart," *New York Times*, August 14, 1879, 2; "Mrs. Stewart Deceived," *New York Tribune*, August 16, 1879, 5; "Mr. A. T. Stewart's Body," *New York Sun*, August 17, 1879, 5.

33. "Unrecovered," *New York Herald*, August 13, 1879, 3; "Stewart's Body Not Found," *New York Tribune*, August 14, 1879, 1; "Mrs. Stewart Deceived," *New York Tribune*, August 16, 1879, 5.

34. "Mr. A. T. Stewart's Body," 5.

35. "Mr. A. T. Stewart's Body," 5.

36. "No Doubt It Would Be Gratifying," *New York Tribune*, August 8, 1879, 4; "Unrecovered," *New York Herald*, August 13, 1879, 3; "The Stewart Grave Robbers," *New York Herald*, August 13, 1879, 6.

37. "Judge Hilton's Tactics," *New York Evening Telegram*, August 13, 1879, 2; "The Unrecovered Body," *New York Evening Mail*, August 13, 1879, 2; "Another Stewart Rumor," *New York Evening Express*, August 13, 1879, 1; "Sensational," *Brooklyn Daily Eagle*, August 13, 1879, 3; "The Stewart Grave Robbery," *Daily Witness* (Montreal), August 13, 1879, 1.

38. "The Body of A. T. Stewart," *New York Times*, August 14, 1879, 2.

39. "The Stolen Body," *New York Herald*, August 14, 1879, 3.

40. "Stewart's Body Not Found," *New York Tribune*, August 14, 1879, 1; "It is with great reluctance," *New York Tribune*, August 14, 1879, 4; "Mrs. Stewart Deceived," *New York Tribune*, August 16, 1879, 5.

41. "Mr. Stewart's Remains," *New York Commercial Advertiser*, August 14, 1879, 3; "Stewart's Body," *New York Evening Mail*, August 14, 1879, 4; "The Late A. T. Stewart," *New York Sun*, August 14, 1879, 3; "City Items," *Daily Witness* (Montreal), August 15, 1879, 5; "Montreal au Jour le Jour," *La Patrie* (Montreal), August 15, 1879, 3; "The Stewart Robbery," *Daily Witness* (Montreal), August 16, 1879, 1; "Tracing the Theft of Stewart's Remains," *Daily Witness* (Montreal), August 16, 1879, 8; "Montreal au Jour le Jour," *La Patrie* (Montreal), August 16, 1879, 3; "Montreal News," *Montreal Witness*, August 20, 1879, 8; "The Stewart's Remains," *New York Evening Express*, August 14, 1879, 2; "A. T. Stewart's Body," *Brooklyn Daily Eagle*, August 14, 1879, 2; "History of a Day," *Daily Graphic*, August 14, 1879, 300; "No Bargaining with Ghouls," *New York Tribune*, August 15, 1879, 4.

42. "A. T. Stewart's Body," *New York Herald*, August 17, 1879, 5.

43. "Mr. A. T. Stewart's Body," *New York Sun*, August 17, 1879, 5; "The Robbers of the Grave," *New York Tribune*, August 18, 1879: 5; "Some of Our Esteemed Contemporaries," *New York World*, August 18, 1879, 4; "Current Events," *Brooklyn Daily Eagle*, August 18, 1879, 2.

44. "Some of Our Esteemed Contemporaries," 4; "The Grave Robbery," *New York Tribune*, August 19, 1879, 5; "The Robbers of the Grave," *New York Tribune*, August 20, 1879, 1; "The Stewart Graverobbers," *Buffalo Morning Express*, August 20, 1879, 4; "Patrick H. Jones," *Buffalo Morning Express*, August 20, 1879, 4.

45. "Mr. Stewart's Body," *New York Evening Express*, August 19, 1879, 4.

46. "General P. H. Jones," *Cattaraugus Republican* (Salamanca and Little Valley, N.Y.), September 4, 1879, 1.

47. Jordan, *Roscoe Conkling*, 309–14; "The Discovery of A. T. Stewart's Body," *New York Star*, June 26, 1881, 4; "A. T. Stewart's Body," *New York Star*, June 26, 1881, 1; "A. T. Stewart's Body," *New York Star*, June 27, 1881, 1; "A. T. Stewart's Body," *New York Star*, June 28, 1881, 1; "A. T. Stewart's Body," *New York Star*, June 29, 1881, 1; "The Body of A. T. Stewart," *New York Star*, June 30, 1881, 1; "The Story of the Robbery," *New York Times*, August 21, 1881, 2.

48. "Stewart's Body Sought," *New York Times*, August 21, 1881, 1–2; "A. T. Stewart's Remains," *New York Times*, August 22, 1881, 8; "The Digging at Cypress Hills," *New York Times*, August 23, 1881, 8; "The Cypress Hill Search Abandoned," *New York Times*, August 24, 1881, 5.

49. "Finished," *Brooklyn Daily Eagle*, February 19, 1883, 4; "A Question of Dollars and Cents," *Brooklyn Daily Eagle*, November 12, 1883, 2; "The Cathedral Accepted," *New York Times*, April 17, 1885, 2; "Is the Body in the Crypt?" *New York World*, April 20, 1885, 8; "Mrs. Stewart's Gift," *New York Times*, May 22, 1885, 5; "Services of Consecration," *New York Times*, May 27, 1885, 4; "The Rich Man's Tomb," *Pittsburgh Dispatch*, April 13, 1885; Elias, *Alexander T. Stewart*, 185, 187.

50. "Mrs. A. T. Stewart Dead," *New York Times*, October 26, 1886, 1; "The Dead Merchant," *New York World*, October 26, 1886, 5.

51. J. North Conway, *Bag of Bones: The Sensational Grave Robbery of the Merchant Prince of Manhattan* (Guilford, Conn.: Lyons Press, 2012), 191–95; "Henry Hilton Is Dead," *New York Times*, August 25, 1899, 1, 3; "Death of Ex-Judge Hilton," *Brooklyn Daily Eagle*, August 25, 1899, 4; Elias, *Alexander T. Stewart*, 197–202.

52. "Mrs. Stewart Deceived," *New York Tribune,* August 16, 1879, 5.

53. "In the Cathedral Crypt," *Brooklyn Daily Eagle,* October 30, 1887, 9; "A City's Great Sensations," *New York Times,* October 30, 1887, 9; "A Story of Police Life," *New York Tribune,* October 30, 1887, 11; "Walling's Tales of Crime," *New York Herald* October 30, 1887, 10; "Stewart's Stiff," *National Police Gazette,* November 12, 1887, 6; George W. Walling, *Recollections of a New York Chief of Police* (New York: Caxton Book Concern, 1887), 231.

54. Walling, *Recollections of a New York Chief of Police,* 230–32; Henry C. Romaine Pension File, National Archives; Phisterer, *New York in the War of the Rebellion,* 375.

55. Walling, *Recollections,* 232–34.

56. Walling, *Recollections,* 234–35.

57. "A City's Great Sensations," *New York Times,* October 30, 1887, 9; "Walling's Story Laughed At," *New York Evening World,* October 31, 1887, 2.

58. Herbert Asbury, *The Gangs of New York: An Informal History of the Underworld* (Garden City, N.Y.: Garden City Publishing Co., 1928), 218–24; Marquis James, "The Corpse of A. T. Stewart," *New Yorker,* December 6, 1941, 70, 72–73, 76, 78, 80–85; Elias, *Alexander T. Stewart,* 209–22, 247; Harry E. Resseguie, "Merchant Prince," MS (219), Resseguie Collection, Baker Library Historical Collection, Harvard Business School, Boston; James Lardner and Thomas Reppetto, *NYPD: A City and Its Police* (New York: Henry Holt, 2000), 80–81. Ruth Reynolds, in "The Merchant Prince and the Grave Robbers," *New York Daily News,* August 12, 1956, 16, ignored Walling's account—and all the other evidence—to present a far-fetched, secondhand version of the story in which Stewart's endeavors disturbed a churchyard, causing retribution.

59. Wayne Fanebust, *The Missing Corpse: Grave Robbing a Gilded Age Tycoon* (Westport, Conn.: Praeger, 2005), 178, 183, 187, 225, 230–33, 241, 243.

60. Conway, *Bag of Bones,* 159–60, 203, 205, 242.

61. "The Stewart and Other Cases," *New York Tribune,* September 9, 1883, 6.

11. DECLINE

1. "The Fall Elections," *Irish-American,* October 6, 1877, 4; "Political Notes," *Irish-American,* January 20, 1892, 5; "A Talk with the Tammany Chief," *New York Tribune,* November 5, 1874, 1–2.

2. McDougall, *Throes of Democracy,* 531; "The November Elections," *New York Times,* October 28, 1878, 2; "National Greenback-Labor Party," *New York Herald,* October 29, 1878, 4; "Congressional Candidates," *New York Herald,* October 30, 1878, 6; "Congressional Candidates," *New York Tribune,* November 2, 1878, 5; "Ninth Congressional District," *New York Herald,* November 3, 1878, 8; "The City Vote," *New York Times,* November 7, 1878, 2; Mark A. Lause, *The Civil War's Last Campaign: James B. Weaver, the Greenback-Labor Party and the Politics of Race and Section* (Lanham, Md.: University Press of America, 2001), 17–38; Erie, *Rainbow's End,* 8, 49; Diner, "The Most Irish City in the Union," 95–99, 101; Gibson, *Attitudes of the New York Irish,* 91–93, 270–75, 296–97.

3. "Republicans in Council," *New York Herald,* July 25, 1879, 10; "The Political Battle," *New York Herald,* November 2, 1879, 9.

4. "And still they come," *Stark County Democrat* (Canton, Ohio), July 22, 1880, 2; "Ex-Postmaster," *Brenham (Tex.) Weekly Banner,* July 29, 1880, 2; "For Hancock," *Daily Cairo (Ill.) Bulletin,* October 28, 1880, 2; "John Kelly's Anxiety," *New York Times,* August 27, 1880, 1; "The

Lottery Concluded," *New York Times*, September 3, 1880, 2; "Hancock's Friendly Phalanx," *New York Herald*, August 28, 1880, 2; "Conservative Republicans," *New York Herald*, September 16, 1880, 4; "Independent Republicans," *Truth*, September 16, 1880, 1.

5. "The Last Legislature," *New York Times*, June 17, 1882, 8; "Uproarious Anti-Monopolists," *New York Tribune*, June 17, 1882, 2.

6. "The National Anti-Monopoly League," *New York Times*, January 1, 1881, 8; "The Anti-Monopoly League," *New York Times*, January 29, 1881, 3; "The Anti-Monopoly Crusade," *New York Times*, February 23, 1881, 4; "The Anti-Monopoly Creed," *New York Times*, September 14, 1882, 5; "The Anti-Monopoly Party," *New York Times*, September 25, 1881; "Favoring the Democrats," *New York Times*, October 4, 1882, 2.

7. Calhoun, *From Bloody Shirt to Full Dinner Pail*, 75–76.

8. Mandelbaum, *Boss Tweed's New York*, 94.

9. Bunting, *Ulysses S. Grant*, 147–55; McFeely, *Grant*, 450–517; Smith, *Grant*, 606–28; Waugh, *U. S. Grant*, 216, 229, 242–46; "A Nation at a Tomb," *New York Times*, August 9, 1885, 1; *National Cyclopedia of American Biography*, 3:52; Wilson and Fiske, *Appleton's Cyclopedia of American Biography*, 2:431; Dilley, *Biographical and Portrait Cyclopedia of Chautauqua County*, 328; Josephson, *Politicos*, 160.

10. Walter H. Hebert, *Fighting Joe Hooker* (Indianapolis: Bobbs-Merrill, 1944), 295–96; Lloyd Lewis, *Sherman: Fighting Prophet* (New York: Harcourt, Brace & Co., 1932), 651–52.

11. *Trow's New York City Directory* (New York: Trow City Directory Co., 1879), 734 (1880), 769 (1881), 785; *Webb's Consolidated Directory of the North and South Shores, Staten Island, 1882–3* (New York: Webb Brothers, 1882), 172 [1884], 172; Daniel P. Libby, comp., *The Standard Directory of Richmond County, for the Year 1893–1894* (New Brighton, N.Y.: Richmond County Standard, 1893), 174 (1897), 150; *Trow's Business and Residential Directory of the Borough of Richmond* (New York: Trow Directory Co., 1899), 83 (1900), 184; PHJ to B. Perry, April 5, 1880, author's collection; SMJ Deposition, August 1, 1904, and James M. Jones Deposition, August 1, 1904, both in PHJ PR, NA. The directories list the Joneses' Port Richmond residence as 2 Ann Street, but Jones's death certificate and the deposition of SMJ of August 1, 1904, give their home address as 3 Ann Street.

12. "Men Who Catch Trains," *New York Times*, July 6, 1890,14.

13. McConnell, *Glorious Contentment*, 143; Gustavus A. Weber, *The Bureau of Pensions: Its History, Activities and Organization* (Baltimore: Johns Hopkins Press, 1923), 4–5; PHJ, Declaration for an Original Invalid Pension, September 28 and October 28, 1881; PHJ Deposition, May 20, 1884; Certificates of Walter R. Gillette, September 22, 1881, and August 17, 1884, and of William O'Meagher, November 1, 1881, and May 21, 1884; Affidavit of Henry Van Aernam, June 9, 1884; all in PHJ PR, NA. On pensions and attitudes of and toward pensioners, see Marten, *Sing Not War*, 199–243.

14. PHJ to Gen. John C. Black, Commissioner of Pensions, January 8, 1886; Examining Surgeon's Certificate, Dr. William O. McDonald, August 20, 1884; H. C. Borden to Hon. J. C. Black, Commissioner of Pensions, August 31, 1885; PHJ Pension Certificate No. 306.530; James M. Jones Deposition, August 1, 1904; Helen E. Hoopes Deposition, August 1, 1904; all in PHJ PR, NA.

15. PHJ, Declaration for the Increase of an Invalid Pension, September 22, 1885; PHJ to Gen. John C. Black, Commissioner of Pensions, January 8, 1886; J. J. Bartlett to Mr. Mack,

Chief Case Division, January 11, 1886; J. D. Morgan, Reviewer, to Mr. Van Matee, Chief, Board of Review, Pension Office, March 9, 1886; Surgeon's Certificate, October 13, 1886; all in PHJ PR, NA; Bell, *Mosquito Soldiers*, 2, 29, 118.

16. Marten, *Sing Not War*, 251.

17. Surgeon's Certificate, October 13, 1886; "The 'Mathew Monument,'" *Irish-American*, June 8, 1872, 6; McCaffrey, "Forging Forward and Looking Back," 220–21; Gibson, *Attitudes of the New York Irish*, 36–40; SMJ Deposition, August 1, 1904, both in PHJ PR, NA; Marten, *Sing Not War*, 100–111, 198.

18. John G. Mitchell Deposition, October 5, 1904; Edgar D. Coonley Deposition, November 17, 1904; Special Examiner J. H. Elliott to E. F. Ware, Commissioner of Pensions, November 19, 1904, all in PHJ PR, NA; Henry Van Aernam to Alfred W. Benson, February 8, 1888, Alfred W. Benson Papers, Kansas State Historical Society, Topeka, Kans.; PHJ to E. D. Northrup, July 1, 1893, EDN Papers.

19. E. D. Northrup diary, February 3, 1892; PHJ to E. D. Northrup, July 1 and October 1, 1893, February 8, February 20, February 23, February 24, September 25, 1894, August 15, 1897; Alexander Bird to E. D. Northrup, September 27, 1894; William Phelps to Messrs. Fitzpatrick and Weller, September 2, 1895; George C. Waterman to E. D. Northrup, February 5, 1896; all in EDN Papers; SMJ Deposition, August 1, 1904, PHJ PR, NA; "Funeral of James Gayler," *New York Times*, June 22, 1897, 7; "Postal Reduction Decried," *New York Times*, January 25, 1898, 5; "No British Alliance," *Irish World*, January 15, 1898, 1; "Petition to the Senate of the United States," *Irish World*, February 5, 1898, 1.

20. Dr. Edgar D. Coonley Affidavit, August 23, 1898; John G. Mitchell Deposition, October 5, 1904; Special Examiner J. H. Elliott to E. F. Ware, Commissioner of Pensions, November 19, 1904, all in PHJ PR, NA; PHJ to James W. Eldridge, September 15, 1899, Eldridge Collection, The Henry E. Huntington Library and Art Gallery, San Marino, Calif.; E. D. Northrup diary, July 6, 1900, and E. D. Northrup to Matthew B. Cheney, January 26, 1903, EDN Papers.

21. Dr. Edgar D. Coonley Deposition, March 29, 1904; SMJ Deposition, August 1, 1904; James M. Jones Deposition, August 1, 1904; James J. Brown Deposition, September 28, 1904; all in PHJ PR, NA.

22. PHJ Death Certificate, July 23, 1900, PHJ PR, NA; "Death of Gen. P. H. Jones," *Richmond County Advance*, July 25, 1900; "General P. H. Jones Dead," *New York Press*, July 25, 1900, 7; "Patrick Henry Jones," *New York Commercial Advertiser*, July 25, 1900, 5; "General Jones Dead at Seventy," *New York Herald*, July 25, 1900, 7; "Patrick Henry Jones," *New York Evening Post*, July 25, 1900, 10; "Death of Gen. Patrick H. Jones," *New York World*, July 25, 1900, 7; "Death of General Jones," *Staten Islander* (New Brighton, N.Y.), July 25, 1900, 1; "General Jones Dead," *Columbus (Ga.) Enquirer-Sun*, July 25, 1900, 5; "Brig. Gen. Jones Dead," *Sioux City (Iowa) Journal*, July 25, 1900, 1; "The Death Roll," *Buffalo Evening News*, July 25, 1900, 6; "Deaths of a Day," *Scranton (Pa.) Tribune*, July 25, 1900, 1; "General Patrick Henry Jones," *Omaha (Neb.) Daily Bee*, July 25, 1900, 4; "Patrick Henry Jones Dead," *New York Times*, July 26, 1900; "Death of a Veteran," *Jamestown Evening Journal*, July 26, 1900, 1; "Death of Gen. P. H. Jones," *Irish-American* (NY.), July 28, 1900, 8; "Jones," *New York Freeman's Journal and Catholic Register*, July 28, 1900, 8; "News Has Been Received," *Ellicottville Post*, August 1, 1900, 8; "Brig.-Gen. Patrick H. Jones, Dead," *Boston Pilot*, August 4, 1900, 5; "Jones," *Irish World*, August 4, 1900, 9; "P. H. Jones," *Dakota City (Neb.) Eagle*, August 9, 1900; "Death of Patrick H. Jones," *Cattaraugus Republican*

(Salamanca, N.Y.), August 10, 1900; Alfred S. Johnson, ed., *The Cyclopedic Review of Current History*, vol. 10, no. 7, September 1900 (Boston: Current History Co., 1901), 685; *Biographical Directory of the State of New York 1900* (New York: Biographical Directory Co., 1900), 233.

23. "Death of a Veteran," *Jamestown Evening Journal*, July 26, 1900, 1; "Pat Jones," *Capital Herald* (Little Valley, N.Y.), August 9, 1900, 8; "General Patrick H. Jones," *Ellicottville Post*, August 15, 1900, 3.

24. "Reunion of Veterans Held at Cattaraugus Last Friday," *Cattaraugus Republican*, October 5, 1900; Matthew B. Cheney to E. D. Northrup, January 20, 1903, EDN Papers; "Patrick Jones Camp, No. 65, Sons of Veterans," *Ellicottville Post*, May 28, 1902.

25. "P. H. Jones and A. T. Stewart's Body," *New York Sun*, July 26, 1900,6; "Stewart's Body," *Fort Worth (Tex.) Morning Register*, August 3, 1900, 6; "A. T. Stewart's Body," *Brooklyn Daily Eagle*, August 3, 1900, 7.

26. SMJ, "Application for Accrued Pension (Widow's)" January 25, 1901; SMJ Affidavit, April 1, 1901; Special Examiner Report, May 3, 1901; SMJ Deposition, August 1, 1904; James M. Jones Deposition, August 1, 1904; all in PHJ PR, NA.

27. G. W. Moore, Special Examiner, to H. Clay Evans, Commissioner of Pensions, February 13, 1902; SMJ, Power of Attorney, May 15, 1902; SMJ Deposition, August 1, 1904; James M. Jones Deposition, August 1, 1904; Helen E. Hoopes Deposition, August 1, 1904; all in PHJ PR, NA.

28. Untitled form listing rate per month; Copy of "H.R. 1062, An Act Granting pension and increase of pension to certain soldiers and sailors of the civil war, and certain widows of such soldiers and sailors"; SMJ Death Certificate; Helen E. Hoopes, "Application for Reimbursement," March 4, 1913; Edward O. Wieters affidavit, April 16, 1913, all in PHJ PR, NA; "Deaths," *Philadelphia Public Ledger*, December 19, 1912.

29. "Gift to the Post Office," *New York Times*, April 25, 1897, 24; Louis M. Lauscher, Information Officer, Office of the Postmaster, United States Post Office, New York, to author, February 15, 1974; Robert Daruk Sr., Postmaster, New York District, to author, February 6, 2008. The image is reproduced in Thomas C. Jefferies, *The Postal System of the United States and the New York General Post Office* (New York: Manufacturers Trust Co., 1922), 33.

30. Items in the author's collection.

31. "Mr. A. T. Sommerville of Ellicottville," *Ellicottville Post*, August 22, 1923; "Catt. Co. Seeks Grant to Preserve War Saddle," undated clipping courtesy of Margaret Arrance, Sanford, N.C., author's collection; "Civil War Saddle to Be Back on Display Soon," *Corner Stone: Quarterly Newsletter of the Cattaraugus County Museum and Research Library* (July 2005): 1; "Civil War Saddle Is Being Exhibited," *Buffalo News*, August 22, 2005.

32. Mark H. Dunkelman, "The Doctored Botticher," *Military Images* 28, no. 5 (March–April 2007): 17–19.

33. Greeley, *Recollections of a Busy Life*, 143.

BIBLIOGRAPHY

MANUSCRIPT SOURCES

Private Collections

Charles W. Abell Letters. Jean Schultz Collection, Westford, Vt.

Homer A. Ames Letters. Carolyn Ames Simons Collection, Phoenix, Ariz.

Mervin P. Barber Diary. Paul A. Lockwood Collection, Newark, Ohio.

Alexander Bird Diary. Janet Bird Whitehurst Collection, Los Banos, Calif.

Joel M. Bouton Letters. Maureen Koehl Collection, South Salem, N.Y.

Francis M. Bowen Diary. Ronald Bowen Collection, Brighton, Mich.

Martin D. Bushnell Letters. Frank M. Bushnell Collection, Napoli, N.Y.

Winfield S. Cameron Letter. Jerome H. Davis Collection, Corry, Pa.

Alonzo A. Casler Letters. Marjorie D. Hazen Collection, Ashland, Ohio.

Newton A. Chaffee Letters. Howard Stearns Collection, Fairhope, Ala.

William Charles Letters and Diary. Jack Finch Collection, Freedom, N.Y.

James W. Clements Letters. Judith Wachholz Collection, River Falls, Wisc.

Fayette Dutcher Letter. Celia M. Krieger Collection, Little Valley, N.Y.

James D. Emmons Letters. Leslie R. Page Collection, Auburn, N.Y.

George Eugene Graves Letters. Ron Meininger Collection, Gaithersburg, Md.

Stephen R. Green Letters (December 8, 1862; and November 21, 1863). Author's Collection.

Stephen R. Green Diary and Letters (December 12, 1862; December 28, 1863; February 18, 1864; and June 20, 1864). Phil Palen Collection, Gowanda, N.Y.

James L. Harding Papers. Ken Ursin Collection, Mechanicsburg, Pa.

William D. Harper Diary. Raymond Harper Collection, Dunkirk, N.Y.

Dana P. Horton Letters. Author's Collection.

Arthur Hotchkiss Letters. Author's Collection.

Patrick H. Jones Letters. Author's Collection.

George J. Mason Letters. Juliet Mason Collection, Russell, Pa.

Richard J. McCadden Letters. Ron Meininger Collection, Gaithersburg, Md.

Richard J. McCadden Letters (May 5, 1863; and May 9, 1864). Author's Collection.

Barzilla Merrill Letters. Doris Williams Collection, Orange City, Fla.

George W. Newcomb Letter (December 4, 1862). Michael W. Schaefer Collection, Gettysburg, Pa.

George W. Newcomb Letter (December 7, 1862). Author's Collection.

George W. Newcomb Letters (January 4 and May 8, 1863). U.S. Army Military History Institute, Carlisle Barracks, Pa.

William W. Norton Letters. Author's Collection.

Joshua R. Pettit Diary. Mary C. Ranney Collection, Ellicottville, N.Y.

John N. Porter Letters. Francis N. T. Diller Collection, Fairview, Pa.

James D. Quilliam Letters. Edithe Nasca Collection, Fredonia, N.Y.

Franklin T. Saunders Letter. Susan M. Martin Collection, Mount Joy, Pa.

Edgar Shannon Letters (August 1862–February 1864). Alberta McLaughlin Collection, Frewsburg, N.Y.

Edgar Shannon Letters (March 1864–April 1865). Timothy T. Shaw Collection, Cheektowaga, N.Y.

Emory Sweetland Letters. Lyle Sweetland Collection, South Dayton, N.Y.

Oscar M. Taylor Letters. Virginia Canella Collection, St. Petersburg, Fla.

Henry Van Aernam Letter (November 22, 1864). Author's Collection.

Hiram Vincent Letters. Robert Vincent Collection, Alpharetta, Ga.

Lewis D. Warner Diary (1863). John L. Spencer Collection, Canandaigua, N.Y.

Lewis D. Warner Diary (1864–65). Charles H. Warner III Collection, Santa Rosa, Calif.

Stephen Welch Diary. Carolyn Stoltz Collection, Tonawanda, N.Y.

Charles E. Whitney Diary. Elizabeth Maher Collection, Mayville, N.Y.

Repositories

Augustana College, Sioux Falls, S.D.
Center for Western Studies
Samuel D. Woodford Letters

Bowdoin College Library, Brunswick, Me.
Oliver Otis Howard Papers

Brown University, Providence, R.I.
John Hay Library
Petition to President Lincoln

Cattaraugus County Clerk's Office, Little Valley, N.Y.
Deed Books

Chautauqua County Historical Society, Westfield, N.Y.
George A. Taylor Letters

CIVIL WAR LIBRARY AND MUSEUM, PHILADELPHIA
Military Order of the Loyal Legion of the United States Records

COLUMBIA UNIVERSITY, NEW YORK
Rare Book and Manuscript Library
John A. Dix Papers

CORNELL UNIVERSITY, ITHACA, N.Y.
Edwin Dwight Northrup Papers, no. 4190, Department of Manuscripts and University Archives

DUKE UNIVERSITY, DURHAM, N.C.
Rare Book, Manuscript, and Special Collections Library
James G. Macomber Letters

ELLICOTTVILLE HISTORICAL SOCIETY, ELLICOTTVILLE, N.Y.
Regimental Letter Book, 154th New York

EMORY UNIVERSITY, ATLANTA
Manuscript, Archives, and Rare Book Library
Green Family Civil War Papers, 1861–63

FENTON HISTORY CENTER, JAMESTOWN, N.Y.
John C. Griswold Letters

HARVARD BUSINESS SCHOOL, BOSTON
Baker Library Historical Collection
Resseguie Collection

HENRY E. HUNTINGTON LIBRARY AND ART GALLERY, SAN MARINO, CALIF.
Eldridge Collection

KANSAS STATE HISTORICAL SOCIETY, TOPEKA
Alfred W. Benson Diary and Letters

LIBRARY OF CONGRESS, WASHINGTON, D.C.
Roscoe Conkling Papers
Hamilton Fish Papers
Horace Greeley Papers
William T. Sherman Papers

Martin County Historical Society, Fairmont, Minn.
William Bird Jr. Letters

Mazomanie Historical Society, Mazomanie, Wisc.
Horace Smith Diary

Minnesota Historical Society, St. Paul
Newell Burch Diary

National Archives, Washington, D.C.
Truman Harkness Letter, Harkness Pension File
Patrick Henry Jones Medical Records
Patrick Henry Jones Military Records
Patrick Henry Jones Pension Records
Letters Received by the Commission Branch of the Adjutant General's Office, 1863–70
Letters Sent, Twentieth Corps, April 1864–May 1865, vol. 20, RG 393, pt. 2, entry 5377
154th New York Descriptive and Order Books
154th New York Muster Rolls
154th New York Returns
Edwin R. Osgood Letter, Osgood Pension File
Passenger Lists of Vessels Arriving at New York, 1820–97, M237
Record of Appointment of Postmasters, 1832—September 30, 1971, M841, roll 88
Records of the Office of the Postmaster General, RG 28
Register of Letters Received and Endorsements Sent, Second Brigade, Second Division, Twentieth Army Corps, RG 393, pt. 2
Register of Letters Received by the Office of the Secretary of War, M22
Thaddeus L. Reynolds Letters, Reynolds Pension File
Henry C. Romaine Pension File
Union Staff Officers Files, 1861–66
James W. Washburn Letters, Washburn Pension File
Devillo Wheeler Letters, Wheeler Pension File
Alansing Wyant Letters, Wyant Pension File

New-York Historical Society, New York
Chester Alan Arthur Letter Press Books
Joshua M. Van Cott Letter

New York Public Library, New York
Horace Greeley Papers, 1831–73

New York State Archives, Albany
Correspondence and Petitions, 1821–96, New York State Adjutant General's Office, B0462

New York State Library, Albany
Jerome Andrews Letters
Marshall O. Bond Diary
Patrick H. Jones Letter
Edwin D. Morgan Papers

University of Iowa Library, Iowa City
Marcellus W. Darling Letters

University of Notre Dame Archives, Notre Dame, Ind.
David Power Conyngham Papers

University of Rochester, Rochester, N.Y.
Rush Rhees Library
Thurlow Weed Letters

U.S. Army Heritage and Education Center, Carlisle, Pa.
U.S. Army Military History Institute
Archives of Commandery in Chief, Military Order of the Loyal Legion of the United States
Civil War Times Illustrated Collection, Fergus Elliott Diary
Nelson Loomis Diary
Henry Van Aernam Letters

PUBLISHED SOURCES

Newspapers

Albany (N.Y.) Argus
Albany (N.Y.) Evening Journal
American Union, Ellicottville, N.Y.

Boston Pilot
Brenham (Tex.) Weekly Banner
Brooklyn Daily Eagle
Buffalo Evening News
Buffalo Morning Express
Capital Herald, Little Valley, N.Y.
Cattaraugus Freeman, Ellicottville, N.Y.
Cattaraugus Republican, Ellicottville, N.Y.
Cattaraugus Republican, Little Valley and Salamanca, N.Y.
Cattaraugus Union, Ellicottville, N.Y.
Columbus (Ga.) Enquirer-Sun
Courrier des États-Unis, New York, N.Y.
Daily Cairo (Ill.) Bulletin
Daily Graphic, New York
Daily Witness, Montreal
Daily State Journal, Alexandria, Va.
Dakota City (Neb.) Eagle
Dakota Herald, Yankton, Dakota Territory
Dakota Republican, Vermillion, S.D.
Ellicottville (N.Y.) Post
Fort Worth (Tex.) Morning Register
Frank Leslie's Illustrated Newspaper
Fredonia (N.Y.) Censor
Gowanda (N.Y.) Reporter
Harper's Weekly
Irish-American, New York
Irish Citizen, New York
Irish World, New York
Jamestown (N.Y.) Journal
Jerseyman, Morristown, N.J.
La Patrie, Montreal
Mayville (N.Y.) Sentinel
Memphis (Tenn.) Daily Appeal
Middletown (N.Y.) Daily Times
Montreal Witness
Nashville (Tenn.) Union and American
National Police Gazette
National Republican, Washington, D.C.
New York Commercial Advertiser

New York Daily News
New York Dispatch
New York Evening Express
New York Evening Mail
New York Evening Post
New York Evening Telegram
New York Evening World
New York Freeman's Journal and Catholic Register
New York Herald
New York Illustrated Times
New York Leader
New York Morning Telegraph
New York Press
New York Republic
New York Spectator and Weekly Commercial Advertiser
New York Star
New York Sun
New York Sunday Mercury
New York Times
New York Tribune
New York World
North Nebraska Eagle, Dakota City
Olean (N.Y.) Times
Omaha (Neb.) Daily Bee
Philadelphia Public Ledger
Pittsburgh Dispatch
Richmond County (N.Y.) Advance
Scranton (Pa.) Tribune
Sioux City (Iowa) Journal
Soldier's Friend
Stark County Democrat, Canton, Ohio
Staten Islander, New Brighton, N.Y.
Trenton (N.J.) Daily State Gazette
Truth, New York
Watertown (N.Y.) Daily Times

Public Documents

A Bill for the Relief of Patrick H. Jones, 45th Cong., 2nd sess., S. 1005.

Congressional Record. 45th Cong., 2nd sess., 1878. Vol. 7, pt. 3.

U.S. House of Representatives. *Report of the Committee on Public Buildings and Grounds*. 45th Cong., 2nd sess., 1878. H. Doc. 890.

———. *Report of the Postmaster General of the United States*. 45th Cong., 2nd sess., 1877. Ex. Doc. 1, pt. 4.

Books and Articles

Adams, William, ed. *The Historical Gazetteer and Biographical Memorial of Cattaraugus County, New York*. Syracuse: Lyman, Horton & Co., 1893.

The Albany Directory. Albany: Sampson, Davenport & Co., 1866, 1867, 1868.

Anbinder, Tyler. *Nativism and Slavery: The Northern Know Nothings and the Politics of the 1850s*. New York: Oxford University Press, 1992.

Anderson, Mary. *A Few Memories*. New York: Harper & Brothers, 1896.

Asbury, Herbert. *The Gangs of New York*. Garden City, N.Y.: Garden City Publishing Co., 1928.

Atlas of Cattaraugus County, New York. New York: D. G. Beers & Co., 1869.

Bayor, Ronald H., and Timothy J. Meagher, eds. *The New York Irish*. Baltimore: Johns Hopkins University Press, 1996.

Bell, Andrew McIlwaine. *Mosquito Soldiers: Malaria, Yellow Fever, and the Course of the American Civil War*. Baton Rouge: Louisiana State University Press, 2010.

Benedict, Bryce D. *Jayhawkers: The Civil War Brigade of James Henry Lane*. Norman: University of Oklahoma Press, 2009.

Bergan, Francis. *The History of the New York Court of Appeals, 1847–1932*. New York: Columbia University Press, 1985.

Biographical Directory of the State of New York 1900. New York: Biographical Directory Co., 1900.

Boyle, Frank A. *A Party of Mad Fellows: The Story of the Irish Regiments in the Army of the Potomac*. Dayton, Ohio: Morningside, 1996.

Breen, Matthew P. *Thirty Years of New York Politics Up-to-Date*. N.p.: Published by the author, 1899.

Browne, Junius Henri. *The Great Metropolis: A Mirror of New York*. 1869. Reprint. New York: Arno Press, 1975.

Bruce, Susannah Ural. *The Harp and the Eagle: Irish-American Volunteers and the Union Army, 1861–1865*. New York: New York University Press, 2006.

Brummer, Sidney David. *Political History of New York State during the Period of the Civil War*. New York: AMS Press, 1967.

Bunting, Josiah, III. *Ulysses S. Grant*. New York: Times Books, 2004.

Burroughs, Edwin G., and Mike Wallace. *Gotham: A History of New York City to 1898*. New York: Oxford University Press, 1999.

Calhoun, Charles W. *From Bloody Shirt to Full Dinner Pail: The Transformation of Politics and Governance in the Gilded Age.* New York: Hill & Wang, 2010.

Calkins, Hiram, and De Witt Van Buren. *Biographical Sketches of John T. Hoffman and Allen C. Beach, the Democratic Nominees for Governor and Lieutenant-Governor of the State of New York.* New York: New York Printing Co., 1868.

Chamberlin, Everett. *The Struggle of '72.* Chicago: Union Publishing Co., 1872.

Clews, Henry. *Twenty-Eight Years in Wall Street.* New York: Irving Publishing Co., 1887.

Connelly, Howard Wallace. *Fifty-Six Years in the New York Post Office.* New York: C. J. O'Brien, 1931.

Conway, J. North. *Bag of Bones: The Sensational Grave Robbery of the Merchant Prince of Manhattan.* Guilford, Conn.: Lyons Press, 2012.

Conyngham, David P. *Sherman's March through the South.* New York: Sheldon & Co., 1865.

Cornell, William M. *The Life and Public Career of Hon. Horace Greeley.* Boston: Lee & Shepard, 1872.

Court of Appeals State of New York. N.p., n.d.

Crapsey, Edward. *The Nether Side of New York; or, the Vice, Crime and Poverty of the Great Metropolis.* New York: Sheldon & Co., 1872.

Crimmins, John D. *Irish-American Historical Miscellany.* New York: Published by the author, 1905.

Davis, William C. *Battle at Bull Run: A History of the First Major Campaign of the Civil War.* Garden City, N.Y.: Doubleday, 1977.

Depew, Chauncey M. *My Memories of Eighty Years.* New York: Charles Scribner's Sons, 1922.

Dickens, Charles. *Martin Chuzzlewit.* New York: Dodd, Mead, 1944.

Dilley, Butler F. *Biographical and Portrait Cyclopedia of Chautauqua County, New York.* Philadelphia: John M. Gresham, 1891.

Diner, Hasia R. "'The Most Irish City in the Union': The Era of the Great Migration, 1844–1877." In *The New York Irish,* edited by Ronald H. Bayor and Timothy J. Meagher, 87–106. Baltimore: Johns Hopkins University Press, 1996.

Dunkelman, Mark H. *Brothers One and All: Esprit de Corps in a Civil War Regiment.* Baton Rouge: Louisiana State University Press, 2004.

———. "The Doctored Botticher." *Military Images* 28, no. 5 (March–April 2007): 17–19.

Dunkelman, Mark H., and Michael J. Winey. *The Hardtack Regiment: An Illustrated History of the 154th Regiment, New York State Infantry Volunteers.* East Brunswick, N.J.: Fairleigh Dickinson University Press, 1981.

Elias, Stephen N. *Alexander T. Stewart: The Forgotten Merchant Prince.* Westport, Conn.: Praeger, 1992.

Ellis, Franklin, ed. *History of Cattaraugus County, New York.* Philadelphia: L. H. Everts, 1879.

Engle, Stephen D. *Yankee Dutchman: The Life of Franz Sigel.* Fayetteville: University of Arkansas Press, 1993.

"An Epic of Early Iowa: Father Trecey's Colonization Scheme." *Iowa Catholic Historical Review* 3 (1931): 3–13.

Erie, Steven P. *Rainbow's End: Irish-Americans and the Dilemmas of Urban Machine Politics, 1840–1985.* Berkeley: University of California Press, 1988.

Fanebust, Wayne. *The Missing Corpse: Grave Robbing a Gilded Age Tycoon.* Westport, Conn.: Praeger, 2005.

Farrell, Mary, ed. *Mullingar: Essays on the History of a Midlands Town in the 19th Century.* Mullingar, Ireland: Westmeath County Library, 2002.

Fellman, Michael. *Citizen Sherman: A Life of William Tecumseh Sherman.* New York: Random House, 1995.

Fiske, Stephen. *Off-Hand Portraits of Prominent New Yorkers.* New York: George R. Lockwood & Son, 1884.

Fitch, John. *Annals of the Army of the Cumberland.* Philadelphia: J. B. Lippincott, 1864.

Fitzgerald, Michael. "From Ballingarry to Fredericksburg: David Power Conyngham (1825–1883)." *Tipperary Historical Journal* (1988): 192–200.

Gibson, Florence E. *The Attitudes of the New York Irish toward State and National Affairs, 1848–1892.* New York: Columbia University Press, 1951.

Gordon, Michael A. *The Orange Riots: Irish Political Violence in New York City, 1870 and 1871.* Ithaca: Cornell University Press, 2009.

Greeley, Horace. *Recollections of a Busy Life.* New York: J. B. Ford & Co., 1868.

Hanchett, William. *Irish: Charles G. Halpine in Civil War America.* Syracuse: Syracuse University Press, 1970.

Harlow, S. R., and H. H. Boone. *Life Sketches of the State Officers, Senators, and Members of the Assembly of the State of New York, in 1867.* Albany: Weed, Parsons & Co., 1867.

Hebert, Walter H. *Fighting Joe Hooker.* Indianapolis: Bobbs-Merrill, 1944.

Heckethorn, Charles William. *The Secret Societies of All Ages and Countries.* London: George Redway, 1897.

Henkin, David M. *The Postal Age: The Emergence of Modern Communications in Nineteenth-Century America.* Chicago: University of Chicago Press, 2006.

Herity, Michael, ed. *Ordnance Survey Letters: County Longford and Westmeath.* Dublin: Fourmasters Press, 2011.

Hickey, Rev. W. "Major David Power Conyngham." *Irish Book Lover* 5, no. 6 (1914): 7–8.

Hunt, Roger D., and Jack R. Brown. *Brevet Brigadier Generals in Blue.* Gaithersburg, Md.: Olde Soldier Books, 1990.

An Introduction to the Architectural Heritage of County Westmeath. Dublin: National Inventory of Architectural Heritage, 2007.

Isely, Jeter Allen. *Horace Greeley and the Republican Party, 1853–1861: A Study of the New York Tribune*. Princeton, N.J.: Princeton University Press, 1947.

James, Marquis. "The Corpse of A. T. Stewart." *New Yorker*, December 6, 1941, 70–85.

Jefferies, Thomas C. *The Postal System of the United States and the New York General Post Office*. New York: Manufacturers Trust Co., 1922.

Jenkins, Brian. *Fenians and Anglo-American Relations during Reconstruction*. Ithaca: Cornell University Press, 1969.

Johnson, Alfred S., ed. *The Cyclopedic Review of Current History*, vol. 10, no. 7, September 1900. Boston: Current History Co., 1901.

Johnson, Allen, and Dumas Malone. *Dictionary of American Biography*. New York: Charles Scribner's Sons, 1931.

Jordan, David M. *Roscoe Conkling of New York: Voice in the Senate*. Ithaca: Cornell University Press, 1971.

Josephson, Matthew. *The Politicos: 1865–1896*. New York: Harcourt, Brace & Co., 1938.

Kapp, Friedrich. *Immigration and the Commissioners of Emigration of the State of New York*. New York: Nation Press, 1870.

Keller, Christian B. "New Perspectives in Civil War Ethnic History and Their Implications for Twenty-First-Century Scholarship." In *This Distracted and Anarchical People: New Answers for Old Questions about the Civil War–Era North*, edited by Andrew L. Slap and Michael Thomas Smith, 123–41. New York: Fordham University Press, 2013.

Kelly, Sister Mary Gilbert. *Catholic Immigrant Colonization Projects in the United States, 1815–1860*. New York: United States Catholic Historical Society, 1939.

Keneally, Thomas. *The Great Shame: and the Triumph of the Irish in the English-Speaking World*. New York: Nan A. Talese, Doubleday, 1999.

Kessner, Thomas. *Capital City: New York City and the Men behind America's Rise to Economic Dominance, 1860–1900*. New York: Simon & Schuster, 2003.

Knobel, Dale T. *Paddy and the Republic: Ethnicity and Nationality in Antebellum America*. Middletown, Conn.: Wesleyan University Press, 1986.

Laidlaw, William King. *St. John's Church of Ellicottville*. Ellicottville, N.Y.: Published by the author, 1977.

Lardner, James, and Thomas Reppetto. *NYPD: A City and Its Police*. New York: Henry Holt, 2000.

Lause, Mark A. *The Civil War's Last Campaign: James B. Weaver, the Greenback-Labor Party and the Politics of Race and Section*. Lanham, Md.: University Press of America, 2001.

Lewis, Lloyd. *Sherman: Fighting Prophet*. New York: Harcourt, Brace & Co., 1932.

Lewis, Samuel. *A Topographical Dictionary of Ireland*. London: S. Lewis & Co., 1837.

Libby, Daniel P., comp. *The Standard Directory of Richmond County*. New Brighton, N.Y.: Richmond County Standard, 1893, 1897.

Lord, Francis A. *They Fought for the Union.* New York: Bonanza Books, 1960.

Lynch, Denis Tilden. *The Wild Seventies.* New York: D. Appleton-Century, 1941.

Mandelbaum, Seymour J. *Boss Tweed's New York.* Chicago: Ivan R. Dee, 1990.

Marszalek, John F. *Sherman: A Soldier's Passion for Order.* New York: Free Press, 1993.

Marten, James. *Sing Not War: The Lives of Union and Confederate Veterans in Gilded Age America.* Chapel Hill: University of North Carolina Press, 2011.

McAdam, David, ed. *History of the Bench and Bar of New York.* New York: New York History Co., 1897.

McCaffrey, Lawrence J. "Forging Forward and Looking Back." In *The New York Irish,* edited by Ronald H. Bayor and Timothy J. Meagher, 213–33. Baltimore: Johns Hopkins University Press, 1996.

McConnell, Stuart. *Glorious Contentment: The Grand Army of the Republic, 1865–1900.* Chapel Hill: University of North Carolina Press, 1992.

McDougall, Walter A. *Throes of Democracy: The American Civil War Era, 1829–1877.* New York: Harper, 2008.

McFeely, William S. *Grant: A Biography.* New York: Norton, 1981.

McKay, Charles W. "'Three Years or During the War,' With the Crescent and Star." *National Tribune Scrap Book,* 121–60. N.p., n.d.

McLaughlin, J. Fairfax. *The Life and Times of John Kelly, Tribune of the People.* New York: American News Co., 1885.

McPherson, James M. *Battle Cry of Freedom: The Civil War Era.* New York: Oxford University Press, 1988.

Merritt, Edwin A. *Recollections, 1828–1911.* Albany: J. B. Lyon, 1911.

"Michael Kerwin." *Journal of the American-Irish Historical Society* 12 (1913): 276–77.

Morgan, Jack. *Through American and Irish Wars: The Life and Times of General Thomas W. Sweeney, 1820–1892.* Dublin: Irish Academic Press, 2006.

Morris, R. Rebecca. *A Low and Dirty Place: The Parole Camps of Annapolis, MD, 1862–1865.* Linthicum, Md.: Ann Arrundell County Historical Society, 2012.

Mushkat, Jerome. *The Reconstruction of the New York Democracy, 1861–1874.* East Brunswick, N.J.: Fairleigh Dickinson University Press, 1981.

Myers, Gustavus. *The History of Tammany Hall.* New York: Boni & Liveright, 1917.

The National Cyclopedia of American Biography. New York: James T. White, 1893.

Neidhardt, W. S. *Fenianism in North America.* University Park: Pennsylvania State University Press, 1975.

Nevins, Allan. *Hamilton Fish: The Inner History of the Grant Administration.* New York: Dodd, Mead, 1936.

Nevins, Allan, and Milton Halsey Thomas, eds. *The Diary of George Templeton Strong: Post-War Years, 1865–1875.* New York: Macmillan, 1952.

New York State. Chief of Bureau of Military Record. *Presentation of Flags of New York Volunteer Regiments and Other Organizations, to His Excellency, Governor Fenton, in*

Accordance with a Resolution of the Legislature, July 4, 1865. Albany: Weed, Parsons & Co., 1865.

O'Brien, Maire, and Conor Cruise O'Brien. *Ireland: A Concise History.* London: Thames & Hudson, 1999.

Pepper, George W. *Personal Recollections of Sherman's Campaigns in Georgia and the Carolinas.* Zanesville, Ohio: Hugh Dunne, 1866.

Phisterer, Frederick. *New York in the War of the Rebellion, 1861 to 1865.* Albany: Weed, Parsons & Co., 1890.

Rawley, James A. *Edwin D. Morgan, 1811–1883: Merchant in Politics.* New York: Columbia University Press, 1955.

"Report of the Clerk of the Court of Appeals." *Documents of the Assembly of the State of New York Eighty-Ninth Session—1866.* Vol. 6, no. 124. Albany: C. Wendell, 1866.

"Report of the Committee of Investigation into the Affairs of the Commissioners of Emigration and Quarantine." *Documents of the Assembly of the State of New York Ninety-Ninth Session—1876.* Vol. 4, no. 33. Albany: Weed, Parsons & Co., 1876.

Riis, Jacob A. *The Making of an American.* New York: Macmillan, 1919.

Rohs, Stephen. *Eccentric Nation: Irish Performance in Nineteenth-Century New York City.* Madison, N.J.: Fairleigh Dickinson University Press, 2009.

Sanders, Charles W., Jr. *While in the Hands of the Enemy: Military Prisons of the Civil War.* Baton Rouge: Louisiana State University Press, 2005.

Schecter, Barnet. *The Devil's Own Work: The Civil War Draft Riots and the Fight to Reconstruct America.* New York: Walker, 2005.

Schlesinger, Arthur M., Jr., ed. *The Almanac of American History.* New York: Bramhall House, 1983.

Scott, James Brown, ed. *Cases on Quasi-Contracts.* New York: Baker, Voorhis & Co., 1905.

Sears, Stephen. *To the Gates of Richmond: The Peninsula Campaign.* New York: Ticknor & Fields, 1992.

Severance, Frank H. "The Periodical Press of Buffalo." *Publication of the Buffalo Historical Society* 19 (1915): 259–60, 264–65.

Shannon, James P. *Catholic Colonization on the Western Frontier.* New Haven: Yale University Press, 1957.

Sheridan, Eugene. *The Parish of Clonmellon/Killallon: Including the Medieval Parishes of Killua, Clonamey and Killallon: Faith, History, Folklore and Memories of Our Parish.* N.p.: Published by the author, 2001.

Shiels, Damian. *The Irish in the American Civil War.* Dublin: History Press Ireland, 2013.

Simon, John Y., ed. *The Papers of Ulysses S. Grant.* Carbondale: Southern Illinois University Press, 1967–2010.

Slap, Andrew L. *The Doom of Reconstruction: The Liberal Republicans in the Civil War Era.* New York: Fordham University Press, 2006.

Slap, Andrew L., and Michael Thomas Smith. *This Distracted and Anarchical People: New Answers for Old Questions about the Civil War–Era North.* New York: Fordham University Press, 2013.

Smith, Jean Edward. *Grant.* New York: Simon & Schuster, 2001.

Snay, Mitchell. *Horace Greeley and the Politics of Reform in Nineteenth-Century America.* Lanham, Md.: Rowman & Littlefield, 2011.

Spann, Edward K. "Union Green: The Irish Community and the Civil War." In *The New York Irish,* edited by Ronald H. Bayor and Timothy J. Meagher, 193–209. Baltimore: Johns Hopkins University Press, 1996.

Stebbins, Homer A. *A Political History of the State of New York, 1865–1869.* New York: Columbia University Press, 1913.

Strickland, Chuck, and Peggy Strickland. *The Road to Red House.* N.p.: Published by the authors, 2007.

"There Shall Be a Court of Appeals . . .": 150th Anniversary of the Court of Appeals of the State of New York. N.p., n.d.

Thorpe, T. B. "New York City Post-Office." *Harper's New Monthly Magazine* 43, issue 257 (October 1871): 645–63.

Tiffany, Joel. *Condensed Digest of the Court of Appeals Reports of the State of New York.* Albany: Weare C. Little, 1866.

Tissot, Rev. Peter. "A Year with the Army of the Potomac." *Historical Records and Studies* (United States Catholic Historical Society) 3, pt. 1 (January 1903): 43–84.

Trow's Business and Residential Directory of the Borough of Richmond. New York: Trow Directory Co., 1899, 1900.

The Union State Ticket: Personal Character and Military Services. New York: Baker & Godwin, 1865.

Ural, Susannah J. *Civil War Citizens: Race, Ethnicity, and Identity in America's Bloodiest Conflict.* New York: New York University Press, 2010.

———. "Ye Sons of Green Erin Assemble: Northern Irish American Catholics and the Union War Effort, 1861–1865." In *Civil War Citizens: Race, Ethnicity, and Identity in America's Bloodiest Conflict,* edited by Susannah J. Ural, 99–132. New York: New York University Press, 2010.

U.S. Congress. *Senate Exec. Journal.* 38th Cong., 1st sess., December 12, 1864, vol. 14; 38th Cong., 2nd sess., February 1, 1865, vol. 14; 41st Cong., 2nd sess., December 6, 13, and 21, 1869, vol. 19; 43rd Cong., 1st sess., March 17, 1873, vol. 21.

U.S. War Department. *The War of the Rebellion: A Compilation of the Official records of the Union and Confederate Armies.* 128 vols. Washington, D.C.: Government Printing Office, 1880–1901.

Van Deusen, Glyndon G. *Horace Greeley: Nineteenth-Century Crusader.* Philadelphia: University of Pennsylvania Press, 1953.

Walling, George W. *Recollections of a New York Chief of Police.* New York: Caxton Book Concern, 1887.

Warner, Ezra J. *Generals in Blue: Lives of the Union Commanders*. Baton Rouge: Louisiana State University Press, 1964.

Warner, M. M. *Warner's History of Dakota County, Nebraska*. Dakota City, Neb.: Lyons Mirror Job Office, 1893.

Waugh, Joan. *U. S. Grant: American Hero, American Myth*. Chapel Hill: University of North Carolina Press, 2009.

Weber, Gustavus A. *The Bureau of Pensions: Its History, Activities and Organization*. Baltimore: Johns Hopkins Press, 1923.

Webb's Consolidated Directory of the North and South Shores, Staten Island. New York: Webb Brothers, 1882–84.

"Westmeath Voters 1832." *Irish Genealogist* 5, no. 2 (1975): 234–49; 5, no. 6 (1979): 772–89; 6, no. 1 (1980): 77–98.

Williams, Robert C. *Horace Greeley: Champion of American Freedom*. New York: New York University Press, 2006.

Wilson, H., comp. *Trow's New York City Directory*. New York: John F. Trow, 1868–74; Trow City Directory Co., 1875–81.

Wilson, James G., and John Fiske. *Appleton's Cyclopedia of American Biography*. New York: D. Appleton, 1887.

INDEX